THE GREAT ENTERPRISE

ASIA-PACIFIC *Culture, Politics, and Society*

Editors: Rey Chow, Michael Dutton, H. D. Harootunian,
and Rosalind C. Morris

The

GREAT ENTERPRISE

Sovereignty and Historiography

in Modern Korea

HENRY H. EM

DUKE UNIVERSITY PRESS

DURHAM AND LONDON

2013

Designed by C. H. Westmoreland
Typeset in Whitman with Franklin Gothic display
by Tseng Information Systems, Inc.
Library of Congress Cataloging-in-Publication Data
Em, Henry.
The great enterprise : sovereignty and historiography in
modern Korea / Henry H. Em.
p. cm. — (Asia-Pacific)
Includes bibliographical references and index.
ISBN 978-0-8223-5357-7 (cloth : alk. paper)
ISBN 978-0-8223-5372-0 (pbk. : alk. paper)
1. Korea — Historiography. 2. Sovereignty. 3. International
relations. I. Title. II. Series: Asia-Pacific.
DS905.7.E44 2013
951.90072 — dc23
2012033723

이 저서는 2007년도 정부(교육과학기술부)의 재원으로
한국학중앙연구원의 지원을 받아 수행된 연구임(AKS-2007-CD-4001)
This work was published with a publication subsidy awarded by the
Academy of Korean Studies Grant, which is funded by the Korean
government (MOEHRD, Basic Research Fund).

For Sue K. Em, Mike M. Em, Noh Ock-shin, and Oh Jae-shik

CONTENTS

ACKNOWLEDGMENTS

This book has taken a long time to write, and over the years it has evolved in directions I did not foresee. After an initial effort at historicizing Korean nationalism and nationalist historiography, it became clear to me that my study of modern Korean historiography would have to provide a more comprehensive account of the relationship between imperialism and nationalism. That realization led me to focus on sovereignty and the sovereign subject (*chuch'e*) as concepts and associated practices that were transformed by Euro-American imperialism. It took a long time to figure out how sovereignty, and the assumed equality that one gains by becoming "sovereign," became as foundational as the concept of nation (*minjok*) to the project of modernity and history writing in Korea.

In the early 1980s, just out of college, I spent nine months in the Philippines working on human rights issues. It was there that I received my education in anti-imperialist revolutionary movements. Several years later, from another eighteen months working on human rights and labor issues at the Urban Industrial Mission in Inchŏn, South Korea, I learned how the experience of partition and the Korean War continue to reverberate powerfully for so many. Those experiences also taught me that the sense of individual agency emerges from communities of solidarity. I am grateful to Patricia Patterson and Michael Hahm for those life-changing experiences.

I could not have imagined a book project like this without the training I received from my teachers at the University of Chicago. Starting as an undergraduate, I learned from Tetsuo Najita and Harry Harootunian how historians can and should pose questions about ideas that seem natural and commonsensical. I am grateful to Tets and Harry for turning my interests to history and to critical modes of history writing. A graduate seminar on nationalism taught by Prasenjit Duara shaped my early work on nationalism and nationalist historiography. My greatest debt is to Bruce Cumings, my friend and teacher, whose scholarship and political stance have inspired my work over these many years.

I first presented my work on nationalism and nationalist historiography at a conference organized by Gi-Wook Shin and Michael Robinson. That was an important conference for me, and in the course of preparing my article for their edited volume, *Colonial Modernity in Korea*, I was forced to grapple with myriad questions regarding the modernity of the nation form. John Duncan, my friend, colleague, and mentor at UCLA, willingly engaged me in many hours of conversation about Korean history and historiography. John helped me to sharpen my argument, and I remain deeply grateful for his incomparable generosity.

In the early 1990s, Choi Jang-jip introduced me to the debates over history following liberation in 1945. My debts to Professor Choi continued when I returned to Korea as a Fulbright Senior Scholar, and again in 2007–8, when I taught in the Department of Korean History at Korea University. It was with his support that I was able to organize an international conference on the colonial period, affording me the opportunity to learn from a remarkable group of scholars working on the colonial period, including Micah Auerback, Takashi Fujitani, Todd Henry, Ken Kawashima, Helen Lee, Jinhee Lee, John Lie, Serk bae Suh, Jun Uchida, Janet Poole, and Theodore Jun Yoo. I am grateful to the many colleagues at Korea University from whom I learned a great deal, especially Professors Cho Kwang and Kang Man-gil, who allowed me to sit in on their lectures and seminars on Korean historiography.

In 1998 Kim Dong-choon invited me to present my work on Sin Ch'ae-ho and postnationalism at Yŏksa munje yŏn'guso. That provided the occasion for conversations over the years with Korean historians of my generation, especially Park Chan-seung. In 2000 Alain Delissen invited me to Paris to spend a month at the Centre de Recherches sur la Corée, EHESS. I am grateful to Alain and Koen de Ceuster for their comments and questions on the papers I presented on Sin Ch'ae-ho and Paek Nam-un. In 2007, as part of the Oxford History of Historical Writing project, Axel Schneider invited me to a conference at Leiden University on the writing of history in twentieth-century East Asia. That provided the occasion for me to map out certain trajectories in history writing in modern Korea. In 2009 Jae-Jung Suh invited me to SAIS-Johns Hopkins University for a workshop on my book manuscript. As the invited respondent, Stefan Tanaka provided valuable comments and counsel. In 2010 Andre Schmid invited me to the University of Toronto for another workshop, and I received very helpful comments from Janet Poole and Ken Kawashima. Andre shares my interest in Korean historiography, and his careful reading and critique of my manuscript were immensely helpful.

I would like to thank the Academy of Korean Studies for providing a publication subsidy. None of the chapters in this book is a reprint of earlier publications, but materials from earlier publications have been incorporated into various chapters. Those earlier publications include "'Overcoming' Korea's Division: Narrative Strategies in Recent South Korean Historiography," *positions: east asia cultures critique* 1, no. 2 (1993); "Minjok as a Modern and Democratic Construct: Sin Ch'ae-ho's Historiography," *Colonial Modernity in Korea*, ed. Gi-Wook Shin and Michael E. Robinson (Cambridge: Harvard University Asia Center, 1999); and "Historians and History Writing in Modern Korea," *Oxford History of Historical Writing*: vol. 5, *Historical Writing Since 1945*, ed. Axel Schneider and Daniel Woolf (New York: Oxford University Press, 2011).

I am happy for this opportunity to acknowledge other friends and colleagues not yet mentioned and with whom I have worked, who encouraged and helped me over the years: Charles Armstrong, Robert Buswell, Cho Eun-su, Choe Min, Chungmoo Choi, Michael Chwe, Alexis Dudden, Han Suk-Jung, Yukiko Hanawa, Marty Hart-Landsberg, Heo Eun, Theodore Q. Hughes, Im Chong-myong, Rebecca Karl, Kwak Jun-Hyeok, Jo Gye-Won, Jung Tae Hern, Elaine Kim, Kyung-Hyun Kim, Lee Beom-jae, Lee Jin-Han, Lee Jung-Shin, Timothy S. Lee, Lydia Liu, Abé Mark Nornes, Seung-Deuk Oak, Se-Mi Oh, Leslie Pincus, Elizabeth Shim, Ryu Si-hyun, J. T. Takagi, Meredith Jung-En Woo, Lisa Yoneyama, Marilyn Young, and Jonathan Zwicker.

I could not have finished this book without the support of a truly wonderful group of friends who read parts of the manuscript, suggested further readings, and provided critical comments. To Christine Hong, Monica Kim, Suzy Kim, Namhee Lee, Jae-Jung Suh, and Youngju Ryu, thank you. My editors at Duke University Press were adept and unfailingly supportive. Two anonymous readers provided extraordinarily precise and knowledgeable critiques. As for mistakes and shortcomings, those remain my responsibility. To Grace Kyoungwon Em, and to Changbin and Aerie, who grew up waiting for this book to be published, I can finally say: it's done. Thank you for your love and patience. With gratitude, I dedicate this book to both Kyoungwon's parents and mine.

INTRODUCTION

In an essay published in *Tongkwang* in September 1932, Kim Ki-rim called on "Miss Korea" to cut her hair. "Someone once described the modern as the era of the 3S's (sports, speed, sex), but I will instead call the first thirty years of our century the era of the short hair. As typified by 'Nora,' the 'Bob' (short haircut) is the ultimate symbol of liberation and of women venturing outside. . . . Cutting your hair announces your departure from that 'harem' to which you have been shackled for thousands of years; it is the sign that you have come out under the blue sky."[1] In Kim's discourse on modernity, he set aside the purportedly familiar characterization of modernity as sports, speed, and sex to focus on bobbed hair, feminists as typified by Henrik Ibsen's Nora, and women of status venturing outside in daytime unconstrained by marriage and motherhood. Indeed by the 1930s one could have seen in colonial Korea baseball games, beauty pageants, exhibitions, display windows fronting the new department stores, street-cars, street lights, and cafés that enabled crowd watching. Starting about a decade earlier, Kim's readers would have seen and felt not just the rapidity of change in the physical, spatial, and cultural ordering of colonial Seoul, a constantly self-negating temporal dynamic, but also the increasing rate of change itself. As for sex, Kim began his essay by acknowledging that in Korea in the 1930s the bob haircut was *still* associated with (feminine) eroticism, along with bright red lipstick, the side glance (*kyŏnnuntchil*), and other vulgar practices that belonged to the world of café waitresses and dance girls in *The Threepenny Opera*.[2] He imagined that if he were to suggest to a coed, "Go on, why don't you cut your hair?," she might turn red in the face, furious, as though he had damaged her dignity.

In addressing young Korean women ("Miss Korea"), Kim tried to substitute those still prevalent associations by drawing contrasts he defined in terms of temporality and civilization as measured by the status of women: women shackled for past millennia in contrast to liberated women of the twentieth century. He granted that their neatly braided hair was, well, neat. But tied to that neatly braided hair hung "the dreams of a backward feudal era." He wanted "Miss Korea" to look at her sisters in China who had kicked away the barbaric custom of foot binding: Look at their strong legs running to the anti-imperialist front ("t'ado XXjuŭi ro Xsŏn ŭl talryŏ").³ He urged "Miss Korea" to look at *their* short hair, and he ended his essay with the question, "Deep in your heart, don't you want to defend the Bob cut that is so vilified?" By titling his essay "'Miss Korea' Cut Your Hair," Kim was able to address young Korean women as if they stood on the world's stage, on view as in beauty pageants that are consciously organized for both national and international audiences. His agitation for Korean women to liberate themselves and to participate in (colonial Korea's) social and political life, offered in a pedagogic tone and without reference to patriarchy, was a common rhetorical strategy for male writers who were asked, frequently, to write about women and women's issues in colonial Korea in the late 1920s and early 1930s.

Published without attribution, Kim Ki-rim's essay was the third of three essays on Korean women and short hair, coming after an essay by Kim Hwal-lan, a professor and vice principal at Ewha (Women's) College, and a second essay by "K. Y.," a student at "X Women's School" who had cut her hair. Until 1939 Ewha College was the only women's college in colonial Korea, and in her essay Kim Hwal-lan noted that Ewha College had two or three students with short hair.⁴ She equated short hair with convenience and predicted that the number of students with short hair would "naturally" increase over time. Kim Hwal-lan, who had received her Ph.D. in education from Columbia University in 1931, let it be known that she neither encouraged her students from cutting their hair nor prevented them from doing so. K. Y. had more to say in her essay. She began with the declaration that she had gained many things after she cut her hair. She noted, however, that people who voiced all kinds of opinions about the bob haircut did so only from a third person's perspective. She also noted that she could not shake off the feeling that men, whether they argued for or against the bob, continued to look at women as visual objects for their pleasure and enjoyment.

A point of departure for this book is Kim Ki-rim's observation that the twentieth century was the era of the short haircut: that the cutting of hair signified the triumph of reason over unreason, the realization of individual autonomy, and the emergence of the modern political subject that established the anti-imperialist front. Kim Ki-rim's exhortation arose from a romantic infatuation that is the subject of this book, a "romance of sovereignty," according to Achille Mbembe, that articulates "a certain idea of the political, the community, [and] the subject." It was (and is) a romance that "rests on the belief that the subject is the master and the controlling author of his or her own meaning . . . [and on the belief that] the exercise of sovereignty, in turn, consists in society's capacity for self-creation."[5] As K. Y. observed, sovereignty as pedagogy also sought to reproduce gender, racial, class, and civilizational hierarchies and was complicit with power. Still, K. Y. made it clear that she liked her hair short: "In truth, I like it. It was when I cut my hair that I learned something about [the power of] social conventions, and people's emotions and rationality."[6] The general aim of this book is to examine this truth and the pleasures that derive from the idea of being sovereign, possessing a subjective will (chuch'esŏng) capable of reconstituting life, language, and labor. This book examines the historicity of sovereignty (chukwŏn), its complicity with power, and its creative, productive capacity, and also the conventions, rationalities, and subjectivities that sovereignty elicited.

Part I focuses on the historicity of sovereignty: how sovereignty functioned as pedagogy for imperialism and colonialism and how it became the paramount signifier for Korea's modern era, productive of desire and subjectivity. Chapter 1 examines sovereignty as a legal concept that structures the modern nation-state and relations between empires and nation-states. Sovereignty was not fully articulated by the Peace of Westphalia and then extended to Europe's periphery. The European conception of sovereignty—that is, equal sovereignty—has a more complicated history. Sovereignty and international law were improvised out of the colonial encounter and given various articulations by European colonizers in conditions of hegemonic contestation with other colonial powers to declare who was sovereign, who was not, and why.[7] That is to say, colonialism was central to the constitution of sovereignty, and one specific aim of this book is to explore the historicity of sovereignty in modern Korea and its deep complicity with both Japanese and Euro-American empires and colonial projects.

As a history of historical writing in modern Korea, part II examines sovereignty's creative, productive power, calling on Korean historians who would privilege and deploy, for their own purposes, the concept of equal sovereignty as the condition for rewriting Korea's past. Korean historians did the imagining, but it was sovereignty that made it possible to imagine the Korean ethnic nation (*minjok*) and to imagine it as a self-same unity that evolved (or developed) through linear time. As nationalist historians rendered the ethnic nation as the sovereign subject (*chuch'e*) of Korean history, they located Korea in global time and helped create a democratic logic, limited by national boundaries, that invited all Koreans — male and female, old and young, high-born and of low status — to become sovereign subjects of national history.

To recognize sovereignty's complicity with imperialism and colonialism, it should be recalled that Japanese authorities had forced King Kojong to issue a royal decree (*tanbalryŏng*) that ordered all adult men to cut off their topknots.[8] Before the royal decree was issued on December 30, 1895, Yu Kil-chun, the home minister, flanked by Japanese troops, had pressured King Kojong and the crown prince to have their own topknots cut.[9] For most adult men in late nineteenth-century Korea and China, the cutting of hair was associated with humiliation and violence against the body, severing one's ties to parents, ancestors, and a civilizational order.[10] In the decades before and after the turn of the twentieth century, one's hair and clothes became intensely visible signs of political and cultural allegiance. Outraged by the topknot decree, from January to April 1896 local literati led Righteous Armies in armed insurrection against officials who enforced the topknot decree. For the Japanese, the avowed objectives behind the topknot order had to do with hygiene and with convenience while working. In the royal decree, however, published by the Home Office, King Kojong associated topknot cutting with the goal of achieving equal standing in the nation-state system: "We, in cutting Our hair, are setting an example to Our subjects. Do you, the multitude, identify yourselves with Our design, and cause to be accomplished the great enterprise [*taeŏp*] of establishing equality with the nations of the earth."[11] Cutting the topknot made manifest one's decision to reject the "cruelty" and "backwardness" that differentiated Korea from the civilized nations of the world. The discarded topknot signaled a severing of the future from the past, because the past could no longer be instructive for action in the present. The topknot order was one among many acts of undoing in late nineteenth-century Korea, and it was Euro-American imperialism, with sovereignty functioning both as political power and police power, which equated such acts of deterritorialization and reterritorialization with the great enterprise of embracing Western civilization and attaining equal standing with other sovereign nations.

The great enterprise, to be carried out by Koreans, required that kind of definitive severing so that Korea could stand autonomous and free, as an equal.[12] Thus there is no irony in the fact that Japanese authorities had to force sovereignty on King Kojong. Sovereignty and international law were more than just complicit in imperialist projects. King Kojong's declaration of independence from China on January 7, 1895, forced on him by Inoue Kaoru, laid the legal basis for increasing Japan's control over Korea.[13] As a reminder of that which existed prior to sovereignty and precolonial history, chapter 1 explains why the state-ness of Chosŏn Korea was not marred in the eyes of the Chosŏn scholar-officials by their monarch's subordinate ritual status to the Ming emperor or, by the eighteenth century, even to the Qing (Manchu) emperor. To be sure, Ming-Chosŏn and Qing-Chosŏn relations were neither predetermined nor static, and the notion of Chosŏn Korea as a model tributary obscures periods of severe tension and conflict, for example, during early Ming-Chosŏn relations (especially between 1408 and 1433), when the Chinese imperial court demanded human tribute (girls for the imperial harem and boys to be eunuchs), or during early Qing-Chosŏn relations when Manchu armies twice invaded Korea, in 1627 and 1636, to force the Korean court to accept vassal status.[14] The Manchu invasion of 1636 was especially devastating, and submission to the Qing was humiliating; for many years after 1636 Chosŏn officials kept using the Ming calendar in internal documents, and they never adopted Manchu clothing or hairstyle. But tribute bought noninterference, and for much of its history Chosŏn Korea successfully maintained its autonomy as well as trade relations by way of this ritually subordinate relationship to China. Moreover, when relations with the imperial court improved, the Chosŏn literati could argue that it was Korea's inclusion in a China-centered world, and their own fierce commitment to the basic categories that defined that world in terms of inner and outer, civilization and barbarism (hwa and yi) that endowed Chosŏn with its distinctive and civilized state-ness. That is to say, it was often through engagement with that China-centered world that Chosŏn scholar-officials imagined Korean civilization (soChunghwa) realizing its full potentiality, its cosmic meaning.

The importance and value for the Chosŏn court of receiving investiture from the Ming or Qing imperial court revolved around domestic politics, and the Chosŏn court time and again displayed a multifaceted persona in its relations with China; for much of the Chosŏn period, Korean scholar-officials could readily acknowledge that a central facet of the state-ness of Chosŏn Korea derived from its subordinate inclusion in a China-centered tributary system, and at the same time identify Tan'gun, who stood outside the Chinese genealogy, as the progenitor of the Korean state. Korea's China-centered sovereignty was not absolute sovereignty, and certainly not equal sovereignty. Its rituals and protocols were very different from the rituals and protocols of post-Westphalian sovereignty based on the notion of equal, separate, and indivisible authority and identity. In the late nineteenth century, King Kojong's default strategy was to utilize to best advantage the protocols of the China-centered tributary system as well as the protocols of the sovereignty-based nation-state system. It was hegemonic contestation—specifically Japan's victory over China in the Sino-Japanese War—that provided the occasion to eliminate this ambiguity, as well as the space for maneuver that it had afforded. While Inoue Kaoru might have forced King Kojong's "declaration of independence," the king and the greater part of reform-minded officials should be seen as coauthors of the Independence Oath taken at the Royal Ancestral Temple. Chapter 1 presents historical substantiation of this claim and prepares the ground for discussion of the relationship between imperialism and nationalism by looking at the relationship between authorship (a claim of sovereignty) and ritual action.

In the sense that the king's ritual performance on January 7, 1895, was doubly prescribed (not just by ritual manuals dating back centuries but also by Inoue Kaoru), it could be said that King Kojong—as Chosŏn Korea's supreme sacerdotal authority, its monarch and bearer of the dynastic mission and Heaven's mandate (ch'ŏnmyŏng)—was, and was not, the author of his actions. It was understood by all that only King Kojong's taking the Oath before his ancestors could make Korea's independence (from China) inviolable. It is in that sense of King Kojong as coauthor of his own ritual performance that chapter 2 takes up the question of how sovereignty as a nation form could be replicated across the globe, chiefly among and by newly emerging bourgeoisies, for Benedict Anderson "the first classes to achieve solidarities on an essentially imagined basis."[15]

Chapter 2 begins with the argument that before the Sino-Japanese War, and before King Kojong's declaration of Korea's "independence," material and discursive conditions already existed within Korea that would allow for the dissemination of not just the idea of national sovereignty but also the presumption that recognition of Korea's sovereignty by the Western imperial powers was a necessary condition for avoiding colonization. Toward this end, intellectuals like Yun Ch'i-ho took it for granted that Korea had to demonstrate commitment to European civilization, as measured by specific "reforms" of political, economic, and cultural institutions and practices (such as sumptuary laws), and also to participate in international events such as the Columbian Exposition in Chicago in 1893. The problem, as Yun saw it, was that Korea's commitment to the great enterprise was as second-rate and dismal as the Korea Exhibit, so much so that he found himself unable to walk away from it.

To the extent that the Korea Exhibit at the Columbian Exposition functioned for Yun as a synecdoche of Korea's abjection, it is possible to understand the sadness as well as genocidal contempt that Yun felt at the sight of Native Americans in the American West congregating around railroad stations along the Central Pacific Railroad: "Indians were seen at almost every station. Some of them painted their faces red and most had red or blue blankets wrapped around their bodies. A sad and somewhat contemptible sight: sad because of their past history, but contemptible because of the inability to improve their condition. A race that fails, from voluntary laziness and ignorance, to avail itself of the advantages of civilization brought so close to its reach isn't worthwhile to live."[16] Yun, a progenitor of the Korean (Christian) bourgeois class that would emerge under Japanese colonial rule, saw Native Americans in terms of a visual regime that paralleled the objectifying and disciplining operations of discourses on "civilization." If Native Americans did not avail themselves of Euro-American civilization—if they voluntarily chose to live in ignorance and "degraded humanity"—then they did not deserve to live. For Yun, the decision to embrace Euro-American civilization was, in itself, proof of a people's capacity for rationality and autonomy. His privileging of freedom, and ruminations on why certain populations do not deserve to live, point to not just the inclusionary pretensions of liberal theory and the exclusionary effects of liberal practices, but also to liberalism's essential link to imperialism and colonialism.[17] His privileging of freedom also points to the centrality of violence in the constitution of (Christian) liberal-bourgeois subjectivity in early twentieth-century Korea and its permutations through the colonial period down to postcolonial anticommunist South Korea.[18]

It must be said that the violence of sovereignty was very productive. In language, sovereignty as a form of command prompted Korean intellectuals, as writers, historians, and translators, to produce new meanings and new narratives through semantic innovation. In the translation of sovereignty in its nation form, chapter 2 focuses on the unavoidable accommodation to Euro-American modernity and on semantic innovation through both productive imagination and the legislative rationality of capitalist sovereignty.[19] Attention paid to the legislative rationality of capitalist sovereignty goes against the grain of scholarship that wants to portray modernity and nation in Korea as Korea's own creation, with Korean intellectuals selecting, translating, and thereby creating their own modernity from the Western archive. If that were the case, the modernity thus created would be sovereign to Korea, dynamic, and ongoing: Korea's modernity as an incomplete project that is both particular and universal. Historians would then have a firm basis for writing the history of Korea's modernity untainted by imperialism and colonialism; historians need only take due account of the historical and political context and "the limitations of his time." This kind of scholarship (also) emerges from desire created by sovereignty itself.

In terms of language, it was the translation of capitalist sovereignty in the late nineteenth century that produced the diachronic identity of national language (*kuk'ŏ*), discernible in the poetry (*hyangga*) of the Silla period down to the language of scholar-officials in late nineteenth-century Seoul. "The Korean language" came to be imagined as singular, a unity even in its great variations over space and time. In analyzing this process of translation, in the literal sense, chapter 2 draws attention to the radical transformations in language and political economy, transformations that were overdetermined by the legislative rationality of capitalist sovereignty. One key example is the word for *economy* used today in China, Japan, and Korea: 經濟 (C: *jingji*, J: *keizai*, K: *kyŏngje*). The lexical unit *kyŏngje* was a contraction of *kyŏngse jemin* (經世濟民): to govern the world and relieve the people. That is to say, prior to the nineteenth century, *kyŏngje* referred to a political economy that was necessarily and overtly moral, a moral economy structured on obligation to the people's welfare. When Japanese intellectuals translated *economy* as *keizai*, however, they associated *keizai* with production, consumption, and the wealth of nations, an intellectual approach that linked public interest with competition and the pursuit of private gain. With *kyŏngje* rendered as *economy*, the extraction of profit would appear as a series of relations of exchange rather than tribute extracted through political domination: the people, as workers and producers, became autonomous and "free" in their poverty and propertylessness. Like capitalism, then, the term kyŏngje could (and did) take a purely economic form.

In the late nineteenth century, Japanese intellectuals also created a series of neologisms in the course of translating from European languages, including the word for nation, minzoku (K: minjok). It is important to note that words like minjok ([ethnic] nation) were incorporated into Korean as it was being nationalized. In other words, the nationalization of the Korean language occurred within a profoundly transnational, translingual context. Christian missionaries, especially Protestant missionaries, helped transform the Korean alphabet into an icon of Korea and an icon for the Korean nation. They inspired and trained many prominent Korean linguists and grammarians, including the brilliant linguist Chu Si-gyŏng. Missionaries sought and obtained international recognition for the scientific value of the Korean alphabet. They promoted respect for and standardization of the Korean vernacular and fostered a spirit of protecting the Korean script.[20] It was within this context that vernacular Korean written with King Sejong's alphabet (created in 1443) was elevated to the status of national script (kungmun), while literary (classical) Chinese was demoted to mere Chinese writing. But while international recognition given to Korean writing might seem to pay homage to Korean genius, as Rey Chow has argued, homage to the West has long been paid in the form of what seems to be its opposite[21]: in this case, the radical insistence on kungmun (Korean written vernacular as the national script). In that sense, it was capitalist sovereignty that promoted Korea's distinction from China and standardization of language practices and populations, with Korean and Koreans constituted as distinct units that identify each other.

Although Japanese authorities saw King Kojong's declaration of sovereignty as a necessary step toward the imposition of a protectorate and eventual annexation, to justify colonization they also had to explain why Korea was never really sovereign and never really capable of maintaining "the sovereignty Japan had obtained for Korea." Chapter 3, which begins part II of this book, shows how, out of ancient ruins, the Japanese colonial state constructed an explanation for why colonization was necessary. Soon after annexation the Japanese colonial state poured money, expertise, and concrete to restore Sŏkkuram, an astonishingly beautiful Buddhist statue seated within a man-made stone grotto "discovered" by a Japanese mailman. The Japanese colonial state also restored a number of Buddhist temples near Kyŏngju and breathlessly extolled Sŏkkuram and the Buddhist art and architecture of the Silla period as the "culmination of the religion and the art of the Orient."[22] The pedagogic lesson had to do with Japan's self-designated role as curator for Asia's art and a colonial lesson on temporality. Sŏkkuram and the art and architecture of the Silla period represented the apex of Korean cultural history, brilliant artistic achievements which stood in stark contrast to the squalor of Korea's present. The story of Sŏkkuram—its creation and subsequent slide into obscurity and ruin— was the sad story of Korea: a beautiful and brilliant cultural past that was as much Asian as Korean, followed by a long downward slide. The colonial authorities did not just teach Koreans about their past; they had to restore it for them.

Ultimately colonial rule depended on coercive power: the power to suppress protest and armed resistance. But Japanese colonialism could not have been sustained with just coercive power. To establish sufficient hegemony, Japanese colonialism had to be, above all, a pedagogic endeavor in which the colonized would come to recognize the relative superiority of the colonizer. Restoring Sŏkkuram to its former glory was part of that pedagogic effort, teaching about the world and Korea's place in it as defined by Japan and the West. In this colonizing project, the Japanese colonial state drew heavily on Euro-American colonial practices. Like the British in India and Americans in the Philippines, the Japanese allocated money and expertise to carry out excavations and surveys, to study Korea's past, and to restore some cultural sites (but not others) in order to establish the categories and narrative strategies by which Korea and Koreans would be understood. Thus there was a proliferation of (competing) discourses on Korean identity that emanated from the Japanese colonial state as well as Korean nationalist intellectuals and organizations. In this competition, the Japanese colonial state was more successful in terms of producing detailed studies of Korean art, customs, language, religion, and history.[23] For the Japanese colonial state, the goal of transforming colonial Korea for its strategic ends went hand in hand with the work of transforming peasants into *Chōsenjin* (Koreans). The logic of its racist colonial policy compelled the Japanese colonial state to reconstitute (disparate) Korean identities into a homogeneous *Chōsenjin* that became both a bureaucratic and a derogatory classification for all Koreans regardless of gender, regional origin, or class background.

Contrary to conventional nationalist accounts which argue that Japanese colonial authorities pursued a consistent and systematic policy of eradicating Korean identity, we should see that the Japanese colonial state actually endeavored to produce Koreans as subjects, subjects in the sense of being under the authority of the Japanese emperor and in the sense of having a separate and inferior subjectivity. This in turn led to a bifurcated discourse, because Korean nationalist historians, in competition with the Japanese colonial state, were engaged in the project of recovering or producing an autonomous and sovereign Korean subjectivity. Nationalist historians would find evidence of this subjectivity in history, but in necessarily incomplete or disfigured form; for nationalist historians, only political independence could render possible the full realization of true (sovereign) Korean subjectivity. Although the power of the repressive and ideological apparatuses of the Japanese colonial state far surpassed that of the Korean nationalist movement, Korean intellectuals were more than capable of ensuring that the discourse on national and individual sovereignty remained a contested field throughout the colonial period.

I do not mean to present a simple binary between Korean nationalists and the Japanese colonial state. The history outlined in this book has to do with competing nationalisms, and readers should be aware that Japanese settlers and their organizations, although I do not discuss them, were also very much involved in producing knowledge about Korea. This is pointed out by Jun Uchida, who cautions against simple identification of Japanese settlers with the Japanese colonial state. Japanese settlers were "brokers of empire" in the sense that, as nonstate actors, they participated and intervened in the colonial project in complex ways that complemented but also complicated the government-general's rule.[24] Thus, and as suggested by K. Y.'s and Kim Ki-rim's essays on the bob, any "Korean" subjectivity created under such conditions had to assume "a world of synchronic temporality"—that is, baseball games, beauty pageants, exhibitions, display windows in the new department stores, as well as history writing, all understood in synchronic "world" time, and subjectivity itself constituted by "historical identification and spatial proximity."[25]

Colonial historians, for their part, represented Japan's annexation of Korea also as a restoration. Based on his reading of the eighth-century texts *Kojiki* and *Nihon shoki*, Kume Kunitake suggested that Japan before Jinmu (the mythical first emperor) was a thalassocracy encompassing Kyūshū, the

Korean peninsula, and southeastern China.[26] Such narratives would depict colonization of Korea as the restoration of Japanese rule, Japan having ruled southern Korea in ancient times. Colonial historians also suggested that Japanese and Koreans were descended from common ancestors. Such narratives, however, created anxiety for colonialists as well as anticolonial Korean nationalists, an anxiety over sameness or lack of essential difference between colonizer and colonized. Colonialist historiography came into its fullness with narrative strategies that could affirm sameness while asserting colonial difference and colonial hierarchy, which were maintained through narratives about absence, lack, and temporality. Colonialist historiography argued that external forces—Chinese, Manchurian, and Japanese—had determined Korea's historical development from its very beginnings. Factionalism was deeply ingrained in the Korean political culture, as evidenced by successive purges of literati and factional strife during the Chosŏn period, preventing the emergence of a unified political will. Korean society prior to annexation had been utterly stagnant. In other words, Koreans were not and could not become sovereign subjects of their own history.

Of these, stagnation theory was perhaps most effective in establishing colonial difference in terms of temporality. Drawing on the authority of the social sciences, specifically Karl Bücher's theories on nonmarket economics, Fukuda Tokuzō argued that feudalism and private ownership of land had failed to emerge in Korea, and thus the level of development in late nineteenth-century Korea was comparable to that in tenth-century Fujiwara Japan. Based on a twenty-day trip to Korea in 1902, Fukuda was able to conclude that Koreans "who lack the courageous warrior spirit that our nation [minzoku] represents" must look to Japan, while the Japanese have no choice but to "acknowledge the weight of our appointed task, a natural fate and duty of a powerful and superior culture to assimilate Korea and Koreans by sweeping away their utterly corrupt and decayed national particularity."[27] It was against the assertion of superiority based on temporal difference—a thousand-year gap between Japan and Korea—that Paek Nam-un wrote *Chōsen shakai keizaishi* (1933) and *Chōsen hōken shakai keizaishi* (1937).[28] Paek's aim was to show that Korean society and economy had developed in accordance with universal stages of development and as a result of socioeconomic forces internal to Korea, that is, Koreans as sovereign subjects of their own history, a history that was as universal in its development as that of Europe or Japan.

Focusing on Paek Nam-un, chapter 4 examines history writing as it became an academic discipline in colonial Korea. Among Korean historians trained at Japanese universities, especially Waseda and later Keijō Imperial University in colonial Seoul, many adopted the narrative framework of colonialist historiography, specifically *Mansenshi*, a Manchuria-Korea spatial conception that negated Korea's historical sovereignty by presenting history as a movement, in waves, into Korea, and more generally that of Oriental history (*tōyōshi*), which presented Japan as uniquely capable, in contrast to moribund places like Korea and China that were saddled with debilitating customs and a long troubled past. As Stefan Tanaka has shown, *tōyōshi* provided justification for Japan's imperial expansion,[29] and historians like Yi Pyŏng-do, the central figure in positivist and critical-textual historiography, conceded a great deal to *tōyōshi*, to its status as objective, academic, and uniquely legitimating historical scholarship. Thus, contemporaneous with Paek Nam-un's work, the 1930s saw Korean historians coalescing around three competing schools: nationalist historiography as it emerged in the first decade of the twentieth century, its claims, central themes, and narrative strategy outlined by Sin Ch'ae-ho; socioeconomic (Marxist) historiography, with Paek Nam-un situating Korean history in world history, and Korean history unfolding in accordance with historical laws (and thus a historiography "that does not know despair"); and positivist historiography, as represented by Yi Pyŏng-do and the Chindan Society, that aimed for an objective, academic approach to history writing.

There are a number of problems with a typology such as this. Much of modern Korean historiography does not fit neatly into these categories, and the categories themselves distort as much as they explain. But this typology does offer a useful starting point for understanding how a majority of South Korean historians, until quite recently, thought about their intellectual genealogy, their relationship to certain modes of historical writing, and their political and ideological stance. Once the Japanese Empire collapsed in 1945, the commitment to objectivity on the part of positivist historians appeared as little more than complicity with colonialism. Many of the historians who had privileged objectivity had participated actively in institutions established by the Japanese colonial state and had helped produce colonial narratives under the banner of academic rigor. In the months following liberation (August 15, 1945), it was Marxist intellectuals like Paek Nam-un who were energized, and they began laying the foundations for postcolonial Korea's higher academic institutions. The day after

Japan's surrender, Paek began organizing the Chosŏn haksulwŏn (Korean Academy of Sciences), welcoming leading progressive scholars across the disciplines, from engineering to literature, science, and art. But the partition of Korea and U.S. military occupation below the 38th parallel stopped this process. In August 1946, when the U.S. Army Military Government in Korea (USAMGIK) announced its plan to merge Keijō Imperial University with nine existing professional schools to form Seoul National University, Paek was vocal in his criticism of the plan: university faculty would have little autonomy from the USAMGIK's Department of Education, and academics who had actively collaborated in support of the Japanese Empire would be included in the faculty. With conservatives in control of the Department of Education, however, the Korean historians appointed to the faculty of Seoul National University were mostly Chindan Society members, including Yi Pyŏng-do. As U.S. occupation forces prepared to create a separate anticommunist state in southern Korea, many Marxist intellectuals, including Paek, went north, pushed by anticommunist repression and pulled by offers of employment and opportunity to take important roles in the national democratic revolution under way on the other side of the 38th parallel.

Chapter 5 presents a brief outline of how positivist historiography came to be reconstituted as nationalist historiography after 1945. In 1961 Yi Kibaek published *Kuksa sillon* (A New History of Korea), written as a history textbook that incorporated the narrative of *kŭndaehwa* (modernization). Echoing W. W. Rostow's emphasis on the importance of creating new social groups—intellectuals, merchants, and military personnel—for economic development in the Third World,[30] Yi attributed dynastic change and historical progress in Korean history to the emergence of new social classes. In thus adopting modernization theory promoted by American academics and advisors, *Kuksa sillon* presented a non-Marxist postcolonial narrative that was anti-Japanese but uncritical of American intervention. This renovation of the textual-critical tradition, in the form of modernization narratives, quickly became the dominant mode of history writing in the context of the cold war. Chapter 5 makes the observation that the question of neocolonialism (the United States in South Korea), suppressed by the anticommunist state, came to be sublimated through developmental time: South Korea was developing with American assistance but also by using its own sources of modernity. The bulk of chapter 5, however, focuses on how and why Marxist historiography of the 1930s was reconfigured as nationalist historiography in the 1970s and 1980s. Because Paek Nam-un went to North Korea in 1948, historians in South Korea could not cite his work, and the only way to integrate and engage his work was by casting him as a nationalist historian. Through their empirical studies of land tenure, growth of commerce (merchant capital), and the development of a commodity-monetary economy in the latter half of Chosŏn, Kim Yong-sŏp and Kang Man-gil revived and confirmed Paek's disclosure of the internal dynamic underlying Korea's historical development, with class struggle central to that process.

Under a nationalist canopy, then, Kim Yong-sŏp and Kang Man-gil reestablished intellectual links to a form of history writing that had been suppressed in South Korea after the Korean War. Their view of history was based on an anticolonial, oppositional nationalism, and their historiography contributed greatly to understanding the dynamic nature of Korea's social and economic development in late Chosŏn. In this limited sense, Kim and Kang shared common ground with nationalist historians who preferred modernization theory; their common agenda was to write a Korea-centered history. But the implications of their historical narrative could not be more different. For modernization historians, the origins of Korea's modernity were to be found in the cultural and scientific developments in the eighteenth century and traced forward to Westernized and Westernizing elites of the nineteenth century and to the noncommunist nationalists in the twentieth century who would eventually establish South Korea. Kim, along with Kang, laid the basis for the argument that there were two possible paths to modernity: a relatively more egalitarian and autonomous path from below, with peasant rebellions providing the main impetus for progressive change, and a more exploitative, dependent path from above, led by elites who would ultimately capitulate to imperialist demands starting in the late nineteenth century.

Kim and Kang located the Westernized and Westernizing elites within a historical trajectory that had roots in the cultural and political world of the landed class in the late Chosŏn period, whose modernization efforts from the late nineteenth century to the present reflected their narrow class interests, and for that reason tended toward dependency on outside powers, that is, collaboration with the Japanese in the colonial period and with the Americans after 1945. This was a trajectory that paved the way for Korea's colonization by Japan, formation of separate states in 1948, and dictatorship and dependent capitalist development in South Korea. This revisionist historical narrative found a broad audience with the publication in 1979 of *Haebang chŏnhusa ŭi insik* (Korean History before and after Liberation), edited by the courageous intellectual and journalist Song Kŏn-ho. This book presented a powerful account of how 1945 marked the beginning of the most horrific chapter in modern Korean history. It exposed the inglorious origins of the South Korean state and negated cold war historiography by positing as *nationalist* the resistance to the UN-sponsored separate elections in 1948 on which South Korea claims its legal basis.

It was the people's uprising in the city of Kwangju in 1980, however, and the massacre perpetrated by South Korean troops that finally broke the South Korean government's ideological hegemony. The magnitude of the state violence drove students and intellectuals to search for the structural and historical origins of South Korea's dictatorship. Drawing on historical narratives like those in *Haebang chŏnhusa ŭi insik*, through *minjung* (people's) art, *minjung* theology, and protest music and performance, students and intellectuals sought to constitute the *minjung* (the subaltern) as a national and nationalist subject, a subjectivity that could be an alternative to and autonomous from nationalist narratives authorized by either the North Korean or the South Korean state. For Kang Man-gil, the historian's most pressing task was to write a history of modern Korea from a perspective unfettered by "the structure of division." Such a perspective is accessible, Kang argued, when historians understand the political struggles of the immediate postliberation period not simply as the denouement of the colonial experience but also as a struggle to overcome national division.

Since the 1980s, then, nationalist historiography in South Korea has been associated with leftist politics. In the last decade of the twentieth century, with the collapse of socialist states in Eastern Europe and the dissolution of the Soviet Union, what might be called postnationalist historiography began to gain ground in South Korea. Weary of nationalism's totalizing power, a number of literary critics, along with historians outside the field of Korean studies, drew on postcolonial theory and took aim at much of modern Korean historiography (that is, not just nationalist historiography), among other things for its fixation on narratives of linear development. But the principal target was nationalist historiography for its erasure of plurality, complexity, and difference. In an interesting twist, the so-called New Right welcomed scholarship inspired by postcolonial theory for its refusal to narrate the colonial period as the Manichaean struggle of a colonizing Japan that was racist and exploitative, opposed by a resisting and enduring people, or nation (*minjung, minjok*). With this, the New Right turned to criticism of nationalism in general, and nationalist historiography of the 1980s in particular, attacking nationalist historiography for questioning South Korea's legitimacy.

In *Haebang chŏnhusa ŭi chaeinsik* (Reexamination of Korean History before and after Liberation), published in February 2006 with enthusiastic coverage from conservative dailies like the *Chosŏn ilbo*, the editors charged that leftist-nationalist historiography, as epitomized by *Haebang chŏnhusa ŭi insik*, was responsible for the "dangerously distorted" historical perspective held by a sizable segment of the public (mostly the younger generation) as well as by the left-leaning Roh Moo-hyun administration. Compiled by four scholars identified with postmodern theory and the New Right, the title of this two-volume anthology deliberately evoked *Haebang chŏnhusa ŭi insik*, signaling the editors' intention of restoring balance to the historical understanding of colonial and postcolonial history. The editors of *Haebang chŏnhusa ŭi chaeinsik* argued that the leftist-nationalist historiography of the 1980s had achieved near hegemony in politics, in spite of later research that should have corrected such a skewed view. They argued that leftist-nationalist historiography remained entrenched, discouraging the publication of more "objective" scholarship.[31] The New Right welcomed postcolonial critiques of nationalism and nationalist historiography as a way to reassert the sovereignty of the individual (!) and to reaffirm the sovereignty of South Korea and the legitimacy of its anticommunist legacy.

As intensely anticommunist as the Old Right but also fiercely liberal in terms of their commitment to individual freedoms and market capitalism, the New Right accommodated postcolonial scholarship as a tactical move, while their strategic target was leftist-nationalist historiography and its political expression. As Bruce Cumings points out, what the New Right saw as a "dangerously distorted" historical perspective appeared time and again in classified reports authored by American military and intelligence officers who were critical of U.S. policy toward Korea.[32] It should also be noted that a number of contributors to *Haebang chŏnhusa ŭi chaeinsik*, either implicitly or explicitly, took issue with the kind of universalism assumed by the editors of *Haebang chŏnhusa ŭi chaeinsik*—a universalism identified as "civilization"[33] —based on triumphalist notions of progress and neoliberal values that conveniently separated the present from histories of violence, expropriation, exploitation, and control. While it is evident that there is no longer an "outside" to the logics of global capitalism, it is also evident from the history of history writing presented in this book that global capitalism creates surpluses that refuse to be disciplined or regimented — specifically, knowledge, experience, and subjectivity, surpluses that constitute a form of wealth to which not just intellectuals but the multitude also has access. As Michael Hardt and Antonio Negri have argued, the poor revolt not because they have nothing to lose, but because they are rich: "Deprivation . . . may breed anger, indignation, and antagonism, but revolt arises only on the basis of wealth, that is, a surplus of intelligence, experience, knowledges, and desire . . . not because the poor are empty and excluded from wealth but because they are included in the circuits of production and full of potential, which always exceeds what capital and the global political body can expropriate and control."[34] In other words, the great enterprise of sovereignty was potent fiction, a fiction that became a head over heels romance that allowed for the production of the language and the coordinates for the critique of sovereignty's complicity with power. Sovereignty provided the conceptual language for writing national histories, but it also constituted the site for the continuous production of oppositional subjectivities and political alternatives.

PART I

Sovereignty

chapter one

SOVEREIGNTY AND IMPERIALISM

> A historically meaningful imperialism is not only or essentially military and maritime panoply, not only economic and financial prosperity, but, also, this ability to determine in and of itself the content of political and legal concepts. . . . A nation is conquered first when it acquiesces to a foreign vocabulary, a foreign concept of law, especially international law.
>
> — CARL SCHMITT, lecture, 1933

On January 7, 1895, King Kojong, accompanied by Queen Min, Crown Prince Yi Ch'ŏk, the Taewŏn'gun (regent), royal princes, cabinet ministers, vice ministers, and hundreds of officials, musicians, dancers, and attendants, was at the *chongmyo*, the Chosŏn dynasty's Royal Ancestral Temple.[1] Performing the grand sacrificial rite at the Royal Ancestral Temple as a direct male descendant of Yi Sŏng-gye, the dynastic founder (King T'aejo), King Kojong stood before the spirit chambers of Chosŏn dynasty kings and their queens as the archetypal filial son, Chosŏn Korea's supreme sacerdotal authority, and as its monarch, the carrier of the dynastic mission and the bearer of Heaven's mandate (*ch'ŏnmyŏng*). In 1895 the nineteen spirit chambers in the Main Hall held the spirit tablets of the major Chosŏn dynasty kings and their queens, starting with the spirit tablet of the dynastic founder and his queen in the westernmost chamber, with descending kings and queens in sequence toward the eastern end. As he performed the great offerings, King Kojong swore to preserve the dynasty that his ancestors had founded and sustained for 503 years. Reading the Oath "in the presence of the Spirits of Our Ancestors in Heaven," Kojong vowed, "We will no longer lean upon another state [*t'abang*] but will lay broad the destiny of the nation [*kukbo*: destiny of the state], restore prosperity, build up the happiness of Our people, and thus secure Our autonomy and independence [*chaju tongnip*]."

> We declare publicly to all the Imperial Ancestors that We, your humble descendant, have received and guarded the mighty heritage of Our Ancestors. . . . But now in our generation, the times are greatly changed. . . . A neighboring

Power and the unanimous judgment of all our officers unite in affirming that only as an independent ruler can We make our country strong. How can We your humble descendant, having received the spirit of the times from Heaven, refuse to conform and thus fail to preserve the heritage bestowed by Our Ancestors? . . . From this time forth We will no longer lean upon another state but will lay broad the destiny of the nation, restore prosperity, build up the happiness of Our people and thus secure Our independence. . . . Therefore, We, Your humble descendant, do now take the fourteen great Laws and swear in the presence of the Spirits of Our Ancestors in Heaven and announce that, relying on the merits bestowed by Our Ancestors, we will bring these to a successful issue, nor will We dare to retract Our word. Bright Spirits, descend and behold!

1. All thought of dependence on China shall be put away so that the heritage of independence may be secured.[2]

Perhaps the scores of musicians, dancers, and attendants did not know, but high-level officials certainly did, that it was the "neighboring Power" (*ubang*: allied country) — specifically, Inoue Kaoru, Meiji Japan's envoy extraordinary and minister plenipotentiary to Korea — who had compelled King Kojong to make this "Oath of Independence." It was Inoue who had taken the lead in using the great offering at *chongmyo-sajik* to render the Western concepts of sovereignty and independence sensible and manifest to the scholar-official class and the broader public. Isabella Bird, who witnessed this "singular ceremony," recounted how the Oath was taken "in circumstances of great solemnity in a dark pine wood, under the shadow of Puk Han [Mt. Pukhan] at the most sacred altar in Korea, in presence of the Court and the dignitaries of the kingdom." "Old and serious men had fasted and mourned for two previous days, and in the vast crowd of white-robed and black-hatted men which looked down upon the striking scene from a hill in the grounds of the Mulberry Palace, there was not a smile or a spoken word. The sky was dark and grim, and a bitter east wind was blowing — ominous signs in Korean estimation."[3]

In the late Chosŏn period, great offerings at the Royal Ancestral Temple and at the Altars of Land and Harvest formed the core of the dynasty's auspicious rites and were performed several times each year. By the nineteenth century the Main Hall of the Royal Ancestral Temple complex, with its long front corridor connecting the nineteen spirit chambers, boasted the world's longest floor space in a wooden structure. At the temple, to the east of the main palace, the Chosŏn dynasty monarch reported to the ghosts of his dead ancestors regarding important matters of state and asked for their help and guidance.[4] At the Altars of Land and Harvest (sajik), to the west of the main palace, the monarch prayed to the gods of earth and grain for his people's security and well-being. Throughout the Chosŏn period, until the very end of King Kojong's reign (1864–1907), Chosŏn dynasty kings as well as scholar-officials (sadaebu) regarded these two ritual sites as the metonym for what we would call the Chosŏn state.[5] Chosŏn dynasty monarchs could, and did, subscribe to the notion that the people (min) constituted the foundation, and that the people's welfare formed the raison d'être of the state. But sovereignty—supreme authority within Korea's borders—belonged to the Chosŏn monarch, and a core function of dynastic rituals had to do with the (re)production of knowledge and sentiment associated with filiality and loyalty as appropriate for a strictly hierarchical and patriarchal social order. Although the power of Chosŏn dynasty monarchs was circumscribed by the scholar-official class, a class that resolutely clung to the conceit that the Chosŏn dynasty was its creation, it was dynastic kingly power as manifested by the Royal Ancestral Temple and the Altars of Land and Harvest (chongmyo-sajik) that stood guard over the progressively lesser prerogatives of the king's subjects.[6] Neither the scholar-official class nor the commoners, and certainly not the slaves (nobi), could presume to claim the chongmyo-sajik as their own. If the Chosŏn monarch spoke French he would have said, "L'état, c'est moi."[7]

While the chongmyo-sajik provided the symbolic and cognitive coordinates for identifying and identification with Chosŏn Korea as a dynastic state, its state rituals also designated Chosŏn as a not-so-exemplary vassal state of China. In 1395, when the Chosŏn dynasty built its Royal Ancestral Temple in the new capital, Hanyang (Seoul), its structure conformed to ancient prescriptions proper to a tributary state. The temple was built according to the "same hall, different chambers" system utilized in the Han dynasty, with the westernmost chamber as the honored position. The original Main Hall was a seven-kan structure with five spirit chambers, the number of spirit chambers stipulated by the Zhōu dynasty as appropriate for a tributary state. But by 1834 the Main Hall had been expanded to a nineteen-kan structure. In China the royal shrines of Tang and Song dynasties had only eleven chambers. Thus, as in other institutions and practices, the Chosŏn dynasty's Royal Ancestral Temple complex, patterned on Chinese precedents, came to take on a uniquely Korean and not so subservient character.[8]

During the previous dynasty, Koryŏ (918–1392) had also entered into some form of tributary relations, often reluctantly, with Song, Liao, and Jin as those dynasties established control over parts of "China" in succession.[9] At the same time, from the very beginning of the Koryŏ dynasty through the latter part of the thirteenth century, many Koryŏ scholar-officials, in both official and private writing, referred to the Koryŏ ruler as a Son of Heaven (K: *ch'ŏnja*, C: *tiānzǐ*) and emperor (*hwangje, sŏnghwang, che*). As Ro Myoung-ho has pointed out, until 1270, when Koryŏ capitulated to the Mongols after thirty years of resistance, early Koryŏ rulers and most of its officials had held a "pluralist" (*tawŏnjŏk*) outlook that recognized greater and equal empires in China and in Manchuria, while positing Koryŏ as the center of a separate and bounded world ruled by the Koryŏ emperor, who claimed a ritual status reserved for the Son of Heaven.[10] Koryŏ rulers from the dynastic founder Wang Kŏn (T'aejo, r. 918–43) to Wŏnjong (r. 1214–74) had the imperial suffix *-cho*, or *-jong* for their posthumous temple names. The Koryŏ Army was organized into five armies rather than the three allowed to a king. During this period Koryŏ rulers were addressed with the imperial *p'yeha* (C: *bixia*), wore the imperial yellow, used their own reign names, invested members of the royal family as kings (*wang*), and conducted sacrifices to Heaven.[11] As Remco Breuker notes, imperial designations for edict, crown prince, palace, and so on are easily found in extant records, while epitaphs and eulogies on steles reveal "diverse and colorful instances of imperial appropriations."[12]

Referring to the Koryŏ ruler as emperor and Son of Heaven seems to have been commonplace in early Koryŏ; for example, among "folk" songs (*sogak*) in the music (*akji*) section of the *Koryŏsa*, "P'ungipsong" eulogizes the Koryŏ ruler as "Son of Heaven in the East" (*Haedong ch'ŏnja*), who as emperor, with the help of Buddha and Heaven, pacifies the world through his transformative instruction (*kyohwa*).[13] Indeed the rise and fall of various dynasties in "China," from the late Tang to the establishment of the Yüan dynasty, encouraged late Silla and early Koryŏ courts to articulate, using ostensibly Sinocentric spatial terms, their own centrality in a multipolar world. Until capitulation to the Mongols, Koryŏ was an "empire" with its own microtributary system. The Koryŏ emperor forced Jurchen tribes outside its borders to pay tribute and accept Koryŏ's suzerainty, and then bestowed titles appropriate to tribute-offering vassals from beyond Koryŏ.[14] Unequal sovereignty did not neatly correspond to borders: it was not a simple matter of being a king abroad and an emperor at home. For late Silla and early Koryŏ rulers, their appropriation, or annexation, of All under Heaven (K: ch'ŏnha, C: tianxia) to assert their vision of different, coexisting "worlds" as a broadly shared idea went hand in hand with the production of complex discursive strategies that affirmed these rulers' possession of full de jure sovereignty, that is, possession of Heaven's mandate. Even as Silla and Koryŏ rulers received investiture from (another) Son of Heaven, it was Heaven itself that ostensibly supported these rulers' authority. As the folk song "P'ungipsong" suggests, Koryŏ was the center of the haedong (East of the Sea) world, and the ruler of Koryŏ ruled as emperor and Son of Heaven. It seems this folk song was sung well into the Chosŏn period.[15]

Haidong (East of the Sea; K: haedong) in Tang dynasty texts referred to a geographic area considered to be separate and distinct from China, a historicized space that encompassed the three kingdoms Koguryŏ, Silla, and Paekche. According to Ch'u Myŏng-ŏp, the term Haedong was appropriated by the Silla court during the "Unified" Silla period to name a bounded world south of the Liao River. While the boundaries of Haedong, or for that matter the boundaries of Samhan (referring to Koguryŏ, Silla, and Paekche), did not remain fixed, the spatial imaginaries Haedong and Samhan constituted the "world" (ch'ŏnha) that the early rulers of the Koryŏ dynasty claimed as emperors and Sons of Heaven.[16] In 933, when Wang Kŏn received investiture from the ruler of later Tang, Tang acknowledged the dynastic founder of Koryŏ as the legitimate successor to King Chumong, the legendary founder of Koguryŏ. At the same time, as Sem Vermeersch points out, Wang Kŏn's reign title ch'ŏnsu (Heaven Bestowed) made it clear that he had received the mandate to rule directly from Heaven.[17]

While this pluralist outlook seems to have prevailed in early Koryŏ, some advocated a more full-throated version of Koryŏ as the center of Haedong. In the early twelfth century, with Liao (of the Khitan) fading and Jin (of the Jurchen) taking its place, the monk Myoch'ŏng advocated war with the Jin to "recover" the heartland of Koguryŏ, extending deep into Manchuria. Myoch'ŏng prophesied that the thirty-six countries (that is, the entire world) would eventually submit to Koryŏ and bring tribute.[18] While a definitive assessment is impossible, given the paucity of records from the Koryŏ period, it seems there was significant sympathy and support for an expansionist, irredentist effort. Arguing that the topography of Kae-gyŏng (Kaesŏng), Koryŏ's capital, was losing its vital energy, Myoch'ŏng argued for moving the capital to the Western Capital (Pyongyang).[19] For Myoch'ŏng, the shifting of the capital to Pyongyang also would have sig-naled a commitment to shift away from a China-centered Confucian cul-ture. In the end, Myoch'ŏng's forces were defeated by Kim Pu-sik, a de-feat that the twentieth-century historian Sin Ch'ae-ho would refer to as one of the greatest tragedies in Korean history. Well aware of Koryŏ's im-perial claims and practices, but also aware of its own limits, (Southern) Song's attitude toward Koryŏ imperial claims and practices was rather tol-erant. As for the Liao and Jin, they were more willing to recognize another Son of Heaven, according to Breuker, "perhaps because they always had to compete with other Sons of Heaven."[20] At times Song reception rituals for Koryŏ envoys and Koryŏ reception rituals for imperial envoys from Song, Liao, and Jin suggested equal rather than hierarchical relations; that is, while Song, Liao, and Jin did not wholly recognize Koryŏ imperial claims and practices, neither did they reject them completely.[21]

In 1270, after thirty years of struggle against the Mongols, Koryŏ finally capitulated to the Yüan. The Yüan established commanderies in Pyong-yang and Ssangsŏng and demoted the titles of the Koryŏ ruler, court, and officials. This capitulation to the Mongols assured dynastic continuity in terms of the Koryŏ name, ancestral shrines, and guardian deities of the state. But starting with King Ch'ungnyŏl (r. 1274–1308), the Koryŏ crown prince was raised in Beijing, Koryŏ kings married princesses of the Yüan imperial house, and Koryŏ became a son-in-law state (puma'guk) of the Yüan empire. During this period the Yüan dynasty exerted a powerful in-fluence over kingly succession in Koryŏ, and the temple names of six Koryŏ kings, from Ch'ungnyŏl to Ch'ungjŏng (r. 1348–51), were made to begin with ch'ung (loyalty), indicating loyalty to the Yüan. The Koryŏ court's son-in-law status—that is, its loss of full sovereignty—lasted until the mid-fourteenth century, when King Kongmin captured Ssangsŏng and declared the Koryŏ throne autonomous.[22]

At the beginning of the Chosŏn dynasty, to reconfirm sovereign au-tonomy that had been lost to the Yüan during the latter part of the Koryŏ period, the Chosŏn court built an Altar to Heaven. The officials on the Board of Rites insisted, however, that the Altar be called wŏndan (Round Altar) rather than wŏn'gudan (Round Hill Altar), to avoid the appearance of asserting the Chosŏn monarch's ritual equivalence with the Ming emperor and thus avoid conflict with Ming China. The majority of the *sadaebu* resisted the wishes of early Chosŏn dynasty kings to personally conduct the sacrifice to Heaven at the *wŏndan*, an act that would have unmistakably constituted the Chosŏn monarch as equal in ritual status with the Ming emperor. Preventing the monarch from conducting sacrifices to Heaven was a duty of the scholar-official class checking the power of Chosŏn dynasty kings.[23] The *sadaebu* repeatedly reminded early Chosŏn monarchs that only the Son of Heaven (the emperor of China) had the requisite ritual status to conduct sacrifices to Heaven.[24] After King Sejo's reign (1455–68), subsequent Chosŏn dynasty monarchs seem to have given up on the *wŏndan*, and it faded away.[25] Thus in 1895 the Chosŏn dynasty *chongmyo-sajik* configuration, delimited by the absence of an Altar to Heaven, unmistakably signified Chosŏn's ritually subordinate status to China. In 1897, when King Kojong declared Korea an empire, an Altar to Heaven was rebuilt on the site where high-level envoys from Qing China used to be lodged. In 1913, three years after annexation, the Japanese colonial government dismantled the Altar to Heaven, and a hotel was built on the site.[26]

In establishing the Chosŏn dynasty in 1392, Yi Sŏng-gye found it necessary to seek tributary status from the Ming emperor, and subsequent Chosŏn dynasty kings had to continue the practice of receiving investiture from the Ming emperor. But at the same time, the capital-based scholar-officials who helped Yi Sŏng-gye establish the Chosŏn dynasty maintained that the dynastic founder had received Heaven's mandate to rule. In August 1392, the founding year of the Chosŏn dynasty, Cho Pak of the Board of Rites submitted a memorial to the throne in which he affirmed a long history of Korean rulers receiving the mandate directly from Heaven: "Because Tan'gun was the first ruler to receive the Mandate of Heaven in Korea (Tongbang), and Kija [C: Jizi] was the first ruler to bring civilization to fruition in Korea, the magistrate in Pyongyang should be instructed to conduct sacrifices to them at appropriate times."[27] In confirming Tan'gun's direct relationship to Heaven and his status as the founder of the first "Korean" state (in 2333 BCE near Pyongyang), and by having the city of Pyongyang conduct sacrifices to both Tan'gun and Kija, the *sadaebu* of the early Chosŏn dynasty chose to buttress a religious and political narrative (and practice) that was already well established during the Koryŏ period: the claim to a distinct and indigenous history of legitimacy (*chŏngt'ong*) that reached far back into the mythic past, indeed to the days of Tan'gun contemporaneous with the Chinese sage kings Yao and Shun.[28]

In the same memorial, however, Cho Pak also requested King T'aejo to put an end to royal sacrifices to Heaven at the Round Hill Altar, pointedly reminding him that only the Son of Heaven (the emperor of China) could perform the sacrifice. Unlike the Ming emperor, King T'aejo could not claim the unique status of mediator between Heaven and the civilized world.[29] The seeming contradiction of proclaiming an indigenous and distinct history of legitimacy for Chosŏn, on the one hand, and insisting that the Chosŏn dynasty monarch observe ritual proprieties appropriate for a vassal state of Ming China, on the other, points to the complex ways in which Yi Sŏng-gye and the capital-based *sadaebu* negotiated power between themselves to overcome both external and internal obstacles when establishing the Chosŏn dynasty. In other words, the capital-based scholar-official class that helped Yi to power was careful to institutionalize structures, practices, and narratives that limited the power and authority of the Chosŏn monarch.[30] This arrangement, or settlement, along with the contingent and dynamic aspects of Ming-Chosŏn and Qing-Chosŏn relations, produced multiple and seemingly conflicting narratives — conflicting, that is, from the modern standpoint of sovereignty in the modern nation-state system.

In the seventeenth century, after two invasions, the second having been truly devastating and humiliating, the Chosŏn dynasty acknowledged Qing suzerainty, but without truly accepting the Manchu dynasty's claim over the Central Plain (K: *chungwŏn*). Scholars like Song Si-yŏl (1607–89), who lived through both invasions as a young man, yearned to overthrow the Qing and restore the Ming. For Song, disrecognition of Qing China was fundamentally linked to the question of civilization, and as adamant a Ming loyalist as he was, he also made it quite clear that civilization was not permanently tied to place or people. Both Confucius and Mencius, for example, were born in states where previously the region and its people had been considered foreign, or barbaric (*tongyi*), and Song argued vigorously that it was the duty of learned men in Chosŏn Korea to continue the civilizational legacy that began with the sage kings Yao and Shun, a precious legacy that was cultivated and transmitted by Confucius, Mencius, and Zhu Xi and taken up by Yi Hwang (Toegye) and Yi I (Yulgok) of Chosŏn Korea.[31] That commitment to civilizational legacy is what prompted Song's disciples to build a shrine to the Ming emperor, both to make amends for the failure to actually launch an attack against the Qing and as an expression of their claim to the Ming mantle of civilization.[32]

To reclaim its authority over rituals and discourse on the state of Chosŏn Korea's civilization, and even as it performed rituals of submission to the Qing, the Chosŏn court took the dramatic step of also establishing a shrine to the Ming. Sukchong (r. 1674–1720) established a shrine to the Ming Wanli emperor on the palace grounds, and eighteenth-century monarchs like Yŏngjo (r. 1724–76) and Chŏngjo (r. 1776–1800) expanded the scope of sacrifices to Ming emperors. This high-stakes politics over ritual practice helped establish a potent narrative of Chosŏn Korea as soChunghwa, a lesser civilization compared to Ming China, but after the Manchu conquest of China, the last bastion of civilization. That is to say, late sixteenth-century and seventeenth-century mortuary rites to the Ming conducted by Chosŏn monarchs and the sadaebu were acts of self-identification that would maintain Chosŏn Korea's distance from Qing China and elevate Chosŏn Korea and its civilization at Qing's expense.[33] In broader historical perspective, Chosŏn officials, from the beginning to the end of the Chosŏn dynasty, often chafed at the demands imposed by the tributary relationship with China. At the very beginning of the Chosŏn period Chosŏn officials repeatedly balked at the amount of tribute to be paid to the Ming. In relation to the Qing, Gari Ledyard wryly notes that Korean diplomats on tribute missions to Beijing seemed strangely graceless and clumsy in their ritual obeisance, at least during rehearsals supervised by the Chinese Board of Rites.[34]

In the late nineteenth century, this complex discursive history surrounding Chosŏn's tributary status—that is, Korea's multiple, seemingly conflicting narratives on legitimacy—presented a conundrum and obstacle to Japanese and Western imperialism. Inoue Kaoru in fact had been a key official in Meiji Japan's first concerted attempt to "deterritorialize" and then "reterritorialize" Chosŏn's zone of contact.[35] As the vice envoy, Inoue was signatory to the 1876 Treaty of Kanghwa, in which the first article avowed that Chosŏn was an independent country (chaju chi pang) with the same sovereign rights (kwŏn) as Japan.[36] It turned out, however, that this first "Western-style" treaty, to which the Chosŏn court was forced to affix its seal, did not succeed in wrenching Chosŏn Korea from its tributary status toward China. Attached to the Treaty of Friendship and Commerce of 1882, which established relations between the United States and Korea on terms of "equality," King Kojong's dispatch stated that Korea was a dependency of China, "but the management of her government affairs, home and foreign, ha[d] always been vested in the (Korean) sovereign."[37] The strategy, of course, was to try to utilize to best advantage the principles of both the China-centered tributary system as well as the sovereignty-based nation-state system.

In discussions with Li Hongzhang leading up to the U.S.-Korea Treaty of 1882, Kim Yun-sik had pressed for the formulation "for China, Korea is a dependent country; for all others, Korea is independent."[38] Between 1885 and 1887, in the dispute with Britain over its occupation of Port Hamilton (Kŏmundo, a group of islands in the South Sea), Korean authorities made references to international law (man'guk kongbŏp) to illustrate the illegality of the British seizure of Korean territory. It was this ambiguity, the space for maneuver afforded by Korea's embrace of both a China-centered world and the nation-state system, which Inoue wanted to negate. As Alexis Dudden has pointed out, by leading the way in utilizing the post-Westphalian, sovereignty-based conception of international relations, Japanese statesmen like Inoue Kaoru positioned themselves as the preeminent translators and enforcers of international law in East Asia.[39] This strategic move, like many Meiji-period domestic reforms and innovations, was "diplomacy carried on by other means." That is, until 1905 the goal of revising the unequal treaties imposed on Japan was never far from the minds of the Meiji leadership, and many of the "reforms" that were instituted in the Meiji era were intended to remake Japan as recognizably similar to the Western powers (for example, the Meiji emperor appearing in public with a Western haircut, strictures against mixed bathing, ending the ban on Christianity).

There were, of course, other strategic considerations. In Britain's competition with Tsarist Russia, the Great Game, Japan could prevent Russia from establishing a warm water port and thus halt Russian imperial expansion southward into East Asia. For such reasons, Britain and the United States did not oppose Japan's efforts to wrench Chosŏn Korea from its tributary status toward China. Moreover Meiji statesmen like Inoue Kaoru used Britain's imposition of a protectorate status on Egypt in 1882 as a model for giving "full sovereignty" and "independence" to Chosŏn. The destruction of the China-centered theory and practice of tributary relations, based on ritual hierarchy and actual autonomy, was to be replaced by the post-Westphalian theory and practice of equal sovereignty, a shift that would facilitate Japanese domination over Chosŏn Korea. Perhaps it should be said that the idea of equal sovereignty both enabled and restrained Euro-American imperialism in nineteenth-century East Asia. In the main, however, both the theory and the practice of symbolic equality and equal sovereignty facilitated actual domination and inequality—as authorized by international treaties and laws.

The Historicity of Confucian Kingship and Sovereign Space

Since the Three Kingdoms period, when Buddhism first received royal patronage—late fourth century CE for Koguryŏ and Paekche and sixth century CE for Silla—Buddhist monks had entreated the Buddhas and bodhisattvas to protect the state. According to Lewis Lancaster, the Buddhism that was embraced by Koguryŏ and Paekche was the royal religion of the Turkic nomadic kingdoms that had dominated northern China in the late fourth century; developed along the Silk Road, Turkic Buddhism led to the deep involvement of Buddhist monks in political matters.[40] From the Three Kingdoms period to the end of the Koryŏ dynasty, the image of the benevolent and compassionate king in possession of divine attributes (a Cakravartin king), arising from the belief in karmic heritage, had defined and enhanced the authority of kings. While Buddhism affirmed the potential of every human being to achieve an enlightened state of mind, it also legitimated Silla's caste system by way of moral causality spanning more than one lifetime, the cycle of death and rebirth in which, based on its karma, a soul transmigrates and is reborn in various states of existence, as animal, human, aristocrat. Such notions legitimated the Silla aristocracy that differentiated itself from the lower orders on the basis of its *kolp'um*, or bone rank. At the very top of the aristocracy was the *sŏnggol* (holy bone) that identified itself as "a lineage of Buddhas, Buddhist rulers about to become Buddhas, and Indian deities."[41] For newcomers to the throne, the king's identification with Cakravartin kings could compensate for shortcomings in the dynastic founder's family background; Wang Kŏn (temple name T'aejo), for example, who founded the Koryŏ dynasty (918–1392), faced down the aristocrats of Silla as the maintainer of the dharma. Thus in the first of his Ten Injunctions, Wang Kŏn instructed his descendents, "For the great enterprise [*taeŏp*] of our country, it is necessary to procure the protective power of all the Buddhas."[42]

During the Koryŏ period, when the power of Buddhist institutions was at its zenith, the insertion of Indian Buddhist and Jain ideas about kingship into preexisting origin and foundation narratives became a part of histories written by Buddhist monks, narratives that asserted correspondences between Buddhist deities, local gods, and heroes that founded kingdoms. The origin narrative for the first "Korean" state centered on Tan'gun, the progenitor of Ancient Chosŏn. In recording this foundation narrative, the thirteenth-century monk Iryŏn asserted an equivalence between Hwanin, the Celestial Emperor; Śakro Devānām Indra, Lord of the Devas, who lives in Svarga, a set of heavenly worlds located on Mt. Meru (in South Asia); and Tan'gun, Hwanin's grandson, as the manifestation of Śrī Mahādevī.[43] This Buddhist gloss on the Tan'gun narrative was but one articulation of spatial and temporal imaginaries informed by Buddhist discourses, including prophecies about Maitreya, the future Buddha who would appear in Koryŏ to enable the construction of a new world. Though Koryŏcentric, the spatial imaginary here is of a much broader world, with Koryŏ as the East and India as the West, as in this mid-tenth-century inscription: "[King Kwangjong] wants to bring peace to the eastern country and greatly upholds the teaching of the western regions. . . . He draws tranquil water from the river of Sŏn [Zen] and spreads the ways of compassion in the palace. The gate of Lanka was broadly opened; the garden of dhāraṇis was brightly expanded."[44] As Vermeersch points out, during King Kwangjong's reign a climate of terror pervaded the court, and "incriminations sufficed to end a career or a life." King Kwangjong executed a great many people, and to atone for the killing he "held Buddhist masses, distributed alms to the poor, organized the release of animals, and forbade the killing of animals."[45]

Koryŏ rulers like Kwangjong undertook Buddhist consecration rituals, similar to bodhisattva ordination, committing them to the dharma. But however much commitment Kwangjong may have had to upholding the dharma, as sovereign, like all kings and emperors, he also claimed the right to kill. That fundamental aspect of kingly sovereign power did not change with the founding of the Chosŏn dynasty, of course, but the capital-based scholar-officials who helped establish the new dynasty saw themselves as the authors who provided meaning and significance to that dynastic change. Staunchly committed to a great transformative enterprise, they launched a sustained attack on Buddhism and the Buddhist church: Buddhist monks and Buddhist rituals were banished from the court and the capital, and Chosŏn rulers were prevented from undertaking Buddhist consecration rituals. In their commitment to the comprehensive Confucian transformation of ideas, institutions, and practices associated with both kingship and dynastic narratives, these scholar-officials constituted themselves as the ruling class and the Chosŏn state as a Confucian bureaucratic state. Confucian rituals became the point of departure for governance (*yech'i*), with ritual propriety understood as having a transformative power, able to constitute people as righteous and loyal subjects, making it less necessary for laws or the king to kill so many. By the late sixteenth century the Chosŏn dynasty could claim success in naturalizing Confucian rituals, rituals that created and mediated status identities (*sinbun*) and affective relations.[46]

How was it that the scholar-officials and aristocrats residing in and around the capital, who were themselves steeped in Buddhist lore, so determined to eradicate Buddhist influence from the political and cultural life of the Chosŏn court and the scholar-official class? The decision to completely purge Buddhism from state rituals, and Buddhist institutions and influence from the Chosŏn court, provided the fledgling dynasty its material basis—in terms of land, labor, and taxes—for consolidating state power. We should not lose sight of the pressing institutional and security concerns behind the campaign against Buddhism. There was a great need to expand the tax base, reward merit subjects with land, and calculate how the new dynastic state could consolidate power. This pushed the *sadaebu* to bring about the destruction of over three thousand Buddhist temples, seize monastery lands and slaves, limit the number of novices permitted to become monks, sell Buddhist statues to Japan or melt them down to mint coins, and prohibit Buddhist monks from entering the capital.

But at the same time it is difficult not to see this particular dynastic change as also emblematic of a purposeful epistemological act. There were sustained and coordinated diatribes not just against Buddhist institutions and practices (particularly mortuary rites) but also against shamans and shamanistic practices. Perhaps the most consequential epistemological move was made by Chŏng To-jŏn (1342–98), one of the intellectual founders of the new dynasty, who so effectively made use of the categories of orthodox and heterodox thought. After Chŏng, the Confucian literati would regularly draw distinctions between orthodox learning and aberrant concepts (*idan*), and such categories provided the intellectual basis for the articulation and dissemination of Confucian notions about sovereignty and selfhood (with its focus on self-cultivation) and the suppression of Buddhist concerns with other-worldliness and salvation.

One could still find in the seventeenth and eighteenth centuries maps showing how the land itself (the topography of the Korean peninsula) continued to be conceptualized in Buddhist terms; for example, Korea's mountains linked to the mountains of Tibet that formed the head of a huge dragon, its long body stretching east along the mountain ranges above Mongolia, with its tail sweeping down south along Korea's T'aebaek mountain range, its tip ending with Mt. Halla on Cheju Island off the southern coast of the Korean peninsula.[47] But sovereign space as imagined by late Chosŏn scholar-officials was definitively bounded, and in spatial terms the embrace of a Neo-Confucian universal order meant a turning away from Koryŏ claims to a culturally distinct empire. As Andre Schmid notes, "By the late Chosŏn dynasty, travelers to China were quite conscious that, in the words of the famous scholar Pak Chiwŏn, 'This river [the Yalu River] is the point of contact and the boundary between them and us.' To cross the Yalu River was to enter into Qing territory."[48] In the eighteenth and nineteenth centuries, writes Schmid, Chosŏn officials demonstrated their considerable talent in performing tribute formalities before Qing officials sent to clarify the border between Chosŏn and China, while remaining adamant about Chosŏn land claims and interpretation of border markers.[49] I think it is possible to understand this spatial imaginary of Chosŏn as a bounded sovereign space as indicative of a continuing sense of being besieged, following the incredible shock of invasions from Japan and then by the Manchus, as Pak Che-ga put it, "when Heaven collapsed and Earth was torn apart" and barbarians (the Manchus) overthrew the Ming dynasty.[50]

In the seventeenth century it had not seemed far-fetched for Song Si-yŏl to advocate war with the Qing empire:

> Today, those who oppose the plan for northern subjugation try to justify their position by stating that our military is too weak to carry out such a task. However, Koguryŏ was able to defeat millions [sic] of Sui and Tang soldiers despite the fact that their territory was only one-third of the land we now call our own. No less a figure than Emperor Taizong of Tang was humbled by our ancestors during the battle for Ansi Fortress. Those barbarians [Manchus] are nothing more than an uncivilized people who do not add up to one ten-thousandth of the worth of Emperor Taizong.[51]

By Pak Chi-wŏn's time, however, it was clear that Chosŏn would not be able to march north to "punish" the Manchus, leaving a situation of continued unease over sharing a border with the Qing Empire. Eighteenth-century scholars-officials like Yu Tŭk-kong (1749–1807), a disciple of Pak Chi-wŏn, wrote histories about Korea's "northern" dynasties Koguryŏ and Parhae, highlighting great military victories over the Sui and Tang Empires. At the same time, Yu did not write *Palhaego* as part of an irredentist project. As Huh Tae-yong explains, the book was a recollection about a powerful kingdom that served a different purpose: to reinforce the notion of Chosŏn as the last bastion of civilization. Early twentieth-century nationalist historians like Sin Ch'ae-ho saw Koguryŏ's military victories against the Sui and Tang as proof of strength and resistance to China. But, as Huh argues, Yu's historiography should not be read as a prototype or precursor to twentieth-century nationalist historiography. His histories of Koguryŏ and Parhae were meant to show "that Confucian-based Sinocentric order could be restored" within the bounded space of Chosŏn.[52]

To be sure, in the early part of the Chosŏn period, the court and the scholar-official class chafed at paying tribute to the Ming—so revered by Song Si-yŏl after its demise—especially human tribute (girls for the harem and boys to serve as eunuchs), since young girls sent to the Ming palace were recruited from among daughters of low- to middle-grade officials.[53] The number of human beings requisitioned was relatively small (several dozen a year), and in 1433 the Ming emperor stopped this practice. Just as in the early Koryŏ period, the Chosŏn court had built a Temple to Heaven and established its own microtributary system, launching punitive expeditions to Tsushima (today part of Nagasaki Prefecture) and border areas inhabited by the Jurchen, forcing these polities to submit as vassals to the Chosŏn ruler and to pay tribute. By the sixteenth century, however, the Chosŏn ruler was clearly not an emperor, nor did the Chosŏn court see itself as the center of a separate and distinct world. The Chosŏn monarch, the *sadaebu*, and the literati in the countryside embraced the civilization-barbarism binary associated with Sinocentrism.[54] This conviction in the correctness of a China-centered world was authorized by a conception of sovereignty that could not be based on the notion of multiple centers or multiple worlds, as in centuries prior.

In the late sixteenth century and early seventeenth, the devastations wrought by the Hideyoshi and Manchu invasions and the political disorientation brought on by the collapse of the Ming dynasty prompted the Chosŏn monarchy and the *sadaebu* to intensify efforts to "Confucianize"

Chosŏn society.[55] When the Manchus demanded that the Chosŏn court transfer to the Qing dynasty the deferential ritual and diplomatic protocols Chosŏn had observed in its relations with the Ming court, the Chosŏn court and the *sadaebu* could not bring themselves to comply, to which the Manchus responded with two invasions, in 1627 and 1636. Having to capitulate to the Manchus in 1636 and witness the "barbarian" Manchus seizing the center of civilization in 1644, mid-seventeenth-century Chosŏn literati could only fantasize about "marching north" to restore the Ming dynasty.[56] Forced to submit, and faced with the immense task of restoring its networks of power and authority, the Chosŏn dynasty's reaction in the intellectual and cultural realm was to (re)invigorate patriarchy and reinforce the categories of civilization (*hwa*) and barbarism (*yi*).[57] For the Chosŏn elite after the seventeenth century, it was Chosŏn's embrace of Chunghwa, a China-centered culturalism, and their own commitment to the basic categories that defined that world in terms of inner and outer, civilization and barbarism (*hwa* and *yi*), that endowed Chosŏn with its distinctive and civilized state-ness. It was through deep intellectual engagement with and fidelity to a China-centered cultural inheritance that the civilization of Chosŏn realized its full potentiality, its cosmic meaning.

That is to say, the collapse of the Ming dynasty in the mid-seventeenth century had the effect of reinforcing Confucian kingship and the perception of Chosŏn's sovereign space as *soChunghwa*, a lesser but the only remaining civilization.[58] The attributes of centrality (*chung*) and civilization (*hwa*) were detached from the historical, geographical China and converted into universal norms that both the Chosŏn court and the *sadaebu* could claim to uphold, alone in the world. Toward the end of the eighteenth century, however, it became increasingly difficult to sustain the pretense that Chosŏn was the last bastion of civilization. Pak Chi-wŏn, for example, called attention to the many favorable aspects of Qing China's material culture (including new modes of manufacture and commerce) and disparaged the moribund quality of Chosŏn's economy.[59] For officials like Pak, who traveled to Beijing and wrote about what he saw, the characterization of Qing China as barbaric was laughable. Placing emphasis on technical utility and the people's welfare (*iyong husaeng*), he advocated a thoroughgoing renovation of Chosŏn's economy and social life on the model of Qing China. Hong Tae-yong, with his appreciation for the Jesuits' knowledge of mathematics and astronomy, sought to bring about an even more radical decentering: the Earth is round, spins on an axis, and circles the sun with the other planets, and thus the concept of "centrality" can only be relative.[60]

Just as complex as this cultural, spatial, and political history, the meaning of the various state rituals did not remain fixed over the five centuries of the Chosŏn period. To be sure, the Chosŏn court never turned away from the notion of yech'i, transforming people into loyal moral subjects through ritual. But it would be inaccurate to see the grand sacrificial rites at the chongmyo-sajik as emblematic of an unchanging or fixed tradition. After the theory and practice of Chosŏn's state rituals were codified during the reign of Sŏngjong, in 1474 in the Kukcho oryeŭi (Manual for Five State Rites), debates over ritual propriety and the meaning of the rites in different circumstances became the central arena of political struggle until the very end of the Chosŏn dynasty. The evolution of the theory and performance of grand sacrificial rites at the chongmyo-sajik bring to light not only the history of conflict over ideas and experiences of Confucian kingship but the history of the Chosŏn elite's understanding of both state sovereignty within a China-centered tributary system and Confucian selfhood—the self that is not private, solitary, and autonomous but positively situated in hierarchic and patriarchic sociality.

In the late nineteenth century, for Russian, Japanese, American, and British diplomats and businessmen intent on acquiring concessions from the Chosŏn court in pursuit of both personal and national gain, the seeming ambiguity in Chosŏn's sovereign status created a number of legal and strategic obstacles. In contrast, as Japanese diplomats knew very well, the post-Westphalian conception of sovereignty—based on the notion of equal sovereignty, supposing a final and supreme authority within a political community delineated by well-defined borders—facilitated the machinations of the imperialist powers. By ruling out pretexts for further Chinese intervention or mediation on behalf of Korea, Japan could supplant China's influence over Korea. More important, Japan's tutelage of Korea could receive the sanction of Britain and the United States.

Rituals of Independence

Among Meiji elder statesmen (genrō), Inoue Kaoru was the most well-versed on the political situation in Chosŏn Korea, and in the autumn of 1894 he volunteered to go to Korea to replace Ōtori Keisuke, the Japanese minister in Seoul who was thought to lack sufficient prestige to deal with Western diplomats.[61] Ōtori was also having trouble dealing with the Tae-wŏn'gun, who began to scheme against the Japanese once the Deliberative Council, led by Kim Hong-jip, began to pass reform measures intended to abolish slavery and do away with status distinctions. Inoue, on the other hand, easily sidelined the Taewŏn'gun with evidence of his plot to enlist the aid of Chinese forces in the north and Tonghak forces in the south. As envoy extraordinary and minister plenipotentiary to Korea, Inoue had the power to negotiate and conclude treaties with Korea. His strategic goals were to sever the tributary ties that had linked China and Korea for centuries and then, without offending the Western powers, convert Korea into Japan's protectorate.[62]

Soon after arriving in Seoul on October 26, 1894, Inoue revealed his twenty-point reform program to King Kojong and the leading members of the Chosŏn government. The first article of the reform program insisted, "All power shall stem from one source, namely, the king." The last article stipulated, "For the purpose of securing the independence of Korea, the above articles of reform and national policy shall be presented at the Royal Ancestral Temple and be published for the benefit of the people."[63] Thus it was that King Kojong's Oath before the ghosts of his dynastic forbearers, not to submit to the dictates of other countries, was dictated to him by Inoue Kaoru. In July 1894, after Japanese troops had taken control of the central palaces in Seoul, a Deliberative Council (Kun'guk kimuch'ŏ) had been established. Led by Kim Hong-jip and Yu Kil-chun, the Council passed hundreds of reform measures intended to abolish status distinctions and "cruel customs." Most of the members of the Council had been involved in Enlightenment efforts since the 1870s. It should also be remembered that, except in those instances where they tried to seize power directly, King Kojong had supported and encouraged the efforts of reformist officials.[64] At the same time, such revolutionary (antifeudal) reforms also took their impetus, in part, from the Tonghak rebellion, with reformist officials hoping to conciliate the Tonghak insurgents in the countryside.[65] Thus, starting with King Kojong, the two decades preceding the Sino-Japanese War (1894–95) had witnessed determined efforts in both the capital and the countryside to do away with status distinctions and to envision alternative structures that would accommodate a much broader section of the populace in political discourse.[66]

As part of the reform measures, the State Council and Six Ministries, including the Board of Rites, were abolished in December 1894. In their place, seven ministries modeled on the Meiji government were established. Interestingly, while most of the reformist officials maintained an unfavorable view of Confucian rituals, Inoue was more attentive to how old rituals might be made to produce new meanings. It was Inoue who took the lead in trying to use the great offering at *chongmyo-sajik* to render the Western concept of sovereignty and independence sensible (and manifest) to the scholar-official class and the broader public. Following Inoue's script, King Kojong was shown using the great offering at the *chongmyo-sajik* as a vehicle for imbuing the old words with new meanings, by associating words such as *tongnip* (independence) with the Western semantics of sovereignty. By so doing, King Kojong in fact confirmed to the literati as well as the Western powers that Chosŏn Korea had all along lacked full sovereignty.

By October 1894, after major Japanese victories over Qing forces on land (the battle at Pyongyang) and at sea, King Kojong and most of his officials were ready to formally cut Chosŏn's ties to China.[67] Inoue might have written the script for King Kojong's "declaration of independence," but the king and the greater part of reform-minded officials, for their own reasons, were coauthors of the Independence Oath taken at the Royal Ancestral Temple. Yu Kil-chun, who in 1890 submitted his manuscript *Sŏyu kyŏnmun* (Observations on a Journey to the West) to King Kojong, had offered this seemingly sympathetic but condescending appraisal of those who argued for continued ritual deference to China:

Occasionally, people unfamiliar with international law [*kongbŏp*] and the trend of the times, and unable to make a distinction between a vassal state [*sokkuk*] and a tributary state [*chin'gongguk*], point to our payment of tribute [to China] as evidence of our country's vassal status. But who would pay tribute if they did not respect their own country and love their own sovereign [*in'gŭm*]? Enmeshed in a difficult situation by the actions of great powers, they had settled on the stratagem of protecting their country through extravagant ritual deference [to China]. Understanding their country's vulnerable situation and overly afraid and fearful of the great powers, they swallow their sense of outrage and undermine the power that can flow from concerted effort. But if we think about the underlying basis, we can surmise that [their actions] stem from anxiety and trepidation rooted in loyalty to their country and love for their sovereign.[68]

Pak Yŏng-hyo and Sŏ Kwang-bŏm were the principal leaders within the Deliberative Council from December 1894 until July 1895, and while the Council passed dozens of reform edicts, it cannot be said that it was autonomous from Japanese control. At the same time, since his role in the Kapsin coup attempt in 1884, Pak had been consistent in his call for Korea's independence from Qing China. While forcing China to acknowledge Korea's complete independence would have been difficult without recourse to war, it can be argued that the king's pledge to "dispense with any thought of relying on Qing China, and to firmly set about laying the foundations for Korea's sovereign independence" was not completely overdetermined by Japanese occupation forces.

It is important to keep in mind that as early as 1883, prior to the signing of a treaty with the United States, the Chosŏn officials who had argued for the establishment of relations with the United States were not oblivious to how power determined international relations and the application of international law. As one writer pointed out in the *Hanyang chubo*, "What are international treaties and laws? They are but a tool of rich and powerful countries to rationalize their own misconduct and to rebuke others. . . . In international commerce only strength matters amid rich and poor, weak and strong, and one cannot rely on international treaties or laws."[69] At the same time, those who advocated establishing diplomatic and trade relations with the United States understood that international law functioned as the only language with which Chosŏn could both engage and deter Japan and the Western powers. As we have seen, the *chongmyo-sajik* had anchored the Chosŏn dynasty to extremely complex discursive traditions of asserting autonomy within a China-centered tributary system. Despite—for some, precisely because of—profound changes forced by mid-nineteenth-century Western imperialism and the treaty-port system, tributary protocols in Qing-Chosŏn relations remained central to both China and Korea in terms of self-representations and representations to the world at large.[70] In that sense, King Kojong's "declaration of independence" at the Royal Ancestral Temple in 1895, in the presence of his ministers and other high officials, and his determination "not to submit to the dictates of other countries" (that is, not to submit to the dictates of China) signaled a radical break not just politically but also in terms of diplomatic and discursive practices.[71]

In the first article of the fourteen-article Oath that he read aloud, King Kojong pledged to "give up all idea of any subjection to China [*ch'ŏngguk*], and to agree to labor to firmly establish [Korea's] independence [*chaju tong-*

nip]."[72] This was the first time that a Chosŏn dynasty monarch explicitly disavowed Chosŏn's commitment to a China-centered geopolitics.[73] Kojong's Oath signaled his commitment to securing Chosŏn's independence in a global nation-state system dominated by the Western imperial powers, a system wherein sovereignty supposed a final and absolute authority in a specific political community, a (nation-)state, with no final or absolute authority existing elsewhere. More significant perhaps than the pledge to sever Chosŏn's ties to China was the language of the Oath itself, in which the meaning and significance of old words like *chaju* and *tongnip* were linked conclusively to contemporary Western legal terminology (*kongbŏp*) and practices,[74] setting in motion a process that would remove Heaven as the source of political legitimacy.

In the second article of the Oath, King Kojong promised to formalize the royal succession. Although making the king even more vulnerable (with the possibility of forced abdication), formalizing the royal succession would stabilize the monarchy, and doing so without an imperial patent of appointment from the Qing emperor would provide further proof of the end of Korea's tributary relationship to China. Instead, and taking the Meiji experience as his model, Inoue endeavored to make Japan the underwriter of the Korean monarchy. In that sense, King Kojong's Oath was a translation of sorts. It was to be the hypothetical equivalent of the Meiji emperor's Charter Oath of 1868.[75] The sweeping reforms, dating from the occupation of Kyŏngbok palace in July 1894, were to be seen as the Korean equivalent of the Meiji Restoration: an *ishin* (K: *yushin*), a term emotively resonant with classical significance.

The Meiji Charter Oath too was issued in the midst of revolutionary chaos, meant to reassure the various domains concerning the aims of the new Meiji government. The figure of the emperor in Kyoto had provided the rationale for overthrowing the Tokugawa *bakufu*. In addition to his ethical and sacerdotal authority, the emperor was to be "restored" to political authority as well (and moved to Edo, the seat of Tokugawa power), and under his gaze domainal sectionalism would be replaced by a new political unity. The Charter Oath, finalized by Kido Kōin of the Chōshū domain and signed by the young Emperor Meiji (then sixteen years old), called for the unity of all classes, high and low, establishment of deliberative assemblies, a promise that matters of state would be decided by public discussion, permission for people of all classes to pursue their aspirations (for example, commoners could seek government employment), the discarding of evil customs, and the search for knowledge throughout the world (that is, the West).[76]

While Inoue tried to portray King Kojong's Oath as Chosŏn's equivalent of the Meiji Charter Oath, Meiji statesmen like Mutsu Munemitsu, Japan's foreign minister, were disdainful of those who sought to represent Japan's motives as being entirely chivalrous. On the topic of sponsoring "reforms" in Chosŏn Korea Mutsu wrote:

> When it became publicly known that we were undertaking these reforms [in Korea] by ourselves, Japanese opinion spontaneously agreed that a chivalrous nation like ours should not hesitate to extend a helping hand to a friendly nation like Korea. . . . Naturally, I myself never saw any significance in the issue of Korea's reform other than its being a matter of political necessity. . . . Nevertheless, once the situation changed and Japan became solely responsible for Korea's reform, reform itself became a vital issue in our foreign policy, and our government was obliged at the very least to attempt its implementation. Whatever circumstances lay behind the unity of opinion in Japan at the moment, I recognized that having such unity and cooperation was extremely desirable for domestic and diplomatic purposes.[77]

Among other things, the "reforms" were meant to curb the power of the Korean king, and on this point Mutsu would have agreed. In the remaining articles of the Oath, King Kojong pledged that all affairs of state (*chŏngmu*) would be decided in consultation with his cabinet, that the queen would not interfere with such decisions, and that the expenses of the royal household would be reduced.[78] So that all the people would become aware of King Kojong's vow to his dynastic ancestors, the royal Oath (*sŏgomun*) was published and disseminated in three different versions: in *han'gŭl*, mixed script, and literary Chinese. Along with King Kojong's birthday and the anniversary of the founding of the dynasty, this "day of independence" was declared a public holiday.[79]

Equal Sovereignty as Colonial Pedagogy

In Europe the knowledge and practice of state sovereignty emerged with the Treaty of Westphalia in 1648, and traditional notions about the Holy Roman Empire were permanently abandoned.[80] In place of overlapping sovereignties—that is, an empire headed spiritually by a pope and temporally by an emperor—the German princes of the Holy Roman Empire gained "absolute sovereignty" in their dominions, and Europe was reconceptualized as a community of sovereign states. Equal sovereignty was identified with the principle that there should be a final and absolute authority in the political community and that "no final and absolute authority exists elsewhere."[81] That is to say, sovereignty of the nation-state did not precede the development of the nation-state system. As Anthony Giddens points out, "International relations are not connections set up between pre-established states which could maintain their sovereignty without them: they are the basis upon which nation-states exist at all."[82]

Just as the idea of a China-centered tributary system was a construct, so too was the post-Westphalian notion of equal sovereignty and, for that matter, the Enlightenment notion of individual personhood, of the unique individual as a self-aware, self-creating subject beyond (or prior to) social status, roles, and obligations. Proponents of equal sovereignty and autonomous personhood tended not to forget the constructedness of both, because, as Stephen Krasner reminds us, there was no golden age when state sovereignty (or personhood) was wholly accepted, respected, or scrupulously practiced. As long as there have been states, states have compromised their own sovereignty and violated that of others.[83] Referring to the experiences in Europe, Krasner points out, "Principles associated with both Westphalian and international legal sovereignty have always been violated. Neither Westphalian nor international legal sovereignty has ever been a stable equilibrium from which rulers had no incentive to deviate."[84]

In spite of this history, the Westphalian idea of sovereignty could and did serve as a cognitive map for nineteenth-century Western (and Japanese) imperialism in East Asia. Treaties, institutions, and discourses on equality between sovereign states, and equality between men, served to open up both China and Japan to trade and diplomacy in the middle of the nineteenth century. While Western diplomats were hypersensitive to rituals and symbols that could be construed as violating their own sovereign equality,[85] the treaties they forced on China, Japan, and Korea were unequal, with the most-favored-nation clause preventing China (and Japan) from playing off one Western power against another. That is to say, extraterritoriality, treaty ports and assorted concessions, control over tariffs, and belief in white supremacy went hand in hand with Western liberal claims about individual equality and equality between sovereign states. Indeed Japanese intellectuals like Fukuzawa Yukichi saw an essential relationship between the two, arguing that Japan's sovereignty and independence depended on individuals who were themselves constituted as independent and equal.[86]

King Kojong's Oath of 1895 was not the first nor the last occasion wherein Japanese and Western diplomats tried to educate the Korean court on how to maintain Chosŏn as an "independent" nation, while at the same time trying to ensure that the Korean court would continue to yield to their demands. Several days before King Kojong made his pledge before his dynastic ancestors, for example, Inoue had also advised the king to recall Korea's legation in Washington, D.C., Korea's only diplomatic legation in a Western country at the time. Inoue advised Kojong to sell the legation property and entrust Korean matters to the Japanese embassy.[87] John M. B. Sill, the U.S. minister to Korea, reported that King Kojong was not pleased by this suggestion: "The king dislikes to lose this chief mark of his independence."[88]

Diplomats in the U.S. legation, such as Horace N. Allen, had been concerned about Japan's intentions in Korea (namely, acquisition of monopolies and concession rights) and in response to King Kojong's appeals wanted the United States to join Britain and Russia in calling for the withdrawal of both Chinese and Japanese troops from Korea.[89] But instructions from Washington held them to "impartial neutrality." Though a diplomat, missionary, and entrepreneur like Allen chafed at America's passive position (from the mid-1880s on), like the other Western diplomats in Korea, he was not displeased with the Oath that King Kojong was induced to make.

According to Martina Deuchler, by 1880 King Kojong, along with his chief state councilor and other high ministers, had become convinced that it was in Chosŏn's interest to sign a treaty with the United States. Such a course was sure to elicit public outrage, however, especially from the Confucian literati in both the capital and the countryside who were still adamantly opposed to opening the ports to Western imperial powers. The policy paper that won over King Kojong and his ministers was *Chaoxian celue* (K: *Chosŏn ch'aengnyak*, A Policy for Korea) written by Huang Zunxian, councilor to He Ruzhang, the first Qing minister to Japan. In Huang's view, Russia posed the chief security threat to Korea, Korea was critical for shielding China's eastern flank, and the Chinese Army and Navy were not capable of defending Korea in case of a Russian attack. To keep the Russians in check, Huang argued, Korea should be encouraged to sign a treaty with the United States.[90] For common security calculations, then, both King Kojong and Li Hongzhang wanted Chosŏn Korea to establish diplomatic relations with the United States.

Li Hongzhang, viceroy of China, did not start the treaty negations with Commodore Robert Shufeldt of the U.S. Navy until Kim Yun-sik, King Kojong's representative, arrived in Tientsin.[91] Deuchler has suggested that one reason for wanting a high Korean official present at the negotiations was Li's fear that China would be held responsible for the fulfillment of the treaty. Nonetheless he wanted to insert into the treaty a clause that acknowledged Korea's dependence on China. As argued by Kwŏn Hyŏk-su, this hybrid tributary-treaty approach sought to maintain tributary relations while grounding commercial and political relations on the basis of international law.[92] At a time when China was itself beset by Western imperial powers, the kind of direct influence and intervention that Yuan Shikai, the Imperial Chinese Majesty's resident in Korea, attempted in the period 1882–94 was quite novel. It was to resist Qing China's attempt to impose on the Chosŏn court the equivalent of a protectorate status that King Kojong became eager to establish and strengthen diplomatic relations with the United States.[93] King Kojong had his own reasons for wanting to underscore Korea's dependence on China at this time. Most immediately he wanted to deflect opposition to the treaty within Korea by making it appear as if it were demanded by China. Thus the formula advocated by Kim Yun-sik in Tientsin was this: "With regard to China, Korea is a dependent country; with regard to all other countries, Korea is independent." But Shufeldt rejected this formulation on the grounds that, while it was of no concern to the United States if Korea needed China's approval for the treaty, a treaty between two countries had to presuppose complete equality between the partners.[94]

When Lucius H. Foote, the first American minister to Korea, finally set foot in Seoul in May 1883, he told King Kojong that the United States was motivated by concern for the "comfort and happiness" of the Korean people and that "the weakness of a nation [referring to Korea] was sometimes its strength." Kojong welcomed the minister, hoping that the American presence would help keep the other imperialist powers at bay. But by the mid-1880s American interest in Korea was already waning; Washington did not bother appointing a minister for a number of years between the mid-

1880s and 1905, and President William McKinley and President Theodore Roosevelt were not concerned about the likelihood that Japan would colonize Korea. After Japan's victory over Russia in the Russo-Japanese War (1904–5) and the signing of the Taft-Katsura agreement, American diplomats led the Western charge out of Korea.[95]

The American-Korean Treaty of 1882, Korea's first (unequal) treaty with a Western power, had not resolved what was seen as ambiguity in Korea's sovereign status. Japan's victory over China in 1895, however, not only put an end to that ambiguity (and the China-centered tributary system), it also confirmed Japan's role as the preeminent translator of the new semantics of sovereignty in East Asia. This, as we shall see, did not herald the disappearance of old categories like inner and outer, civilization and barbarism (*hwa* and *yi*) in Japanese public discourse. For scholars and government officials alike, the satisfaction derived from translating the new semantics of sovereignty was, it seems, mostly intellectual (as an instrumental form of rationality): it was the satisfaction of making transparent the calculus (or rationality) of power, in quantitative measurement, in both the old and new rhetoric, and depicting international relations as a realm of pure politics based on equal sovereignty.[96]

It was difficult to mobilize and at the same time manage public support for the government's international relations. Mutsu Munemitsu, Japan's foreign minister during the Sino-Japanese War, explained this limitation succinctly in *Kenkenroku* (A Record of Arduous and Selfless Service to the Throne):

> The government quite naturally wished to foster patriotic sentiment and saw no reason to repress it. Patriotism, however, is something coarse which runs to excess; and if great care is not taken in controlling it in specific situations, it may cause serious difficulties for the authorities. Herbert Spencer once wrote at the conclusion of an essay on the profound patriotic spirit of the Russian people, that patriotism is the legacy of a barbaric age. While his critique is perhaps too severe, there are cases where the injudicious encouragement of patriotic feelings may be inimical to the achievement of a state's long-range objectives.[97]

After victories at Pyongyang (September 15, 1894) and on the Yellow Sea (September 17, 1894), the Japanese public had become certain of an early victory and wondered only when the standard of the Rising Sun would fly from the Gates of Heavenly Peace in Beijing. Animated by "coarse patriotism," the public did not realize that the government had no choice but to capitulate to the Triple Intervention.[98] Because the people were emotionally aroused, they could not objectively assess the international situation: "While our prestige rose, the need to act responsibly in world affairs grew at a corresponding rate. However, our people at the time were so aroused that they acted purely on the basis of subjective judgments, without any objective regard for the international ramifications of the policies they advocated. Judging matters only from their own limited perspective, they had no sense of how far Japan could go without provoking serious complications abroad."[99]

Thus the patriotism of the people, while useful, can also cause problems in state-to-state relations and even governability. Because of uninformed and highly jingoistic public opinion, stirred up by irresponsible opponents of the government, Japan was obliged to push the Chinese forces beyond the prudent limit, that is, beyond the point acceptable to Russia, Germany, and France. The government's capitulation to the Triple Intervention was a policy of last resort, a decision that could have been avoided had it not been for the vagaries of European diplomacy (which Japan had little control over) and the ignorance of the government's opposition. Mutsu's implied demand for absolutism in domestic politics thus went hand in hand with his understanding of international relations. The privileging of rationality, a type of rationality that would disclose the foreign Other in quantitative measurement, would make possible the establishment of clear, determinate goals as the sole basis for action. Only this kind of rationality could safely guide Japan in its (late) emergence as an imperial power within the nation-state system dominated by the West. The new semantics of sovereignty, ostensibly monopolized by those in the Meiji government trained in law, could not, by itself, organize, mobilize, and control public opinion. It was at the end of the nineteenth century that Meiji statesmen like Mutsu Munemitsu articulated the basis for the emperor system, idealizing the One Individual that Hegel identified with Oriental despots, not in the language of myth but in the language of instrumental rationality.

Authorship and Ritual Action

In the days leading up to the great offering at the Royal Ancestral Temple in January 1895, King Kojong had to be prudent in his speech and action, to cleanse his mind and purify his body.[100] On the day of the great offering, before entering the precinct of the Main Hall, Kojong and the crown prince stepped into a walled enclosure (*chaesil*), where they washed themselves with water drawn from a round well (*chejŏng*) and arranged their vestments. Proceeding northwest along the royal path (*ŏro*) toward the Main Hall (*chŏngjŏn*), Kojong walked alone along its raised middle passage and entered the Main Hall through the eastern gate. Court officials, musicians, and female dancers entered the *chŏngjŏn* through two pillars outside the western gate. The foundation of one pillar was round, signifying Heaven, and the foundation of the other was square, signifying Earth, thus forming the unity of Heaven, Earth, and humankind. Inside the *chŏngjŏn*, the court officials formed long lines on the upper stone terrace (*sang-wŏldae*), and following the principles of yin and yang, the musicians formed two orchestras, one on the upper stone terrace (*dŭngga*) and the other on the lower stone terrace (*hŏn'ga*).[101]

After the placing of the ancestral tablets, the royal ancestral spirits were welcomed, the ghosts entering the *chŏngjŏn* through the central gate in the south wall (*sinmun*).[102] As the first cup of wine was offered, the upper orchestra performed eleven music pieces (*pot'aep'yŏng*) and dancers performed the civil dance (*munmu*) holding two flutes, *yak* and *chŏk*, the latter made from a pheasant feather, as singers praised King T'aejo's founding of the Chosŏn dynasty and the civil accomplishment of subsequent Chosŏn kings. With the offering of the second and third cups, the lower orchestra performed eleven music pieces (*chŏngdaeŏp*), and dancers performed the martial dance (*mumu*) holding wooden swords and spears, as singers praised the military feats of King T'aejo and subsequent Chosŏn kings.

The sentimental and cognitive attributes of such ritual action formed the basis for the pedagogic and legitimating functions of grand sacrificial rites at the *chongmyo-sajik*, enabling the monarch to enact the story of the Chosŏn dynasty as *his* story, reminding himself and his officials of the dynasty's raison d'être.[103] Performing the sacrifices at the *chongmyo* and the *sajikdan* in the presence of his ministers and lesser officials, the Chosŏn monarch mediated between Heaven and Earth, between the dead and the living. Through the act of invoking Heaven and welcoming the spirits of his dead ancestors at the *chongmyo*, or invoking the gods of land and grain at the *sajikdan*, praying for rain, the Chosŏn monarch affirmed his legitimacy, his responsibility for the welfare of his subjects (the moral criterion for exercising power), and the metaphysics of hierarchy that defined

Chosŏn's unique political and social order. Rather than simply reflect (and confirm) existing political and social relations, the sacrificial rites were supposed to reconstitute those relations—the ruler and the ruled constituting each other as such—by demonstrating how human feelings were to be channeled into proper hierarchical and patrilineal channels.[104] By replicating state rituals at the local level, in appropriately lesser forms, the people were to be incorporated into the existing (imagined) hierarchical, male-centered political and social order as filial sons and loyal subjects, positively situated in their sociality.[105]

When King Kojong performed the great offering on January 7, 1895, we do not know what he thought or how he felt. In the sense that all of his actions were prescribed in detail, in ritual manuals dating back to the late fifteenth century, it could be said that King Kojong, as the principal performer of the state ritual at the *chongmyo-sajik*, was, and was not, the author of his actions.[106] Whatever the inner state of the king and others at any single point in the ritual, however, it was understood by all that his Oath before his ancestors made the pronouncement of independence inviolable. In other words, whether or not King Kojong and his scholar-officials believed in ghosts, they would not have denied that the political economy of knowledge in late nineteenth-century Chosŏn still validated the notion that rituals, properly performed, provided unique access to essential knowledge about one's place in the world, with appropriate feelings and values. In that sense, King Kojong's inner state did not matter as much as the fact that he performed the ritual as prescribed. His Oath was a speech-act, an utterance that immediately produced a new reality precisely because he alone possessed requisite authority. His ritual performance and speech-act that day were doubly prescribed, not just by centuries of ritual manuals but also by Inoue Kaoru's script. This did make a difference. Chosŏn-period scholars of ritual recognized, of course, that rituals are historical (human) creations. But blatant attempts to use dynastic rituals as vehicles to create and communicate new meanings helped foster a more willful, unrestrained attitude (and rivalry) toward the manipulation of signs. Such acts of translation not only destroyed the China-centered theory and practice of tributary relations but also demolished the dynastic (feudal) incorporating logic and set loose new desires.

As with any act of translation, Inoue's attempt at translation did not occur between two distinct systems of signs and meanings, Japanese and Korean.

In fact his attempt at translation necessitated a prior gesture: the portrayal of Korea and Japan as distinct, unified spaces, each with its unique system of signs and meanings. Here was the distinctively productive (as opposed to repressive) aspects of Japanese colonialism at this historical juncture: the collaboration with reformist officials to resignify the past and to mobilize the past to authorize projects that would break with tradition. The productive imagination of this particular translator was conditioned by the narrative of Western liberalism and the nation-state system into which Korea was to be incorporated. Such acts of translation helped produce new subjectivities, imagined communities, and ostensibly transparent relations between present and past in late nineteenth-century Chosŏn as well as in Meiji Japan and eventually denied Heaven as that which confers the right to rule.

King Kojong's 1895 Oath before the spirits of dead Chosŏn dynasty kings and the use of translated words like *tongnip* in the last decades of the nineteenth century had much in common and reveal a great deal about the nature of Korea's translated modernity and the process by which Korea became colonized by Japan (1910–45). New meanings were invented that would serve as hypothetical equivalents of the (Western) semantics of sovereignty involving terminology and practices that validated Western imperialism, colonialism, and capitalist penetration. Through the use of neologisms and manipulation of centuries-old dynastic rituals, the made-up quality of orthodox conceptions of the world was brought to the fore, and the search for intellectual certitude turned increasingly toward instrumental reason. But perhaps the spirits of dead Chosŏn dynasty kings could not be so easily swayed, or King Kojong's body was not yet so docile. On the day of the Winter Solstice, when the visit to the Yi Ancestral Temple should have taken place, King Kojong's body had broken out in a rash.[107] Thus Inoue Kaoru and Korea's declaration of independence from China had to wait sixteen days until the king's body returned to a ritually clean state.[108]

The king's body breaking out in a rash can serve as a metaphor not only for the process of deterritorialization but also for the process by which the nationalist desire for equal sovereignty was created by the violent, destructive, and constructive workings of imperialism. Inoue's manipulation of Chosŏn dynastic symbols and rituals to create and communicate new meanings aimed to conjure spirits—but spirits rendered mute, reduced to visuality, and locked in a past severed from their future. After the Triple

Intervention and the retreat of Japanese influence in Chosŏn, King Kojong continued the manipulation of dynastic rituals, leading in 1897 to the building of a wŏn'gudan (Round Hill Altar), the elevation of Chosŏn to the Great Han Empire (Taehan cheguk), and the elevation of his own status to that of emperor.[109] But this short period of relative autonomy would be brought to an end with the Russo-Japanese War and the Japanese imposition of a protectorate in 1905. Thereafter the modern desire for independence and equal sovereignty would be nurtured by nationalist historians like Sin Ch'ae-ho. While the initial conjuring of that desire took place before Heaven and the spirit tablets of Chosŏn dynasty kings and queens, with the dynastic state on its death bed and Heaven removed as the source of political legitimacy, it is perhaps understandable why historians like Sin Ch'ae-ho and Pak Ŭn-sik would turn to the most elemental, the most quintessential as the point of departure for reconstituting the whole.

It should be remembered that mortuary rituals, among other things, help gather the life force (K: ki, C: qi), and it is the gathering and dispersing of this force that set in motion the cycle of living and dying. Other than mortuary rituals, and as prerequisite to self-strengthening and anticolonial resistance, what practice could gather this force to reconstitute the whole? For Sin Ch'ae-ho, it was history writing that could revive the people's quintessential spirit (chŏngsin), and it would be on the basis of that inner force that the whole could be reconstituted—the people's spirit, shaped by history but also transcending it, channeling and transforming ki into a modern, historical, and material force. Like the monarch who is also the officiant of mortuary rituals at the Royal Ancestral Temple, nationalist historians would tend to the Korean Geist. Taking up ideas related to social Darwinism and the organic theory of the state, Sin Ch'ae-ho and other nationalist historians in the first decade of the twentieth century would (re)imagine Chosŏn Korea as an organic entity, the ethnic nation, rather than a dynastic state. Like mortuary rituals and the exercise of one's moral capacity, history writing in early twentieth-century Korea was remembrance, an act of mourning, and ethical practice, an act that gathers ki, the ethnic nation's life force, facilitating movement toward anticolonial struggle and the birth of another living body, this time as a sovereign nation-state. Thus for Sin, one of the first to narrate Korea's past in the mode of nationalist historiography, historians had a heavy responsibility.

The historical and semantic links between imperialism and nationalism are obviously quite complex, and the chapters that follow try to unravel some of that complexity. Historians who insist on maintaining a sharp distinction, analytical and otherwise, between imperialism and nationalism make a simple but important point. Whereas imperialism sought to establish domination over Korea, Korean nationalism in the late nineteenth century and much of the twentieth century was defensive. In opposing imperialist encroachment, Korean nationalists sought to unite and mobilize the people through more egalitarian, inclusive politics. But in dismantling status distinctions, in teaching people of all classes the idea and practice of citizenship, and in pursuing the goal of development, nationalists also succeeded in naturalizing the nation-state form and legitimating its totalizing power.[110] At the same time, focusing on the concept of sovereignty and the historical and material linkages between imperialist violence and nationalist imagination, the historical analyses presented here show how the past could also become the space of democratic reimagining, inspiration, and endurance.

chapter two

IMPERIALISM AND NATIONALISM

Questions answered: "Korea" and "Corea" are both correct, but the former is preferred. Korea is not a part of China, but is independent. The Koreans do not speak the Chinese language and their language resembles neither the Chinese nor the Japanese. Korea made treaties in 1882. Korea has electric lights, steamships, telegraph, but no railroads. Koreans live in comfortable tile-roofed houses, heated by flues under the floor. Korean civilization is ancient and high; area, 100,000 square miles; population 16,000,000; climate like that of Chicago. — Sign over the Korea Exhibit, World's Fair in Chicago, 1893

In its brief description of the Korea Exhibit at the Chicago World's Fair — named the World's Columbian Exposition to celebrate the four-hundredth anniversary of Christopher Columbus's "discovery of the New World" — the *Chicago Record* quoted in its entirety the sign that hung over the Korea Exhibit and surmised, correctly, that the Koreans staffing the exhibit had gotten tired of answering the same questions over and over.[1] In December 1893, when Commissioner Chŏng Kyŏng-wŏn returned to Korea and reported to King Kojong about Korea's participation in the World's Fair, he noted that there were so many visitors from so many countries asking questions that they had to place a label on every item they displayed, explaining its use.[2] Providing a distinctly national backdrop to the small descriptive labels — Korea is not a part of China; the Korean language resembles neither Chinese nor Japanese; Korean homes are kept warm in the winter by flues under the floor — the sign over the exhibit likely had a more ambitious pedagogical intent, anticipating not just questions fairgoers might ask about Korea, but also the questions that they *should* be asking about Korea's place in the world.

Whether the author of this sign was the commissioner of the exhibit, Chŏng Kyŏng-wŏn, or perhaps Horace Allen, appointed by King Kojong to advise and assist the Korean delegation to the World's Fair, the delegation took pains to emphasize Korea's distinguishing characteristics.[3]

Korea's distinctiveness from China and Japan and the very act of its self-representation at the World's Fair were meant to give evidence of its independence and sovereignty. The sign above the Korea Exhibit can be read as a somewhat glum attempt to educate fairgoers—the exhibit itself proving inadequate—that Korean civilization was "ancient and high" and that, at the same time, Korea was becoming modern. As an attempt to insert a legal and moral dimension into the description of Korea as a nation-state, as well as to serve as an informational backdrop for the tobacco pipes and other artifacts of everyday life on display, the sign over the exhibit spoke directly to what many fairgoers might have recognized as a legal principle operative in capitalist modernity: only autonomous individuals and nations can enter into binding contractual agreements; only autonomous individuals and nations are truly advanced (and masculine), capable of making mature moral decisions.[4]

A decade earlier, a year after the signing of the Treaty of Commerce and Amity between the United States and Chosŏn Korea, an eight-man diplomatic mission had been dispatched to the United States. Led by Chief Envoy Min Yŏng-ik, the mission visited two industrial fairs in Boston.[5] By the time of the World's Fair in Chicago, Qing China still had no intention of abandoning Chinese claims of suzerainty over Korea and Chosŏn Korea remained in a seemingly ambiguous "dependent-yet-autonomous" status.[6] Participation in international events like the World's Fair provided evidence of state-led efforts that Benedict Anderson referred to as official nationalism.[7] To put it differently, a year before the first Sino-Japanese War and King Kojong's declaration of Korea's "independence," material and discursive conditions already existed within Korea that would allow for the dissemination of not just the idea of national sovereignty but also the presumption that recognition by the Western imperial powers was a necessary condition for avoiding colonization—whether by China, Russia, or Japan.

As Lydia Liu has observed, sovereignty in the late nineteenth century was based on a constitutive notion of sovereign right.[8] In other words, sovereignty required recognition from the Western imperial powers. To receive recognition, non-European polities had to demonstrate commitment to European civilization, as measured by specific "reforms" of political, economic, and cultural institutions and practices, including participation in international events like the Chicago World's Fair. The product of centuries of colonial expansion and conquest, late nineteenth-century sovereignty was capitalist sovereignty, functioning, as Hardt and Negri argued, both as political power and police power: "a political power against all external political powers" and a police power that worked to subsume "singularities in the totality, of the will of all into the general will."[9] At a time when European colonies covered roughly half of the mainland of the earth (subjugating roughly two-fifths of the earth's human population),[10] when European superiority seemed indisputable and sovereignty-based international law facilitated Euro-American imperialism, sovereignty had become a machine, and Korea's participation in the World's Fair expressed both compliance and the staging of new forms of subjectivity and desire—for example, desire for inclusion in the nation-state system dominated by the West.

Extraordinarily popular and influential, the Columbian Exposition had more than 27 million visitors over its six-month run, a number equivalent to more than 40 percent of the population of the United States at the time. As Richard Seager notes, the Chicago World's Fair "functioned as a pilgrimage site for millions . . . enthralled by its evocation of history, its panoramic displays of global culture and modern technology."[11] Exposition planners created three separate spheres that together encompassed their vision for the World's Fair: the monumental White City, the Midway Plaisance (an amusement area officially under the auspices of the exposition's Department of Ethnology), and eight miles north of the Exposition, in downtown Chicago, the newly constructed Art Institute to host the various congresses, including the World Parliament of Religions. The White City was so called because of the white plaster that formed the façade of the Exposition buildings. Lit up by ninety thousand incandescent lamps and constructed along a lagoon and reflecting waterways covering 686 acres, the buildings themselves were immense and ornate neoclassical Beaux Arts structures. Housing gigantic machines while alluding to the glories of Augustus Caesar, these structures elicited in the leading national periodicals countless essays that pointed to the future with "an imperial cast of mind."[12]

The author of the sign over the Korea Exhibit asserted not just Korea's selfhood and autonomy but also unambiguous agreement with the belief that such an assertion was appropriate and moral. At the same time, the Korea Exhibit itself was seemingly deficient, embarrassingly so, at least for Yun Ch'i-ho.[13] Yun had just completed his graduate studies in Christian education and systematic theology at Emory College and was on his way to China, with a three-week stop in Chicago to see the Columbian Exposition and the World Parliament of Religions. His first trip outside of Korea had been in 1881, when he was sixteen. His father, a military official, had arranged for him to join the Inspection Mission to Japan (*chosa sach'aldan*) as an assistant.[14] Sent by King Kojong, the officials who toured Japan were to observe and report on institutional and technological changes being pushed through by the Meiji state and to assess the threat to Korean security. When the Inspection Mission returned to Korea, Yun stayed on in Japan to study Japanese.[15] A year later, in 1882, he began studying English, because "with English, Koreans would be able to directly import Western civilization without having to go through Japan."[16]

In 1883 the Japanese foreign minister Inoue Kaoru recommended Yun to Lucius Harwood Foote, America's first envoy and minister plenipotentiary to Korea.[17] Returning to Korea with Minister Foote, Yun received an appointment as a clerk in the newly established Office of Extraordinary Affairs (T'ongni kimu amun, the antecedent to a foreign ministry) and was assigned as Foote's translator. Later, as a protégé of the "progressives" who launched a failed coup attempt in 1884, Yun had to go into hiding, and when Minister Foote left Korea in January 1885, Yun went with him.[18] Upon reaching Nagasaki, Yun cut off his topknot and bought a suit of Western clothes. He went on to Shanghai, where he enrolled in a school run by the American Methodist Episcopal Church, South, and in April 1887 converted to Christianity. In late 1888, with the help of American missionaries, he went to the United States to study theology at Vanderbilt and at Emory College.[19] His chief interest at the World's Fair was the World Parliament of Religions, the first formal attempt to create a global dialogue between faiths, where the representatives of Eastern and Western spiritual traditions helped establish the notion of "world religions," a category that expressed a vague commitment to religious tolerance, while reinforcing a logic of classification.[20]

World Religions and Tolerance

Delegates to the Parliament of Religions were to engage in dialogue premised on tolerance, the rules specifying that delegates should "state their own beliefs and reasons for them with the greatest frankness" but refrain from criticism of others.[21] In his diary, however, Yun Ch'i-ho did not refrain from criticizing some of the delegates. Between summary descriptions of delegates' speeches, Yun took swipes at those who argued for religious pluralism. Of Hirai Ryuge Kinzō, a delegate from Japan, Yun wrote that his style was beautiful, his thoughts "expressed as they were in vague and metaphysical terms." He noted that Hirai "caught the audience" but judged his paper "morally useless on account of its fallacies." "He advocating a synthetic religion defined religion as an 'apriori belief in an unknown entity.' Then he proceeded to consider the nature of the unknown entity. 'Nonsense!' For if the entity is 'unknown' how can he consider its nature? . . . He tried to show that the creator of conditioned and finite beings could not be infinite and unconditioned. He might as well have said that the maker of unintelligent dolls can't be intelligent!"[22] Yun noted that the delegates of all the non-Christian creeds presented a united front to Christianity and that the Unitarians and Universalists sided with them. Hirai's paper was sharply critical of Christian missionary work in Japan, but many of his declarations were followed by loud applause.[23] In his entry for September 27, the last day of the Parliament, Yun mentions Hirai again: "Harai [sic] of Japan talked about the Japanese priest's [sic] shedding tears for leaving America. I call this an Asiatic lie pure and simple."[24]

As John P. Burris notes, some of the strongest voices from Asia, in exquisite English, belonged to delegates from India and Ceylon: "The lengthy British occupation of India had caused deep animosities, and the foremost thing on the Indians' minds was not to enunciate transcendental truths, which they also did, but to talk religious politics."[25] But Yun was not sympathetic. He quoted Virachand Raghav Gandhi from Gujarat, who represented Jains, and commented, "Gandhi, a Bombay lawyer [sic]. 'Do I wish a Hindoo [sic] or a Buddhist turn a Christian? God forbid! Do I wish a Christian turn a Hindoo or a Buddhist? God forbid!' Thus in the very name of liberty, toleration etc. etc. this man forbids the freedom of choice."[26] It should be noted that one of the goals of this first World Parliament of Religions was to "inquire what light each religion has afforded, or may afford to other religions of the world." While desiring racial inclusion,[27] Yun was not a little skeptical about whether Hindus and Buddhists might be able to shed any light on divine truth. His privileging of freedom (the freedom to choose one's faith) dovetailed closely with the Christian-centric vision of John Henry Barrows, the chairman of the General Committee on Religious

Congresses of the World's Congress, for whom one of the objects of the Parliament was to "change [the] many-colored radiance back into the white light of heavenly truth." The white light of heavenly truth was, of course, Christianity. Barrows charged that "those who ha[d] the full light of the cross should bear brotherly hearts towards all who grope in a dimmer illumination."[28]

Two weeks later, arriving in Vancouver after four days of a "tedious ride over prairies, wild mountains, canyons, valleys of varied scenes and temperature," Yun had this to say about the Native Americans he saw in the stations along the Central Pacific Railroad: "Indians were seen at almost every station. Some of them painted their faces red and most had red or blue blankets wrapped around their bodies. A sad and somewhat contemptible sight: sad because of their past history, but contemptible because of the inability to improve their condition. A race that fails, from voluntary laziness and ignorance, to avail itself of the advantages of civilization brought so close to its reach isn't worthwhile to live."[29] Yun's perspective on Native Americans thus paralleled the objectifying operation of discourses on "civilization," associating a moral and political complex of meanings with white supremacy. If Native Americans did not avail themselves of Euro-American civilization — if they voluntarily chose to continue living in ignorance and "degraded humanity" — then they did not deserve to live. No matter how constrained or forced that "choice" might be, the act of choosing Euro-American civilization was, in itself, proof of a people's capacity for rationality and autonomy — that is, autonomy from tradition and ignorance. Yun's privileging of freedom, along with ruminations on why certain populations did not deserve to live, point to not just the inclusionary pretensions of liberal theory and the exclusionary effects of liberal practices, but also the centrality of violence in the constitution of (Christian) liberal-bourgeois subjectivity in the late nineteenth century and its permutations through the colonial period down to postcolonial anticommunist South Korea.[30]

While in Chicago, when not attending the Parliament of Religions, Yun also visited the Columbian Exposition. He observed that the China Exhibit seemed "more concerned about selling its merchandise." Yun does not mention it, and it is quite possible that he did not know, but the Qing government had turned down President Benjamin Harrison's invitation to participate in the Columbian Exposition to protest the extension of the

Chinese Exclusion Act of 1882. There were a number of earlier Chinese exclusion laws, but the Act of 1882, insofar as it was a federal law, established a comprehensive legal barrier to Chinese immigration and made Chinese already in the United States permanent aliens. In 1892 the Chinese Exclusion Act was renewed for another ten years, and that is what prompted the Qing government to boycott the Chicago World's Fair in 1893. Without China's participation, the Chinese Exhibit was organized by five private groups, three of which were not Chinese, including a New York jeweler and a Swedish-led committee that designed the Chinese "temple." Well away from the magnificent buildings and exhibits around the Court of Honor, referred to as the White City, the Chinese Exhibit was located in the Midway Plaisance. "Sandwiched between entertainment facilities," the Chinese displays "became a source of amusement, not respect."[31]

Set apart from the White City by a rail bridge, the Midway Plaisance extended west, a strip of land a mile long and about six hundred feet wide, "organized linearly . . . providing a lesson in racial hierarchy."[32] The historian Hubert Howe Bancroft described the Midway:

> Entering the avenue a little to the west of the Woman's Building [the visitor] would pass between the walls of medieval villages, between mosques and pagodas, past the dwellings of colonial days, past the cabins of South Seas islanders, of Javanese, Egyptians, Bedouins, Indians. . . . Then, as taste and length of purse determined, for fees were demanded from those who would penetrate the hidden mysteries of the plaisance, they might enter the Congress of Beauty with its plump and piquant damsels, might pass a house in one of the theatres or villages, or partake of harmless beverages served by native waiters. Finally they would betake themselves to the Ferris Wheel, on which they were conveyed with smooth, gliding motion to a height of 260 feet, affording a transient and kaleidoscopic view of the park and all it contains.[33]

On or near the Midway Plaisance, there were exhibits of Dakota Sioux, Navajos, Apaches, and various northwestern tribes. According to Robert Rydell, the Native Americans became objects of abuse and ridicule: "With Wounded Knee only three years removed, the Indians were regarded as apocalyptic threats to the values embodied in the White City. . . . The White City and the Midway were truly symbolic, but not antithetical, constructs. Rather, the vision of the future and the depiction of the nonwhite world as savage were two sides of the same coin."[34]

Among foreign participants, Japan received a great deal of attention and had the largest presence in terms of space, including a 40,000-square-foot building and garden complex on Wooded Island, several buildings and attractions on the Midway, and some 90,000 square feet of display space in the White City. In return for an early, substantial contribution to the Chicago organizers and a promise to reproduce a building of "the most ancient style of architecture," Japan had been given prime real estate on Wooded Island. Costing nearly $500,000, the Japanese pavilion included a reproduction of the Phoenix Hall of the Byōdō-in temple near Kyoto, with a teahouse and gardens.[35] It must be noted that the Japanese presentation at Chicago was strictly controlled by an imperial commission headed by Foreign Minister Mutsu Munemitsu, who spent "virtually every waking hour" pondering the problem of how to renegotiate (unequal) treaties with Western imperial powers.[36] The pursuit of this state objective was woven into the narrative strategy of representing Japanese Buddhism at the World Parliament of Religions.[37]

In his opening address for the Japanese delegation, Noguchi Zenshirō, a Buddhist layman, artfully touched on the themes of Western aggression and the illegality of the treaties. Judith Snodgrass writes, "Maintaining his ironical message of gratitude, Noguchi thanked America for sending Perry and presented Japanese Buddhism as the most precious gift that Japan could offer." Comparing Commodore Perry to Columbus, Noguchi hinted at the continuing movement of civilization westward, from Europe to America to Japan. As Snodgrass points out, his paper, in a very subtle way, criticized Euro-American imperialism: "The Japanese erected a statue to Perry, as the Americans had done to Columbus, but beside it they placed a statue of Ii Naosuke, the chancellor of the Tokugawa *bakufu* who had been assassinated as a traitor, Noguchi explained, because 'he opened the door to a stranger without waiting for the permission of the emperor' . . . [alluding] to the invalidity of the treaties forced upon Japan by the United States."[38]

The majority of the fairgoers were working-class and farming families, and as they marveled at the latest scientific and technological innovations exhibited in ornate, massive neoclassical buildings, they were also introduced to innovative and entertaining ways of representing racial and civilizational hierarchies. In 1890 nearly 78 percent of the population of Chicago were either foreign-born or the children of foreign-born,[39] and it would be safe to say that the White City and the idea of America as united and progressive did not convince every fairgoer. The working-class movement was strong and militant; seven years earlier a rally in support of striking workers had led to what has come to be known as the Haymarket Massacre, and Chicago had the reputation of being "the most radical of American cities."[40] Black Americans were denigrated and excluded, as Ferdinand L. Barnett noted: "Only as a menial is the Colored American to be seen. . . . It remained for the Republic of Hayti [sic] to give the only acceptable representation. . . . That republic chose Frederick Douglass to represent it as Commissioner through which the Colored American received from a foreign power the place denied him at home."[41]

The Chicago of Upton Sinclair, the Chicago of sweatshops and tenements, habitats without plumbing or light—that "real" Chicago conflicted with the Exposition directors' vision of the future. In that sense, as Alan Trachtenberg has pointed out, the White City was not only physically separated from Chicago, but also aesthetically differentiated.[42] For Yun Ch'i-ho, that physical and aesthetic distance only intensified the distance he perceived between Korea and civilized nations. On seeing the Korea Exhibit, Yun wrote that it was so second-rate and dismal that he could not turn away from it. The Exhibit did not present Chosŏn Korea as a nation that a modern citizen might admire. It was altogether unable to articulate Korea in any compelling way within that symbolic universe that privileged industrialization, progress, and empire. Yun wrote in his diary that he could not help but "blush at the poverty of Corean arts." He spent two days viewing the Columbian Exposition. In his entry for September 28 he wrote, "After breakfast went to the Fair. Felt humiliated not to find a Corean flag in any of the buildings from whose roofs fly the colors of almost every nation. Ah! Yet I shall not know the depth and breadth of the degradation and shame of Corea till I get into her capital. . . . Went to the Corean Pavilion at 11 a.m. and stayed there until 5 p.m.! Why and what for? I can't explain; only I couldn't get away from there, miserable as the exhibit is."[43]

Korea's participation in the Columbian Exposition and its mode of national self-representation illustrate the pathways by which Korea was imbricated with the cultures of Euro-American empire and the (re)structuring of racial and civilizational hierarchies in the intellectual and political terrain of late nineteenth-century semicolonial Korea. They illustrate how imperialism and the global articulation of sovereignty by the Western imperial powers created the material and discursive conditions that rendered Korea and Koreans "wretched and slavish."[44] While a student at Vanderbilt and Emory, Yun had spent his summers giving sermons at churches throughout the South.[45] In his diary entry for June 26, 1893, in Lincolnton, North Carolina, he wrote, "Had a full house last night. Met Mrs. M. A. Wildman of Richmond. She introduced herself to me as a cousin of Miss Linnie Davis a Presbyterian missionary to Corea. God bless her; a missionary to Corea has more to endure than one in the African jungles." His diary records many delightful hours spent playing the game of quotation with wives, daughters, and widows of pastors, and the daughter of his landlord while in Chicago. In his entry for August 11, 1893, in Lynchburg, Virginia, Yun recorded his "wandering thoughts": Miss F. E. was "aristocratic in feeling and bearing though not in circumstances. . . . [She] asked me if I ever get mad! Have I deceived her in hiding and controlling my passions? Certainly not. It is no sin to hide our passions as long as we design no harm *behind* those who may offend us."

His diary makes it clear that Yun was offended numerous times by the racism he encountered in the United States. But in hiding his anger he insisted that he harbored no design to harm those same (white) Americans. On the other hand, toward those groups of people (nonwhites) whom he judged willfully in ignorance and barbarity, such as the Native Americans he saw in the American West, his anger, indeed his casual genocidal remark, could be stated freely and openly. Intellectuals like Yun Ch'i-ho — Korean, male, bourgeois, and Christian, practiced in public speaking, afternoon teas, and parlor games with white women, his passions firmly controlled as befit a civilized man — helped set in motion political and cultural movements under the rubric of Civilization and Enlightenment (*munmyŏng kaehwa*) that ushered in a modern public sphere and a racialized and nationalized abstracted subjectivity.[46]

From Vancouver, via Japan, Yun arrived back in Shanghai in mid-November 1893 to await political changes in Korea that might permit his return.[47] That opportunity came with the outbreak of the Sino-Japanese War, the Japanese occupation of Seoul, and Inoue Kaoru's support for a reformist government. Yun returned to Korea in February 1895 and received an appointment first as vice minister of education, and then as vice minister of foreign affairs.[48]

Translating Sovereignty

It is not clear when Yun Ch'i-ho began keeping a diary. What has been pre-served begins on January 1, 1883. At the time he was studying English in Japan with Lizzie Goodhue Millet, the wife of Ernest Francisco Fenollosa, a professor of philosophy and political economy at Tokyo Imperial University, and Kanda Naibu, a lecturer in English at Tokyo Imperial University. Yun's early diary entries were in literary Chinese. However, on November 25, 1887, while studying at the Anglo-Chinese College in Shanghai,[49] he switched to vernacular writing in the Korean alphabet with the simple declaration "From today I will keep my diary in Korean [kungmun]." On December 7, 1889, a year after arriving in Nashville to study at Vanderbilt, he changed his language again, this time to English. He wrote, in English, "My Diary has hitherto been kept in Corean. But its vocabulary is not as yet rich enough to express all what I want to say. Have therefore determined to keep the Diary in English." His English entries were much longer, and he immediately took up topics he had not written about before: about Jacob ("the Armenian"), a friend who was poor ("poorer than I") but who had "simplicity in manner and kindness of heart"; about the southerner who "looks down on a negro with as much contempt as on a brute"; and about the southern church that "favored slavery."[50]

When Yun switched from Korean to English, the questioning, feeling, self-conscious self that emerges from the diary seems to emerge fully formed. In the Korean-language entries of the days and weeks prior to the shift, the language does not—cannot—give evidence of that kind of in-teriority, of a masculine and singular consciousness. Even for Yun, who obviously had a knack for languages and writing, the Korean vernacular at the time proved inadequate for self-presentation. It was not the poverty of the Korean vocabulary that made written vernacular Korean inade-quate. Vernacular Korean in the late 1880s, as a written language, did not have the kind of literary conventions that English developed after the eighteenth century, that could interpellate Yun as author and narrator of a self-narrative. Central to his diary keeping was the figure of the sover-eign subject in the post-Enlightenment West that was informed by notions of self-interest, self-consciousness, and self-knowledge.[51] In his switch to English, his diary became a self-defining story, and Yun a self-determining author who could write about his own subjectivity from externalized and internal points of view, constituting himself as both subject and object.

While Yun may have constructed his subjectivity in English, it was also clear to him, as it was to the Western missionaries in Korea, that a distinctly Korean subjectivity—that is, a Korean national subjectivity—would have to be constructed in the Korean vernacular. This would necessitate an immense cultural shift. William E. Griffis, an American Orientalist and Congregational minister, recalled how, more than once, he had urged "Korean literary men" to "cultivate their own mother tongue," but in vain: "They were safely immune, inert and unashamed, for they considered the subject of cultivating their vernacular beneath their notice. . . . If De Quincey's dictum, that next to the flag of his native country, a scholar should be loyal to his own language, be true, then it seems little wonder that Korean sovereignty was lost and that Japanese may yet become the official language of Cho-sen."[52] There were, of course, Korean literary men who had sought to forge a link between written Korean vernacular and patriotism, men like Yu Kil-chun, Sŏ Chae-pil, Chu Si-gyŏng, and Yun Ch'i-ho, all of whom had extensive exposure to Western languages, especially English.[53] To not only articulate and disseminate news and new ideas, but to convince its readership of the moral and ethical significance of recognizing that (seemingly) essential link between civilization, sovereign thinking, and a "national" language constituted the primary motivation behind the creation of Korea's first vernacular newspaper, *Tongnip sinmun* (literally, the Newspaper Independent).[54]

Beginning publication on April 7, 1896, printed in the Korean alphabet, with occasional articles and editorials in English, *Tongnip sinmun* referred to the Korean alphabet created during King Sejong's reign (1418–50) as the national script (*kungmun*).[55] A creation of Sŏ Chae-pil, and later with Yun Ch'i-ho as publisher and editor-in-chief, the newspaper was published by the Independence Club.[56] It was printed by the Trilingual Press run at the Paejae Boys' High School by the American Methodist Episcopal Mission.[57] The inaugural issue included an editorial written by Sŏ Chae-pil:

> The reason that our newspaper uses only the Korean alphabet [*kungmun*], and not Chinese [*hanmun*], is so as to have it read by all the people without regard to their social status [*sangha kwich'ŏn*]. Space is provided between words in the hope that people might read the paper with ease and understand what is recorded in the paper more fully. In foreign countries [*kakkuk*], people [*saram tŭl*], without regard to their sex, first learn their own writings and only after they have acquired a good command of their language do they begin to learn

a foreign language [oe'guk kŭl]. But in Korea, people study the Chinese writing system even though they did not learn the Korean alphabet [Chosŏn kungmun], and therefore it is rare to find people [saram] who know the Korean writing system well. When we compare Korean and the Chinese writing system, Korean letters are superior. First, they are easier to learn. Second, they are Korean letters [Chosŏn kŭl] and therefore if the Korean people [Chosŏn inmin] use them for all things, the people of all ranks, without regard to their positions, can understand them with ease. The people have long been accustomed to the use of Chinese orthography and have failed to use the Korean writing system, so that the Korean people [Chosŏn inmin] have now become unfamiliar with their own letters. Instead they are more familiar with the Chinese writing system. Is this not lamentable![58]

Sŏ Chae-pil was twenty years old when he had to flee to Japan, along with Kim Ok-kyun, Pak Yŏng-hyo, and Sŏ Kwang-bŏm, after the failure of the 1884 coup attempt. Receiving a cold shoulder from Inoue Kaoru, Sŏ went to the United States the following year. After working in various menial jobs, he was accepted into the Columbia University Medical School (now George Washington University) and received his medical degree in 1892. Soon after, he married Muriel Armstrong, the daughter of Colonel George Buchanan Armstrong, founder of the U.S. Railway Mail Service and a cousin of President James Buchanan. Sŏ had U.S. citizenship when he returned to Korea in 1896 to participate in the movement to transform Korea under the banner of "civilization and enlightenment."[59] His American name, Philip Jaisohn, was itself a translation, based on a combination of the first character of his given name, Chae (載), with his family name, Sŏ (徐), to create Jaisohn. The second character of his given name, p'il (弼), became Philip. The recombination of the various signifiers Sŏ, Chae, p'il into Philip Jaisohn may appear to us forced and mechanical because of its obedience to the way American names are ordered. But obedience to Euro-American norms allowed Sŏ Chae-pil to acquire a hybrid name, an American wife, and U.S. citizenship. The making of this hybrid name illustrates how modernity and the nation form first came to be translated in late nineteenth-century Korea: the unavoidable accommodation to Euro-American modernity and semantic innovation through both productive imagination and the legislative rationality of capitalist sovereignty.[60]

Translating modernity and the nation form suggests beginnings: the inauguration of the Korean alphabet as the national script in the last decade of the nineteenth century, the beginning of modern Korean historiography in the first decade of the twentieth century, the emergence of modern Korean literature, and a host of other beginnings. Together these provided evidence of the simultaneous emergence of the ethnic nation (*minjok*) and modernity in Korea. There is a temptation to depict Korean intellectuals in the late nineteenth century and early twentieth as sovereign subjects of such beginnings, not just present at the creation but there as the active subjects creating new meanings as they translate from one language to the host language and in the process create new identities, new institutions, and new practices that are of their own making. Formulated in this way, the act of translation might suggest a historical narrative quite different from that suggested by attention to Western and Japanese hegemony: modernity and nation in Korea as Korea's own creation, with Korean intellectuals selecting, interpreting, and creating their own modernity from the Western archive. The modernity thus created would be Korean (encompassing different intellectual traditions), dynamic, and ongoing—an incomplete project that is both particular and universal. Historians would then have a firm basis for writing the history of Korea's modernity; this history would be the retelling of the intellectual's consciousness, while taking due account of the historical and political context, that is, "the limitations of his time."

But such a historical narrative is the product of a type of desire created by sovereignty itself, as Hardt and Negri put it, sovereignty as "a form of command that overdetermines the relationship between individuality and universality as a function of the development of capital."[61] A more critical historiography might locate acts of translation in a specific space and time, a crossroad where "things happen" by way of imagination and political dynamic. One of the things that happened was the production of new meanings and new narratives through semantic innovation. To see how semantic innovation might have occurred in specific moments, in specific texts, it can be argued that "combinatory rationality" was put into play by structural semantics, while a "legislating rationality" was at work at the level of narrative.[62] Things happened through the productive imagination of the translator, but the rationalities to be noted here were, for the most part, not under the control of the translator. To the extent that these rationalities were beyond the reach of the translator, we have to concede that language itself has a certain agency. We can talk about translating from some language to Korean, but only if we do not assume that this act of translation occurs between two distinct systems of signs and meanings.

Prior to standardization and modernization begun in the late nineteenth century, Korean could not have functioned as an effective means for shared communion.[63] As Ross King points out, "The language situation in 1880s Korea was one of diglossia and digraphia." The official written language was *hanmun*—"classical Chinese in its Korean guise"—while the spoken vernacular was "a series of related, unstandardized dialects of Korean, the most prestigious being that of the capital, Seoul." As for writing, there were four major "styles": *ŏnmun, ŏnhanmun, idumun,* and *hanmun*.[64] It was when Korean intellectuals translated capitalist sovereignty in the late nineteenth century that the diachronic identity of Korean came to be assured—from the language of *hyangga* of the Three Kingdoms period down to the language of officials in late nineteenth-century Seoul—and Korean imagined as singular, a unity even in its great variations over space and time.[65] To historicize this act of translation, then, it is crucial to attend to the epistemological as well as political possibilities that presented themselves as nation, the "West," and the "world" as an international community (*man'guk*: literally, ten thousand countries) came to be constructed in late nineteenth-century Korea.

Legislative rationality, capitalist sovereignty functioning like a machine, the unavoidable accommodation to Western norms and laws, and semantic innovation—how might we conceptualize these as processes of translation and in translation? There were a number of ways by which new words were created and old words given new meanings. For example, neologisms such as *ethnic nation* (J: *minzoku*) were created in Japan in the process of translation. In the early 1880s Miyazaki Muryū translated the French Assemblée Nationale as *minzoku kaigi*. It took a decade or so for this neologism, *minzoku*, to attain a certain degree of stability in its meaning as ethnic nation.[66] The compound *minzoku* (K: *minjok*), understood as *ethnic nation*, began to circulate in Korea in the early 1900s. As usage of the term became more fixed in East Asian political discourse, its meaning approached the German *Volk* or *Volkschaft*.[67] An "old" compound like *kokumin* (國民), used internally to refer to the people of one's domain (J: *han*, 藩) during the Tokugawa period, accrued new associations after the Meiji Restoration and began to circulate throughout East Asia in the early twentieth century, its meaning vacillating between the conservative "national subject" and the more liberal "national citizen." There were other compounds used throughout East Asia whose meanings were radically altered by their association with certain terms in Western social science texts.

Another revealing example is the word for *economy* used today in China, Japan, and Korea (經濟; K: *kyŏngje*, C: *jingji*, J: *keizai*). The lexical unit *kyŏngje* is a contraction of *kyŏngse jemin* (經世濟民, to govern the world and relieve the people), found in classical Chinese literature. That is to say, prior to the nineteenth century, *kyŏngje* referred to a political economy that was necessarily and overtly moral in the sense of obligation to people's welfare.[68] In 1827 Satō Nobuhiro in his work *Keizai yōroku* (The Essence of Economics) rendered *keizai* in terms of production, consumption, and the wealth of nations, an intellectual approach that linked public interest with competition and the pursuit of private gain, almost certainly in the context of studying and translating Dutch texts.[69] As Justin Rosenberg has pointed out, whereas tribute (taxes or rents, in money or kind) was extracted through direct political relations of domination prior to capitalism, in a capitalist economy "profit [is] appropriated through a series of relations of exchange." When the people (*min*, 民) had been subordinated as the king's subjects, they were the object of both governance and sometimes compassion. With capitalist sovereignty, and *kyŏngje* rendered as *economy*, political inequality was no longer inscribed in the relations of production. The extraction of profit appears as a series of relations of exchange rather than tribute extracted through political domination; the people, as workers and producers, became "free" in their poverty and propertylessness. Like capitalism, then, the term *kyŏngje* could (and did) take a "purely economic" form.[70]

For our purposes, I will limit the examination of semantic innovation to the question of how Korean intellectuals like Philip Jaisohn, Chu Si-gyŏng, and others could have "shortened the distance" between words like *ŏnmun* (諺文, vulgar script)—the Chosŏn literati's designation for vernacular writing using the Korean alphabet invented in the mid-fifteenth century, today referred to as *han'gŭl* (in South Korea)—and *Chosŏn kŭl* (Korean letters, 朝鮮글) and *kungmun* (national script, 국문, 國文). For the Chosŏn literati, vernacular writing in Korean was *ŏnmun* in the sense that the Korean alphabet recorded vulgar speech. But in November 1894, in the wake of the Kabo reforms, a royal edict referred to vernacular writing in the Korean alphabet as the national script and decreed, "All laws and edicts shall have

Korean as their base; one may attach a translation in literary Chinese [*han-mun*] or in mixed script [*kukhanmun*]." Here, it should be noted that this royal edict gave recognition and enormous prestige to not just vernacular writing in the Korean alphabet but to the very concept of a "national script."

When first promulgated in 1443 under the directive *hunmin chŏngŭm* (instruct the people on the correct sounds), the vernacular writing system that came to be belittled as *ŏnmun* was a true alphabet that represented phonemes, units of sound that distinguish meanings. It was easy to learn, but the Chosŏn literati opposed the use of this alphabet in official texts on epistemological grounds. Literary Chinese (*hanmun*) was the writing system of power and universal truth. It was not foreign. It was the script that secured Korea's place in civilization. The Chosŏn literati expressed intense anxiety that the widespread use of *ŏnmun* would inevitably result in many turning their back on a vast universe of cultivated learning.[71] Thus laws, indeed anything of importance, could not and should not be written in the Korean alphabet. Prior to the late nineteenth century, then, it would have made little sense to place *country* (國) before *mun* (文). To the extent that a "national script" (國文) made any sense at all, it would have suggested a "country" mode of writing unable to shake off its parochialism: *country* would have rendered *mun*—letters, but also literature in the larger sense—into its other, that is, the local written vernacular, the "other" of true knowledge.[72]

When referring to their country, the Chosŏn literati often used the term *Eastern Country* (K: *Tongguk*, 東國), the geographical point of reference, of course, being China.[73] But the formal name for this dynastic state was Chosŏn,[74] and in referring to *Chosŏn kŭl* (Korean letters) Philip Jaisohn had combined the "pure" Korean word *kŭl*, for writing, with the name for Korea that did not locate it spatially with regard to China. The huge gulf between writing that is *kŭl* (글) and writing and literature that is *mun* (文) was bridged by *kŭl*'s association with Chosŏn and *mun*'s association with *kuk* (country) in the space and time of Korea's becoming "sovereign" from China.[75] That is to say, it took more than just productive imagination to shorten the distance between the national and *mun* and to posit an equivalence between the local vernacular (*Chosŏn kŭl*) and national (*kungmun*) script. The declarative sentence "They are Korean letters [朝鮮글]" derived its meaning, significance, and power from imperialism and capitalist sovereignty that had de-centered and provincialized China and shattered the

notion of all-under-heaven (C: *tianxia*, K: *ch'ŏnha*), a concept which placed
the Chinese emperor at the center and defined political sovereignty in relation to that center. Within the rationality of capitalist sovereignty, it now
made good sense to combine Chosŏn with *kŭl* and *country* with *mun*: Korea
is different from China; *kŭl* cannot come after China or Japan or France;
country and *mun* belong together. It was that *international* context — sovereignty's legislative rationality — which enabled intellectuals like Jaisohn to
imagine Korea as a singular linguistic community and to urge all Koreans
to read and write in the Korean vernacular.

We saw how this rationality worked in the case of Yun Ch'i-ho's diary
writing when, in 1887, he switched from literary Chinese to vernacular
writing in the Korean alphabet and referred to it as *kungmun*. It was not
an accident that Yun switched from literary Chinese to the Korean script
while studying at the Anglo-Chinese College in Shanghai. Through personal and institutional networks that were transnational, through church
services and Bible study groups, and by inspiring and training many prominent Korean linguists and grammarians — including the brilliant linguist
Chu Si-gyŏng — Christian (especially Protestant) missionaries made possible international recognition of the scientific value of the Korean vernacular script, promoted respect for and standardization of Korean, and
fostered a spirit of protecting the Korean script.[76] Protestant missionaries
helped transform the Korean vernacular script into an icon of Korea and
an icon for Korea. The status given to Chosŏn *kŭl* as national script might
seem to pay homage to Korean genius. But as Rey Chow has argued, the
homage to the West has long been paid in the form of what seems to be its
opposite:[77] in this case, the insistence on national language. That is to say,
imperialism and capitalist sovereignty compelled Korea's distinction from
China, Japan, and all the other countries, and the West was very much
present in constituting the Korean language and Korean people as inherent
attributes of a distinct unity.[78]

Sovereignty and Peoplehood

In English-language historiography on modern Japan and modern China,
many of the groundbreaking histories written in the early years of the
cold war dealt with Western "impact" and Japanese and Chinese response.
While this historiography, for the most part, presented Western impact as

modernization — a social scientific reworking of the earlier "civilizing" process — in Korea's case Western impact was rendered even more benign, because Korea was colonized by Japan in 1910. That is to say, historians (outside of North Korea) have not considered, in a critical way, the colonizing *effect* of not just Western impact on late nineteenth-century Korea but of the nation-state system into which Korea was forcibly incorporated. The nation-state system interpellated intellectuals like Chu Si-gyŏng, Philip Jaisohn, and others as nationalized subjects who produced semantic innovations and demarcated Korea as a unified space with a distinct system of signs and meanings. This semantic innovation was overdetermined and marked a beginning, not just in the sense that *Tongnip sinmun* was the first newspaper published in vernacular Korean and English. The *Independent* became a "national" newspaper *because* it was printed in the vernacular. This newspaper, disseminated "nationally," enabled new ways of experiencing time and space.[79] It helped create, as Rebecca Karl found for China at the turn of the twentieth century, "a world of synchronic temporality emphasizing historical identification and spatial proximity."[80]

The point to be made here is that a new consciousness of history and globality — for example, the plight of the Vietnamese under French colonial rule, or lessons to be learned from Italian or Polish history — helped establish a logic of equivalence based on a racial geography of the world and a concomitant desire for a unified nation space predicated on a unity of Korean language and Korean people. While this imagined unified nation space enabled "historical identification" with other countries and peoples, *how* that identification would be articulated — who and what would be made visible and audible — was central to a new political aesthetic of subject-making. In Philip Jaisohn's editorial in the *Tongnip sinmun*, readers were told that people in foreign countries (*kakkuk saram tŭl*), regardless of sex, study foreign languages only after they have acquired a good command of their own language (*pon'guk kungmun*). By inference, Jaisohn constructed a civilizational hierarchy, and Koreans were to emulate those people most civilized — Euro-Americans — who knew to value their own national language.[81] In calling on all Koreans (*Chosŏn inmin*), without regard to position or social status, to read and write in vernacular Korean, Jaisohn was echoing a central tenet of liberalism and capitalist sovereignty: that formal political inequality among men should not be basic to Korea's sovereignty.[82]

Jaisohn's editorial problematized not just the profound gap separating literary Chinese from vernacular Korean but also the profound social, cultural, and political gap that separated the social classes in Korea. To put it differently, while *Tongnip sinmun* enabled a consciousness of simultaneity with one's countrymen and with peoples elsewhere, it also highlighted and problematized the hierarchically fragmented state of the Korean people. For Jaisohn and many other intellectuals in ensuing years, it was clear which social class constituted the main obstacle to unifying and standardizing both the language and the people. For younger political activists like Rhee Syngman, the main impediment was posed by the scholar gentry steeped in classical training, while hope lay in the common people (*paek-sǒng*). In the introduction to *Tongnip chǒngsin* (Spirit of Independence), written in 1904 while he was in jail, Rhee wrote:

> To make this book as readable as an old [vernacular] novel, I provided lengthy explanations in simple everyday language and did not write down the names of many people and places. So that a large number of people throughout the country could read this easily, I have only used the Korean script [*kungmun*] to record [my thoughts]. Much discussion is addressed to the common people [*paeksǒng*] in particular, because the future of Korea [TaeHan] is entirely dependent on them. By and large, people [*saram*] of middle and higher status, or those who know some literary Chinese, are for the most part rotten, set in their ways, and beyond hope. Not only are these people [beyond hope], but the places they inhabit are also beyond salvation.[83]

It should be noted that the future Rhee invoked for Korea was a future (possibly quite disastrous) different from Korea's past and present. The scholar gentry steeped in Confucian learning were "rotten, set in their ways, and beyond hope." The past, now identified with the world of the scholar gentry, could not be instructive for Korea's present or for the future. But what about the common people whom Rhee presumably addressed and on whom the future of Korea depended?

In an essay titled "To Establish the Nation Teaching and Transformation Is the Key," written in literary Chinese roughly in the same period, Rhee referred to the people (*paeksǒng*) as dolls made of wood (*mok'u*) or grass (*ch'ou*).[84] In this essay, as in *Tongnip chǒngsin*, Rhee repeated an assertion that would have been familiar to anyone with a modicum of knowledge of classical Chinese literature: the people are the foundation of the country.

But he cast the people as the country's foundation not just in the old sense that they are the producers of all things essential to life (thus their moral stature) but also in the very novel sense that the common people are the historical agents that usher in the future. The problem, for Rhee, was that their minds (*chŏngsin*) were stiff and preoccupied by petty interests; their minds had no feeling or movement. As narrative, we might call this the poetics of degeneration. This kind of poetics had already been well established around the time Rhee became an activist, as illustrated by this editorial in the *Independent* in March 1897:

> Whether a country is progressing [*chinbo*] or not progressing has to do, above all, with whether its countrymen seek their rights as a people [*paeksŏng*]. By people, we are not just talking about those who hold no government office: all who live in the country are *paeksŏng*. . . . When the people exercise their rights the authority of the monarch [*ingŭm*] becomes enhanced and the country's standing [*chich'e*] is elevated.[85] But the people of Chosŏn, having been oppressed by their own countrymen for hundreds of years, have long forgotten their rights [*paeksŏng ŭi kwŏlli*], and do not even know what it means.[86]

Just as *Tongnip sinmun* conferred (inter)national status on vernacular Korean, so this editorial sought to reconstitute *paeksŏng* in a world of synchronic temporality, abstracted through a logic of equivalence: *paeksŏng* no longer in the sense of people who do not hold office but inclusive of all who live in Korea, the people not as the object of governance but as bearers of rights.

Seven years later, however, in Rhee's *Tongnip chŏngsin*, the category *paeksŏng* still retained that character of requiring edification (*hwa*). Rather than describe the people as the bearer of rights, however, Rhee constitutes them as fallen kin, brothers and sisters gripped by ignorance and poverty—and, it should be added, sinfulness. "My only fervent wish is for the ignorant and despised, young and weak brothers and sisters in the country to pay special attention, to become interested on their own initiative, to step by step try to move to action, and also to guide others, so that day by day people's attitudes will change and manners reformed, so that transformation [*hwa*] will come from below."[87] While Rhee hoped for transformation to come from below, and while he was certain that the future of Korea depended entirely on the people (*paeksŏng*), there was no unity among the millions of Koreans: the children of rich families saw the world as a paradise on earth, caught up in licentiousness, given to drink, sex, and gambling (*chusaek-chapki*); the children of poor families thought only of filling their stomachs, if necessary by stealing and deception.[88] Rhee wrote *Tongnip chŏngsin* precisely because he thought the Korean people were not up to the task of defending Korea's independence, and his view, as reflected in his political practice, hardly changed.

Prior to his imprisonment, Rhee had been one of the youngest and most ardent activists in the Manmin kongdonghoe (People's Assembly), which grew out of debating forums first organized by the Independence Club at huge outdoor assemblies in the heart of Seoul that drew thousands, if not tens of thousands, evolving from public gatherings for deliberative dialogue to what might be called street parliaments.[89] On October 30, 1898, in an assembly held in front of the palace organized jointly by reformist officials and the Independence Club, the assembly discussed a six-point resolution to be presented to Emperor Kojong, with two of the points related to the campaign for a legislative assembly: treaties and agreements with foreign powers should require legislative ratification, and appointment of all high officials should require the approval of the majority of Emperor Kojong's ministers.[90] On November 4 the arrest of Independence Club activists began. In January 1899 the Independence Club was forcibly dissolved, Yun Ch'i-ho was sent into internal exile in Wŏnsan, and nine months later *Tongnip sinmun* stopped publication.[91]

Rhee was charged and then jailed for involvement in an alleged conspiracy to have Emperor Kojong abdicate in favor of Yi Kang (1877–1955), Kojong's fifth son, and then to bring back Pak Yŏng-hyo (1861–1939) from Japan to head a reformist cabinet.[92] Rhee was sentenced to die, but after heavy pressure from American missionaries living in the capital (Rhee had attended Paejae Boys' High School and converted to Christianity while in jail), his sentence was commuted to life in prison; he was released when the Russo-Japanese War began, and then he was on his way to the United States.[93] His trip to the United States was reportedly arranged by two high officials, Min Yŏng-hwan and Han Kyu-sŏl, who wanted him to seek American help in safeguarding Korea's independence. Rhee met Secretary of State John Hay and President Theodore Roosevelt, but there was no chance that he could have succeeded. Roosevelt brought together representatives of Russia and Japan to negotiate at Portsmouth, producing a treaty which ended the Russo-Japanese War, with Russia agreeing not to interfere with

Japan in matters related to Korea.[94] A month before the conclusion of the Treaty of Portsmouth, Secretary of War William Howard Taft and Prime Minister of Japan Katsura Tarō came to an agreement regarding Korea. In the Taft-Katsura memorandum, Roosevelt agreed to Japan's control of Korea, and Japan recognized America's paramount interest in the Philippines. In November 1905 Korea became a protectorate of Japan.

In 1906 Rhee began his studies in the United States and earned three academic degrees in record time: a bachelor's degree from George Washington University in 1907, a master's degree from Harvard in 1910, and a doctorate from Princeton in 1910. Until he returned to Seoul in 1945 on a U.S. military plane, and throughout the Korean War and beyond, he continued to look to the United States for political, economic, and military support.[95] His critique of Korea's aristocracy, his condescending attitude toward the common people, and his faith in both Christianity and the United States trace the outlines of what I have been calling the (Christian) liberal-bourgeois subjectivity that emerged in Korea at the turn of the twentieth century.

For Rhee, politics remained primarily a pedagogic project, a top-down process of edifying the ignorant masses in order to constitute a unity. He was quite clear about the necessity of the civilizing process. Where the problems of ignorance, superstition, and lethargy among the people were intractable, Rhee warned against actual independence. As he put it, "To grant independence [chaju kwŏlli] to [an unenlightened nation] would be like giving a sharp sword to an immature child. So that it will not harm him, the sword ought to be taken away. Just as a child should not be allowed to wield a sword at his whim, the unenlightened nation, regardless of its size or strength, cannot receive the protection of international law nor retain its sovereign rights, not because the law is unfair [p'yŏn-byŏk]."[96] Rhee's conception of sovereignty and peoplehood, while seemingly inclusive of everyone, was profoundly undemocratic and colonial. As Uday Mehta has pointed out, such exclusion was not the result of liberalism practiced incompletely. The exclusionary basis of liberalism derived from its theoretical core: the legitimacy of political authority requires consent; consent, to be meaningful, requires the people giving that consent to be possessed of reason; certain groups of people (children, madmen, and idiots) are incapable of exercising that kind of reason; such people can be excluded, governed without their consent.[97] Rhee's Spirit of Independence outlined those cultural, social, and even psychological attributes that constitute the preconditions for political inclusion. Like liberalism's prescription for colonized peoples — where the colonized were rendered equivalent to children or semicivilized or simply incompetent — Rhee's people should be attentive, obedient, industrious, and sit patiently in the waiting room of History until the day they are ready for sovereignty.

More democratic articulations of sovereignty and peoplehood would emerge from other productive imaginations, including those of historians turned revolutionaries immersed in mass-based anticolonial struggles in colonial Korea and in the Korean diaspora. As historians adopted narrative strategies that sought to explain Korea's loss of sovereignty and point the way toward recovery of sovereignty, history writing became an integral part of anticolonial struggles. Rather than positing an inherent lack, these histories pointed to the existence of an autonomous national subject in Korean history, variously identified with a Korean spirit—*sim* (心), *hon* (魂), or *ŏl*, the equivalent of *Geist*—or with different conceptions of peoplehood: *minjok* (ethnic nation, 民族), *minjung* (people, 民衆), or *inmin* (people, 人民). Inviting the people into history, modern national(ist) histories reified sovereignty, rendering the present condition as a moment in the telos of History.

History Writing and Nationalism

If the impetus for the creation of a public sphere and the nationalizing of both language and people originated with imperialism, capitalist sovereignty, and liberalism that was deeply implicated in both, then what kind of conception of the whole existed within Korea prior to the late nineteenth century? The case can easily be made that "Korea" as a civilization, or as a cultural and social formation, had a history dating back well over a thousand years. As the political and religious elite of "Unified" Silla (676–935), Koryŏ (936–1392), and Chosŏn (1392–1910) reacted to and participated in intellectual movements within the larger cosmopolitan world centered around "China," they were compelled to generate various forms of collective identity — representations of their state and their people as being separate and unique. Through the practice of state-sponsored rituals, the building of monuments, and the compilation of official histories, narratives about the collective self were continuously generated. As such narratives were generated, other (competing) narratives were repressed or contested.

That is, narratives on "Korean" identity did not simply accumulate over time; not all such narratives got transmitted, and those that were were invariably translated (that is, reinvented) for use in the present.[98]

It is in this sense that the concept of Koreans as constituting an ethnic nation (*minjok*) is a modern construct which, in the historical context of its emergence at the turn of the century, enabled more democratic, more inclusive forms of political action. As noted earlier, the word *minjok* (read as *minzoku* in Japanese) was a neologism created in Meiji Japan.[99] When Korean (and Chinese and Japanese) nationalists wrote in English in the first half of the twentieth century, the English word they generally used for *minjok* was *race*. In the late nineteenth century and early twentieth, as Walker Conner points out, numerous writers in the West (incorrectly) employed *race* as a synonym for *nation*. And, as Andre Schmid points out, when intellectuals throughout East Asia appropriated the neologism, *minjok* became not only a powerful political concept but also "a powerful conceptual tool . . . to rewrite [the] historical past."[100]

This is not to ignore Lydia Liu's injunction to those engaged in cross-cultural studies to eschew a conceptual model "derived from a bilingual dictionary."[101] Following Liu, I do not assume that languages are commensurate or that equivalents exist naturally between them. Although the word *minjok* entered the Korean vocabulary in the late 1890s and became widely used two decades later, this is not sufficient proof that the *minjok* is a modern construct. Son Chin-t'ae (1900–Korean War?) made this point in 1948 when he wrote, "Although the word 'minjok' was not used in the past—because it was the quintessential character of Korea's court-centered, aristocratic states to obstruct the development of such [national] consciousness [*sasang*] and concepts—the [Korean] minjok certainly did exist even if the word did not."[102] Similarly Cho Tong-gŏl applauds the pioneer of nationalist historiography, Sin Ch'ae-ho (1880–1936), not for creating a historical narrative based on a new construct called the *minjok* but for creating a historical narrative based on the *discovery* of the *minjok*—suggesting that prior to its discovery the *minjok* was already (and always) present.[103] In contrast to these views, I am arguing that *minjok* is a modern construct, and not to recognize it as such is to miss the crucial link, in early twentieth-century Korean historiography, between nationalism and democratic thought.

To understand this linkage, we might begin with the question of when and how peasants of Kyŏngsang Province, for example, became "Koreans."

Of a very different historical context, Eugen Weber has argued that the French peasant was "nationalized" (that is, made French) only in the 1880s. "The French" were produced in the last decades of the nineteenth century through the creation of a national language (standard French) and national customs. To be more precise, the transformation of peasants into French-men became possible after the establishment of universal schooling, unifi-cation of customs and beliefs by interregional labor migration and military service, and subordination of political and religious conflicts to an ideology of patriotism. In other words, it was only after the emergence of modern state structures that distinctive social, political, and linguistic practices be-came "local variations" of a newly created national culture.[104]

If the French became "French" in the 1880s, when did Koreans become "Korean"? In asking this question, I must emphasize that Korea, perhaps as early as the Koryŏ period, had far more linguistic and cultural unity than did prerevolutionary France. There were, however, significant linguistic and cultural differences among the various provinces in Korea. Even more im-portant than these regional (lateral) differences, status distinctions between *yangban*, *chungin* (middle people), commoners, and *ch'ŏnmin* (base people) had created horizontal lines of cultural cleavage in which each status group had its own idiom, norms, and social role. It can be argued, for example, that Confucianism "belonged" to the ruling (*yangban*) class in the sense that it served to underscore, legitimize, and make authoritative the different worlds inhabited by the horizontally segregated layers in premodern Korean society.[105] As Carter Eckert notes, prior to the late nineteenth century,

> there was little, if any, feeling of loyalty toward the abstract concept of "Korea" as a nation-state, or toward fellow inhabitants of the peninsula as "Koreans." Far more meaningful at the time, in addition to a sense of loyalty to the king, were the attachments of Koreans to their village or region, and above all to their clan, lineage, and immediate and extended family. The Korean elite in particular would have found the idea of nationalism not only strange but also uncivilized. Since at least the seventh century the ruling classes in Korea had thought of themselves in cultural terms less as Koreans than as members of a larger cosmopolitan civilization centered on China. . . . To live outside the realm of Chinese culture was, for the Korean elite, to live as a barbarian.[106]

Eckert is not suggesting that Korean elites were ignorant of differences (political, linguistic, and cultural) between themselves and, say, the Chinese. For more than a thousand years, Korea had a central bureaucratic state that employed a class of people whose job was to maintain and articulate their difference from competing, neighboring states (most often in Manchuria, sometimes Japan, and of course, China itself).[107] However, unlike the modern nation-state, the kingdoms of "Unified" Silla, Koryŏ, and Chosŏn were not interested in homogenizing their subjects. In fact it can be argued that the premodern state's (extremely effective) solution to the problem of maintaining political stability was to tolerate local distinctiveness and to maintain status distinctions.[108]

The people of Chosŏn knew that they shared certain ties with other people living in the Chosŏn kingdom, as well as with ancestors they had never seen. But, as Benedict Anderson would argue, these "ties" would have been imagined particularistically, "as indefinitely stretchable nets of kinship and clientship."[109] At the turn of the century, however, a new generation of political activists and intellectuals felt they had to redefine Korea in terms of internal homogeneity and external autonomy. The historical juncture for this epistemological break came after the Korean monarchy proved incapable of keeping imperialist powers at bay and after Japan made Korea its protectorate, undermining the notion of Pan-Asianism based on racial solidarity. Organizing movements for independence, self-strengthening, and people's rights, these intellectuals reimagined Korea's collective identity in terms of a "deep, horizontal comradeship"—regardless of, or because of, the actual divisions and inequalities that prevailed in Korean society.

It was ethnic national historiography (minjok sahak), then, born in the early twentieth century, that for the first time narrated the history of Korea as the history of the Korean minjok, a category inclusive of every Korean without regard to age, gender, or status distinctions.[110] The first nationalist historian responsible for centering the ethnic nation—both as the subject of history and as the object for historical research—was Sin Ch'ae-ho.[111] His essay "Toksa sillon" (A New Way of Reading History), published in 1908, set forth the first and most influential historical narrative equating Korean history (kuksa) with the history of the Korean nation (minjoksa). As a history of the ethnic nation rather than a dynastic history, "Toksa sillon" traced the origin of the Korean nation to the mythical figure Tan'gun.[112] The first "modern" history textbooks published in 1895 had treated Tan'gun as a deity (sinin, 神人) who descended (降) from Heaven. Starting in 1906, after

Korea became a protectorate of Imperial Japan, Tan'gun became human-
ized in the history textbooks, as having been born (生).

Christian missionaries in late nineteenth-century Korea were anxious
to make distinctions between historia, logos, and mythos. While presenting the stories in the Bible as history, they treated the story of Tan'gun as
myth, in the sense of "fable," "invention," "fiction," "what could not have
happened." In 1901, the missionary and historian Homer B. Hulbert, who
evinced high regard for Korean historical sources, nevertheless argued that
events prior to the Three Kingdoms period belong to the time of myth.
"Authentic Korean history may be said to begin with the year 57 B.C. . . .
From the year 57 B.C. the history of Korea is recorded in a clear and rational manner."[113] For Hulbert, the beginnings of the Three Kingdoms period
marked the advent of Korean history. Starting with Sin Ch'ae-ho, the initial
nationalist response to the discrediting of the Tan'gun story was to separate
out the mythic elements from the historical and on the ground of historical
actuality trace Korean ethnic national origin and essential culture back to
Tan'gun as a historical figure who had established ancient Chosŏn.[114]

The Tan'gun legend had an ambiguous place in premodern Korean historiography. It is not mentioned in Korea's oldest extant history, the *Samguk
sagi* (Historical Record of the Three Kingdoms), compiled by Kim Pu-sik
in 1145.[115] According to Han Yŏng-u, the political intent of Kim's *Samguk
sagi* was to bolster bureaucratic authority centered around the Koryŏ
court (936–1392). Compiled ten years after Kim suppressed a revolt led
by Myoch'ŏng, *Samguk sagi* also makes no reference to Parhae (699–926;
P'ohai in Chinese), a kingdom established by a former Koguryŏ general encompassing much of Manchuria, southern Siberia, and northeast Korea.[116]
In writing the history of the Three Kingdoms,[117] Kim Pu-sik depicted Koryŏ
as the successor to Silla (which by 676 controlled the southern two-thirds of
the peninsula). In contrast, the forces led by Myoch'ŏng regarded Koryŏ as
the successor state of Koguryŏ and advocated an (incautious) expansionist
policy to recover onetime Koguryŏ land.[118] The suppression of Myoch'ŏng's
revolt went hand in hand with policies of peacefully coexisting with the Jin
and bolstering the authority of the Koryŏ court by promoting Confucian
principles, particularly loyalty to the king. Likewise the narrative strategy
as well as the methodology of Kim's *Samguk sagi*, including the invocation
of the Confucian historiographic principles of rationality (*mujing pulsin*)
and fidelity to historical sources (*suli pujak*, that is, transmission without

creative elaboration), cannot be understood apart from the political context of mid-twelfth-century Koryŏ.

The Tan'gun legend does appear in the thirteenth-century texts *Samguk yusa* (Memorabilia of the Three Kingdoms, 1285?), written by the Buddhist Sŏn master Iryŏn, and in *Chewang un'gi* (Rhymed Record of Emperors and Kings, 1287), written by Yi Sŭng-hyu.[119] But these histories were compiled under very different historical circumstances. Both began their histories with Tan'gun, a significant assertion that traced Koryŏ's origin directly to Heaven. Because Iryŏn and Yi Sŭng-hyu witnessed the suffering of the people during the Mongol invasions and domination of Koryŏ, Yi Ki-baek surmises that this "strengthened their sense of identity as a distinct race [*minjok*] and gave force to the concept of their descent from a common ancestor."[120] Among the events that Iryŏn and Yi Sŭng-hyu witnessed was King Ch'ungnyŏl's marriage to a daughter of Khubilai in 1274 and the Koryŏ royal family's becoming a cadet branch of the Mongol imperial house.[121] The meaning of the Tan'gun legend in these thirteenth-century texts, then, cannot be isolated from the historical context of the Mongol domination of Koryŏ from 1259 to 1356. Indeed it is reasonable to interpret Iryŏn's narrative strategy of making Tan'gun as ancient as the legendary Chinese emperor Yao and his willingness to talk about "extraordinary forces and capricious spirits" and "wondrous tales" (religiously ignoring the Confucian principle of *mujing pulsin*) as a narrative of resistance.[122]

Sin Ch'ae-ho's use of the Tan'gun legend in the twentieth-century context was similarly a narrative of resistance, but it was also a reinvention—and not simply a revival—of this old and recurrent narrative in premodern Korean historiography. The claim to a distinct history of legitimacy (*chŏngt'ong*) that reached far back into the mythic past did not naturally or teleologically give rise to nationalist modes of narrating territory, temporality, and peoplehood. The best evidence that any "transmission" of the past must also be a reinvention is Sin's "Toksa sillon" itself. If Korea as a homogeneous ethnic nation had been a well-established, abiding concept, then there would have been no need to write "Toksa sillon," and it would not have caused such excitement among his readers in 1908. By identifying the *minjok* rather than the monarch as the subject of an evolutionary history (where the strong survive and the weak perish), "Toksa sillon" displaced traditional forms of Confucian historiography—*p'yŏnnyŏnch'e* (chronicles) and *kijŏnch'e* (annal biographies)—with the (tragic) epic form. Sin adopted a novel way of telling what Confucian historians had already known; his narrative utilized new codes to produce new structures of meaning quite different from that found in histories written in the chronicle style and the annal biography style.[123]

Confucian historiography had constituted itself not as a separate discipline but as an integral part of the study of classics and statecraft. Its function was to serve as a mirror and as a repository of knowledge that would enable the monarch and all scholar-officials to act morally and ethically in the present. As a political tool, history writing had the solemn ethical function of assigning praise and blame. As texts considered central to subject-formation, Confucian histories served a pedagogic function in the practice of self-cultivation that was to be both self-directed and yet profoundly social. Although both official and private histories existed, both were written by bureaucrats for other bureaucrats (either holding office or aspiring to do so).[124] Moreover in terms of access to court documents and official histories (with the exception of the Collected Statutes), these could be consulted only by a small group of scholar-officials.[125]

Although nationalist historiography was constituted as a modern and scientific discipline, it preserved certain aspects of Confucian historiography, for example, the concept of history as a mirror for the present and history as serving an ethical function, assigning praise and blame. But the critical difference had to do with the profound epistemic break caused by Korea's incorporation into the nation-state system dominated by the West in the late nineteenth century and the social position of the historian and his intended readership in colonial modernity. Few of the nationalist historians came from high *yangban* status; many were regularly hounded by the colonial police; and most wrote their histories in their capacity as "public intellectuals." When Sin Ch'ae-ho wrote "Toksa sillon," for example, he was a member of the secret society Sinminhoe (New People's Association) and employed by the newspaper *Taehan maeil sinbo* (Korean Daily News), and the essay itself was serialized in the *Taehan maeil sinbo* from August to December 1908.[126]

On the eve of Korea's being colonized by Japan, to achieve political independence and to reclaim dignity and "authentic" identity in reaction to colonialist discourses on Korea, nationalists such as Sin Ch'ae-ho sought to arouse, unite, and mobilize the entire Korean population.[127] In place of loyalty to the king and attachments to the village, clan, and family, and in place of hierarchic status distinctions among *yangban*, *chungin*, commoners, and *ch'ŏnmin*, nationalist historiography endeavored to redirect the people's loyalty toward a new, all-embracing identity of Koreans as a unique ethnic group. It was with this political intent that Sin wrote "Toksa sillon" for an emerging "general public," tracing Korea's ethnic and cultural origins as far back as possible to a geographic area that extended far beyond the Korean peninsula into Manchuria.

In 1908 Sin's indictment of Kim Pu-sik's *Samguk sagi* for its deletion of Manchuria from Korean history and his reconceptualization of state history (*kuksa*) as the history of the Korean nation (*minjoksa*) were radical conceptual acts. Sin's identification of the *minjok* as the subject of an evolutionary history marked a watershed in modern Korean intellectual history.[128] In a much later essay, serialized in *Tonga ilbo* from October 1924 through March 1925, where Sin continued his polemic against Kim Pu-sik, Kim's many faults were condensed to *sadaejuŭi* (事大主義), a mentality of subservience—the antithesis of a sovereign, autonomous subjectivity. For Sin, the defeat of Myoch'ŏng by Kim in 1135 and the subsequent erasure of Tan'gun and Parhae (and thus Manchuria) from Korean history was *the* disastrous turning point in Korean history and ushered in a thousand-year legacy of *sadaejuŭi*.[129] With this, Sin created new possibilities for imagining the ethnic nation: as autonomous subject, a primordial unity, a complete figure of sovereignty absent in the present but present at the very beginning of history and recoverable in the future.

This was a strategy of disavowal similar to and yet different from that of Yun Ch'i-ho. Like Sin's, Yun's disavowal was temporal. He could have tea with white Christian ladies in the Jim Crow South, sympathizing with the cousin of Miss Linnie Davis, a Presbyterian missionary in Korea, who "ha[d] more to endure than one in the African jungles." In this intensely racialized private space, a congregation point for supporting those who bear the white man's burden,[130] Yun could be differentiated from those Koreans who desperately needed American missionaries through the shared fiction that his sociality in that space (his Christian faith, his demeanor, his skill at word games) removed him temporally from his brethren. But living in American time, the disavowal was difficult and complicated given how intensely racialized were the spaces he inhabited. His emotional life saturated by racial and civilizational hierarchies that produced feelings of fascination and revulsion, Yun found himself unable to walk away from the

Korea Exhibit at the Columbian Exposition *because* it was so second-rate and dismal. To the extent that for Yun, the Korea Exhibit functioned as a synecdoche of Korea's abjection, it is possible to understand his sadness and contempt for Native Americans in the American West as springing from recognition and identification.

Sin Ch'ae-ho's disavowal was different; the ethnic nation he located at the very beginning of history already contained within itself an autonomous subjectivity, its own sovereignty. Subsequent historians, especially Marxist historians like Paek Nam-un writing in the early 1930s, would be critical of Sin, historicizing his historiography as an "antique inheritance" from the nineteenth century. Because Sin grounded his historical narrative on concepts like *sim* (心), *hon* (魂), and *ŏl* (Spirit, Mind, or *Geist*), Paek Nam-un rendered Sin's historiography as an idealist-particularist history that in the end only reinforced colonialist historiography. By emphasizing Korean uniqueness, nationalist historiography reinforced the view of precolonial Korea as outside of world history. Be that as it may, history writing after Sin continued to revolve around the problematic of sovereignty, and sovereignty continued to be privileged precisely by the claim that the ethnic nation preceded sovereignty. The problematic of sovereignty and autonomous subjectivity rendered the past flexible and the present changeable.

PART II

History Writing

chapter three

NATIONALIZING KOREA'S PAST

> The history of a state is that which renders a precise record of the rise
> and/or fall, prosperity and/or decay of the [ethnic] nation. Without the
> nation there is no history; without history, the nation cannot have a clear
> perception of the state, and thus the historian has a heavy responsibility.
> —SIN CH'AE-HO, "Toksa sillon," *Taehan maeil sinbo*, 1908

A year before Japan's annexation of Korea, while climbing the eastern slope
of Mt. T'oham in Kyŏngju, a Japanese mailman made a great discovery.[1]
Near the summit, as he took in the beauty of the mountain shaped like a
great folding screen and in the distance the Eastern Sea, he chanced upon
what looked to be a cave. Inside he encountered a Buddhist statue of aston-
ishing beauty. Following this "discovery" of the Sŏkkuram, constructed in
the mid-eighth century, Japanese authorities began an extensive restoration and pedagogic effort. Today the Sŏkkuram is a major tourist destination in South Korea, a national treasure recognized by UNESCO as a World
Heritage Site, giving testimony to the brilliance of Korea's cultural and religious past. The restoration effort began in 1913, and it was the Japanese
colonial state that first brought Sŏkkuram to the attention of the world.
Why would the Japanese colonial state spend money and resources to restore Sŏkkuram and sing odes to the beauty of not just Sŏkkuram but also
Pulkugsa and the Silla capital of Kyŏngju? Was Sŏkkuram forgotten during
the Chosŏn period? Didn't the Chosŏn state recognize its historic and artistic importance? What made it easy for Japanese writers like Yanagi Sōetsu,
founder of the folk craft movement in Japan, to take the lead in praising
Sŏkkuram as the "culmination of the religion and the art of the Orient"?[2]

Questions like these go to the heart of understanding the complexity of
colonial domination and power and the multifaceted history of colonialism, starting with Euro-American and Japanese colonialism. Ultimately
colonial rule depended on coercive power: the power to eradicate or re-
press armed resistance and protest. But Japanese colonialism could not
have been sustained with just coercive power; Japan had to establish sufficient hegemony, the creation of a political and cultural environment in

which the colonized recognized the relative superiority of the colonizer. In other words, colonialism had also to be a pedagogic endeavor in which the colonized were taught to live, and to want to live, in a world created by the colonizer and to see that world as natural. Restoring Sŏkkuram to its former glory formed a part of that pedagogic endeavor, teaching about the world and Korea's place in it as defined by Japan and the West. That is to say, an essential part of Japanese colonial rule involved knowledge production that drew heavily on Euro-American colonial practices. Like the British in India and the Americans in the Philippines, the Japanese colonial state invested time, money, and human resources to carry out excavations and surveys, to study Korea's past and restore some cultural sites (but not others) in order to establish the categories and narrative strategies by which Korea and Koreans would be understood. This Korea, contemporaneous with the time and discursive space in which Japanese scholars working for the colonial authorities produced knowledge about Korea's past, is what I refer to as colonial Korea.

The Japanese discovery of Sŏkkuram in 1909 coincided with massive and brutal suppression campaigns in the southern provinces to eradicate armed resistance by Righteous Armies. The Righteous Armies were a response to the forced abdication of King Kojong and the disbanding of the Korean Army in 1907. Up and down the Korean peninsula Righteous Armies launched attacks against Japanese and pro-Japanese individuals and organizations, also targeting infrastructure such as bridges, railroads, and telegraph lines. In North Kyŏngsang Province, Righteous Armies were most active around Mt. Ilwol. It was during his inspection of the suppression campaign in Taejŏn that the Japanese resident general Sone Arasuke heard news about Sŏkkuram, visited the site himself, and immediately ordered Sekino Tadashi, an expert on antiquities, to conduct a thorough study of the site.[3] Sone's initial plan for Sŏkkuram was to take it apart and ship it to Japan—in other words, to loot it.

A road was constructed between Pulguksa and Sŏkkuram, and the resident general had plans drafted to construct a rail line from Kampo to the top of Mt. T'oham and to enlarge the port at Kampo. Sŏkkuram was to be taken apart piece by piece and sent by train and then by ship to Japan. But in the end the costs involved turned out to be prohibitive, in terms of money but also in terms of the resistance that would have been waged by Koreans. In 1910, the year Japan annexed Korea, Sekino Tadashi published a study in which he explained to the Japanese reading public the artistic value of Sŏkkuram. In the same year photos of Sŏkkuram were published for the first time—in Japan.[4] After annexation, with colonial Korea formally part of the Japanese Empire, the head of the colonial government, Governor-General Terauchi Masatake, dropped plans for dismantling and shipping Sŏkkuram to Japan. In 1912 he visited Sŏkkuram and approved the plans and budget for its restoration. The restoration work, begun in 1913, took three years to complete. With a road built connecting Pulguksa and Sŏkkuram, school trips were organized, with teachers bringing students down from Seoul to Pusan by train. Under Japanese tutelage, Koreans would come to learn about the beauty and significance of Sŏkkuram. This shift in policy—from plunder to restoration—would showcase not just Sŏkkuram but also Japan's sophistication and modernity, its mastery of the (Western) disciplines of archaeology, architecture, and art history. This restoration work would demonstrate Japanese knowledge and commitment to studying, restoring, and appreciating "Asian art." Japan would be the curator, uniquely able to preserve and present Asian art as equally compelling as Western art to both Asia and the West.

Except for the wood used for structural supports, the workmen, tools, and materials for the restoration were all brought from Japan. The main Buddha in the rotunda faced east with an ethereal smile, his robe draped over his left shoulder, sitting cross-legged on a raised central pedestal, his left hand open in the gesture of bearing witness. This Buddha was left in place, but everything else was taken apart. The granite stones, "woven like silk," that formed the outside wall of the rectangular anteroom, where ceremonies were conducted; the rotunda beyond where the main Buddha was enshrined; the eight guardian deities carved in relief on stone slabs that formed the inner wall of the anteroom; the two massive stone pillars at the entrance to the rotunda; the curved stone slabs along with knuckle stone that formed the vaulted dome, serving as a canopy over the main Buddha; a carving of Indra on the right and Brahma on the left; and lining the wall around the rotunda two Bodhisattvas and the Ten Disciples[5]—all these were taken apart and then put back together again. But it turned out that the restoration effort was not entirely successful.

To provide more structural support the Japanese restorers used concrete to put the pieces back together again. The stone slabs still formed a canopy over the Buddha, but these were now part of a concrete dome over the rotunda. Soon after restoration moisture became a problem. The original structure, the granite stones "woven like silk," had allowed for both circulation of air and indirect sources of light into the rotunda.[6] With a concrete dome, however, moisture trapped in the rotunda condensed and trickled down the face of the Buddha, as if the Buddha was sweating, and moss began to grow on the stone reliefs.[7] In spite of this debacle, the Japanese colonial state went to great lengths to showcase its cultural preservation efforts. Reporting on the start of restoration work, *Maeil sinbo*, the Korean-language newspaper published by the colonial government, described Sŏkkuram as a brilliant example of the Korean nation's artistic character (*minjokjŏk kaesŏng*).[8] Thus it was the Japanese colonial state that definitively identified Sŏkkuram as an example of Korea's cultural and religious past.

On July 4, 1916, the Japanese colonial state promulgated the Regulations on the Preservation of Ancient Sites and Relics of Chōsen. As Hyung Il Pai has pointed out, these regulations stipulated that any discoveries of historic ruins or buildings, sites of palaces or temples, Buddhist images, earthenware, and other objects of Korean art, archaeology, and history were to be reported to the nearest police captain. The colonial state also established the Commission for Investigating Historic Relics (Chōsen koseki kenkyūkai), charged with the task of implementing the regulations and "investigating archeological remains, planning exhibitions, preserving and reconstructing monuments, registering national remains, and publishing the results of their research activities." Pai also notes that these regulations were adaptations of regulations and guidelines first passed in Meiji Japan.[9] But it should be stressed that Meiji heritage-management laws grew out of the Meiji state's own "discovery" of "Japan's" artistic past. In 1884 a commission sponsored by the Meiji government catalogued the temples, shrines, and artifacts in Nara Prefecture. This commission, led by Okakura Kakuzō, Kanō Tessai, and Ernest F. Fenollosa, "discovered" the Guze Kannon, a seventh-century gilt-wood sculpture at Hōryūji temple.[10]

It was a discovery in the sense that the Guze Kannon had been locked inside a shrine that had not been opened for centuries. Ernest Fenollosa, at the time a professor of philosophy and political economy at Tokyo Imperial University,[11] described the discovery this way:

> The greatest perfect monument of Corean Art that has come down to us, without which we could only conjecture as to the height reached by the peninsula creations, is the great standing Buddha, or possibly Bodhisattwa, of the

Yumedono pavilion at Horiuji.[12] This most beautiful statue, a little larger than life, was discovered by me and a Japanese colleague in the summer of 1884. I had credentials from the central government which enabled me to requisition the opening of godowns and shrines. The central space of the octagonal Yumedono was occupied by a great closed shrine. . . . The priests of the Horiuji confess that tradition ascribed the contents of the shrine to Corean work of the days of Suiko, but that it had not been opened for more than two hundred years. . . . They resisted long, alleging that in punishment for the sacrilege an earthquake might well destroy the temple. Finally we prevailed, and I shall never forget our feelings as the long disused key rattled in the rusty lock. Within the shrine appeared a tall mass closely wrapped about in swathing bands of cotton cloth, upon which the dust of ages had gathered. It was no light task to unwrap the contents, some 500 yards of cloth having been used. . . . Seen in profile it seemed to rise to the height of archaic Greek art. . . . But the finest feature was the profile view of the head, with its sharp Han nose, its straight clear forehead, and its rather large—almost negroid—lips, on which a quiet mysterious smile played, not unlike Da Vinci's Mona Lisa's.[13]

Fenollosa's account presents a singular masculine voice, acknowledging a Japanese colleague but not naming him, displaying imperial credentials that overpower local resistance, unlocking and entering forbidden sacred places, stripping away the cloth to reveal the Bodhisattva's mysterious smile.[14]

Okakura Kakuzō's account of this discovery is different in a number of ways.[15] In 1884 Okakura was working in the art section of the Ministry of Education. Eighteen years later, while staying in India, he recounted the discovery this way:

In 1884 along with Fenollosa and Kanō Tessai, I approached the priests asking that they open the door. The priests replied that if they did so thunder would certainly be heard. They opened it at the beginning of Meiji during the clamor over the separation of Buddhism and Shintō. Instantly the heavens clouded over and thunder roared; the masses became frightened and fled. With such a memorable experience they did not easily acquiesce. . . . After we removed the cloth we reached white paper. This is where the masses stopped when they were frightened off by the thunder.[16]

Published well after Okakura's death, in the immediate aftermath of Japan's invasion of China in 1937, *The Awakening of the East* presents powerful denunciations of Western imperialism.[17] Okakura's account locates the Guze Kannon in its local and contemporaneous significance, as meaningful and connected to early Meiji religious and political life and conflict. In a different work, written in the same period but published in 1903 as *The Ideals of the East*, Okakura narrated the past incorporation of Buddhist art and ideals from India, via China and Korea, as exemplifying the intellectual and artistic waves that had washed ashore in Japan over millennia, making Japan "the real repository of the trust of Asiatic thought and culture." In that sense, Okakura continued, "Japan is a museum of Asiatic civilization; and yet more than a museum because the singular genius of the race leads it to dwell on all phases of the ideals of the past."[18]

Japan was the spiritual repository of Asia over millennia, the only place in Asia where the best of Asian thought and culture "in all their purity" was incorporated into Japanese life "in the spirit of living Adwaitism"—Adwaita meaning "the state of not being two . . . [consistent with] the great Indian doctrine that all which exists though apparently manifold, is really one."[19] Therefore the Japanese people were bound to shoulder the responsibility of serving as the voice of Asia. Okakura explained how the Japanese came to this responsibility in terms of "unbroken sovereignty," a sovereignty that endowed the Japanese with "the spirit of living Adwaitism which welcomes the new without losing the old": "the strange tenacity of the [Japanese] race, nurtured in the shadow of a sovereignty unbroken from its beginning, that very tenacity which preserves the Chinese and Indian ideals in all their purity amongst us, even where they were long since cast away by the hands that created them."[20]

While a student at Tokyo Imperial University Okakura had studied with Fenollosa and came to share his deep interest in Japanese art. In the same year that they discovered the Guze Kannon in their capacity as imperial art commissioners, Okakura and Fenollosa founded Kanga-kai, an art society that endeavored to awaken the Japanese public to the significance of Japan's national treasures. Together they helped establish the Tokyo Fine Arts Academy and the Tokyo Imperial Museum, and they helped draft the law for the preservation of temples, shrines, and art treasures. It was Okakura's rendering of Japan as "the real repository of the trust of Asiatic thought and culture" that allowed him to begin *The Ideals of the East* with the declaration "Asia is one."

In *Chōsen bijutsushi*, a 1932 publication on Korean art history, Sekino

Tadashi, who had been the chief consultant on the Sŏkkuram restoration project, identified the origins of Korean art with the Chinese-influenced art of the Lelang Commandery (K: Nangnang), negating any notion of an autochthonous origin. Published a year after Japan's invasion of Manchuria, Sekino's history of Korean art fit comfortably with the Manchuria-Korea spatial conception of *Mansenshi*, a colonialist narrative that presented Korean cultural history in terms of movement, in colonizing waves, into the Korean peninsula. Sekino's history of Korean art, its origins identified with both Manchuria and China, used a narrative strategy well established by the early 1930s, of brilliant origins and then decline. With the adoption of Buddhism during the Three Kingdoms period Korean art reached its zenith in Silla and then "Unified" Silla. But then began a long decline starting in the Koryŏ period, reaching its nadir in the dry and trivial art of the Chosŏn period.[21] Within that narrative, Sŏkkuram became a great artifact of Japan's Asia: Asia as One. That is, in taking responsibility for Korea's cultural and artistic past, and unlike Okakura, who took care to situate the Guze Kannon in its local and contemporaneous significance, the Japanese colonial state's restoration of Sŏkkuram in Kyŏngju emptied that site of local and contemporaneous meanings, while colonial scholarship reterritorialized Sŏkkuram and other Three Kingdoms–period sites and artifacts, helping to produce new historical and spatial imaginaries (for example, the binary of Western art and Eastern art) for an expanding Japanese empire.

Colonialist and Nationalist Historiography

The pedagogic endeavors of the Japanese colonial state situated Chosŏn Korea in a temporality in which Korea's brilliant artistic achievements in ancient times stood in stark contrast to its recent precolonial past. Sŏkkuram, presented as the "culmination of the religion and the art of the Orient," also rendered Buddhist art and architecture of Silla as the apex of Korean cultural history. The story of Sŏkkuram—its creation and subsequent slide into obscurity—was the story of Korea: a brilliant past that was Asian rather than Korean, followed by a downward slide into the vulgar and trivial art of the Chosŏn dynasty, pointing to the necessity of Japan's tutelage of Korea and Koreans. Japan's annexation of Korea was a restoration at many levels, including restoration of ancient kinship ties and of Japanese rule over Korea—Japan having ruled southern Korea in ancient times, as asserted by nativist (*kokugaku*) readings of the eighth-century texts *Kojiki* (Record of Ancient Matters) and *Nihon shoki* (The Chronicles of Japan). Colonialist historiography, then, written mostly by Japanese historians but also by a number of Korean historians, provided justification for Japanese control over Korea by narrating Korean history in terms of decline and lack. Contemporary Koreans lacked the capacity for autonomous development, lacked a progressive spirit. Colonialist historiography suggested, and at times stated unequivocally, that because of such inherent deficiencies Japan had no choice but to lead Korea into modern civilization.

Contemporary South Korean historians identify four themes which characterize colonialist historiography on Korea: that external forces — Chinese, Manchurian, and Japanese — had always determined Korea's historical development (*t'ayulsŏngnon*); that premodern Korean society had been utterly stagnant, nineteenth-century Korea being equivalent to twelfth-century Japan (*chŏngch'esŏngnon*); that factionalism was deeply ingrained in the Korean political culture, as evidenced by continuous factional strife during the Chosŏn period (*tangp'asŏngnon*); and that Japanese and Koreans shared a common ancestry, and therefore Japan's colonization of Korea represented the restoration of ancient ties (*Il-Sŏn tongjoron*).[22]

In this way colonialist historiography suggested, and later stated unequivocally, that because of such inherent deficiencies Japan was compelled to extend imperial rule over Korea so as to lead it into modern civilization. According to Hatada Takashi, the origins of what many contemporary Korean historians characterize as colonialist historiography on Korea can be traced to mid-Meiji efforts to write a national history for Japan. One very influential work was *Kokushi gan* (A Survey of Japanese History), published by Tokyo Imperial University in 1890. Written by Shigeno Yasutsugu, Kume Kunitake, and Hoshino Hisashi, *Kokushi gan* was intended as a primer in the teaching of Japanese history, and it was long used as a university textbook. According to Numata Jirō, it was Shigeno Yasutsugu who played the leading role in establishing the "modern Tokyo tradition" of history writing. Stressing the native origins of "mainstream" historiography in modern Japan, Numata argues that the Tokyo tradition resulted from a fusion between the critical methods of Western historical science (as introduced by the German historian Ludwig Riess in 1887) and the scholastic tradition of evidential research, or *kōshō gaku* (K: *kochŭnghak*, C: *k'ao cheng*), which had been well established during the Tokugawa period.[23]

What Hatada Takashi would point out, however, is that if the birth of modern historical science in Japan owed its methodology to the Tokugawa tradition of evidential research, the narrative framework for Japan's national history was also greatly influenced by Tokugawa nativist (*kokugaku*) views on Japan's origins. According to Hatada, *Kokushi gan* drew on the nativist reading of the *Kojiki* and the *Nihon shoki*, which asserted that Japanese and Koreans had a common ancestry (*Nissen dōssoron*), but only in the sense that long ago the Japanese had controlled the southern part of Korea. *Kokushi gan*, as intended, provided the narrative framework for Japan's national history textbooks used in primary and secondary schools, creating a historical imaginary (*rekishi zō*) wherein the colonization of Korea in modern times represented the restoration of an ancient relationship.[24] This kind of expansionist historical imaginary, along with media portrayals of Korea following Japan's victory in the first Sino-Japanese War (1894–95), created a historical imaginary whereby the Japanese came to believe that Japan had ruled Korea in ancient times and that the Japanese colonization of Korea in modern times represented the restoration of an ancient relationship.[25]

This imperial imaginary in Japan's national histories was reproduced in histories of Korea. Hayashi Taisuke's *Chōsenshi* (History of Korea), published in 1892, argued that in ancient times the northern part of Korea had been a colony of China (with Han Chinese commanderies of Lelang, Lintun, and Chenfan controlling areas that had belonged to Wiman Chosŏn) and the southern part of Korea had been controlled by Mimana (Kaya), a Japanese colony. Hayashi's *Chōsenshi* set the framework for other studies on Korea that sought to explain its historical development as having been determined by external forces. Hyŏn Ch'ae's *Tongguk saryak* (1906), which was used as a Korean history textbook in the newly established public schools, was published as a translation of Hayashi's *Chōsenshi*, perhaps as an expedient way to get around Japanese censors. As Andre Schmid has pointed out, in his translation of *Chōsenshi* Hyŏn changed the narrative in important ways, downplaying Empress Jingū's alleged invasion of Korea as one of many battles between competing Korean kingdoms and between Korean kingdoms and Japan.[26] Nevertheless this act of "translation" scandalized Sin Ch'ae-ho, because Hyŏn did not seem mindful of the consequences of such expediency, either in terms of historical scholarship or politically.[27] To cite one more example, Fukuda Tokuzō's *Kankoku no kei-*

zai soshiki to keizai tani (Economic Units and Economic Organization in Korea), published in 1904, asserted that the most salient characteristic of Korean history was its stagnancy. Fukuda found Chosŏn of the late nineteenth century comparable to tenth-century Japan (Fujiwara period).[28]

These studies of Korea set the tone for other studies on the Orient. Stefan Tanaka has shown that Japanese historians created the category of *tōyōshi* (Oriental history) so as to narrate Japanese history as different from but equal to European history. One strategy used by Tokugawa intellectuals to deal with the prevailing China-centered East Asian world order and to assert Japan's equivalence with China had been to replace Chūgoku with Shina as the Japanese appellation for China. This name allowed nativist (*kokugaku*) scholars to separate Japan from the barbarian and civilized or outer and inner implications of the name Chūgoku.[29] However, after Japan's victory in the first Sino-Japanese War (1894–95), historians such as Shiratori Kurakichi employed the name Shina to signify China "as a troubled place mired in its past, in contrast to Japan, a modern Asian nation."[30] The symbolic shift in names for China had its counterpart in Korea as well. Sin Ch'ae-ho's use of Jina rather than Chungguk reflects what Schmid has called the "decentering of the Middle Kingdom." After Japan's victory in the first Sino-Japanese War, this de-centering reversed inherited notions of civilization and shifted the locus away from China and toward Japan and the West. This point is illustrated by a revealing editorial in the *Tongnip sinmun*, the organ of the Independence Club, uncovered by Schmid: "The only thing [we Koreans] knew was to revere China as the central plain [*chungwŏn*], scorn Japan as the country of *wae*, and call all other countries barbarians [*orangk'ae*]. Now, for more than ten years, our doors have been open and we have welcomed guests coming from all places. With our ears we can hear, and with our eyes we can see the customs and laws of western countries. We can now generally judge which countries are the civilized ones and which countries are the barbarous ones."[31]

In Japanese historiography, the substitution of Shina for Chūgoku and the creation of a new spatial category called Tōyō (the Orient) and a new academic discipline called *tōyōshi* (Oriental history) marked the emergence of a comprehensive ideological system regarding Japan's position and destiny in relation to the West and the rest of Asia.[32] Behind the creation of *tōyōshi* was the political desire to portray the Japanese as uniquely capable of meeting the European nations on an equal plane, and thus uniquely capable of leading Asia. *Tōyōshi* enabled Japanese intellectuals to conceptualize the West as "merely another culture (though in some aspects still a superior one), a fellow competitor on [the] rocky path toward progress."[33] The creation of *tōyōshi* was motivated by defensive considerations in that it sought to deflect notions of permanent Western superiority. At the same time, *tōyōshi* had its aggressive side. In the hands of Japan's Orientalists, China and Korea came to embody all the negative aspects of the West's Orient, and *tōyōshi* provided justification for Japan's imperial expansion. As argued by Tanaka, "modern" Japanese historiography emerged as a response to the Orientalism of the West—that is, as an attempt to de-objectify Japan and Asia. The strategy adopted by historians like Shiratori (and institutions like the Department of Oriental History at Tokyo Imperial University) was to prove that the Japanese were not Oriental, as defined by the West, by using the *same* (Orientalist) epistemology.[34] As a new academic field, *tōyōshi* legitimated itself on the basis of its "scientific," "rationalistic" methodology and on the basis of its practical application in the "administration of southern Manchuria" and the "protection and development of Korea."

For historians like Sin Ch'ae-ho, the violence of imperialism and colonialist historiography was justification enough for writing a nationalist historiography. Sin's historiography set the themes for later nationalist historiography, which insisted that Korea had always had a distinct culture and society, testified to the veracity of the Korean nation by chronicling the long history of the Korean people's resistance to foreign aggression, and narrated the emergence of the Korean nation as an essential part of world history. Many contemporary historians locate the emergence of modern history writing in Korea with Sin's "Toksa sillon," published in 1908. On what basis can this essay claim such status? In 1894, under the aegis of the newly established Education Ministry (Hakmun amun, later hakbu), "modern" textbooks, including history textbooks, were published. However, as Sin himself notes, although the history textbooks listed Kim T'aek-yŏng, Hyŏn Ch'ae, and others as authors, these textbooks were, on the whole, translations of history books on Korea written by Japanese scholars.[35]

Examining history books used at different schools, I've found hardly any of value. In the first chapter, Koreans [*minjok*] are described as if they were part of the Chinese people; in the second chapter, Koreans appear almost like part of the Sŏnbijok [Hsien-pi]; and reading the entire book Koreans are variously made out to be part of the Malgaljok [Moho], part of the Mongojok [Mongols], part of the Yŏjinjok [Jurchen], or part of the Ilbonjok [Japanese]. If this were true, our land, which encompass several tens of thousands *li*, would be in pandemonium with barbarians from north and south milling around, and [our] accomplishments of four thousand years would be credited to the Liang in the morning, and in the evening to the Ch'u.[36]

In criticizing these textbooks, Sin identified the history of Korea with the fortunes of the *minjok* as constituted by the descendants of Tan'gun; gave the geographic length of Korea as about ten times the customary three thousand *li*, thus appropriating nearly all of Manchuria; took great pains to assert a distinct, separate ethnicity for the Korean people, tracing a precise, singular genealogical history, beginning with Tan'gun and continuing through Ancient Chosŏn, Puyŏ, Koguryŏ, Parhae, Koryŏ, and Chosŏn; and characterized, without equivocation, history as an instrument for instilling patriotism among youth.

On the first point, Sin's identification of a country's history with the history of the people (*minjok*) parallels the revolutionary shift that occurred with the French Revolution, the shift from *L'état c'est moi* to *L'état c'est le peuple*. The opening sentence of "Toksa sillon" reflects the republican ideal held by Sin and many other leading nationalist intellectuals of that time. Later in this text he wrote, "A state does not belong to one individual, it belongs to the entire people."[37] As a tactical matter, however, he did not attack the Korean monarch.[38] Nevertheless the republican position staked out in "Toksa sillon" gives evidence of what Kang Man-gil has described as the shift from patriotism based on loyalty to the king to a nationalism based on popular sovereignty.[39] This *democratic* predisposition became much more obvious in Sin's later writing (see the discussion below of the *minjok* in relation to the *minjung*).

As Schmid has pointed out, when Sin asserted a distinct, separate ethnicity for the Korean people that originated with Tan'gun and descended through Puyŏ, his aim was to subvert weak and limited conceptions of Korea's national space. His lament over the erasure of Parhae from official historiography had historical precedent. In *Parhae ko*, completed in 1784, Yu Tŭk-kong lamented the fact that Koryŏ did not compile a history of Parhae. Because Kim Pu-sik had not included Parhae's history in the *Samguk sagi*, instead tracing Koryŏ's legitimacy only through "Unified" Silla, Koryŏ had in effect given up its claim over the territory Parhae had once controlled. (In the Confucian historiographic tradition, it is the duty of successive dynasties to compile the history of preceding dynasties from the material left by their predecessors.) To reclaim Parhae's history as part of Korean history, Yu argued that Parhae and "Unified" Silla should be seen as forming northern and southern states. This argument was repeated by Kim Chŏng-ho in the mid-nineteenth century in his *Taedong chiji* (Geography of Korea).⁴⁰ During the colonial period, this way of periodizing Korean history was adopted by Chang To-bin, An Hwak, and Kwŏn Tŏk-kyu. After liberation, in North Korea, Pak Si-hyŏng, Chu Yŏng-hŏn, and others characterized Parhae as the successor state of Koguryŏ, but they did not refer to this era as the Period of Northern and Southern States (*nampukguk sidae*).⁴¹

Schmid notes that confrontations over territorial access—such as resource concessions to foreign powers, circulation of foreign currencies, extraterritoriality, and unregulated Japanese immigration—had already undermined inherited conceptions of territorial authority. Sin's "Toksa sillon" "became the first in a long line of Korean history writing that wielded the Manchurian connection to create a nationalist history that reveled in the grandeur of an ancient past."⁴² In thus problematizing Chosŏn-period orthodox conceptions of Korea's national space, Sin drew on irredentist themes that existed in earlier historiography. In *Chosŏn sanggosa* (History of Ancient Korea), written sixteen years later (1924), Sin praised Han Paek-kyŏm's *Tongguk chiriji* (Korea's Topographic Record) as having inaugurated (proper) historiography. Completed in 1615, Han narrated two lines of descent for Korean history: in the north, from Tan'gun and Kija down through Koguryŏ; in the south, from Samhan down through Paekche, Silla, and Kaya. Han's narrative privileged the northern line of descent over the southern. Writing at a time when another invasion from the south (from Japan) seemed unlikely, a time when the Ming seemed weak even as the Jurchens were gathering their forces in the north, Han had argued for a strong policy toward the Jurchens and included (reinstated) Manchuria within the territorial boundaries of Korea's ancient past. Adopting Han's narrative strategy, Sin panegyrized the northern line of descent.

It is also important to note that, two decades prior to "Toksa sillon," Japanese historians had begun to question the "limited" conception of Japan's national space. In an article published in 1889, Kume Kunitake criticized the notion of "Japan as an island nation that had not changed in thousands of years," and he reminded his readers of an ancient Japan that had encompassed Korea and southeastern China. Eventually, as Tanaka notes, "arguments like Kume's [served] as a historical justification for the annexation of Korea."[43] In 1891 Kume published an article in *Shigaku zasshi* in which he referred to Shintō as "a primitive custom of sacrifice to heaven." Kume came under such heavy attack from Shintoists and nationalists that he was obliged to relinquish his post at Tokyo Imperial University.[44] The spatial imagining of a greater Japan and Sin's greater Korea shared a similar strategy, but their political aims were, for the most part, diametrically opposed: Kume was creating a modern and "rational" historical framework for Japanese colonialism, and Sin a historical framework for Korean resistance.

With this defensive motivation, Sin identified the Korean *minjok* as the descendants of Tan'gun and reconstituted Manchuria as the birthplace of the *minjok* and a powerful reminder of Korea's past glory. Although his appropriation of Manchuria can be seen as a defensive response, this historical narrative also sustained and duplicated a potent totalizing tendency.[45] We can also detect in his adoption of categories like *Jina* (J: *Shina*) and *tongyangsa* (J: *tōyōshi*) a paradox inherent in nationalist discourse in the colonial world: the subjugated people, in the very act of resisting colonial rule, speak the language of their oppressors—the language of empire. The problematic in nationalist thought forces it relentlessly to demarcate itself from the discourse of colonialism, but even as nationalist discourse seeks to assert the feasibility of entirely new political possibilities, it remains a prisoner of the modes of thought characteristic of rational knowledge in the post-Enlightenment age—thus the lack of autonomy of nationalist discourse.[46]

Perhaps precisely because of its derivative nature, as a twentieth-century construct the discourse on *minjok* could become a powerful mobilizing force.[47] But while acknowledging the inclusive and egalitarian propensity of the Korean nationalist movement, we should be on guard against the appropriating and totalizing power of nationalist historiography. As Elie Kedourie cautions, nationalist historiography would deceive most readers: "Men who thought they were acting in order to accomplish the will of God, to make the truth prevail, or to advance the interests of a dynasty, or perhaps simply to defend their own against aggression, are suddenly seen to have been really acting in order that the genius of a particular nationality should be manifested and fostered."[48] Or, as argued by Prasenjit Duara, while in reality the "nation" is a contested and contingent identity, national (as well as nationalist) historiography secures for the nation "the false unity of a self-same, national subject evolving through time."[49] Kedourie's and Duara's critiques of national historiography are pertinent to the Korean case. With too much confidence, contemporary Korean national historiography (minjok sahak) secures for the nation a long list of "national" heroes from as early as the Three Kingdoms period, heroes like Ŭlchi Mundŏk (mid-sixth century to early seventh century) of Koguryŏ. But as John Duncan points out, it is "extremely unlikely that the peoples of Koguryŏ, Paekche and Silla all thought of themselves as members of a larger, 'Korean' collectivity that transcended local boundaries and state loyalties." Duncan rejects the premise common in nationalist histories that a Korean ethnic nation was already in existence at the dawn of historical time. Accordingly he is skeptical of the notion that the contest between the Three Kingdoms—the wars between Koguryŏ, Paekche, and Silla—represented a struggle for the political unification of the Korean minjok. While pointing to the capacity of the premodern state to break down local cultural and linguistic barriers, Duncan also cautions against nationalist historiography that seeks "to elide potentially competitive forms of identification such as class, region, or gender in favor of a totalizing national identity."[50]

Nevertheless, on the basis of certain assumptions made about blood and soil, national (and nationalist) historiography endows a succession of cultural and military heroes with a common "national" identity. As Etienne Balibar explains, this national identity "is always already presented to us in the form of a narrative which attributes to [this entity] the continuity of a subject. The formation of the nation thus appears as the fulfillment of a 'project' stretching over centuries, in which there are different stages and moments of coming to self-awareness."[51] Through the power of this ideological form, national histories can portray even Paleolithic inhabitants of the peninsula as "early Koreans," their culture as "pre-national," and the modern Korean nation-state as the culmination of a long process of development.[52] The same holds for North Korean historiography, except that Koguryŏ and Parhae would be substituted for "Unified" Silla in tracing the development of subsequent "mainstream" Korean history. But as Balibar reminds us, we should not read this history as "a line of necessary evolution but [as] a series of conjunctural relations which has inscribed them after the event into the pre-history of the nation-form."[53]

Even as some historians acknowledge the discontinuities and breaks in

Korean history, nearly all still accept the nation-state as the "normal" or "natural" form of political community.[54] This, Duara argues, is a central facet of Western hegemony: the assumption that the nation-state is the only legitimate form of polity.[55] We are as yet unable to imagine alternative political forms, and by writing narratives of the nation, which constitute much of modern historiography, historians help maintain the illusion of a nation's necessary and unilinear evolution. The nation form, as ideology, presents itself to us as ontological necessity; our desire that history will confirm our belief that the present rests on profound intentions and necessities prompts the production of a linear, continuous history that begins in the ancient past and culminates in the establishment of the Republic of Korea or (depending on one's politics) the Democratic People's Republic of Korea.

Almost all general histories of Korea begin with the Bronze Age, if not earlier, suggesting that the people who used bronze daggers and built dolmen tombs more than 2,500 years ago were early Koreans. To cite but two examples, the university-level general Korean history textbook *Han'guksa kaesŏl* (Outline of Korean History), written by South Korea's Compilation Committee for National History Textbooks, begins the narrative of Korean history with this sentence: "The Korean nation [*minjok*] emerged from the Neolithic period and the Bronze Age as an exceptional, homogeneous people possessing a unique culture, and established a tradition that was different from that of the Chinese."[56] In volume 1 of *Chosŏn t'ongsa* (History of Korea), published in Pyongyang by the Social Science Academy, the national narrative begins with the appearance of "primitive bands" in Northeast Asia and the Korean peninsula during the Paleolithic era about a million years ago.[57] It remains for a democratic historiography to show how the nation threatens to impose immutable articulations in an authoritarian way. Strange as it may sound, the basis for a much less totalizing historiography may, I think, be found in Sin Ch'ae-ho's later historiography and certainly in his anarchist writings.

Coauthors of Nation

The proliferation of discourses on Korean identity, which emanated from both the Korean nationalist movement and the Japanese colonial state, stemmed from the *necessity* to "nationalize." For both Koreans and Japanese, the necessity of producing Korean subjects was prompted by the development of the global nation-state system. In the process of trying to compete, or simply survive, in the nation-state system, *both* the colonial state and the Korean nationalist movements and organizations had to study, standardize, and thus reinvent (or just invent) everything we now associate with the Korean nation, including such cardinal elements as the Korean language and Korean ethnicity. Imperialist rivalry over Korea and eventual colonization by Japan intervened in Korea's nation-building process, and the process of nationalizing Koreans was, in a sense, taken over by the Japanese colonial state. Starting with the restoration of Sŏkkuram, it was the Japanese colonial state that went on to establish controls over print capitalism as well as national systems of schooling, transportation, and communication that produced colonial Chōsenjin (Koreans). The transformation of Japanese peasants into Japanese (*kokumin*) had begun several decades earlier, after the consolidation of the Meiji Restoration and the establishment of a strong central state. By the time of Korea's annexation, the Japanese state had accumulated substantial experience with the technologies of both nation-building and colonization, including the production of national consciousness. Those who became colonial administrators (for example, Gotō Shinpei in colonial Taiwan) had made a careful study of Western colonial institutions and methods.

Compelled to deny any "constructive" role in Japanese colonialism, contemporary Korean nationalist accounts draw attention to the last decade of the colonial period, when the colonial authorities, under the banner of Naisen Ittai (Japan and Korea as One Body), pursued a policy of forced assimilation: eliminating the use of Korean in school instruction (1934), requiring attendance at Shintō ceremonies (1935), and forcing the adoption of Japanese surnames (1939). The slogan of Naisen Ittai, however, reveals the ambivalence of Japan's racist policy throughout the colonial period, marked by the combination of exteriorization and internal exclusion. Japan, as the Interior (*Nai*), excludes Korea (*sen*) as the "outside"; at the same time, this outside (Korea) must become one with the Interior, which is always already there.[58] It was in this sense that Japanese colonialism was "constructive" for both the colonizer and the colonized: the construction of Japanese superiority as demonstrated by the inferiority of Koreans and the superiority claimed by the colonizer generating a self-image of inferiority among Koreans.

Coercion, prohibition, and censorship, then, were not the only (or even primary) forms through which colonial power was exercised. The Japanese colonial state did establish new rules and controls over the enunciation of Korean national identity, and there were topics that were off-limits or required strict observance of protocol, tact, and discretion. At the same time, there was a steady *proliferation* of discourses concerning Korean identity emanating from the Japanese colonial state itself, including studies of Korean history, geography, language, customs, religion, music, and art in almost immeasurable detail. What are we to make of this? For the Japanese colonial state, the goal of exploiting Korea and using it for Japan's strategic ends went hand in hand with the work of transforming peasants into Koreans. In other words, the logic of its racist colonial policy compelled the Japanese colonial state to reconstitute (disparate) Korean identities into a homogeneous Chōsenjin. Thereafter *Chōsenjin* became both a bureaucratic and derogatory classification that applied to all Koreans regardless of gender, regional origin, or class background.

Thus, contrary to conventional nationalist accounts which argue that Japanese colonial authorities pursued a consistent and systematic policy of eradicating Korean identity, we should see that the Japanese colonial state actually endeavored to produce Koreans as subjects, in the sense of being under the authority of the Japanese emperor and in the sense of having a separate (and inferior) subjectivity. This in turn led to a bifurcated national (and racial) discourse because Korean nationalist historians, in competition with the Japanese colonial state, were engaged in the project of recovering or producing an autonomous Korean subjectivity. Nationalist historians would find evidence of this subjectivity in history, but in necessarily incomplete or disfigured form. They presumed an essential link between national sovereignty and individual sovereignty and regarded nonnational forms of community and solidarity as partial, incomplete grounding, asserting that only national liberation could render possible the full realization of authentic subjectivity.

Thus we have both the Japanese colonial state and Korean nationalists researching and writing Korean history, preserving and interpreting Korean customs and religious practices, and laboring to create a standard Korean language. Although the power of the repressive and ideological apparatuses of the Japanese colonial state far surpassed that of the Korean nationalist movement, the contradictions inherent in Japan's racist colonial policy, along with the capacity of the Korean nationalist movement to (re)generate discourses of identity and liberation, ensured that the discourse on nation remained a contested field throughout the colonial period.[59] Thus any "Korean" subjectivity created under such conditions—whether loyal or defiant to the Japanese Empire—had to be profoundly unstable and constantly threatened by the contradictions of colonial experience.[60]

In analyzing discourses that are hegemonic on a global scale, such as the nation form, we must consider nondiscursive macroprocesses, processes that have to do with the capitalist world economy, or what Immanuel Wallerstein has called the "World System." According to Wallerstein, hegemony in the World System has to do with "productive, commercial and financial preeminence of one core power over other core powers," a preeminence that is not enduring because there is both upward and downward mobility in core-periphery relations.[61] The nation-state system emerged as the political superstructure of this World System. The interstate system is competitive because nation-states in the periphery may succeed in attaining core status, and core nations can slip to semiperiphery status.[62]

Bruce Cumings makes use of World Systems theory to argue that for most of the twentieth century (with the exception of the seven months from Pearl Harbor to the Battle of Midway), Japan had been a subordinate part of either a trilateral American-British-Japanese hegemony or a bilateral American-Japanese hegemony.[63] In other words, even as it ruled Korea, Japan was a subimperial power, a "core" power in relation to Korea and China but a dependency of Britain and the United States in both the regime of technology and world politics. Cumings illustrates this by citing the example of Japanese textile firms, the leading sector in Japan's first phase of industrialization, which bought their machines from England until about 1930. In the 1930s Japan began producing better machines and quickly became the most efficient textile producer in the world. In the mining industry, however, Japan was still dependent on American technology throughout the 1930s, allowing American gold-mining companies to profit from Korean gold mines. In sum, according to Cumings, Japan's position in the World System changed according to the following timeline:

1900–22: Japan in British-American hegemony
1922–41: Japan in American-British hegemony
1941–45: Japan as regional hegemon in East Asia
1945–70: Japan in American hegemony[64]

Cumings is not proposing a reduction of national narratives to some abstract capitalist relations of production. Rather, along lines suggested by

Balibar, Cumings's approach to understanding national narratives might be described as "bound up not with the abstraction of the capitalist market, but its concrete historical form: that of a 'world-economy' which is always already hierarchically organized into a 'core' and a 'periphery,' each of which has different methods of accumulation and exploitation of labor power, and between which relations of unequal exchange and domination are established."[65] In other words, as Balibar explains, it is "the concrete configurations of the class struggle and not 'pure' economic logic which explain the constitution of nation states."[66] On the relationship between discourses on ethnic identity and the logic of the World System, Wallerstein notes that the capitalist system is based not merely on the capital-labor antinomy but on a complex hierarchy within the labor segment. This hierarchy within labor generates the "ethnicization" of the workforce within a given state's boundaries. There are certain advantages to the ethnicization of occupational categories because different kinds of relations of production require different kinds of "normal" behavior. The advantages have to do with the fact that the state need not do all the work; the oppressed group will *voluntarily* defend its ethnic identity and socialize its membership. This resolves "one of the basic contradictions of historical capitalism — its simultaneous thrust for theoretical equality and practical inequality."[67]

The concrete, historical form of this World System, which is always hierarchically organized into a core and a periphery, provided the framework for the hegemony of the nation-state system. The ability of historians like Shiratori to define, limit, and authorize a certain view of the rest of the Orient, and then impose it, was made possible by an emerging industrial mode of production in Japan whose success was verified in Japan's victories over China (1895) and Russia (1905). And yet Japan's version of Orientalism could not achieve full hegemonic status in the sense that even as Japan colonized Korea and established a puppet state in Manchuria, it remained a dependency of Britain and the United States. Thus we might say that there were overlapping and competing hegemonies operating in Korea, producing competing discourses on race, nation, gender, modernity, and culture. Moreover these hegemonies dissipated as one moved from the core (London, Washington, Tokyo) to the major intellectual centers in the periphery (Beijing, Shanghai). In Beijing and Shanghai, urban centers where a multitude of intellectuals and political activists in some form of exile were thrown into unexpected contact, hybrid spaces with complex, international financial and intellectual ties yielded new possibilities for change and innovation, for both thinking and organizing. From this periphery, intellectuals like Sin Ch'ae-ho succeeded in subverting or displacing the dominant (colonial) framework in important ways.[68]

In Sin's anarchist writings (from 1925 on), the all-embracing identity of *minjok* is replaced by the more partisan category of *minjung*. In historical studies written in the early twentieth century, Sin presented a less essentialist way of conceptualizing the nation. Perhaps as a self-critique of his earlier position in "Toksa sillon," his introduction to the *Chosŏn sanggosa* (History of Ancient Korea) has moments of ambivalence in signifying the *minjok*, that is, moments of slippage in the opposition of self and Other. Why was *Chosŏn sanggosa* published in Korea in 1931, about a decade after it was written? In 1931 the general crisis in the world economic system had pushed the Soviet Union toward the policy of "socialism in one country" and the United States toward the New Deal. In Europe and Japan fascism reemerged as a powerful movement, presenting itself as an alternative to the problems of a market economy. In 1931 Japanese forces invaded Manchuria, and Korea began to be transformed into an economic and military base for Japanese penetration of the Chinese mainland. That same year the Sin'ganhoe voted to dissolve, acknowledging its failure to create an effective united front of Korean communists, nationalists, and anarchists within Korea. On the intellectual scene, the Chōsenshi henshūkai (Society for the Compilation of Korean History; SCKH), whose work was directed and funded by the office of the governor-general in Korea, was about to begin publication of its massive, detailed study of Korean history, the outcome of a project begun by Governor-General Saitō Makoto in 1922.

In 1932, after ten years of work, SCKH published the first five volumes of what became the thirty-eight-volume *Chōsenshi* (Korean History). In addition, SCKH published a three-volume *Chōsen shiryō shushin* (Collection of Korean Documents) and a twenty-one-volume *Chōsen shiryō sōkan* (Archive of Korean Documents). The SCKH was clearly an organ of the Japanese colonial state, but its members included Korean historians like Ch'oe Nam-sŏn, the man who drafted the "Korean Declaration of Independence" in 1919, and Yi Nŭng-hwa, a renowned historian of Korean Buddhism. Yi was one of the original fourteen members when the SCKH was organized in 1922 by Arikishi Tadaichi, and Ch'oe joined in 1928.[69] It was at this historical juncture that Sin Ch'ae-ho's *Chosŏn sanggosa* was serialized in Korea in the *Chosŏn ilbo*.[70] The day after *Chosŏn sanggosa* ended, the *Chosŏn ilbo* began publishing Sin's *Chosŏn sanggo munhwasa* (Cultural History of Ancient Korea), which ran in forty installments. An Chae-hong (1891–1965), a historian in his own right and the president of *Chosŏn ilbo*, was instrumental in publishing Sin's work inside Korea.[71] Because Sin had not compromised with the Japanese — at the time he was incarcerated in a Japanese prison in Lūshun (Port Arthur) — and because the work itself had been written outside the geographical and intellectual perimeter of Japan's hegemony, Sin's historiography was presented as a much needed corrective to colonialist historiography's distortions of Korea's ancient past. But in writing from the periphery, Sin succeeded in subverting not only colonialist historiography, but many of the assumptions associated with the nation form. Ironically this counterhegemonic move was made possible by Sin's appropriation of Hegel's subject-object distinction. It is worth quoting at length from Sin's introduction to *Chosŏn sanggosa*:

> What is history? It is the record of the state of mental activity in human society wherein the struggle between the "I" [*a*] and the "non-I" [*pi-a*] develops through time and expands through space. World history, then, is a record of such a state for all of mankind, while Korean history is a record of such a state for the Korean people [*Chosŏn minjok*].
>
> Who do we refer to as "I" and the "non-I"? Simply put, we call the person situated in the subjective position "I," and all others we call "non-I." For example, Koreans call Korea "I" and call England, America, France, Russia, and others the "non-I." But the people of England, America, France, Russia, and other countries each call their countries "I" and call Korea a "non-I." The proletariat refers to itself as "I" and to landlords, capitalists, and others as the "non-I." But the landlords, capitalists, and others each refer to their own group as "I" and to the proletariat as the "non-I." Not only this but in learning, in technology, in occupations, and in the intellectual world — and in every other area — if there is an I there will be a non-I as its opposite; and just as there is an I and the non-I within the I position, so there is an I and the non-I within the non-I position. Therefore, the more frequent the contact between the I and the non-I, the more heated will be the struggle of the I against the non-I. And so there is no respite in the activity of human society, and there will never be a day when the forward advance of history will be completed. It is for this reason that history is the record of struggle between I and the non-I. . . .
>
> If the people of Myo, Jina, etc. — the non-I — constituting the other [*sang-*

daeja] had not existed, it is unlikely that "I" would have existed. That is, naming the state as Chosŏn, building the three capitals, keeping the five armies, etc.—this manifestation of the "I" would not have occurred.[72]

Here, in reference to Jina (J: Shina), we might detect the presence of Japanese Orientalism. But although Sin may have used *Jina* rather than *Chungguk* to distance Korea from the barbarian and civilized, outer and inner implications of China as the Middle Kingdom, his use of *Jina* in *Chosŏn sanggosa* did not (indeed could not) invoke the kind of Orientalist assumptions present in Shiratori's historiography. National identity (Korean, English, or French) is historically constructed and changes over time;[73] it may have been constructed in opposition to a foreign other, but it is also (necessarily) fragmented from within. Thus we find the subject-object distinction made by Hegel, but it is clear that the philosophical structure "which uncannily simulates the project of nineteenth-century imperialism," as Robert Young puts it, has been taken over, made "universal" from the point of view of the colonized.[74]

Beyond Nationalism

Immersed in the intellectual ferment of Shanghai and Beijing, especially in the wake of the May Fourth Movement, Sin Ch'ae-ho was able to appropriate Hegel's dialectic in a way that asserted not a triumphant, rational subject but a contingent and open-ended one. When the Korean provisional government in Shanghai elected Rhee Syngman as president in absentia and proved unwilling to take up armed struggle against Japanese colonialism, Sin denounced it in the newspaper *Sin Taehan* (New Korea) and returned to Beijing in 1920. In 1923, when Sin wrote the "Declaration of the Korean Revolution" for the Korean revolutionary organization Ŭiyŏldan, he did so in consultation with Yu Cha-myŏng, who was an anarchist and the leading theorist in the Ŭiyŏldan.[75] Even had we not known that Sin became an anarchist after writing these histories, the texts themselves suggest moments of ambivalence in signifying the *minjok*, that is, *moments of slippage in the opposition of self and other*: "If there is an I there will be a non-I as its opposite; and just as there is an I and the non-I within the I position, so there is an I and the non-I within the non-I position."[76]

In his later anarchist writings, Sin tried to construct a new collective subjectivity capable of subverting the modernist program, which he saw as oppressive, exploitative, and brutal. The nation form as imagined by the West was hegemonic, in the sense that the global nation-state system set the boundaries of political discourse, defining the nation-state as the "normal" or "natural" form of political community. And yet no construct can be completely or permanently hegemonic, and hegemony dissipated as one moved from the core to the periphery. From the periphery, then, intellectuals like Sin succeeded in subverting or displacing the dominant framework in important ways.

Nationalist readings of Sin's work focus on the anti-Japanese aspects. In the "Manifesto of the Korean Revolution" (1923), Sin did list "Bandit Japan" (*kangdo Ilbon*) as the primary target of the revolution, understood as the Japanese emperor, the governor-general of Korea and other high officials, "traitorous politicians," and any and all facilities belonging to the enemy. By smashing Japan, Koreans could recover an "indigenous Korea" (*koyu ŭi Chosŏn*) which lay beneath Japan's despotism. (Sin places quotation marks around *Korea* and *Japan*.) But the recovery of an indigenous Korea did not mean the restoration of old social forms. Along with foreign rule, "slavish culture and servile mentality" were to be destroyed. All religious beliefs, ethics, culture, art, customs, and habits of traditional culture produced by the strong for their enjoyment had to be dismantled so that the people (*minjung*) could break out of their abject fate and construct a people's culture (*minjungjŏk munhwa*).

Sin excoriated those Koreans who were lobbying for an "independent domestic administration" (*naejŏng tongnip*), "participatory government" (*ch'am chŏngkwŏn*), or "self-rule" (*chach'i*). They were forgetting that Japan had devoured Korea "even as the ink was drying on [Japanese] slogans that had guaranteed 'Peace in Asia,' and the 'Protection of Korean Independence.'" Sin also ridiculed those nationalists who advocated a "cultural movement" (*munhwa undong*). Writing editorials that would not offend the colonial authorities was all the cultural movement amounted to. For Sin, 100 million pages of newspapers and magazines could not equal the power of one uprising in awakening the *minjung*.

Sin also denounced those nationalists who advocated "diplomacy" (*oegyoron*) or "preparation" (*chunbiron*). He did not name specific individuals, but it would have been clear to his readers that the targets of his polemics were Rhee Syngman and An Ch'ang-ho. Rhee was "stupid" (*ŏlisŏkgo yongryŏl hada*) for banking on foreign intervention to solve the problem of national survival. As for An and others who argued for "preparation," Sin reminded them that they should be preparing for a war of independence. Arguing that Koreans must ready themselves for independence, the advocates of preparation actually advocated political quietism, turning their energies to education, industry, and a whole list of things that had to be readied prior to direct, uncompromising struggle. These activists made the rounds in Beijing, Siberia, Hawaii, and the United States to collect money for their programs, but all they could show for their efforts were a few precarious schools and inept organizations.[77]

What did Sin Ch'ae-ho advocate in the 1920s? As Sin Yong-ha argues, Sin's disgust with nationalists in the Korean provisional government, plus his reading of Pyotr Kropotkin, turned him from nationalism to anarchism.[78] Today most conservative intellectuals in South Korea gloss over the fact that rather than the nation (minjok), the historical subject in Sin's revolution was the people, or the multitude (minjung), a broad political grouping of the oppressed and exploited "propertyless masses" (musan taejung).[79] The minjung, as Sin used the term, was a more amorphous category than Marx's proletariat, but it was not synonymous with the Korean people as a whole, that is, minjok. As Marx did for the proletariat, Sin granted ontological privilege to the minjung.

Throughout Korean history, argued Sin, the minjung formed the wretched majority—exploited, beaten, starved, lulled into subservience and obedience. For that very reason, the minjung was uniquely capable of sweeping away all oppressive and exploitative institutions and practices, and in that sense the minjung was a universal subject. But unlike the Marxist-Leninists, Sin refused to distinguish between the vanguard and the masses, or between leaders and the led, and the revolution was therefore a "minjung revolution" or a "direct revolution." The minjung formed the "grand headquarters" of the revolution (Minjung ŭn uri hyŏngmyŏng ŭi taebonyŏng ida). Through a program of assassinations, bombings, and uprisings, Sin believed, the "conscientized" segment of the minjung could succeed in imparting "resolve" (kag'o) to the rest of the minjung. When the minjung as a whole resolved to take the path of revolution, all the cunning and savagery of the colonial state would not be able to stop the revolution.

Thus Sin differentiated between the "awakened" minjung and the "not awakened" minjung, but this distinction was not at all similar to the kind of external and manipulative relationship that characterized the Leninist conception of relations between the "vanguard" and the "masses." Sin resisted the Leninist idea that the "for itself" of the revolutionary subject was accessible only to the enlightened vanguard. Indeed even as he called for a revolution, his language echoed the moralistic tone of Kropotkin. The exploitative economic system swallows up the people (*minjung*) in order to fatten thieves, but this system of plunder must be destroyed in order to improve the lives of the people. In all societies with inequalities, the strong oppress the weak, the high-born stand above the humble, and the people have to plunder, excoriate, and envy one another. At first the majority of the people are harmed for the happiness of a few. But later the privileged few struggle among themselves so that the people are harmed even more. Thus the happiness of *all* the people can be attained only with the eradication of social inequalities.[80]

In spite of this seemingly immutable commitment to an egalitarian ideal, many conservative intellectuals assume that had Sin lived to see Korea liberated he would have abandoned his anarchism.[81] But it was his assertion that an unfettered people would construct communities based on equality, cooperation, and reason. Although Korea's liberation from colonial rule was a fundamental goal of the revolution, the "privileged classes" (*t'ŭkkwŏn kyegŭp*) which oppress the "Korean people" (*Chosŏn minjung*, in quotations in the original text), including the colonial administration, were to be overthrown so as to recover an "unfettered people" (*chayujŏk Chosŏn minjung*). The emergence of an unfettered people, and the communities they would create based on equality, cooperation, and reason, could not be brought about through the power of any nation-state.

Here, then, was a political program that went beyond national and individual sovereignty and a historical view that undermined the continuous, unified narrative of the nation. To those who fear the unraveling of capitalist sovereignty Sin might say, "Those who do not know how to build do not know how to destroy, and those who do not know how to destroy do not know how to build. Construction and destruction are different only in appearance. In the mind, destruction is immediately construction."[82] After the Korean War, state nationalism as it emerged in both North and South Korea all but overwhelmed and swamped such autonomous forms of imagination. Sin's turn to anarchism (where the all-embracing identity of *minjok* is replaced by the more partisan category of *minjung*) already suggested that *minjok* by itself could no longer serve as a democratic imaginary, was no longer able to reveal and subvert a wide range of subordinated subject positions such as woman, worker, tenant farmer, and illiterate. Before the end of the colonial period, a more democratic historiography would emerge as a critique of nationalist historiography, by showing how claims staked out by other identities have often been suppressed or marginalized by the discourse on *minjok*.

chapter four

UNIVERSALIZING KOREA'S PAST

> Beyond critical readings of those classical [dynastic] histories, we have
> taken on the task of gathering and analyzing, consistent with the highest
> standards of modern historiography, all the materials that were scattered
> or ignored, all kinds of shards and fragments, to establish a progressive his-
> toriography of the entirety of national life. That [kind of historiography]
> does not simply present the past for self-critique; it constitutes our per-
> spective on what lies ahead. It is this that gives historiography its political-
> ity [*silch'ŏnsŏng*], and prescribes the general direction [of political struggle].
> —PAEK NAM-UN, *Chōsen shakai keizaishi*, 1933

In a Korean-language article published in *Chungang* in November 1933,
three months after the publication of his first major work, *Chōsen shakai
keizaishi* (A Social Economic History of Korea), Paek Nam-un sought to
reach out to a broad Korean audience in his approach to writing Korean
history. Written in Japanese and published in Tokyo, *Chōsen shakai keizaishi*
was the first comprehensive socioeconomic history of ancient Korea, and
its publication was promptly celebrated by intellectual circles in both Japan
and colonial Korea. In the *Chungang* article, consistent with his materialist
stance, Paek refused to portray *Chōsen shakai keizaishi* as groundbreaking
scholarship, insisting instead that the book should be read as an initial articulation of an already existing societal (class) consciousness arising from
present-day realities confronting Koreans. At the same time he insisted
that he had to be free to present a critical reading of historical sources and,
"as a Korean scholar," free to engage in "scientific debate" with "ordinary
popular conceptions."[1]

The tension between Paek's claim that his work articulated an already
existing consciousness and his contention that Korean historians must
challenge ordinary popular conceptions gives some indication of the for-
bidding intellectual terrain that he and other Korean Marxists occupied in
the early 1930s in colonial Korea. The Peace Preservation Law of 1925, as
amended in 1928, had made it a capital offense to organize or lead any or-

ganization that threatened the *kokutai* (national body/structure). Militant leftists and *futei senjin* (malcontent Koreans) were the main targets of the Peace Preservation Law in Japan, as well as in colonial Korea. In Japan, *futei senjin* was a frequently used pejorative term that gained currency when, in the wake of the forced abdication of Emperor Kojong in 1907, Righteous Armies (*ŭibyŏng*) in Korea launched armed struggle against Japanese forces. In the immediate aftermath of the Great Kantō Earthquake of 1923, the fear and anxiety among the Japanese public that had accompanied Korean resistance to colonization gave way to wild rumors that Koreans were taking advantage of the catastrophe by perpetrating rape, arson, and seditious riots. Vigilantes set up checkpoints and massacred over six thousand people in the Tokyo-Yokohama area whom they identified as Korean.[2]

With the onset of the Great Depression in 1929 the price of rice dropped precipitously, leading to even greater hardship in the Korean countryside. In 1930, 50 to 60 percent of farm income came from rice, and when prices dropped, the loss in income was passed down to the tenant farmers. After the invasion of Manchuria in 1931, censorship and police surveillance became more intense, and with the elimination of many socialists and communists from various movements and institutions Marxist intellectuals like Paek Nam-un were, to a large extent, isolated from institutions that could shape ordinary popular conceptions. Between 1925 and 1928 there had been four attempts to establish a Korean Communist Party inside of colonial Korea, but all ended in mass arrests. Colonial police kept former Korean Communist Party members and fellow travelers under more or less permanent surveillance even after they had served their prison terms. By 1928 it had become impossible to sustain a revolutionary movement within colonial Korea—the Japanese authorities were too efficient—and the locus and leadership of the Korean communist movement shifted to overseas bases.[3]

Many of the institutions that attempted to shape ordinary popular conceptions were ideological apparatuses of the Japanese colonial state: the public school system, certain religious institutions, and, as described by Chulwoo Lee, the police, who "conducted surveys, supervised public hygiene, directed residents in road building and repair, gave instructions on farming, exhorted people to take side-jobs and to save money, acted as conciliators in private disputes, enforced court judgments, organized meetings for ideological propaganda, and so on."[4] The Buddhist organization Chōsen

Bukkyōdan (K: Chosŏn Pulgyodan), for example, was founded as part of the colonial project of Japanese-Korean reconciliation. As Micah Auerback points out, however, Chōsen Bukkyōdan never overcame the tensions between the Japanese and Korean Buddhist communities. Based on a close reading of both Japanese- and Korean-language articles in *Chōsen Bukkyō*, the newsletter of the Chōsen Bukkyōdan, Auerback concludes that because of the Japanese sense of entitlement and ethnic and cultural superiority, publications like *Chōsen Bukkyō* ultimately failed to generate among Korean readers a sense of intimacy with the Japanese, known as *ch'in-Il*, commonly translated as *pro-Japanese*.[5]

For a little more than a decade after the March First Movement of 1919, a "cultural policy" had replaced the patently coercive policies of the first decade of colonial rule. Under the banner of "Harmony between Japan and Korea" (*Naisen yūwa*), flogging as a form of punishment was abolished, the Corporation Law that had prevented Koreans from starting modern enterprises was abolished,[6] and permits were granted for independent Korean-language newspapers and magazines. Korean-language publications proliferated and tested the limits of censorship laws. As Michael Robinson points out, until 1932 the colonial state maintained a dual set of publication laws: one for Japanese-language publications, another for Korean-language publications. Whereas Japanese-language materials were subject to post-publication censorship, Korean-language newspapers and magazines were subject to prepublication censorship. Moreover the police applied a secondary dual policy of censorship toward Korean publications, repressing radical publications and tolerating apolitical expressions of national pride and aspiration. Of the publications that were suspended permanently in the 1920s—magazines like *Sinsaenghwal*, *Shinch'ŏnji*, and *Kaebyŏk*—all had relentlessly advanced leftist or uncompromising nationalist views.[7]

Even though they often questioned colonial policy and popularized national narratives that seemingly countered colonialist narratives, nationalist newspapers like *Tonga ilbo* and *Chosŏn ilbo* were seen as less threatening and allowed to carry on. For the nationalist press, there was a market for counternarratives within colonial Korea, and the stature and circulation of *Tonga ilbo* and *Chosŏn ilbo* rose in tandem with its "nationalist/anti-colonial quotient." By the early 1930s, as Robinson notes, a process of financial attrition and police repression had eliminated politically oriented journals, while *Tonga ilbo* and *Chosŏn ilbo* became major publishing groups that profited from the publication of slick magazines for a mass audience.[8] It was this commercialized, politically restrained publishing industry that helped shape "ordinary popular conceptions" at the time Paek Nam-un wrote *Chōsen shakai keizaishi*.

From the point of view of Marxists like Paek, the national narratives disseminated in newspapers like *Tonga ilbo* did not fundamentally subvert the hierarchies and categories of knowledge established by the Japanese colonial state. On the one hand, the Bolshevik Revolution and subsequent sniping from Korean Marxists had forced many nationalist intellectuals to "discover society" (*sahoe*) and the impoverished masses (*minjung*) as historical, political, and ethical categories that had to complement the discourse on the ethnic nation (*minjok*). On the other hand, after the dissolution of the united front organization Sin'ganhoe (New Trunk Society, 新幹會) in 1931, nationalist intellectuals had become even more hostile to Marxists. The Sin'ganhoe, organized in 1927, had sought to bridge the gap between a dwindling number of communists and unwavering nationalists. Both communists and nationalists had called for unity since the early 1920s, but the catalyst for actually creating a broad united front came in late 1925, when it seemed that some of the principal leaders in the "cultural nationalist" camp were contemplating more "realistic" goals in place of outright independence.

The influential writer Yi Kwang-su had gone on record calling for home rule (*chach'i*), thereby accepting Japan's sovereignty over Korea. In late 1925 reports surfaced that Ch'oe Rin, the leader of a Ch'ŏndogyo faction, along with Kim Sŏng-su and Song Chin-u, who ran *Tonga ilbo*, were engaged in serious discussion with the colonial authorities about the possibility of home rule.[9] It was this that prompted the first real agreement between communists and unwavering nationalists like An Chae-hong, editor of *Chosŏn ilbo*, to create a broad united front organization.[10] An had become the chief editor of the Korean-language daily in 1924, and in 1927 he had played a leading role in organizing Sin'ganhoe. In 1931 he opposed the communists' call for the dissolution of the Sin'ganhoe, but to no avail. Nationalists like An shared a similar dilemma with communists: how to create and sustain an effective united front between the communists and nationalists but at the same time maintain their distinct ideological "identity," continue their polemics against the other's ideological stance, and extend hegemony over the entire united front.[11] Among communists, those whose "national-

ist quotients" were high were labeled "petit bourgeois" and "right-wing op-
portunists." Those whose "class militancy" led to the collapse of the united
front (and political isolation) were labeled "left-wing extremists."[12]

When Sin'ganhoe was founded in February 1927, the *Tonga ilbo* management (Kim Sŏng-su and Song Chin-u) were obliged to support it, and
its unambiguous goal of continuing the struggle for Korea's independence
through political resistance effectively shelved any plans for organizing a
movement for home rule. Even after joining the Sin'ganhoe, however, Kim
and Song did not abandon the idea of home rule, and before the organization's dissolution in 1931, a less intractable leadership flirted with the idea.
When the alliance between the Kuomintang and the Chinese Communist
Party collapsed in 1927, resulting in the deaths of thousands of Chinese
communists—and many Korean communists as well[13]—the fourth execu-
tive committee of the Korean Communist Party (1928) tried to prevent a
comparable catastrophe by creating a powerful worker-peasant bloc within
the Sin'ganhoe to prevent the "reformist bourgeoisie" from gaining hegemony over the united front, but without success. The Japanese authorities, for their part, were sympathetic and yet guarded about the idea of
home rule for Koreans. Serious consideration of home rule stopped with
the implementation of the Naisen Ittai policy in the mid-1930s.[14] By 1931
the communists and the Japanese colonial authorities were ready to dissolve the Sin'ganhoe. Not all leftists agreed with this decision, and most
nationalists in the Sin'ganhoe, including An Chae-hong, tried to prevent
the dissolution. The communists' decision to dissolve the organization in
1931 was anticipated in the Comintern's December Theses of 1928, which
pointed to the error of ceding leadership of the united front to the nationalists. But the actual dissolution came as a response to the sharply different
context of 1931: Japan's invasion of Manchuria, the strengthening of fascist
movements around the world, and the heightened necessity of differenti-
ating revolutionary international solidarity from nationalist politics. After
the dissolution of the Sin'ganhoe until the beginning of the Pacific War, the
remaining Korean communists focused their effort on carrying out revolution from below.

It was in this political and intellectual context, as ideological divisions
among Korean intellectuals became much more pronounced, that Paek
Nam-un published *Chōsen shakai keizaishi* in 1931 and *Chōsen hōken shakai
keizaishi* (Economic History of Korean Feudal Society) in 1937.[15] In both
books Paek took issue with "stagnation theory," then prevalent in Japanese

socioeconomic historiography on Korea, reacting specifically to Fukuda To-kuzō's assertion that feudalism and private ownership of land had failed to emerge in Korea. For Fukuda, despite dramatic social and dynastic changes in Korean history, such as the transition from the Koryŏ dynasty to the Chosŏn dynasty, Korea's social-economic structure had failed to change, and thus the level of development in late nineteenth-century Korea was comparable to that of tenth-century Fujiwara Japan. Fukuda's assumptions regarding the stages of economic development came from the work of Karl Bücher, who wrote that economic development advances in stages, from a natural econ-omy to a city or burg economy to a national economy. Based on a twenty-day trip to Korea in 1902, Fukuda was able to conclude that, without a feudal class, transactions between producer and consumer could not evolve from credit to a fully monetary economy, and Korea remained stuck at the stage of an ancient village economy (Bücher's natural economy).[16] In opposition also to Japanese Marxist historiography on Korea, which tended to view Korean society as truly "Asiatic," Paek's aim was to show that the Korean society and economy had developed in accordance with universal stages of development and as a result of social-economic forces internal to Korea.

Paek also took to task Korean nationalist historians like Sin Ch'ae-ho and Ch'oe Nam-sŏn (1890–1957) for their idealist, particularist view of his-tory, which he saw as an antique inheritance from the nineteenth century, suited to the needs of emerging capitalist nations like Germany and Japan in their confrontation with advanced capitalist powers like England. But this historiography, which depicted Korea's past as if it formed a unique "mikrokosmus," did not suit the political needs of the people in colonial Korea; it suited the needs only of "wandering scholars" (p'yŏnnyŏk hakdo; fahrender Shüler) fond of collecting "antiques." By grounding their histori-cal narrative on idealist concepts like hon or ŏl (Spirit, Mind, or Geist), Paek argued, the idealist and particularist histories in the end only reinforced colonialist historiography by emphasizing Korean uniqueness.[17] For Paek, the particularity of Korean social formations represented only the particu-larity of universal history as manifested in Korea.

Paek Nam-un's Social Economic History

The characterization of leftists as embracing universalism and national-ists as embracing particularism reduces to a simple but nevertheless useful dichotomy what is actually a very complicated intellectual terrain in the early 1930s. Many aspects of *Chōsen shakai keizaishi* went against the grain of nationalist historiography, including Paek's treatment of Tan'gun (檀君), the mythical progenitor of the Korean nation. In the precolonial period, starting in the latter half of the 1890s, the story of Tan'gun was central to the historical narrative that de-centered China and established Korean sovereignty in the nation-state system. Since its establishment in 1895, all of the history textbooks published by the Korean government's Ministry of Education (hakmun amun, hakbu) presented Tan'gun as the founder of the first Korean state. Textbooks published until 1906 presented Tan'gun as a deity (*sinin*, 神人) and the founding of ancient Chosŏn as a sacred event. *Chosŏn yŏksa*, the first history textbook published by the newly established Ministry of Education, referred to Tan'gun as a deity. Published in 1895, the Tan'gun story in *Chosŏn yŏksa* was taken from Kwŏn Kŭn's text *Ŭnjesiju* (1396). Confucian literati like Kwŏn claimed Tan'gun as the first ruler of the Korean state. The passage taken from *Ŭnjesiju* reads, "Long ago when the deity [*sinin*] descended by the pakdal tree [*Betula schmidtii*] the people [*kugin*, 國人] accepted him as their sovereign."[18]

Japanese historians, on the other hand, starting in the late nineteenth century and continuing through the end of the colonial period, treated the Tan'gun story as myth (mythos) not just in the sense of not being history (historia and logos), but as a fable created only centuries earlier. In the 1890s Naka Michio and then Shiratori Kurakichi dismissed the Tan'gun story as a story fabricated in the thirteenth century by the Buddhist monk Iryŏn. In the 1920s historians like Inaba Iwakichi continued to dismiss the Tan'gun story as a narrative created in the thirteenth century, even while speculating about the shamanistic elements in the story that belonged to a much more distant past. For Japanese historians to give historical veracity to the Tan'gun story would have meant confirming not just the sovereign origins of the first Korean state but also Korea's claim to a much older history: Tan'gun's birth dated to 2333 BCE; Iwarebiko, or Emperor Jimmu, the first legendary emperor of Japan, was said to have established his throne in 660 BCE.

Starting with Sin Ch'ae-ho, the initial nationalist response to Japanese (and Western) discrediting of the Tan'gun story was to separate out the mythic elements from the "historical," to trace Koreans' ethnic-national origin, and essential culture, back to Tan'gun as a historical figure who had established Ancient Chosŏn. In the 1920s, with greater freedom in publishing afforded by the colonial government's "Cultural Policy," and with ethnographic and folklore studies introduced by Japanese scholars that reconstituted myth, and the study of myth, as anything but an antithesis to science, Korean historians found new ways of historicizing the Tan'gun story.[19] Drawing on scholarship on totems, taboos, and shamanism, Ch'oe Nam-sŏn drew attention to the practice of heaven worship and theocracy as exemplified in the Tan'gun narrative. As a nationalist historian, Ch'oe Nam-sŏn read the Tan'gun story as the expression of religious practice dating to prehistoric times, an ancient narrative that indicated a common cultural sphere for all of northeast Asia centered around Ancient Chosŏn, which he referred to as a *Purham* cultural sphere, a cultural sphere that in its importance and geographic scope rivaled that of the Chinese, Indian, and European cultural spheres.[20]

In *Chōsen shakai keizaishi*, Paek also treated the Tan'gun foundation story as a myth, but a myth that opens a window into *social relations* in Korea's prehistoric era. Paek rejected both nationalist (religious) readings of Tan'gun that were "far-fetched" and colonialist readings that were "fraudulently rational."[21] In the genealogy of Tan'gun that begins with Hwanin (Ruler of Heaven), Hwanung (son of Hwanin), and the bear whom Hwanung transformed into a woman and whom Hwanung married, giving birth to Tan'gun, the founder of ancient Chosŏn, Paek saw evidence of the beginnings of both class differentiation and the privileging of the male over the female descent line in primitive times. Drawing on theories of phonological change in historical linguistics, Paek argued that the name Tan'gun was originally an honorific title for a male aristocratic chieftain (*wŏnsi kwijokin namgye ch'ujang*).[22]

In addition to his interpretation of the Tan'gun story, Paek also thought he had found evidence of matrilineality and promiscuity in Korea's primitive communal society. He thought he had found evidence of a Punaluan family structure in Korea's ancient past based on his philological study of kinship terms such as *menuri* (daughter-in-law), *manura* (wife), and *nui* (sister); according to Paek, these terms all originated from an older Korean word—not derived from Chinese compounds—that meant *sleeping companion*. For Lewis H. Morgan, Hawaiian kinship terms like *Punalua* referred to the earliest marriage forms in human evolutionary history.[23] Drawing on Morgan's work, via Frederick Engels, Paek assumed that kinship terminology referred to consanguinity and family structures; he assumed, in other words, that terms like *menuri, manura,* and *nui* were the "precipitates" of extinct forms of sexual practices and family structures. For Paek, the Korean equivalent to the Punaluan family was the *tongsŏ kajok* of Korea's distant past.[24] As in Morgan's work, Paek's could provide little evidence that specific nomenclature indicates consanguinity rather than simply terms of address or labels for social relations. Moreover Paek did not problematize the kind of historicism that rendered sexual practices and family organizations associated with contemporary "primitive" societies as survivals of early historical stages.

Like many others in the mid-nineteenth century, Morgan aimed to articulate a grand theory of human history, a theory of cultural evolution that would replace the "theory of human degradation to explain the existence of savages and barbarians": "As it is undeniable that portions of the human family have existed in a state of savagery, other portions in a state of barbarism, and still others in a state of civilization, it seems equally so that these three distinct conditions are connected with each other in a natural as well as necessary sequence of progress."[25] Adopting Morgan's vision of human cultural evolution in toto, Engels argued in *Origin of the Family, Private Property and the State* that the concept of incest and the emotion referred to as jealousy emerged as humanity evolved out of the primitive stage. In primitive society, promiscuous sexual intercourse was the rule: every woman belonged equally to every man, and every man to every woman. In the evolution of the family, then, the first stage was the Consanguine Family, wherein parents and children were proscribed from having sexual relations. At this stage, marriage groups were arranged according to generations: all the grandfathers and grandmothers within the limits of the family were all mutual husbands and wives, the same being the case with their children; brothers and sisters, male and female cousins of the first, second, and more remote degrees were all mutually brothers and sisters, and precisely because of this, they were all mutually husbands and wives.

The second stage in the evolution of the family was the Punaluan Family (the Hawaiian system of consanguinity). At this stage, not only parents and children but brothers and sisters were proscribed from having sexual relations. This was accomplished gradually, commencing with the exclusion of brothers and sisters (on the maternal side) from sexual relations; one or more groups of sisters became the nucleus of one household, their natural brothers the nucleus of the other. This meant that a group of natural or collateral brothers held in common marriage a number of women, who were not their sisters, and these women addressed one another as *punalua*. Similarly a number of sisters, either natural or collateral, were the common wives of their common husbands, excluding their brothers.[26] Paek's (erroneous) discovery of the Punalua Family structure prior to the Three Kingdoms period was nevertheless significant not only in the sense that it initiated social economic studies of Korea's ancient past, but also because it placed Korea within a linear evolutionary narrative that coincided with "historical laws" at work in all societies: the Korean nation (*minjok*) started from primitive communal tribes, giving rise to the slave society in the Three Kingdoms period (first to seventh centuries), Asiatic feudal society beginning with the "Unified" Silla period (seventh to tenth centuries), with incipient capitalism emerging in late Chosŏn starting in the eighteenth century.

Paek expected an angry reaction from nationalist intellectuals, since he had deliberately set out to demolish, in one stroke, the epistemological foundations of colonialist historiography and Korean nationalist historiography, asserting that they shared a common epistemological ground.[27] Elsewhere he stated unequivocally that, in his trek back and forth over four to five thousand years of Korean history, he did not discover anything that particularly distinguished the Korean social system from that of other "cultured nations" (*munhwa minjok*).[28] He admitted, however, that the particularist view of Korea's past had stubbornly persisted. In truth, the "culture movement" (*munhwa undong*) of the 1920s had taken on new life in the aftermath of the dissolution of the Sin'ganhoe in 1931. Korean-language dailies like the *Tonga ilbo* and *Chosŏn ilbo*, under the leadership of Song Chin-u (1889–1945) and An Chae-hong (1891–1965), respectively, were able to mobilize broad public support in the early 1930s for the Movement to Preserve Historical Relics (Kojŏk pojŏn undong) and the Movement to Revitalize Korean Studies (Chosŏnhak undong).[29] These movements, launched in defense of Korean culture, drew strength from and in turn bolstered reactionary politics and nationalist-essentialist (*kuksujuйijŏk*) historiography that reified a unified, continuous past.

Two fairly typical editorials in the *Tonga ilbo* and an essay by Yi Kwang-su made the case for building a national culture this way. In 1932 Yi wrote, "Religion and ideology emerge, vanish, and change. [But] the nation [*minjok*] is unchangeable! The nation is an enduring entity, and the term *minjok* should not be belittled." In January 1934 an editorial in *Tonga ilbo* declared, "National culture cannot be completed with one class or region, and it should not be completed with one class or region. . . . The whole nation [*minjok*] has to gather its strength and work together to build a national culture that would not be inferior to that of any other nation."[30] Regardless of their intention, from Paek's point of view, the essentialist views of Korean nationalists, along with calls for unity, integrity, and trust, dovetailed with the Japanese colonialist discourse on "Korea's unique condition" (*Chōsen tokushū jijō*), which also served as ideological justification for coercive and autocratic methods employed by the colonial state. Paek, of course, was careful to distinguish between the two. But to the extent that both rejected the applicability of laws of historical development (that is, the Marxist worldview), fundamentally their politics ran parallel to each other and consequently both were reactionary.[31] Thus, although Paek's polemics seemed to be directed at multiple targets, he was in fact suggesting that Korean nationalists shared a common philosophical and political ground with the Japanese colonial state. He chose to call this common ground "particularism."

Paek's indictment of particularism was not a mere academic exercise. The Wanpaoshan Incident of 1931 illustrated the complicity between the particularism of Korean nationalism and the Japanese Empire. In the late 1920s and early 1930s, as the Korean population in Manchuria expanded to about two million, the persecution of Koreans by Chinese authorities intensified; Koreans were seen as an instrument of Japanese land investors and a pretext for expansion of Japanese control over Manchuria. The Chinese government had tried to prevent the acquisition of land by Japanese individuals or corporations. On the other hand, Koreans who obtained Chinese citizenship, numbering 48,000 in 1931, were allowed to reside anywhere—that is, they were not limited to the Chientao region—and to purchase or lease land. According to Chinese reports, Koreans with Chinese citizenship frequently resold, mortgaged, or leased the land to Japanese investors. Unofficial sources suggest that, of the total 643,242 acres of land cultivated by Koreans in Manchuria in 1929, at least 40 percent was really under the control of Japanese land speculators and mortgage companies.[32] Japanese consular police based in Chientao intervened on behalf of Koreans in disputes between Koreans and Chinese, based on the argument that Koreans living in China were Japanese subjects and thus entitled to the protection and privileges of extraterritorial status granted under the Treaty of 1915. Indeed many Korean settlers in Manchuria who had obtained Chinese citizenship in order to reside there and purchase or lease land outside of the Chientao district shifted back to Japanese citizenship in order to claim protection from the Japanese consular police.[33]

In 1931, in a small town called Wanpaoshan in Manchuria, violent clashes took place between Chinese and Koreans. Exaggerated accounts of "Chinese landlords massacring Korean peasants" were reported in Korean-language newspapers in Korea (*Tonga ilbo*, *Chosŏn ilbo*). The newspapers failed to point out that Japanese consular police were dispatched to protect the Korean farmers. It seems likely that the rush to sensationalize the incident was fueled by competition between *Tonga ilbo* and *Chosŏn ilbo*. Anti-Chinese riots broke out in nearly all the major urban areas. In Inch'ŏn, Chinese stores were targeted. In Pyongyang, organized mobs attacked the Chinese quarter, breaking into houses and hacking to death scores of people, including women and children. Approximately 127 Chinese were killed and 393 were injured.[34] The nationalist press had whipped up a frenzy of anti-Chinese sentiment that suited Japanese plans for creating the puppet state of Manchukuo. Paek Nam-un's polemic against both nationalist and colonialist historiography was very much grounded in concrete political questions of the day. The communists took the line of *minjung yŏnhap*: unity between the oppressed Chinese and Korean peoples. It was in this context that Paek criticized Korean nationalist (especially nativist) historiography as being a mirror image of colonialist historiography in that it sought to narrate Korean history in terms of its ancient origins and former glory and power. Irredentist yearnings (recovery of Manchuria as the ancient birthplace of the Korean *minjok*), on the one hand, and Orientalist representations of the Chinese, on the other, displaced attention and resentment away from Japanese imperialism. In this way, nationalist discourse could (and did) complement or reinforce Japan's imperial project. By opposing Japanese exceptionalism with Korean exceptionalism, nationalist historiography only reinforced the modes of thought that legitimated Japanese imperialism.

Nationalist Historiography in the 1930s

After Japan's invasion of Manchuria in 1931, open and legal forms of political resistance became impossible, and "unwavering nationalists" focused their efforts on defending the knowledge and practice of things Korean—

especially Korean language and history. Forced to resign from *Chosŏn ilbo* in 1932,[35] An Chae-hong turned his full attention to the study of Korea's past, writing historical narratives that affirmed difference and particularistic claims in contradistinction to both Japanese policies of assimilation and Marxist politics of class struggle. His inspiration came from Sin Ch'ae-ho, the brilliant nationalist historian who went into self-imposed exile in 1910. An's appropriation of Sin's earlier nationalist historiography resulted in a socially grounded nationalist historiography and a political program that he would later call "new nationalism" (*sin-minjokjuŭi*). As a nationalist historian who thought seriously about the category of subjugated masses (*minjung*) exploited by capitalism, An created "new nationalism" as a progressive form of nationalism that would strive to resolve conflict between social classes, even as it continued to privilege the unity of the nation and maintain an anticommunist stance.

For An, Korea's ancient past was a kind of golden age. While his narrative differed sharply from colonialist historiography on the ancient period, there was also a similarity, as in Sin Ch'ae-ho's historiography, in narrating subsequent Korean history in terms of a decline. Rejecting Marxism and Marxist historiography, An maintained that materiality and subjectivity were always mutually constitutive, and he sought to locate in Korea's ancient past an intellectual, religious, and cultural *chŏngsin* (*Geist*) that both identified and unified the Korean ethnic nation in relation to other peoples. Just as subjectivity could constitute a material force in history, universality and particularity were also mutually constitutive. In that sense, the particularity of Korea's past was already universal, and Korean historians need not be self-conscious about accentuating the Korean nation's distinctive subjectivity that linked contemporary Koreans to their (brilliant) ancient past. An identified this distinct subjectivity as *tasari chuŭi*, from the ancient Korean word for the number five ("all digits of one hand") that he claimed also meant "make all live." This communitarian and democratic ethos produced in Korea's ancient past a democratic aristocracy, a community in which all free native males were active, participatory citizens. In contemporary times, then, *tasari chuŭi* could serve as the historical basis for a new nationalism and new democracy that would obviate class exploitation and conflict.

In defense of Korea's sovereign past, An refuted the notion that Kija was a nobleman of Shang who went east to establish (Kija) Chosŏn toward the end of the second millennium BCE. According to texts such as the *Shang-*

shu dazhuan and the *Shiji*, following Zhou's conquest of Shang, King Wu of Zhou enfeoffed Kija as a ruler of Chosŏn. Such texts, written centuries after the event, when incorporated into the narrative framework of *Mansenshi* and *tōyōshi*, presented Kija Chosŏn as a "Chinese" colony, undercutting any notion of a sovereign, autochthonous origin for Korea. This was especially so because Kija was an object of reverence from the Three Kingdoms period up through the end of the Chosŏn dynasty. From the early years of the Chosŏn dynasty, Kija became an object of the dynastic state's veneration, as the Sage King who elevated rites and civilization.[36] An Chae-hong, like Ch'oe Nam-sŏn and Paek Nam-un, turned to historical linguistics and the study of phonological change, and taking those texts as an interpretive springboard, arrived at the conclusion that Kija must have been a common noun rather than a proper noun, denoting a feudal vassal of Tan'gun (ancient) Chosŏn.[37] In this way, An's historiography defended Korean claims to a national, sovereign past and identified a uniquely Korean *chŏngsin*, relevant to the present, that was not only transmitted down through time but also manifested concretely in Korean institutions and practices.

Nationalist narratives such as An's did not make any obvious impact on university-trained historians who were affiliated with the Chindan Society, an academic society organized in 1934 to "compete" with the Japanese in rigorous empirical research in Korean history and culture. Trained in *silchŭng sahak* (positivist historiography) that built on the historiographic tradition of *munhŏn kojŭng sahak* (critical-textual historiography; J: *kōshōgaku*),[38] most historians affiliated with the Chindan Society during the colonial period distanced themselves from both nationalist and Marxist historiography in their academic writing. Among historians who formed the core of the Chindan Society most were graduates of Waseda University and Keijō Imperial University. Organized by Yi Pyŏng-do along with the folklorist and historian Son Chin-t'ae and other leading scholars of Korean history, language, linguistics, and classical literature, the Chindan Society provided a focal point of institutional affiliation in the mid-1930s for Korean scholars working in Korean studies (*Chindan* being a sobriquet for Korea), consolidating networks that had formed among graduates of select universities, especially Waseda and Keijō.[39] *Chindan hakbo*, the journal published by the Society, provided a venue for these Korean scholars to publish, in Korean, scholarly work in Korean studies.

While Yi Pyŏng-do took the leading role in organizing the Chindan Society and published much of his work in *Chindan hakbo*, he also maintained his membership in Seikyō gakkai (青丘學會), an academic society led by Japanese scholars, and published in Japanese academic journals. Although the Chindan Society and its journal were outside the direct control of the colonial Japanese academy, Yi remained committed to "pure" (that is, non-political) scholarship, and until it was closed down in 1940 colonial censors did not need to closely monitor *Chindan hakbo*.[40] That is to say, from the 1930s until the end of the colonial period, most university-trained Korean scholars in Korean studies were not dissidents; they did not challenge colonial rule or, for that matter, colonialist scholarship in any fundamental way. Toward the end of the colonial period, however, Chindan hakhoe members like Son Chin-t'ae began to rethink certain historiographic questions by way of theories and methodologies taken from anthropology, archaeology, and folklore studies, and from the late 1930s onward it is not possible to wholly conflate positivist historiography (*silchŭng sahak*) with textual-critical historiography (*kojŭnghak*). Moreover in comparing the work of Ikeuchi Hiroshi and Kim Sang-gi, Remco Breuker has argued that while textual-critical historiography was highly derivative of *tōyōshi*, Chindan hakhoe historians like Kim Sang-gi were still able to portray Koreans as historical subjects: relations between China and Korea had been based on reciprocity; Koreans participated in the tributary system for the purpose of international trade; and while foreign power and influence were still central themes, Kim Sang-gi shifted the focus from invasion to resistance.[41] Without doubt Chindan Society scholars chafed at disparaging or condescending views of Korean history, people, and culture that were quite palpable in Japanese colonialist discourse on Korea. In 1942 the Chindan Society was dissolved when several of its leading members were arrested in connection with the Society of Korean Language Research incident, including Yi Yun-jae, Yi Hŭi-sŭng, and Ch'oe Hyŏn-bae.

In 1927 Yi Pyŏng-do began working for the Chōsenshi henshūkai (Society for the Compilation of Korean History), an organization directed and funded by the office of the Japanese governor-general.[42] At Waseda (1916–19) he had studied under Tsuda Sōkichi and also Ikeuchi Hiroshi, the first lecturer of Korean history at Tokyo Imperial University. It was on Ikeuchi's recommendation that Yi was hired on a part-time basis in 1927 by the Chōsenshi henshūkai. Ch'oe Nam-sŏn joined Chōsenshi henshūkai in 1928. As the central figure in positivist and critical-textual historiography among Korean scholars, Yi conceded a great deal to the narrative framework of *Mansenshi* and *tōyōshi* and to that mode of historical writing as objective, academic, and uniquely legitimating historical scholarship.[43] While the Chindan Society provided an institutional platform and venue for publishing academic papers written by Korean academics, an additional motivation for organizing the Chindan Society had to do, in part, with countering Marxists like Paek Nam-un.[44] Staying largely within the framework of *Mansenshi* and *tōyōshi*, historians who self-identified with the positivist and textual-critical school helped create new archives, gathering texts and writing histories that focused on very narrow, specific topics, to fill what Walter Benjamin called the "homogenous, empty time" of the nation's past, in marked contrast to Paek's effort to blast apart that history to reveal class conflict and the material basis for Korea's historical development. In South Korea, after liberation and the Korean War, the work of Yi and other scholars affiliated with Chindan hakhoe formed the basis for academic studies of Korean art, architecture, folklore, history, language, literature, and religious traditions. Cho Tong-gŏl suggests that criticism of positivist historiography in contemporary South Korea may stem more from the textual-critical school's submission to, if not complicity with, authoritarian governments in South Korea after 1945 than from complicity with colonialist historiography under Japanese colonial rule.[45]

Universalizing Korea's Past

There were a few Marxist scholars in the Chindan Society, most notably, Pak Mun-kyu, an economic historian, and Kim T'ae-jun, a scholar of Chosŏn-period literature, both graduates of Keijō Imperial University. In an article published in 1933, Pak pointed to the colonial land survey conducted between 1910 and 1918 as pivotal in establishing exclusive property rights, commodification of land, and thereafter capitalist relations in the countryside. In the immediate postliberation period (1945–48), Pak became a member of the Central Committee of the South Korean Workers' Party and then went north in 1948. Kim T'ae-jun studied Chinese and Korean literature at Keijō Imperial University and in 1939 became a lecturer in Korean literature there. In 1931, at the age of twenty-six, he published *Chosŏn hanmunhaksa* (History of Chinese Literary Studies in Chosŏn), and in 1933 he published *Chosŏn sosŏlsa* (History of Chosŏn-period Fiction), serialized in *Tonga ilbo*. Beyond being a brilliant scholar, Kim was also an activist, more so than Paek Nam-un or Pak Mun-kyu. While a lecturer at Keijō Imperial University, he was a member of the Kyŏngsŏng kom group (Seoul communists) in charge of the Bureau of People's Front. Arrested in 1941, he was released from prison in 1944 for health reasons. Soon after his release Kim made his way to Yenan, returning to Korea soon after liberation. He was (re)appointed to the faculty of Kyŏngsŏng University (formerly Keijō Imperial University, later Seoul National University), and he was one of three faculty members recommended by the faculty, students, and alumni for the position of university president. But he was fired from the faculty in connection with protests against USAMGIK's plans for reorganization of Kyŏngsŏng University, and in 1949 he was executed by the South Korean Army for his links with armed partisans.[46]

Paek Nam-un (1894–1979) studied in Japan at Tōkyō Kōshō (today, Hitotsubashi University) from 1919 to 1924 and returned to Korea in 1925 to teach economic history at Yŏnhŭi chŏnmun (later, Yonsei University). Outside of teaching, he joined the Chosŏn sajŏng chosa yŏn'guhoe (Association for Research on Korea's Situation). Aside from one article on the *kye* system (credit societies organized for aid or mutual benefit), all of Paek's published writings from this period are relatively simple articles on economic issues and contemporary events, and he was not active in the Sin'ganhoe. *Chōsen shakai keizaishi*, published in 1933, was Paek's first book, and very soon after its publication he became Korea's foremost scholar. When he wrote *Chōsen shakai keizaishi*, he conceived it as the first book of a comprehensive history of Korea's historical development. To provide the basis for such a history, he outlined in the preface to *Chōsen shakai keizaishi* six issues he hoped to eventually address:

1. Forms of primitive tribal communism
2. The slave economy in the Three Kingdoms period
3. The character of Asiatic feudal society in Korea from the end of the Three Kingdoms period to contemporary times
4. The disintegration of Asiatic feudal society and the sprouts of capitalism
5. International relations and the agenda behind the development of transplanted capitalism
6. A comprehensive survey of the development of ideology

After the publication of his second book, volume 1 of *Chōsen hōken shakai keizaishi*, in 1937, Paek was not able to follow through on the rest of his research agenda: locating the "sprouts of capitalism" in the latter part of the Chosŏn period and delineating the historical development of ideology in Korea and the development of "transplanted [colonial] capitalism." In 1938 he was imprisoned for violation of the Peace Preservation Order; he was subsequently released in 1940 but forced to relinquish his position at Yŏn-hŭi chŏnmun. As outlined here, Paek's project had been to rewrite Korean history from the perspective of historical materialism, starting with the primitive communal stage all the way up to Korea's annexation by Japan. As opposed to Japanese Marxist historiography on Korea, which tended to view Korea as truly "Asiatic" (that is, stagnant, not having reached even the feudal stage of historical development), Paek's aim was to show how each stage of Korean history emerged as a result of social forces *internal* to Korea.

Paek's agenda of demonstrating Korea's universal and yet autonomous subjectivity led him to participate in the centennial commemoration of the death of Chŏng Yag-yong (1762–1836; pen name Chŏng Tasan). The commemoration was part of a nationalist effort to develop Korean studies (Chosŏnhak), a project spearheaded by An Chae-hong and others.[47] While Marxists like Yi Ch'ŏng-wŏn were contemptuous of such projects, Paek took part with the intention of establishing Chŏng Tasan as a transitional figure. According to Paek, Chŏng Tasan was the leading light among Sirhak (practical learning) thinkers, advocating, in nascent form, what some post-colonial scholars would characterize as "communistic, socialistic economic theory." Certainly Chŏng Tasan could fully transcend his historical milieu. He was a great scholar who was not completely emancipated from feudal thinking. He could not have produced modern revolutionary ideas, and yet, being born in the feudal age, he was critical of feudalism, and though trained in the Confucian classics, he was not a mere Confucianist (*sun yu-hakja*). The tribute that Paek paid to Chŏng Tasan, then, had to do with Chŏng's prescient and progressive political and epistemological stance, a stance worth adopting even in the present.[48]

Thus, time and again, Paek argued that despite local variations and con-sistent with all of human history (including European and Japanese his-tory), Korean history developed in accordance with historical laws and by way of universal stages of development. The particularity of Korean social formations, starting from primitive tribal communities and continuing to the slave society of the Three Kingdoms period, to the Asiatic feudal society beginning with the "Unified" Silla period, and the transplanted capitalist society (*isik chabonjuŭi sahoe*) of Paek's time, represented the particularity of universal history as manifested in Korean history. Paek rejected the notion of Korean uniqueness—that is, Korean history as outside of universal historical development—with the argument that while Korean society may be "Asiatic," the development of the productive forces in Korean history was entirely "world-historical." He wrote, "In historical science, the only particularity to be accounted for is the particularity of the stage of a society's historical development, and [Korea's] particularity has to do with a specific reality, rather than a phantasmic uniqueness. Moreover, due to its manifestly progressive quality, [the particularity of Korean history] constitutes a single fundamental correlation [with world history]."[49] What we have here is a clear rejection of the most insulting aspects of the "Asiatic mode of production" as conceived by Marx and Engels.

Marx and Engels used the term *Asiatic society* to describe not only China and India, but also Spain, the Middle East, Java, and pre-Columbian America. That is, the concept of the Asiatic society, or the Asiatic mode of production, was used to describe almost any society based on communal ownership and self-sufficient villages where capitalist market relations are absent. As described in the *German Ideology*, *Grundrisse* (unpublished notes), *Critique of Political Economy*, and *Anti-Dühring*, the essential characteristics of the Asiatic society were communal ownership of land by self-sufficient villages (that is, the absence of private property), unity of handicrafts and agriculture, simplicity of production methods, and dominance of the state over public (irrigation) works. In creating the category of Asiatic society, Marx sought to explain and contrast the dynamic and progressive character of the West with the static and despotic character of the Orient. But aside from numerous empirical objections that can be raised with respect to the concept of an Asiatic mode of production, it also contained theoretical contradictions internally as well as externally with regard to historical materialism. Within the framework of the Asiatic mode of production, self-sufficient, autonomous villages seemed to argue against a centralized state that intervenes in the village economy. As for historical materialism, its inapplicability outside of Europe could be explained only in terms of geographic (that is, ecological) incongruity with Europe.

At the Leningrad Conference of 1931, the concept of a distinct Asiatic mode of production was rejected by Soviet scholars.[50] Thereafter the unilinear (or monistic) scheme—moving from primitive communism to slave, feudal, capitalist, and socialist societies—became the prevailing orthodoxy, and various aspects of Asiatic society were subsequently subsumed under the categories of slavery or feudalism. In *Chōsen shakai keizaishi*, Paek located class differentiation and class domination at the very origin of the Korean ethnic nation: it was the effort to establish durable class domination that drove the process of unifying various tribal federations by a centralizing state. In general agreement with Mikhail Godes's critique of the Asiatic mode of production, Paek argued that Korean feudal society might have been "Asiatic," but not in the sense that there could be a distinct mode of production particular to Korea, or Asia. In *Chōsen hōken shakai keizaishi*, he finessed the (colonialist) assertion about state ownership of land by characterizing feudalism in Korea as a particular (Asiatic) manifestation of the same form in Europe's historical development. In this way, he disposed of the notion of the Asiatic mode of production that echoed the colonialist narrative of a dynamic and progressive West and Japan contrasted with a static and despotic Orient saddled with debilitating customs and a long troubled past. In fact Paek's monistic view of history took aim at two different targets: colonialist historiography but also the particularistic view of history that dominated Korean nationalist historiography.

Paek's *Chōsen shakai keizaishi* (1933) and *Chōsen hōken shakai keizaishi* (1937) were both written in Japanese and published in Japan. In both books, he took issue with "stagnation theory" then prevalent in Japanese historiography on Korea, especially the historiography of Fukuda Tokuzō. At the same time, he polemicized against nationalist historians like Sin Ch'ae-ho and Ch'oe Nam-sŏn for their "idealist" approach, faulting them for adopting outdated German methodologies. By grounding their historical narrative on essentialist concepts like *hon* and *ŏl*, he argued, these idealist histories in the end only reinforced colonialist historiography by emphasizing Korean uniqueness. In Paek's work, we see a consistent and sustained polemic against nationalist historiography for its commitment to a particularistic (idealist, culturalist) view of history. The alternative, as proposed by Paek, was to narrate Korean history from a materialist stance, as part of monistic (universal) history wherein Korea is seen as having developed along universally applicable principles or laws.

We should remember that particularism in Japan (especially in the 1930s) appeared as a rejection of the West and as a critique of "universalism" which was in fact European particularism imposed on the rest of the world. But Japanese particularism (or exceptionalism) was presented as being fated to absorb the other "particularities" in Asia (Korea, China, etc.). By opposing Western imperialism, Japanese particularism assumed a moral superiority toward the rest of Asia. But ultimately it was the (temporary) military and economic superiority toward the rest of Asia which made Japanese exceptionalism a hegemonic discourse. Korean particularism pitted itself against Japanese particularism, but because the rationales underlying both were so similar, Korean particularism was fated to be subsumed. Indeed when repression heightened with the second Sino-Japanese War (beginning in 1937) and Japanese particularism demanded homogeneity both in Japan and Korea (*Naisen ittai*), many of the cultural nationalists argued that Korea should actively support the war effort in order to ensure its proper place in the Japanese Empire.[51]

It is in this sense that Paek saw the danger of particularistic historiography in Korea. Only a materialist view of history could truly resist colonialist claims. Historical materialism offered a monistic view of history that did not permanently privilege the capitalist West. The capitalist West (and Japan) did not represent the end of History. The wealth and power these capitalist nations had accumulated from the exploitation of their working class (at home as well as in their colonies), the maintenance of which ultimately depended on the power of their armies and police forces, would give way to a higher civilization and a new universalism created by a revolutionary working class united across national boundaries. This universalism offered the possibility that a backward Korea could become the sovereign subject of its own history, on an equal plane with the forces of revolution in the West and elsewhere in the world.

In *Chōsen shakai keizaishi*, Paek equated the primitive communal stage with the pre–Three Kingdoms period, the classical stage based on slavery with the Three Kingdoms period, the feudal stage with the period beginning in "Unified" Silla up through the late nineteenth century, and the capitalist stage with incipient capitalism which emerged in late Chosŏn that was displaced by transplanted capitalism following Japan's annexation of Korea. When *Chōsen shakai keizaishi* was published in 1933, Marxist intellectuals like Paek were marginalized not only by the colonial state but also by Korean nationalist (especially nativist, *kuksujuǔija*) intellectuals. But it should be noted that Paek's book also came under criticism from the Left. Yi Ch'ŏng-wŏn, for example, attacked it as a mechanical application of Japanese Marxist (*Kōza-ha*) historiography (on Japanese history) to Korean history.[52] Yi's critique of nationalistic (nativist) historiography was much more sweeping and dismissive. In 1936 he wrote:

> The recent chain of events both on the international front and domestically have necessitated the promotion of efforts to understand "Korea's past and present." But "Korean Studies," which is Confucian-moralistic, pre-ordained, and semi-feudal, constitute Korea's historical development as entirely autonomous of world history, passionate [only] in its investigation of Korea's sacred and inviolable "five thousand years old ŏl." The genius[es] behind this discourse (kongsik: formula) who paint themselves [in the likeness of] "Tan'gun," the tyrannical heroes [chŏnch'ejŏk yŏngung] who borrow the clothes of "Yi Sunsin," and those with ability who put on the mask of "Chŏng Tasan," are all falsifying Korean history. This is how history as mystified by ŏl emerged.[53]

This kind of aggressive polemic, directed against Paek Nam-un as much as against nationalists like Chŏng In-bo, might be explained by the fact that Yi wrote and published his book in Japan, where his primary task was organizing Korean students studying in Tokyo. But in terms of both temperament and circumstance, Paek was much more sensitive to how his work was received by nationalist (nativist) intellectuals, especially since Chŏng In-bo was a close colleague and friend at Yŏnhŭi chŏnmun and Paek benefited greatly from his remarkable mastery of literary Chinese.[54]

As a member of Yŏnhŭi chŏnmun's faculty, and as a public intellectual (rather than an underground activist in Tokyo) under close surveillance by the colonial police, Paek suffered from his doubly marginalized position in terms of both the colonial state and conservative nationalists associated with Tonga ilbo. His anxiety is quite evident in an interview he gave following Chōsen shakai keizaishi's publication. He expressed sadness over the fact that he had the "freedom" to assert that Tan'gun was merely an honorific title for a primitive aristocratic chieftain and not the father of the Korean minjok, whereas he was not free to direct the same kind of critical perspective to contemporary history. Here he was referring to the "freedom" granted by the colonial authorities to debunk nativist claims about Korea's ancient past, a freedom that did not extend to debunking Japanese claims about its role in colonial Korea. But Paek also felt obliged to make the point that a rigorous and critical approach to understanding Korea's past was the true manifestation of a love for Korean history. In an article published in the Tonga ilbo in 1934, Paek wrote, "Rather than boasting about our past, we should rigorously criticize it. This [critical approach], I believe, is truly the pure-minded means to 'loving' our past."[55]

In the interview in November 1933, however, he had gone even further, insisting that, "as a Korean scholar" (*Chosŏnin hakdo ro sŏ nŭn*), he must be free to present a rigorously critical reading of genealogies, that is, clan histories, private histories (*yasa*), and official histories, and be prepared to engage in a scientific debate with ordinary popular conceptions.[56] While there is something poignant about Paek's assertion of his Korean ethnicity as sanctioning his critical approach to Korean history, it should be noted that for Paek, the Korean nation (*minjok*) was an objective historical entity. He referred to the Korean people as a "precocious" nation (*chosuksŏng ŭi minjok*) because they developed quite early on those national character-istics associated with modern nationalism, that is, a unified culture, lan-guage, and customs.[57]

Paek shared with other Asian Marxist historians of his time an approach to history writing wherein the objective was to reveal how laws which govern universal historical development were manifested in a particular nation's history at various stages of its development. His discovery of the Punalua family structure prior to the Three Kingdoms period and his study of slavery in the Three Kingdoms period were significant not only in the sense that they posited a radically different view of Korea's ancient past (radically different from the nativist conception) but also because they sig-nified Korea's conformity with historical laws which govern all societies — including that of Europe. In that sense, the discovery of the Punalua family structure and the specific nature of the social formation at a particular stage were less important as evidence of what was happening. Rather they were important because they were evidence of certain classes of phe-nomena that in turn confirmed the regularity (or universality) of laws that govern history.

While Paek's agenda was to constitute Korean historiography as a "sci-ence," he was not oblivious to the ideological implications inherent in this category. Pointing to the historicity of science (*kwahak ŭi yŏksasŏng*), he ar-gued that while the natural sciences did not inherently contain a class bias, their historical development was linked to the development of the pro-ductive forces and was at times hampered by limits imposed by the ruling class of each epoch. Moreover if the natural sciences were susceptible to becoming a tool for class exploitation, then the social sciences much more readily served class interests. But even as Paek considered science as a practice with determinate conditions, and to a great extent as an ideological reflection of those historical (social) conditions, he retained a commitment to the liberating promise of science and the historical teleology that Marxism, as science, illuminates: a historical direction that was both inevitable and emancipatory, with the dispossessed (the proletariat) as the sovereign subject of history. By demonstrating the historical laws at work in Korean history, Paek showed that Marxist historiography was a "historiography that does not know despair."

chapter five

DIVIDED SOVEREIGNTY AND
SOUTH KOREAN HISTORIOGRAPHY

> If Japan had won rather than lost the Pacific War, what would we be think-
> ing? In that moment, what would be going through our minds as each of
> us pondered how to go on with our lives? I think this has to be the basis for
> our self-criticism. Would we [still] have had the resolve to live out our lives
> as backwoodsmen, buried in the remote countryside?
> —IM HWA, "Declaration of Conscience"

In late December 1945, in Seoul, now occupied by the U.S. Army, a group of
prominent writers and critics—Kim Nam-ch'ŏn, Yi T'ae-jun, Han Sŏl-ya, Yi
Ki-yŏng, Kim Sa-ryang, Yi Wŏn-jo, Han Hyo, and Im Hwa—came together
for a key session of criticism and self-criticism.[1] As politically engaged
intellectuals they were all intensely involved in political and organiza-
tional struggles of the day. That particular day, however, the object of their
struggle was their conception of themselves, and the truth of how they had
lived under Japanese colonial rule. Who were they when liberation came
upon them, and what should be the basis for criticism and self-criticism of
what they had done, said, and wrote during the colonial period? Im Hwa's
question went to the heart of the matter. If Japan had won the war, what
would they be doing? What would they be thinking? If Japan had been
victorious, would they not have felt tempted to compromise, and to embrace the victorious empire? Turning from the hypothetical to a definite acknowledgment of their collective and individual responsibility, Im argued
that even if a writer had not outwardly supported imperial Japan in action,
speech, or writing, and even if no one had noticed one's concealed, latent
urge to compromise, the self-reflective and self-critical "I" cannot help but
know. Therefore, in struggling for Korea's postcolonial present and future,
it was imperative that writers publicly acknowledge and struggle against
such defeatist, reactionary potential in themselves.

The other writers agreed with Im that only a thorough self-examination
that yielded a complete, detailed, and truthful accounting of one's offenses,

weaknesses, and shortcomings, along with sincere acknowledgment and contrition for those offenses and shortcomings in a collective or public setting, constituted a rigorous self-critique. Indeed these writers were at the forum because they agreed with the contention that self-critique had to be the point of departure for dealing with the personal and collective past and constructing a sovereign, postcolonial, emancipatory future. Calls for self-criticism, or "declarations of conscience," had appeared in a variety of publications almost immediately after liberation.[2] With the collapse of the Japanese Empire and the euphoria and public celebrations that followed, the Korean people's aspiration to usher in a sovereign, postcolonial future was made manifest, wholly palpable, and unequivocal. For these writers, criticism and self-criticism were not debilitating and were not meant to be debilitating. Through criticism and self-criticism, the writer, and by extension the proletariat and the multitude (inmin), would become more aware of how and to what extent their thoughts and urges had been shaped (distorted) by their historical (colonial) condition. As the writer constituted himself or herself as an object of collective and self-scrutiny, the possibility opened up for an ongoing transformation wherein the writer, alongside the masses, would become a truly self-conscious, historical (revolutionary) subject. In this process of subjectification, ethical responsibility to nation and class was to precede and establish the ground for (re)shaping one's subjective being in the world, in turn making possible decolonization of society and culture, and the assumption of national sovereignty.

The necessity of a thorough self-critique in a public setting and the presumption of collective fault pointed to at least two realities that leftist intellectuals like this group of writers had to confront soon after liberation from Japanese colonial rule. All of the writers at the forum had been complicit to some degree with Japanese imperial policies, especially after the invasion of China in 1937 and the intensification of war mobilization. Moreover liberation had been conferred rather than won. If Koreans had won their own liberation, the issue of complicity with Japanese colonial rule would have been settled in the course of the anti-imperialist struggle itself, with collaborators sidelined, and the worst collaborators executed, as the national liberation movement overthrew Japanese colonial rule and established its own hegemony. But as it happened, the liberation on August 15 "came like a thief in the night."[3] In the aftermath of a liberation that was given to Koreans by the Allies, following Japan's (too early) surrender, and in the context of occupation by Soviet and American troops who had agreed on the 38th parallel as their dividing line for occupation, Koreans who had actively supported the Japanese Empire as officials in the colonial government or as officers in the Japanese Imperial Army and police were still in positions of power in southern Korea, this time aiding and protected by the U.S. occupation forces.

Marxists were central to confirming criticism and self-criticism as principled practice, as the way to subvert "commonsense" notions about the world and one's place in it, referred to in shorthand as a (petit) bourgeois outlook or a slavish mentality, notions that worked to naturalize selfishness, opportunism, or the idea that Koreans had no choice but to rely on imperial powers — Imperial Japan previously, and now, as it was becoming increasingly apparent in southern Korea, the United Sates. For Marxists, the point of criticism and self-criticism was to establish an unshakeable unity based on "scientific truth" and absolute dedication to national and class emancipation, a unity to be established among members of the Korean Communist Party (KCP), and then a broader unity in the form of a united front encompassing workers, peasants, and intellectuals capable of carrying out a national democratic revolution.[4] But with the People's Committees forcibly "disestablished" by the U.S. Army Military Government, and the USAMGIK exercising all sovereign power previously held by the Japanese colonial state south of the 38th parallel, it was the leftists who were being sidelined and pushed underground in southern Korea.[5]

This was the context to which Yi T'ae-jun referred in a roundabout way early on in the forum with his observation, "Genuine liberation and freedom still seem remote." Not raised explicitly was the question, the political question, of what it meant to (still) refer to August 15 as Liberation Day, as did all the writers at the forum, if genuine liberation still seemed remote. Han Sŏl-ya's comment indirectly acknowledged such uncertainty over how to assess the present: he found it easy to write about the period before August 15, but he found it very difficult to grasp and write about "reality after liberation." For Yi Ki-yŏng as well, August 15 was an ambiguous marker, a fissure or break that confounded narrativization. Yi remarked that it would be strange to write only about the period before August 15 or to write only about the period after August 15. But, he asked, as if raising a rhetorical question, how does one link the period before August 15 to what comes after liberation? What narrative strategy could connect the colonial past to a postliberation present in which genuine liberation and freedom still seemed remote? In lieu of a ready answer the focus shifted to the purpose at hand.

It was Kim Sa-ryang, the youngest writer in the group, who first offered specific self-criticism. In early 1940 Kim's short story "Hikari no naka ni" (Into the Light) had been nominated for the prestigious Akutagawa Prize.[6] The story was written in 1939, soon after Kim graduated from Tokyo Imperial University; the protagonist, like the author at the time, is a Korean student at a prestigious university in Tokyo and a teacher at a night school. In addition to being a university student, the Japanese *kun* reading of the protagonist's family name is Minami, making it relatively easy for the teacher to pass as Japanese. In the end, his inner conflict over ethnic passing finds a resolution of sorts as one of his students, whose mother is Korean, pronounces the teacher's family name using the *on* reading *Nan*, close to the Korean pronunciation *Nam* rather than *Minami*.[7] This reciprocal recognition, up to the point of attempting to pronounce a Korean name, and acceptance and embrace of biethnicity, follows a literal coming-out as the teacher and the student enjoy a day at Ueno Park and shopping. The short story can be read as an indictment of Japanese racism and the policy of having Koreans adopt Japanese family names. But it also suggests that recognition of ethnic difference, and a near future when stigma attached to Koreans might be overcome, become possibilities (only) in the light of empire—thus the title "Into the Light."

In his self-criticism, Kim Sa-ryang explained that he had written "Hikari no naka ni" with grit and zeal to convey in a very real way the emotions of Koreans in Japan in their everyday encounters with Japanese racism, social isolation, and poverty. But looking back, he confessed that "in terms of the content," he had committed an error. He did not elaborate on what made the content problematic. Perhaps it was obvious to the other writers that Kim's depiction of poverty, discrimination, and social isolation of Koreans in Japan could have had the effect, ultimately, of affirming rather than subverting Japan's imperial aims. More than content, however, Han Sŏr-ya seized on the issue of language: even if the content had not required any blame or censure, the fact that the author had written in Japanese required self-criticism. Later in the forum Yi T'ae-jun returned to the issue of language by pointing to a structural relationship between language, literature, and culture. More than literature, and more than culture, Yi saw the attempted obliteration of the Korean language as the principal crisis that should have been all too evident to Korean writers. In the late 1930s and 1940s, with Korean-language newspapers and magazines shut down and Korean-language education eliminated, how could one even talk about (other) predicaments facing Korean literature or culture?

Following Kim Sa-ryang's self-criticism and the focus of criticism shifting to Korean writers writing in Japanese — that is, writing in the language of the colonizer — a number of writers at the forum chimed in on the kind of self-criticism that should be undertaken but in most cases was not. Kim Nam-ch'ŏn, who oversaw the process for approving membership in the newly formed Chosŏn munhakga tongmaeng (Federation of Korean Writers), expressed disappointment at many writers who failed to engage in criticism and self-criticism or whose self-criticism was inadequate or insufficient.[8] Han Hyo agreed: too many writers went to great lengths to try to rationalize what they wrote or did prior to August 15. During the Pacific War it could be said that there was not a single Korean who didn't cooperate in some way with Japan's war effort. It was at this point that Im Hwa intervened. Self-criticism should not devolve into a discourse of *We were all guilty*; that is, the (end) point of self-criticism is not to say *Others were bad and I was bad too*. Even with the knowledge that no one was entirely exemplary, one's attitude toward self-criticism nevertheless has to be *Others were virtuous (ch'akhada) and exemplary (hulryunghada), whereas I was the worst*. For Im, this was the type of attitude necessary for self-(re)making, and from one's conscience (*yangsim*) one had to draw the courage and the will needed to engage in that kind of painful self-examination and contrition. That is, in spite of structural reasons for consciousness, one's *conscience* is not wholly determined by historical or material circumstances, thus the possibility of reconstituting oneself anew.

In contrast to the other writers at the forum, Im's approach to self-criticism was to ground it in reflexive interiority. It was an approach that refused to relativize one's complicity with colonial rule. Indeed if one's complicity was evaluated against a defined hierarchy of offenses, from the most terrible (treason) to the not so terrible, then criticism and self-criticism, the purpose of which is self-(re)making, can be misdirected. Ultimately the self's other has to be an exemplary (imagined) self-consciousness which alone can act as a witness to confirm the truth of one's confession, contrition, and subjective transformation. Perhaps Im's admonition was utopian.

Perhaps such an ethic of self-(re)making could never have been put into practice in an organized way, on a mass scale. Even if such an ethic could have been interpolated into public discourse, perhaps the inevitable result would have been a disciplinary system, a form of modernity as totalizing as the wartime system of controls in the last years of the colonial period. But with Korea divided and occupied by Soviet and American troops, doubt about Korea's sovereign, postcolonial future coalesced around the fear that refusal of self-criticism, especially on the part of intellectuals, would perpetuate a political culture that in the past had acquiesced to imperial powers and surrendered the dream of sovereignty, of postcolonial self-realization.

Yi Wŏn-jo pointed out that some Korean writers wrote in Japanese because it became impossible to publish in Korean, and one could more easily avoid censorship if the text was written in Japanese. Just because a writer wrote in Japanese didn't mean that he or she cooperated with Japan. But, he added, the right decision was to have not written anything at all. Han Hyo agreed. The colonial authorities did not persecute writers for writing. As long as writers rationalized the imperialist war it did not matter how much they wrote. In that sense, not writing anything at all was a form of resistance. Kim Sa-ryang tried to shift the focus of critique: In what sense can a writer talk about conscience or dedication if he or she did not write anything? As writers, what one wrote and how one wrote had to be the focus of discussion. Kim admired the writer who retreated into a hovel and kept on writing. Yi T'ae-jun had the last word and turned the focus back to language. More so than the writer who put away his brush and kept silent, he admired the writer who, without causing harm to the people (*minjok*), wrote in Korean simply to keep the Korean language alive.[9] The writers who participated in this forum, all of them, went to North Korea prior to the outbreak of the Korean War.

Historiography after Liberation

For historians, self-criticism was more problematic. Positivist historians' claim to objectivity had rested on the notion that the narratives they produced were immanent in the empirical evidence: the facts forming the story, facts confirmed by careful and dispassionate reading of the sources, the sources themselves having been subjected to rigorous scrutiny, and causal relations (which structure the narrative) arrived at through scientific principles.[10] To the extent that these historians remained rigorous and objective in their research and methodology, what would they have to apologize for? On what basis could historians who had been committed to positivist historiography disavow their previous work, other than discovery of additional sources or minor revisions in explanations of causal relations? In other words, how could historians who had written histories that fit the narrative framework of colonialist historiography, under the banner of scientific objectivity, now reinvent themselves as postcolonial nationalist historians? In the immediate postliberation period it seems most historians, including Marxist historians, were not ready to present a systematic critique of positivist historiography and the narrative strategies it helped legitimate in the form of *Mansenshi* and *tōyōshi*. A systematic critique of colonialist historiography would come later in South Korea, starting in 1961, eight years after the end of the Korean War and in the immediate aftermath of the April 19 revolution that forced President Rhee Syngman from office. Subsequently, and as a cold war nationalist project, positivist and idealist strands in historiography were brought together as nationalist and anticommunist historiography, largely in the form of cultural history.[11]

For historians who were well regarded during the colonial period and at the same time managed to keep some distance between themselves and Japan's imperialist project, liberation from Japanese colonial rule presented an opportunity to take the leading role in reconstructing historical narratives and reorganizing Korea's educational and academic institutions. In the months following liberation, Paek Nam-un focused his efforts on laying the foundations for Korea's higher academic institutions. The day after Japan's surrender, Paek began organizing the National Academy of Sciences (Chosŏn haksulwŏn), which was to comprise leading scholars across the disciplines and across the political spectrum in the natural sciences, social sciences, and humanities.[12] This academy would have had tremendous influence over the reorganization of higher education and research institutions in Korea. That is to say, in the immediate postliberation period Marxist intellectuals, with Paek taking the leading role, sought to establish hegemony over intellectual production, reaching out to non-Marxist scholars, including nationalist historians who had not capitulated to colonial power. But this reaching out did not preclude Marxists from taking a polemical and partisan stance: even Paek, who was critical of the "excessively leftist" line taken by the Korean Communist Party, depicted all non-Marxist historiography as reactionary.[13]

Most of the leading scholars who had been Chindan hakhoe members chose not to affiliate with Paek's National Academy of Sciences. On August 16, 1945, the same day Paek launched the academy, Son Chin-t'ae and Cho Yun-jae took the lead in reconstituting the Chindan hakhoe, and according to Pang Kie-chung, they did so in order to establish and maintain a nationalist (that is, noncommunist) stance while participating in Left-Right coalition efforts.[14] In reconstituting the Chindan hakhoe, Cho called for the expulsion of "pro-Japanese scholars" from its ranks. The target of his critique included historians like Yi Pyŏng-do. Excluded from a leadership position in Chindan hakhoe, Yi organized a separate organization, the Association for Korean History Research (Chosŏnsa yŏn'guhoe), but nevertheless maintained an influential presence in Chindan hakhoe. Younger historians, however, did not join Yi's association; they either sought membership in the Marxist League of Scientists (Kwahakja tongmaeng) or the newly organized Korean Historical Association (Yŏksa hakhoe), which included Marxist and non-Marxist historians.[15]

The haste with which these historians sought to distance themselves from scholars like Yi Pyŏng-do is understandable in light of an intense antipathy that emerged in the immediate postliberation period toward those who had held positions of authority under Japanese colonial rule. As Tocqueville had observed about hatred toward the aristocracy—that the people hated aristocrats who were about to lose their authority—so too in the immediate postliberation period it seemed as if those who had flourished and had held official positions under the Japanese would no longer be able to exercise their authority, as popular sentiment toward collaborators shifted radically. Collaborators who were not only tolerated but respected during the colonial period came to be reviled precisely because, as Hannah Arendt put it, "wealth without visible function is much more intolerable because nobody can understand why it should be tolerated": "What makes men obey or tolerate real power and, on the other hand, hate people who have wealth without power, is the rational instinct that power has a certain function and is of some general use. Even exploitation and oppression still make society work and establish some kind of order. Only wealth without power or aloofness without a policy are felt to be parasitical, useless, revolting, because such conditions cut all the threads which tie men together."[16] When the

Japanese colonial state lowered its flag in August 1945, collaborators came to be viewed as parasites on the national body. It was in that sense that the demand for land reform and the purge of collaborators became central to postliberation politics, precisely because those who had lost real power when the Japanese Empire collapsed still possessed considerable wealth.

With Yi Pyŏng-do excluded from its leadership, some Chindan hakhoe historians cooperated closely with the USAMGIK, while others participated in organizations led by the Left, including the Committee on Science that was part of the National Democratic Front (Minjujuŭi minjok chŏnsŏn).[17] The National Democratic Front in southern Korea was established in February 1946 and led by a five-person secretariat that included Yŏ Un-hyŏng, Pak Hŏn-yŏng, Hŏ Hŏn, Kim Wŏn-bong, and Paek Nam-un. To the extent that one can impute a political orientation to Chindan hakhoe as a whole, in the immediate postliberation period its political orientation was similar to the strategy charted by An Chae-hong; in 1947 Son Chin-t'ae and Yi In-yŏng explicitly referred to their historiographic stance as "new nationalist historiography" (sin-minjokjuŭi yŏksahak).[18] Cho Yun-jae's charge against Yi Pyŏng-do and other historians focused on their collaboration with colonial government institutions, specifically the Chōsenshi henshūkai. It was generally accepted that the fundamental aim of Chōsenshi henshūkai as an organ of the colonial state was to legitimize Japanese colonial rule, and that it did so by distorting Korean history, specifically by suppressing or delegitimizing important texts (for example, the Samguk yusa) and by producing histories that downplayed the degree to which Koreans were subjects of their own history.[19]

One focal point for this kind of criticism was the thirty-eight-volume Chōsenshi (Korean History) published by Chōsenshi henshūkai, a work that was both a history and a compilation of primary sources. Yi Pyŏng-do's self-defense ran along a theme similar to those presented by Ch'oe Nam-sŏn, Yi Kwang-su, and other prominent intellectuals who had actively collaborated with Japan's imperial project. He had worked for the Chōsenshi henshūkai to prevent a worse outcome: to the degree that he could, he tried to prevent Japanese distortion of Korean history.[20] Unlike Paek Nam-un and many other historians who were deeply involved in political work in the immediate postliberation period, taking leadership positions in political parties, Yi continued to write history. The Korean history textbook Kuksa kyobon, for example, adopted and published by the USAMGIK in 1946 for use in junior and senior high schools, was written by Yi and Kim Sang-gi. For the modern period *Kuksa kyobon* highlighted the March First Movement, activities of the Korean provisional government in Shanghai, and the Kwangju student movement in 1929. *Kuksa kyobon* did not mention armed struggle waged by the communists in Manchuria in the 1930s, nor did it mention the Kwangbokgun (Restoration Army).[21]

In August 1946, when USAMGIK announced its plan to merge Keijō Imperial University with nine existing professional schools to form Seoul National University, Paek Nam-un was vocal in his criticism of the plan (Kukdaean): university faculty would have little autonomy from the USAMGIK's Department of Education, and academics who had actively collaborated in support of the Japanese Empire would be included in the faculty. During the colonial period, at Keijō Imperial University as in other imperial universities, the faculty of each school had significant autonomy from the Ministry of Education. Almost all issues relating to faculty, for example, were decided by the faculty of each school, although decisions involving curriculum, research, and personnel were subject to approval by the Ministry. This autonomy was largely affirmed after 1918, when, in practice, the university president was appointed after nomination by secret ballot of the faculty. The changes introduced by the USAMGIK shifted the organization of the university from the chair system of the nineteenth-century German university to the department system in U.S. universities, but in this instance was centrally organized by the USAMGIK's Department of Education.[22] With conservatives in control of the Department of Education, the Korean historians who became Seoul National University faculty were mostly Chindan hakhoe members, including Yi Pyŏng-do, who became the chairman of the History Department. Those appointed to the social sciences faculty were close colleagues of Paek Nam-un, and they dominated the Economics Department.[23]

As stated earlier, the political strategy of An Chae-hong's "new nationalism" had called for the creation of a Left-Right coalition that would exclude communists. In September 1945 An demanded Pak Hŏn-yŏng's exclusion from the Korean People's Republic (KPR), organized by Yŏ Un-hyŏng. When Yŏ refused to exclude Pak, then general secretary of the Korean Communist Party, An left the KPR.[24] As the "middle ground" quickly disappeared in the context of a divided occupation by Soviet and American troops, An accepted the position of director of the Interim South Korean

Government under the USAMGIK. As the USAMGIK and Rhee Syngman took measures to establish a separate state south of the 38th parallel, Paek Nam-un went north in 1948, ostensibly to attend a political conference. But he stayed on to become the first minister of education (1948–56) in the Democratic People's Republic of Korea (DPRK, North Korea), established later that year. When he died in 1979 at the age of eighty-six, Paek was still a member of the Central Committee of the Korean Workers' Party, ranked forty-sixth in the leadership hierarchy. By 1948 many Marxist intellectuals had left Seoul and gone north of the 38th parallel, pushed by anticommunist repression in the South and pulled by offers of employment and opportunity to take part in the DPRK's national democratic revolution. Between 1946 and 1947 historians like Kim Kwang-jin from Kim Il Sung University in Pyongyang went south to recruit many of the best historians in southern Korea. Yi Ch'ŏng-wŏn, Kim Sŏk-hyŏng, Pak Si-hyŏng, Chŏn Sŏk-dam, and others went north, and historiography in the DPRK came to be dominated by "historians from the South." When the DPRK's Chosŏn ryŏksa p'yŏnch'an wiwŏnhoe (Korean History Compilation Committee) was established in 1949, Paek Nam-un was its chairman.[25] At the same time, intellectuals and politicians who had struggled for a Left-Right coalition—especially those who had opposed the UN-sponsored election in 1948 which created South Korea—were subjected to repression and terror from the South Korean police and right-wing groups. With American backing, those who had championed "objective" empirical research and "nonpolitical" historiography during the colonial period seized nearly all the major academic posts in the Republic of Korea (ROK, South Korea).

Soon after the establishment of separate states in 1948, Marxists in South Korea either had to flee to the North or go underground. The Republic of Korea was established on August 15, 1948, with Rhee Syngman as president. The Democratic People's Republic of Korea was established on September 3, 1945, with Kim Il Sung as premier. With the passage of the National Security Law in South Korea in November 1948, anticommunism was institutionalized as South Korea's overriding political principle, and praising or supporting North Korea in any way became an act of treason. In June 1949, less than a year after its sovereignty was established through UN-sponsored elections, the South Korean state created the Kungmin podo yŏnmaeng (National Guidance League, NGL). *Podo* literally translates to *caring and guiding*. In the late 1930s and 1940s, leftists who renounced their political beliefs had great difficulty finding work and caring for their families, and the Japanese colonial state organized the League for Servicing the State to guide and care for these former political prisoners. According to Kim Dong-choon, this colonial policy served as the model for the NGL as South Korean authorities, especially prosecutors, established laws and institutions to maintain surveillance and control over political dissidents. Membership in the NGL was supposed to be voluntary, but in actuality former communists and political dissidents were forced to register. By late 1949 membership in the NGL had reached 300,000. As an institutional innovation from the late colonial period revived by the South Korean state, the NGL not only maintained surveillance over political dissidents; it also institutionalized, in a comprehensive way, social isolation and political containment of former militants and fellow travelers, including leftist intellectuals. In 1950, soon after the outbreak of the Korean War, South Korean security forces systematically executed thousands of NGL members.[26]

In November 1949 Yi Pyŏng-do became the chairman when the Association for Korean History Research (Chosŏnsa yŏn'guhoe) merged with Chindan hakhoe. In late 1949 the remaining progressive scholars on the Seoul National University faculty were fired. After the Korean War, with Son Chin-t'ae dead, the remaining Marxists turned, and nationalist historians who had participated in Left-Right coalition efforts were now isolated. Yi Pyŏng-do and Chindan hakhoe absolutely dominated South Korean historiography. Beyond the horrific anticommunist witch hunts during and after the Korean War, Yi's return to Chindan hakhoe was made possible, in part, by money from the United States. Both before and after the Korean War, Chindan hakhoe received financial support from the Rockefeller Foundation. In 1954 Yi was named as the primary investigator in an ambitious project of publishing a comprehensive history of Korea, funded by a large grant from the Rockefeller Foundation. The seven-volume history, published between 1959 and 1965, focused on political, institutional, and cultural history, starting with the question of Tan'gun and ancient Chosŏn, and ending in 1910 with Korea's annexation by Japan. Yi wrote the bulk of volume 1 and all of volume 2, from ancient Chosŏn to the end of the Koryŏ period. It was not until the student revolution of April 19, 1960, which toppled the Rhee regime and created for a brief moment a democratic opening, that nationalist historians of a younger generation could challenge the political and intellectual authority of Yi and the positivist and textual-critical tradition.

Postcolonial Historiography: 1960–1980

Although the student revolution of April 19, 1960, that toppled the Rhee regime was crushed by a military coup in 1961, that democratic opening nevertheless allowed a younger generation of historians to narrate history in new ways. In the introduction to *Kuksa sillon*, published in 1961 (just prior to Park Chung Hee's military coup), Yi Ki-baek, who had studied under Yi Pyŏng-do, presented a comprehensive account of colonialist historiography, specifically *Il-Sŏn tongjoron*, the narrative of Japanese and Koreans sharing common origins, and thus Japan's colonization of Korea in 1910 as the restoration of ancient ties; *tangp'asŏngnon*, factionalism as deeply ingrained in the Korean political culture, evidenced by successive purges of literati and factional strife during the Chosŏn period; *chŏngch'esŏngnon*, the notion that the Korean economy and society had been stagnant for a thousand years; and *t'ayulsŏngnon*, a narrative denying autochthonous development, focusing on how external forces from China and Manchuria had determined Korea's historical development.[27]

Written as a history textbook, *Kuksa sillon* aimed to dismantle such "prejudiced views and theories that impede a correct understanding of Korean history." Yi Ki-baek used the word *kŭndaehwa* (modernization), the first Korean historian to make reference to modernization theory that was being promoted by American academics and advisors. *Kuksa sillon*, in other words, created a narrative framework that was safely postcolonial: anti-Japanese but uncritical of American intervention in post-1945 Korea. This type of historiography, a marriage of modernization theory with the positivist and textual-critical tradition, quickly became the dominant mode of narrating Korean history in the context of the cold war. The question of neocolonialism (a critique of the United States), suppressed by the anti-communist state, would be sublimated through developmental time: South Korea was developing with American assistance but also from its own sources of modernity.[28]

As the effort to "overcome" colonialist historiography gathered momentum, however, closet Marxists began to venture beyond the ideological boundaries imposed by South Korea's place in the cold war system under the banner of "nationalist" historiography. It was in that context that Yi Ki-baek took to task historians like Kim Yong-sŏp for drawing on the work of Paek Nam-un and other Marxist historians, and for "turning a blind eye" to the fact that Paek had been hostile to nationalist historiography during the colonial period.[29] But ignoring Paek's critique of nationalist historiography was a self-preservation measure. For progressive historians like Kim Yong-sŏp and Kang Man-gil, Paek's historiography offered a way not just to overcome the legacy left by colonialist historiography but also to reinsert class struggle in historiography.

Because he had left South Korea to go to the North, Paek could not be cited in print nor claimed as an intellectual forbear; the only way to appropriate his work was by casting him as a nationalist historian who took part in the Korean studies movement (Chosŏnhak undong) in the mid-1930s. Through their empirical studies of land tenure, the growth of commerce (merchant capital), and the development of a commodity-monetary economy in the latter half of Chosŏn, Kim Yong-sŏp and Kang Man-gil revived and confirmed Paek's disclosure of the internal dynamic underlying Korea's historical development, in which class struggle was central. Under a nationalist canopy, Kim and Kang reestablished intellectual links to a form of history writing that had been suppressed in South Korea after the Korean War. Their view of history was based on an anticolonial, oppositional nationalism, and their historiography contributed greatly to understanding the dynamic nature of Korea's social and economic development in late Chosŏn. In a very limited sense, Kim and Kang shared common ground with nationalist historians who preferred modernization theory; their agenda was to write a Korea-centered history. But the implications of their historical narrative could not be more different. For modernization historians, the origins of Korea's modernity was the cultural and scientific developments in the eighteenth century, traced forward to Westernized and Westernizing elites of the nineteenth century and to noncommunist nationalists in the twentieth century who would eventually establish South Korea.

In contrast, Kim Yong-sŏp, along with Kang Man-gil, laid the basis for the argument that there were two possible paths to modernity: a relatively more egalitarian and autonomous path from below, with peasant rebellions providing the main impetus for progressive change, and a more exploitative, dependent path from above, led by elites who would ultimately capitulate to imperialist demands starting in the late nineteenth century.[30]

Thus Kim and Kang located the Westernized and Westernizing elites within a historical trajectory that had roots in the cultural and political world of the landed class in the late Chosŏn period, whose modernization efforts from the late nineteenth century to the present reflected their narrow class interests, and for that reason tended toward dependency on outside powers: collaboration with the Japanese in the colonial period and with the Americans after 1945. This was a trajectory that paved the way for Korea's colonization by Japan, the formation of separate states in 1948, and dictatorship and dependent capitalist development in South Korea.

By the late 1970s the argument that there were two possible paths to modernity was an academic formulation of more bracing narrative strategies employed by student activists and dissident intellectuals in South Korea as they reimagined the present as a conjuncture of conflicting historical trajectories. In the lead essay of *Haebang chŏnhusa ŭi insik* (Korean History Before and After Liberation), published in 1979, Song Kŏn-ho presented an ethical critique of how 1945 marked the beginning point of the most horrific chapter in Korean history.[31] Liberation, coming after decades of colonial rule, should have marked the beginning of a new history wherein the oppressed people, the *minjung* (the masses, the multitude), could finally and rightly become the sovereign subject (*chuch'e*) of history. Instead, with the partition of Korea along the 38th parallel coming simultaneously with liberation, former collaborators and those willing to serve the new occupying powers—the Soviet Union and the United States— diverted history from its true path and brought about a terrible ordeal for the Korean people.[32]

The primary target of Song Kŏn-ho's essay was not American imperialism but Rhee Syngman, the arch anti-communist, conservative politician who became the first president of South Korea in 1948. While avoiding detailed discussion of the role of Pak Hŏn-yŏng and the Korean Communist Party (KCP) (later, the Korean Workers' Party), Song reminded his readers that it was Rhee who had allowed notorious collaborators to evade punishment, including former Korean police officials who had hunted down, tortured, and killed independence activists. As a whole, the essays in *Haebang chŏnhusa ŭi insik* drew a link between Rhee's refusal to punish collaborators with other acts that aborted justice and stripped liberation of any real meaning: delaying land reform and weakening its impact; sabotaging the work of the U.S.-Soviet Joint Commission to prevent the formation of a unified coalition government; and taking the lead in manipulating anticommunist discourse to establish a separate state in the South, thus making the 38th parallel drawn by the United States and the Soviet Union a permanent (and militarized) line dividing the Korean nation in two.[33]

Through this critique of Rhee, *Haebang chŏnhusa ŭi insik* reinterpreted history after 1945 in terms of powerful binaries that inspired opposition discourse: genuine nationalism versus mindless anticommunism, and *minjung*-oriented democracy versus mere formal democracy.[34] Song's essay not only exposed the rather inglorious origins of the South Korean state; it also negated cold war historiography by positing as *nationalist* resistance to the UN-sponsored separate elections in 1948 on which the ROK claimed its legal basis. Song's essay was part of a sustained and courageous effort by dissident intellectuals in South Korea to constitute the *minjung* as a national (and nationalist) subject and to imagine a subjectivity that could be an alternative to and autonomous from nationalist narratives authorized by either the North or the South Korean state.[35]

It was the people's uprising in Kwangju in 1980, however, and the massacre perpetrated by South Korean government troops, which broke the state's ideological hold over the democratic movement in South Korea.[36] The magnitude of the state violence drove young intellectuals to search for the structural origins of their predicament. Whereas dissident intellectuals like Song Kŏn-ho had previously skirted the issue of communism and the role played by Pak Hŏn-yŏng and the KCP, for example, by the mid-1980s such taboos no longer evoked automatic self-censorship.[37] In introducing the second volume of *Haebang chŏnhusa ŭi insik*, published in 1985, Kang Man-gil noted that history departments in Korean universities had up to then avoided the modern period.[38] Past attempts to write the history of colonial and postcolonial Korea from an "objective" viewpoint had been repressed, while histories that did get published either consciously or unconsciously conferred legitimacy on the political forces responsible for the division of Korea. Such historiography naturalized the present. They were written from within the *structure of division*.

The historian's most pressing task, then, was to write a history of modern Korea from a perspective unfettered by this structure of division. Such a perspective was accessible, Kang Man-gil argued, when historians understood the political struggles of the immediate postliberation period not simply as the denouement of the colonial experience but also as a struggle to overcome national division. Beyond objective analysis of the history that led to national division, a unification-oriented historiography (*t'ongil chihyangjŏk yŏksa insik*) had to pay special attention to efforts at creating a united front between the Left and the Right at the end of the colonial period and efforts to overcome national division after 1945. Similar to Song Kŏn-ho's essay, Kang Man-gil's essay was a historical narrative that vindicated movements in opposition to the establishment of separate states, including the boycott of UN-sponsored elections in 1948, led by communists as well as nationalists like Kim Ku.

If Kang Man-gil's narrative strategy aimed to recenter Koreans (rather than foreign powers) in history after 1945, the lead chapter in the fourth volume of *Haebang chŏnhusa ŭi insik*, published in 1989 and cowritten by Choi Jang-jip and Chŏng Hae-gu, looked at the Korean War in terms of its structural origins, both domestic and international, while not losing sight of the dynamic character of political struggle.[39] In describing this dynamic, Choi and Chŏng began with explanations of why liberation brought forth a revolutionary situation. Simply put, it was the breakdown of the colonial state at the end of the Pacific War which unleashed demands for revolutionary change. These demands were anti-imperialist and antifeudal in nature: the vast majority of the people wanted former collaborators purged from government posts and nationalization of land, factories, and businesses that had been owned by the Japanese and comprador capitalists.[40]

In marked contrast with anticommunist historiography, the appearance of People's Committees throughout Korea immediately after liberation marked the first steps toward the establishment of a postcolonial government which would have carried out the anti-imperialist, antifeudal revolution. On the question of the American role in postliberation Korean politics, Choi and Chŏng agreed with the arguments made by Bruce Cumings in *Origins 1*: while Soviet troops did not need to force a revolutionary program on northern Korea, the tide of revolution was reversed in southern Korea only with considerable coercive power by the USAMGIK.[41] Moreover, in the period 1945–47, even as the United States participated in the Joint Commission talks, which were to have laid the basis for a unified Korean state, the USAMGIK had pursued a policy of containment, as evidenced by the outlawing of the KCP, strengthening of the repressive state apparatuses, and support for right-wing youth groups.

North of the 38th parallel, immediately after liberation, both the Soviet

Army and Kim Il Sung wanted to establish the party center in Pyongyang, and Choi and Chŏng linked this to what later came to be called *minju kijiron*, the strategy of creating a democratic base area as a preliminary to seizing the whole.[42] The use of conventional military force to overcome Korea's division was not inherent in *minju kijiron*. But after the failure of the U.S.-Soviet Joint Commission talks and the establishment of separate states in 1948, the formal leadership structure of the North Korean Workers' Party and the South Korean Workers' Party were merged into one, and thereafter *minju kijiron* was understood in military terms. Thus, from liberation to the eve of the Korean War, the intent and effect of *minju kijiron* produced, in sequence, an independent KCP leadership in northern Korea, political consolidation by way of anti-imperialist and antifeudal struggles, central leadership for the united front struggle against the U.S.-sponsored movement to establish a separate state in the South, and finally North Korea as a military base from which a war of national liberation could be launched.

On the question of who started the Korean War, Choi and Chŏng dismissed both *namch'imnon* (North attacked South) and *pukch'imnon* (South attacked North) as exercises in assigning blame. But they did express more interest in speculations about entrapment (*hamchŏngsŏl*) by way of NSC 68 and Dean Acheson's Press Club speech and the North Korean attack as limited war meant to force quick negotiations.[43] This volume of *Haebang chŏnhusa ŭi insik* was important for the number of issues it raised and was instructive in how it recaptured the dynamic nature of postliberation politics even while pointing to the structural causes for the Korean War.[44]

A Rightist Critique of Nationalist Historiography

As "revisionist" historical narrative gained currency in the 1980s, conservative historians became increasingly frustrated at historiography that conceded nationalist credentials to North Korea and seemingly denied historical legitimacy to South Korea.[45] But the fall of communism in Eastern Europe in 1989 and the dissolution of the Soviet Union in 1991 brought about a shift, and so did the emergence of postcolonial theory in Korean academic scholarship. The New Right welcomed scholarship inspired by postcolonial theory for its refusal to narrate the colonial period as a Manichaean struggle between a colonizing Japan that was racist and exploitative and a resisting and enduring people, or nation (*minjung, minjok*). With this the New Right turned to criticism of nationalism in general, and nationalist historiography of the 1980s in particular, attacking the latter for being "critical of South Korea."

Haebang chŏnhusa ŭi chaeinsik (Reconsideration of Korean History Before and After Liberation) was published in February 2006 with enthusiastic reviews from conservative dailies like the *Chosŏn ilbo*. Compiled by four scholars identified either with postmodern theory or with the New Right, the title of this two-volume anthology deliberately evoked *Haebang chŏnhusa ŭi insik* as its polemical target, signaling the editors' intention of restoring balance to a historical understanding of colonial and postcolonial history. In their introduction, the editors charged that leftist-nationalist historiography, as epitomized by *Haebang chŏnhusa ŭi insik*, was responsible for the "dangerously distorted" historical perspective held by a sizable segment of the public (mostly the younger generation) as well as by the left-leaning Roh Moo-hyun administration.[46] For the editors of *Haebang chŏnhusa ŭi chaeinsik*, leftist-nationalist historiography of the 1980s, as epitomized by *Haebang chŏnhusa ŭi insik*, had achieved near hegemony in politics, and in spite of subsequent research that should have corrected such a skewed view, leftist-nationalist historiography remained entrenched, discouraging the publication of more "objective" scholarship, attacking those who strayed beyond leftist-nationalist narratives of colonial exploitation, anti-Japanese resistance during the colonial period, and the privileging of leftist-nationalist struggles in the postliberation period.

As Cumings points out, what the New Right saw as a "dangerously distorted" historical perspective in fact appeared time and again in U.S. classified reports leading up to the Korean War, in reports written by American military and intelligence officers who were critical of America's decision to divide Korea and distressed about American involvement in political assassinations, for example, during counterinsurgency operations in Yŏsu in 1948 and Cheju Island in 1948–49.[47] *Haebang chŏnhusa ŭi chaeinsik* did include a number of essays, both older and more recent, that presented evidence as well as compelling narratives on a range of issues that add complexity to narratives about the colonial experience and history after 1945.[48] Some essays challenged *Haebang chŏnhusa ŭi insik* and leftist-nationalist historiography much more directly. On land reform, for example, Chang Si-wŏn's chapter argued that South Korea's land reform succeeded in transforming peasants into independent farmers and helped put an end to status distinctions.[49] On the creation of separate states, Yi Chŏng-sik's chapter, originally published in 1998, presented evidence that as early as October 1945 the Soviet Union was committed to establishing a separate state in the North.[50]

According to Kim Chul (Kim Ch'ŏl), one of the editors of *Haebang chŏnhusa ŭi chaeinsik*, political discourse had shifted to such an extent during the Kim Dae Jung and Roh Moo-hyun administrations that scholars who questioned leftist-nationalist narratives experienced a backlash comparable to the anticommunist witch hunts of the past.[51] The immediate political context to which Kim and the other editors were referring had to do with the twenty or so Truth Commissions established since the year 2000. The first was the Presidential Truth Commission on Suspicious Deaths, formed to investigate suspicious deaths of citizens between 1975 and 1987 and to identify perpetrators for prosecution. Other Truth Commissions investigated the killings on Cheju Island in 1948 (when approximately 30,000 people were killed), collaboration during the colonial period, and responsibility for massacres and killings of civilians by U.S. and South Korean military and police before, during, and after the Korean War. For the editors of *Haebang chŏnhusa ŭi chaeinsik*, these investigations into the past were aimed at consolidating leftist hegemony and undermining South Korea's legitimacy through a one-sided attack on anticommunist conservatives in South Korea—because conservatives were much more likely to have had family members who had collaborated with Japanese imperialists as well as close personal ties to authoritarian regimes of the past.[52]

Thus, in the conservative press, *Haebang chŏnhusa ŭi chaeinsik* was presented as a full-throated and much needed corrective to leftist-nationalist historiography. That the leading conservative newspaper in South Korea was at the forefront of criticizing nationalism and nationalist historiography, and actively cultivating (and supporting) postcolonial scholarship, testifies to how closely nationalism had come to be associated with leftist politics and historiography. The New Right embraced postcolonial theory's critique of nationalism and nationalist historiography as totalizing and undemocratic. Economic historians like Yi Yŏng-hun welcomed postcolonial theory for subverting unities such as class and nation imposed by nationalist narratives. For Yi, postcolonial scholarship provided the opening for recentering the individual and as a way to restore legitimacy to South Korea's anticommunist legacy, now reconfigured as civilizational progress.[53]

Intellectually, however, the accommodation between the New Right and postcolonial scholarship was tenuous, resting solely on their common antipathy toward nationalism and nationalist historiography. For the New Right, intensely anticommunist and fiercely unapologetic about capitalism and capitalist development in South Korea, accommodation with postcolonial scholarship was tactical, and the strategic target was leftist, nationalist historiography and its political expression. On the other hand, a number of contributors to *Haebang chŏnhusa ŭi chaeinsik*, either implicitly or explicitly, took issue with the kind of "universalism" advocated by the New Right, a universalism based on uncritical notions of progress and capitalist development that sought to sweep under the rug histories of racism, violence, class exploitation, and the reinvention of patriarchy both under Japanese colonial rule and under U.S.-supported South Korean governments.

In Lieu of a Conclusion

While the genealogies presented here were unavoidably schematic, the aim of this chapter was to situate different, competing modes of history writing within and against the distinctive political and intellectual configurations that dominated a particular conjuncture in modern Korean history. In socioeconomic (Marxist) historiography, for example, Paek Nam-un's critique of both colonialist and nationalist historiography in the early 1930s drew on and reinforced the idealist / materialist and universality / particularity binaries that nationalist historians like An Chae-hong had to contend with later. Even as Paek affirmed a unilinear view of historical development, his rendering of Korea's ancient past as consistent with universal development included finding what he thought was Korea's equivalent of the Punaluan family structure, thus transforming ancestors into (interesting) strangers.

In the immediate postliberation period, with Korea under divided occupation by Soviet and American forces, Paek's stance became more nationalist, calling for a broad united front that could bring about a unified and sovereign nation-state. In this revolutionary context, Chindan hakhoe members such as Son Chin-t'ae and Yi In-yŏng turned to narrating the nation's past on the basis of a "new nationalism," trying to identify an essential and abiding unity that might transcend and mitigate class conflict. It was the revolution on April 19, 1960, however, that prompted Yi Ki-baek to offer a systematic critique of colonialist historiography, at last rendering positivist historiography safely postcolonial and more effective in naturalizing capitalist modernity, that is, critical of colonialist historiography and Marxist historiography but uncritical of American intervention in Korea after 1945.

As the effort to "overcome" colonialist historiography gathered momentum, in tandem with an increasingly vibrant democracy movement, historians like Kim Yong-sŏp and Kang Man-gil reengaged with Paek's disclosure of an internal dynamic underlying Korea's historical development, wherein class struggle was central to that internal dynamic. It was the people's uprising in Kwangju in 1980, however, and the massacre perpetrated by government troops, which pushed historians like Kang to narrate colonial and postliberation history from outside the "structure of division." This historiography was explicitly nationalist. But it should be kept in mind that, for Kang, this convergence of Marxist historiography with nationalist historiography was historically contingent.[54]

Postnationalist scholarship, which emerged in the first decade of the new millennium, began with studies of the colonial period. Rather than taking ethnicity, sexuality, and class as fixed, objective categories, a younger generation of historians and literary scholars focused attention on the process by which ethnicity, sexuality, and class came to be (re)constituted under colonial rule. As these scholars eschewed a simple colonizer/colonized binary, their work elicited hostile reaction from leftist-nationalist historians but enthusiastic interest from the New Right, in large part because of their deployment of the notion of colonial modernity, in which the colonial sometimes receded into the background, leaving only the modern—but not always as an object of critique. As suggested here, the accommodation between New Right intellectuals and postnationalist scholarship was also contingent, and it remains to be seen whether postnationalist historiography can remain critical of the workings of power without strong links to socioeconomic (Marxist) historiography.[55]

What began in the late nineteenth century as an effort on the part of the dynastic state to attain equal sovereignty developed into a mass enterprise that demanded perseverance and fidelity. Many historians dutifully did their part by sustaining a normative understanding of sovereignty as both the embodiment and the exercise of reason, autonomy, and freedom. Through narratives they compiled, activist historians sought to induce the subject that would be the master and sole author of that enterprise. To paraphrase Alain Badiou, from nationalist historians like Sin Ch'ae-ho to Marxist historians like Paek Nam-un, or New Right historians in contemporary South Korea, historians imagined sovereignty to be not just a goal but an axiom, an idea that demands fidelity.[56] As a record of that fidelity, this book presented an outline of the situation that elicited various modes of history writing, but very little in terms of what that fidelity meant as lived experience. As a legal and ideological principle in capitalist modernity, equal sovereignty as an axiom engendered attachment and attendant range of emotions, including joy, exhaustion, and what Laurent Berlant calls "cruel optimism." For Berlant, a relation of cruel optimism emerges when the object that drew your attachment begins to impede the aim that brought you to it initially. "It is cruel insofar as the very pleasures of being inside a relation have become sustaining regardless of the content of the relation."[57] From "K. Y.," a student at "X Women's School" in the 1930s who could like her short hair but only at the cost of contending with social conventions, to writers like Im Hwa, who, in the immediate postliberation period, felt that only a thorough self-examination and self-critique within a collective setting could produce a genuinely revolutionary and sovereign subject, fidelity to sovereignty, as lived experience, was (and is) at once threatening and profoundly confirming.

APPENDIX 1

Names and Vital Dates:

Akiba Takashi	1888–1954	秋葉隆
An Chae-hong	1891–1965	安在鴻
An Hwak	1886–1946	安廓
Chang To-bin	1888–1963	張道斌
Cho Pak	1356–1408	趙璞
Ch'oe Nam-sŏn	1890–1957	崔南善
Chŏng To-jŏn	1342 (?)–98	鄭道傳
Chŏng In-bo	1893–1950	鄭寅普
Chŏng Yag-yong	1762–1836	丁若鏞 (茶山)
Chu Si-gyŏng	1876–1914	周時經
Fukuda Tokuzō	1874–1930	福田德三
Fukuzawa Yukichi	1834–1901	福澤諭吉
Han Paek-kyŏm	1552–1615	韓百謙
Han Sŏl-ya	1900–1976	韓雪野
Hayashi Taisuke	1854–1922	林泰輔
Hong Tae-yong	1731–83	洪大容
Hoshino Hisashi	1839–1917	星野彬
Huang Zunxian	1848–1905	遵
Hwang Hyŏn	1855–1910	黃玹
Hyŏn Ch'ae	1856–1925	玄采
Im Hwa	1908–53	林和
Imamura Tomo	1870–1943	今村
Inoue Kaoru	1836–1915	井上馨
Iryŏn	1206–89	一然
Itō Hirobumi	1841–1909	伊藤博文
(Empress) Jingū	ca. 169–269	神功天皇 (legendary figure)
Kanda Naibu	1857–1923	神田乃武
Kija (C: Jizi)		箕子
Kim Chŏng-ho	1804 (?)–1866 (?)	金正浩

Kim Hong-jip	1842–96	金弘集
Kim Hwal-lan	1899–1970	金活蘭 (Helen, 天城活蘭)
Kim Ki-rim	1908–?	金起林
Kim Nam-ch'ŏn	1911–53	金南天
Kim Ok-kyun	1851–94	金玉均
Kim Pu-sik	1075–1151	金富軾
Kim Sa-ryang	1914–50	金史良
Kim T'ae-jun	1905–49	金台俊
Kim Yun-sik	1835–1922	金允埴
Kojong (Yi Chae-hwang)	(r. 1863–1907)	
Kume Kunitake	1839–1931	久米 邦武
Li Hongzhang	1823–1901	李鴻章
Liang Qichao	1873–1929	梁「超
(Queen) Min (Min Cha-yŏng)	1851–1895	明成皇后
Min Yŏng-ik	1860–1914	閔泳翊
Minami Jirō	1874–1955	南次「
Murayama Jijun	1891–1968	村山智順
Mutsu Munemitsu	1844–97	陸「宗光
Myoch'ŏng	d. 1136	妙淸
Okakura Kakuzō	1862–1913	岡倉「三 (Okakura Tenshin)
Paek Nam-un	1894–1979	白南雲
Pak Che-ga	1750–1805	朴齊家
Pak Chi-wŏn	1737–1805	朴趾源
Pak Hŏn-yŏng	1900–1955	朴憲永
Pak Si-hyŏng	1910–2001	朴時亨
Pak Ŭn-sik	1859–1925	朴殷植
Pak Yŏng-hyo	1861–1939	朴泳孝 (Yamazaki Eiharu 山崎永春)
Rhee Syngman	1875–1965	李承晚
Saitō Makoto	1858–1936	「藤「
Sejong (Yi To)	(r. 1418–50)	
Sekino Tadashi	1868–1935	「野貞
Shigeno Yasutsugu	1827–1910	重野安繹
Shiratori Kurakichi	1865–1942	白鳥庫吉
Sin Ch'ae-ho	1880–1936	申采浩
Sŏ Chae-p'il	1864–1951	徐載弼 (Philip Jaisohn)
Sŏ Kwang-bŏm	1859–97	徐光範

Son Chin-t'ae	1900–1950	孫晋泰
Son Pyŏng-hŭi	1861–1922	孫秉熙
Sone Arasuke	1849–1910	曾禰 荒助
Song Si-yŏl	1607–89	宋時烈
Suiko	554–628	推古天皇 (Empress Suiko)
Taewŏn'gun (Yi Ha-ŭng)	1820–98	大院君 (李昰應)
Tan'gun	(r. 2333 BCE–)	檀君 (legendary figure)
Terauchi Masatake	1852–1919	寺┌正毅
Torii Ryūzō	1870–1953	鳥居 龍┌
Wang Kŏn	(r. 918–43)	王建 (高麗太祖)
Yanagi Sōetsu	1889–1961	柳 宗┌
Yi Ch'ŏng-wŏn	?–?	李淸源
Yi Hwang	1501–70	李滉 (courtesy name Toegye)
Yi Ki-yŏng	1895–1984	李箕永
Yi Kwang-su	1892–1950	李光洙 (香山光郎)
Yi Nŭng-hwa	1869–1943	李能和
Yi Pyŏng-do	1896–1989	李丙燾
Yi Sang	1910–37	李箱
Yi Sŏng-gye	(r. 1392–98)	李成桂 (朝鮮太祖)
Yi Sŭng-hyu	1224–1300	李承休
Yi T'ae-jun	1904–56	李泰俊
Yi Yi	1536–84	李珥 (courtesy name Yulgok)
Yu Kil-chun	1856–1914	兪吉濬
Yu Tŭkkong	1749–1807	柳得恭
Yuan Shikai	1859–1916	袁世凱
Yun Ch'i-ho	1865–1945	尹致昊 (Itō Jikko 伊東致昊)
Zhu Xi	1130–1200	朱熹 (K: Chu Hŭi)

APPENDIX 2

Character List

chaju chi pang	自主之邦	independent country
chaju tongnip	自主獨立	autonomy and independence
che	帝	emperor
chehu'guk	諸侯國	vassal state
(C: Chenfan)	唇番郡	(K: Chinbŏn) Han Chinese commandery
ch'in-Il	親日	Japanophile
chin'gongguk	進貢國	tributary state
chŏngch'esŏngnon	停滯性論	theory about stagnation
chongmyo	宗廟	Royal Ancestral Temple
chongmyo cherye	宗廟祭禮	grand sacrificial rite
chŏngsin	精神	mind, spirit, *Geist*
chŏngt'ong	正統	legitimate line, legitimate succession
ch'ŏnha	天下	world, All under Heaven
ch'ŏnja	天子	Son of Heaven
ch'ŏnmyŏng	天命	Heaven's mandate
(J: Chōsenjin)	朝鮮人	Koreans
Chosŏn	朝鮮	1392–1910
chuch'e; chuch'esŏng	主體, 主體性	(sovereign) subject, subjectivity, subjective will
chukwŏn	主權	sovereignty
chungin	中人	hereditary class of technical specialists
ch'ung ŏ kukka	忠於國家	loyalty to the state
chungwŏn	中原	Central Plain (North China Plain)
(J: futei senjin)	不逞鮮人	malcontent Koreans
(J: genrō)	元老	Meiji elder statesmen
Haedong	海東	East, Korea
hanmun	漢文	literary Chinese
hon	魂	soul, spirit; its vitality comes from Heaven, and thus can be detached from the body

hongik in'gan	弘益人間	devotion to welfare of humankind
Hunmin chŏngŭm	訓民正音	published in 1443, Instruct the people on the proper sounds,
hwangje	皇帝	emperor
hwa-yi	華 夷	civilization-barbarism
Hwangsŏng sinmun	皇城新聞	September 5, 1898–1910
hyangch'al	鄉札	local letters, archaic Korean vernacular that used Chinese characters for meaning and sound
hyangga	鄉歌	poems from the Three Kingdoms period to the Koryŏ period recorded in *hyangchal*
hyangyak	鄉約	community compacts
hyo ŏ pumo	孝於父母	filiality toward parents
idan	異端	heresy, deviance
idu	吏讀 / 吏頭	archaic writing systems that used Chinese characters and their abbreviations to transcribe Korean
Il-Sŏn tongjoron	日鮮同祖論	(J: Nissen dōsoron) theory about Japanese and Koreans sharing common origins
inmin	人民	the people
(J: *Jiji sinpo*)	時事新報	*Current Events*, a newspaper started by Fukuzawa Yukichi
(J: Keijō)	京城	Seoul
ki	氣	life force or breath, energy
(J: *Kojiki*)	古事記	Record of Ancient Matters, completed in 712
Koguryŏ	高句麗	37 BCE–668
(J: kokumin)	國民	national citizen, subject
(J: kokutai)	國體	national body/structure
Koryŏ	高麗	918–1392
kukka	國家	the state, polity
kŭndaehwa	近代化	modernization
kun'guk kimuch'ŏ	軍國機務處	deliberative council
kungmin	國民	national citizen, subject
kungmun	國文	national script
kunmin ilch'e	君民一體	ruler and his people as one body
kyŏre	겨레	ethnic nation
kwanbo	官報	*Official Gazette* (1894–1910)

kwangmu	光武	era name, August 17, 1897 to August 11, 1907
kwinsin	鬼神	ghost
kwŏlli	權利	authority, privilege, rights
kwŏn	權	rights, prerogative
(C: Lelang)	樂浪郡	(K: Nangnang) 103 BCE–313 CE, Han Chinese commandery
Liao	遼	(Khitan Empire) 907–1125,
(C: Lintun)	臨屯郡	(K: Imdun) 107–82 BCE, Han Chinese commandery
man'guk kongbŏp	萬國公法	international law
Manmin Kongdonghoe	萬民共同會	Assembly of All (People)
(J: Mansenshi)	滿鮮史	history of Manchuria and Korea
min	民	people
minjok	民族	ethnic nation
minjung	民衆	people, the subaltern
mujing pulsin	無徵不信	fidelity to historical sources
munhŏn kojŭng sahak	文獻考證史學	critical-textual historiography
(J: Naisen ittai)	內鮮一體	Japan and Korea as one body
(J: Naisen yūwa)	鮮融和	harmony between Japan and Korea
(J: *Nihon Shoki*)	日本書紀	The Chronicles of Japan, completed in 720
kuk'ŏ	國語	national language
ŏl	얼	mind, spirit
ŏnmun	諺文	disparaging term for Korean letters invented by King Sejong
Paekche	白濟	18 BCE–660
ŏp	業	work, enterprise
paeksŏng	百姓	the people
Parhae	渤海	(C: Bohai) 696–926
Parhaego	渤海考	history of Parhae by eighteenth-century scholar Yu Tŭk-kong
pongkŏn	封建	feudal
puma'guk	駙馬國	son-in-law state
P'ungipsong	風入松	a Koryŏ period "folk" song
p'yeha	陛下	Your Majesty (form of address)
sadae	事大	serve the superior

sadaebu	士大夫	scholar-official class
sajikdan	社稷壇	Altars of Land and Harvest
sangha kwich'ŏn	上下貴賤	people of all ranks
sarim	士林	literati in the countryside
Silla	新羅	57 BCE–668 CE; "Unified" Silla, 668–935
sim	心	mind, heart
sinkungmin	新國民	new citizen-subject
sinyŏsŏng	新女性	new woman
soChunghwa	小中華	Korea as a lesser (but only remaining) civilization
sŏgomun	誓告文	royal oath
sokkuk	屬國	vassal state, dependency
Sŏkkuram	石窟庵	man-made stone grotto with Buddhist statue
sŏnghwang	聖皇	emperor
Sŏyu kyŏnmun	西遊見聞	*Observations on a Journey to the West*
Ssangsŏng	雙城(摠管府)	Yüan commandery
suri pujak	述而不作	transmission without creative elaboration
Taehan cheguk	大韓帝國	Han (Korean) Empire (October 12, 1897–August 29, 1910)
taeŏp	大業	great / grand enterprise
taesa	大祀	great offerings
tanbalryŏng	斷髮令	topknot decree
tangp'asŏngnon	黨派性論	factionalism (ingrained in Korean political culture)
t'ayulsŏngnon	他律性論	heteronomous evolution, lack of autochthonous development
Tongbang	東方	Eastern Country, Korea
Tongguk	東國	Eastern Country, Korea
tongnip	獨立	independence
Tongnip hyŏphoe	獨立協會	Independence Club, July 1896–December 25, 1898
Tongŭi pogam	東醫寶鑑	completed 1613, Precious Mirror of Korean Medicine
(J: tōyōshi)	東洋史	Oriental history
ŭm, yang	陰陽	yin, yang
wae	倭	Japan (pejorative)

Wanpaoshan Incident	萬寶山事件	(K: Manbosan) July 1931
wŏndan	圜壇	Round Altar
wŏn'gudan	圜丘壇	Round Hill Altar
(C: Xuantu)	玄菟郡	(K: Hyŏndo) Han Chinese Commandery 107 BCE–302
yushin	維新	restoration

NOTES

Introduction

1. *Sŭpotssŭ*, *sŭpidŭ*, and *saeksŭ*, along with the explanation for the bob haircut, are in parentheses in the original. Other foreign words like *Nora*, *the Bob*, and *harem* are in quotation marks. Kim Ki-rim was a modernist poet and literary critic. His essay "'Missŭ Koria' tanbal hasio" ("Miss Korea," Cut Your Hair) appeared in *Tongkwang*, no. 37 (September 1932) without attribution.

2. The text refers to *sŏppun tchari ka'gŭk*, Kurt Weil and Bertolt Brecht's *Die Drei-groschenoper*, first performed in Berlin in 1928.

3. X's were inserted to avoid censorship. The Kwantung Army had seized Manchuria in September 1931 and invaded Shanghai in January 1932. Thus when Kim Ki-rim wrote the essay anti-imperialism had taken precedence in Chinese politics.

4. Established in 1886 by Mary Scranton, Ehwa began as a mission school for girls. In the early 1930s Ewha College admitted about a hundred students each year. Of the thirty-seven faculty members, twenty-one were Korean. Kim Hwal-lan was a graduate of Ewha, and in 1922 she helped organize the Korean YWCA. Yun Ch'i-ho, who founded the YMCA in Korea, was her mentor. She was also a member of the Kŭnŭhoe, a nationalist women's organization founded in 1927. But she resigned soon afterward, unwilling to work with women who were Marxists and socialists. Kim Hwal-lan, "Na nŭn tanbal ŭl irrŏkkye ponda," *Tongkwang*, no. 37 (September 1932). See also Ihwa Yŏksagwan, *Ewha Old and New: 110 Years of History (1886–1996)* (Seoul: Ewha Woman's University Press, 2005), and Insook Kwon, "Feminists Navigating the Shoals of Nationalism and Collaboration: The Post-Colonial Korean Debate over How to Remember Kim Hwal-lan," *Frontiers: A Journal of Women Studies* 27, no. 1 (2006).

5. Achille Mbembe, "Necropolitics," *Public Culture* 15, no. 1 (2003), 13. I thank Alexis Dudden for referring me to this article.

6. K. Y., "Tanbalhan kamsang," *Tongkwang*, no. 37 (September 1932).

7. On the historical relationship between imperialism and international law, see Antony Anghie, *Imperialism, Sovereignty, and the Making of International Law* (Cambridge: Cambridge University Press, 2004). See also Martti Koskenniemi, *The Gentle Civilizer of Nations: The Rise and Fall of International Law, 1870–1960* (Cambridge: Cambridge University Press, 2001).

8. There were other, less dramatic changes to sumptuary laws, for example, laws that regulated the length of the pipe and the length and width of the sleeves.

9. According to Hwang Hyŏn, King Kojong turned to Chŏng Pyŏng-ha, an official who was born in the nonaristocratic *chungin* class, and told him to cut the topknot.

Yu Kil-jun cut the crown prince's hair. Cited in Lee Kwang-rin (Yi Kwang-rin), *Yu Kil-chun* (Seoul: Tonga ilbosa, 1992), 122–23.

10. Across East Asia, writers wrote about hair. In Lu Xun's "Toufa de gushi" (A Story about Hair, 1920), for example, a student cut his queue when he went to Japan to study. Upon his return to China he purchased a fake queue in Shanghai. But it was 1910, and he was ridiculed for wearing a fake queue. He took off the queue and put on a Western suit. He was jeered in the streets. He put on the long Chinese gown, and he was still ridiculed. The protagonist in the story, N, finally lashed out at his tormentors with his cane, after which he was left alone. N says, "It [hitting others] made me feel sorrowful." In an essay published in 1935, Lu Xun revealed that "Toufa" was autobiographical. See Evan Shan Chou, "'A Story about Hair': A Curious Mirror of Lu Xun's Pre-Republican Years," *Journal of Asian Studies* 66, no. 2 (2007).

11. In the English translation released by the Home Office and signed by Yu Kil-chun, *taeŏp* was translated as "the great work." Cited in Isabella L. Bird, *Korea and Her Neighbors* (1897; Boston: KPI, 1985), 363. The phrase "Our subjects" (*sinmin*) is actually a compound that refers to two groups: "subjects" or officials (*sin*), and the rest (*min*, or people). For the Korean text, see *Kojong sillok*, 33-kwŏn, 32-nyŏn (1895), 11/15. Kuksa pyŏnch'an wiwŏnhoe (National Institute of Korean History): http://sillok.history.go.kr/main/main.jsp. For *Kojong sillok*, as with other annals in the *Chosŏn wangjo sillok* (Annals of the Chosŏn Dynasty), the citation begins with the ruler's temple name identifying the record (sillok), followed by volume number (kwŏn), the reign year (nyŏn) with the Common Era year in parentheses, the month and day by lunar calendar, and when necessary the entry's location on the page. November 15 by the lunar calendar, 32nd year of Kojong's reign, was December 30, 1895, in the Gregorian calendar.

12. The best work on this period is Andre Schmid's *Korea between Empires, 1895–1919* (New York: Columbia University Press, 2002).

13. Regarding Japanese use of international law to legitimate Japan's empire, see Alexis Dudden, *Japan's Colonization of Korea: Discourse and Power* (Honolulu: University of Hawaii Press, 2004).

14. Human tribute began during the Yüan dynasty. The number of children requisitioned was small, and they were taken on an irregular basis. The girls were selected from daughters of low- to middle-grade officials. Donald N. Clark, "Sino-Korean Tributary Relations under the Ming," *The Ming Dynasty, 1398–1644*, part 2, ed. Denis Twitchett and Frederick W. Mote, *The Cambridge History of China*, vol. 8 (Cambridge: Cambridge University Press, 1998).

15. Benedict Anderson, *Imagined Communities: Reflections on the Origin and Spread of Nationalism* (London: Verso, 1983), 77.

16. Yun Ch'i-ho, *Yun Ch'i-ho ilgi* (Seoul: Kuksa py'ŏnchan wiwŏnhoe, 1973–1989), entry for October 14, 1893, 3:187–88.

17. See Uday Singh Mehta, *Liberalism and Empire: A Study in Nineteenth Century British Liberal Thought* (Chicago: University of Chicago Press, 1999).

18. My argument here has an affinity to the historical trajectories suggested by Kim Yong-sŏp. See below, and note 30 in chapter 2.

19. See note 60 in chapter 2, my reference to Paul Ricoeur's *The Rule of Metaphor: Multi-disciplinary Studies of the Creation of Meaning of Language* (Toronto: University of Toronto Press, 1975).

20. See Ross King, "Western Protestant Missionaries and the Origins of Korean Language Modernization," *Journal of International and Area Studies* 11, no. 3 (2004).

21. Rey Chow, *Women and Modernity: The Politics of Reading between East and West* (Minneapolis: University of Minnesota Press, 1991), xv.

22. The Sŏkkuram is one of South Korea's national treasures and recognized by UNESCO as a World Heritage site. It was constructed in the mid-eighth century on Mt. T'oham near Kyŏngju.

23. See Hyung Il Pai, *Constructing "Korean" Origins: A Critical Review of Archaeology, Historiography, and Racial Myth in Korean State-Formation Theories* (Cambridge: Harvard University Asia Center, 2000).

24. See Jun Uchida, *Brokers of Empire: Japanese Settler Colonialism in Korea, 1876–1945* (Cambridge: Harvard University Asia Center, 2011). See also Uchida Jun, "Ch'ongnyŏkjŏn sigi chae-Chosŏn Ilbonin ŭi 'NaeSŏn Ilch'e' chŏngchaek e taehan hyŏmnyŏk," *Asea yŏn'gu* 51, no. 1 (2008), and Micah Auerback, "'Ch'in-Il Pulgyo' yŏksahak ŭi chae'go: Chosŏn Pulgyodan kwa 1920-nyŏndae Chosŏn esŏ ŭi sŭngryŏ kyŏlhon e taehan nonjaeng," *Asea yŏn'gu* 51, no. 3 (2008).

25. See Rebecca Karl, *Staging the World: Chinese Nationalism at the Turn of the Twentieth Century* (Durham: Duke University Press, 2002), 5–7.

26. See Kume Kunitake, "Nihon fukuin no enkaku," *Shigakkai zasshi* 1 (December 1889), and also Stefan Tanaka, *Japan's Orient: Rendering Pasts into History* (Berkeley: University of California Press, 1993), 71–75.

27. Fukuda Tokuzō, "Kankoku no keizai soshiki to keizai tani," *Keizaigaku kenkyū*, (Tokyo: Dōbunkan, 1904), 147. My English translation is based on Yi Ch'ŏl-sŏng's Korean language translation. See Yi Ch'ŏl-sŏng, "Singminjisigi yŏksainsik kwa yŏksasŏsul," *Han'guksa* 23 (Seoul: Han'gilsa, 1994), 129. See also Owen Miller, "The Idea of Stagnation in Korean Historiography," *Korean Histories* 2, no. 1 (2010): 4–5.

28. Both were written in Japanese and published in Japan to avoid the more stringent censorship laws in colonial Korea.

29. Tanaka, *Japan's Orient.*

30. W. W. Rostow, *A Proposal: Key to an Effective Foreign Policy* (New York: Harper and Brothers, 1957), and *The Stages of Economic Growth: A Non-Communist Manifesto* (Cambridge: Cambridge University Press, 1960). See also Tae-gyun Park, "Different Roads, Common Destination: Economic Discourses in South Korea During the 1950s," *Modern Asian Studies* 39, no. 3 (2005).

31. See Pak Chi-hyang et al., eds., *Haebang chŏnhusa ŭi chaeinsik*, vols. 1 and 2 (Seoul: Ch'aek Sesang, 2006).

32. Bruce Cumings, "The Korea War: What Is It That We Are Remembering to Forget?," *Ruptured Histories: War, Memory, and the Post–Cold War in Asia*, ed. Sheila

Miyoshi Jager and Rana Mitter (Cambridge: Harvard University Press, 2007), 283–84.

33. Pak et al., "Taedam," *Haebang chŏnhusa ŭi chaeinsik*, vol. 2.

34. Michael Hardt and Antonio Negri, *Multitude: War and Democracy in the Age of Empire* (New York: Penguin Books, 2004), 212.

1. Sovereignty and Imperialism

1. The source of this chapter's epigraph, Carl Schmitt's 1933 lecture, was republished in *Positionen und Begriffe* and cited in G. L. Ulmen's introduction to Carl Schmitt, *The Nomos of the Earth in the International Law of the Jus Publicum Europaeum* (New York: Telos Press, 2003), 18–19.

2. The official English translation quoted here suitably makes use of the royal "We." For the Korean text, see *Kojong sillok*, 32-kwŏn, 31-nyŏn (1894), 12/12, first article. Kuksa pyŏnch'an wiwŏnhoe: http://sillok.history.go.kr/main/main.jsp. The thirty-first year of Kojong's reign was 1894. But December 12 (1894) by the lunar calendar was January 7, 1895, in the Gregorian calendar.

3. Isabella L. Bird, *Korea and Her Neighbours* (1897; Boston: KPI, 1985), 247.

4. Grand sacrificial rites (*chongmyo cherye*) were conducted each year in January, April, July, and October. Special rites were also performed on auspicious occasions or difficult times. The Hall of Eternal Peace (*yŏngnyŏngjŏn*), located about fifty meters southwest of the Main Hall (*chŏngjŏn*), is smaller and houses the spirit tablets of the four ancestors of King T'aejo, short-reigned kings, queens, and consorts. Both the Main Hall and the Hall of Eternal Peace stand on two-tiered stone terraces, each enclosed by a square wall. Great offerings at the Altars of Land and Harvest (*sajikdan*) were conducted three times a year.

5. In the Oath, King Kojong used the term *kukka*: "Only as an independent ruler can We make our country [*a-kukka*] strong." The term *kukka* referred directly to the dynastic state and was used long before the nineteenth century. Mid-Chosŏn thinkers like Yi I (pen name Yulgok, 1536–84), for example, used the term to denote the dynastic state, as in *ch'ung ŏ kukka* (loyalty to the dynastic state). See Martina Deuchler, "The Practice of Confucianism: Ritual and Order in Chosŏn Dynasty Korea," *Rethinking Confucianism: Past and Present in China, Japan, Korea, and Vietnam*, ed. Benjamin A. Elman, John B. Duncan, and Herman Ooms (Los Angeles: UCLA Asian Pacific Monograph Series, 2002).

6. It should be noted, however, that for scholars like Chŏng Yag-yong (1762–1836) there was a fundamental distinction to be made between the Royal Ancestral Temple and the *sajikdan*: unlike the Royal Ancestral Temple, which served as a shrine to the spirits of deceased ancestors, the *sajikdan* was a shrine to heavenly deities. Thus, unlike the Royal Ancestral Temple, the *sajikdan* is a shrine with a transcendent status: the Altars of Land and Grain do not belong to a particular dynasty, and they should not be torn down or replaced when a new dynasty comes to power. See Kŭm Chang-t'ae, "Tasan ŭi sajikje wa ch'eje kojŭng," *Chongkyohak yŏn'gu* 16 (1997).

7. *Nobi* were not organized in familial or lineage kinship groups; after all, adult as well as adolescent *nobi* were bought and sold, and they could not perform mortuary rituals. James Palais estimates that *nobi* of all kinds together made up nearly one-third of the population throughout the Chosŏn period. See James B. Palais, *Confucian Statecraft and Korean Institutions: Yu Hyŏngwŏn and the Late Chosŏn Dynasty* (Seattle: University of Washington Press, 1996), 208–70.

8. During King Sejong's reign (1418–50) a separate annex, the Hall of Eternal Peace (*yŏngnyŏngjŏn*), was constructed to house the spirit tablets of the ancestors of King T'aejo as well as short-reigned kings and their queens. In 1545, the year King Myŏngjong took the throne, four *kan* were added to the east end of *chŏngjŏn*. In 1592, the first year of Hideyoshi's invasion of Korea, both the Main Hall and the Hall of Eternal Peace were completely destroyed. The Main Hall was rebuilt as an eleven-*kan* structure in 1608, and the Hall of Eternal Peace in 1668. In 1726 the Main Hall *chŏngjŏn* was expanded to a fifteen-*kan* structure, and in 1834 expanded again to its current size of nineteen *kan*. See Dong-Uk Kim, "Chongmyo," *Korea Journal* 40, no. 3 (2000).

9. In his Ten Injunctions, T'aejo refers to the Khitan as "beasts," and it was not until 960, after the first Khitan invasion, that Koryŏ accepted the suzerainty of the Liao. *Koryŏsa*, kwŏn-2, sega-2, T'aejo 15-nyŏn (932), 5/3. (Kuksa p'yŏnch'an wiwŏnhoe) http://db.history.go.kr/KOREA/.

10. See Ro Myoung-ho (No Myŏng-ho), "Tongmyŏng Wangpyŏn kwa Yi Kyu-bo ŭi tawŏnjŏk ch'ŏnhakwan," *Chindan hakbo* 83 (1997), and "Koryŏ sidae ŭi tawŏnjŏk ch'ŏnhakwan kwa Haedong Ch'ŏnja," *Han'guksa yŏn'gu*, no. 105 (1999).

11. In terms of Koryŏ rulers personally conducting the sacrifice to Heaven (*chech'ŏnnye*), the *Koryŏsa* mentions only fourteen instances.

12. Remco E. Breuker, "Koryŏ as an Independent Realm: The Emperor's Clothes?," *Korean Studies* 27 (2004), 53.

13. This folk song most likely originated prior to the period of military rule, that is, before 1170. In the *Koryŏsa*, as edited by the National Institute of Korean History (Kuksa p'yŏnchan wiwŏnhoe), the first stanza is punctuated in such a way that *che* (帝, emperor) and *pul* (佛, Buddha) appear as a compound, a generic term for Buddha: 海東天子, 當今帝佛, 補天助敷化來. *Koryŏsa*, kwŏn-71, chi-25. Based on other references to the emperor in both the lyrics and many other texts from this period, Ro Myoung-ho argues that *che* and *pul* do not form a compound and that the stanza should be punctuated thus: 海東天子, 當今帝, 佛補天助敷化來. See Ro, "Tongmyŏng Wangpyŏn kwa Yi Kyu-bo ŭi tawŏnjŏk ch'ŏnhakwan."

14. The Jurchen referred to Koryŏ as their "father and mother," and in the *Koryŏsa* the Wan-yen clan refers to Koryŏ as *taebang* (great country). Cited in Breuker, "Koryŏ as an Independent Realm," 27n34.

15. Ro, "Koryŏ sidae ŭi tawŏnjŏk ch'ŏnhakwan kwa Haedong Ch'ŏnja." The *akji* section of the *Koryŏsa* includes three types of music: *aak*, ritual music in the "authentic" style; *tangak*, music originating from Tang and Song; and *sogak*, folk songs sometimes referred to as *hyangak*.

16. In that sense, the Chinese emperor was *haesŏ ch'ŏnja*, the emperor of the West (of the Sea). Ch'u Myŏng-yŏp, *Han'guksa yŏn'gu*, no. 129 (2005).

17. Sem Vermeersch, *The Power of the Buddhas: The Politics of Buddhism During the Koryŏ Dynasty* (Cambridge: Harvard University Asia Center, 2008), 83–84.

18. See Yi Pyŏng-do, *Koryŏ sidae ŭi yŏn'gu: T'ŭkhi chiri toch'am sasang ŭi palchŏn ŭl chungsim ŭro* (1954; Seoul: Asea munhwasa, 1980), cited in Breuker, "Koryŏ as an Independent Realm," 83n121.

19. At the beginning of the Chosŏn dynasty, similar geomantic considerations prompted Yi Sŏng-gye to move the capital from Kaesŏng to present-day Seoul.

20. Breuker, "Koryŏ as an Independent Realm," 78n73.

21. Ro, "Koryŏ sidae ŭi tawŏnjŏk ch'ŏnhakwan kwa Haedong Ch'ŏnja," 14–16.

22. As the crown prince, Ch'ungnyŏl was married to a daughter of Khubilai Khan, the founder of the Yüan dynasty. On Koryŏ as a son-in-law state, see Hyŏn-ku Min, "Koryŏ Politics under Mongol Control: Dynastic Continuity During the Period of Royal Absence," *International Journal of Korean History* 1 (2000).

23. Among Chosŏn dynasty monarchs, Sejo was the only king to personally conduct sacrifices to Heaven at the *wŏndan*. In the case of other early Chosŏn monarchs, during times of severe drought the *sadaebu* acquiesced only to the extent of allowing the king to send one of the state councilors to offer prayers at the *wŏndan*. Pokee Sohn, *Social History of the Early Chosŏn Dynasty: The Functional Aspects of Governmental Structure* (Seoul: Jisik-sanup Publications, 2000).

24. Cho Chun-ha, "Uri nara ŭi chesa munhwa wa chongmyo taeje," *Han'guk sasang kwa munhwa* 12 (2001), 320.

25. This *wŏndan* seems to have been located in present-day Hannam-dong, in Seoul.

26. Hwanggung'u, the structure that remains today, was built in 1899 to house the tablets used in sacrifices to Heaven.

27. *T'aejo sillok*, 1-kwŏn, 1-nyŏn (1392), 8/11, second article. Kuksa pyŏnch'an wiwŏnhoe: http://sillok.history.go.kr/main/main.jsp.

28. Tan'gun named the state he founded (purportedly in the area around Pyongyang) Chosŏn. Historians today refer to this state as Ancient Chosŏn, but there is insufficient archaeological evidence that Ancient Chosŏn actually existed. On Tan'gun and Kija worship, see Han Young-woo, "Kija Worship in the Koryŏ and Early Yi Dynasties: A Cultural Symbol in the Relationship between Korea and China," *The Rise of Neo-Confucianism in Korea*, ed. W. M. Theodore de Bary and JaHyun Kim Haboush (New York: Columbia University Press, 1985). The best known account of Tan'gun appears in the *Samguk yusa* (Memorabilia of the Three Kingdoms) written by the Buddhist monk Iryŏn (1206–89). Iryŏn writes that in the fiftieth year of the Emperor Yao, Tan'gun established a walled city at Pyongyang and called his country Chosŏn. He then moved the capital to Asadal, where he ruled for 1,500 years. When the king of Zhou enfeoffed Jizi (K: Kija) to Chosŏn, Tan'gun went into the mountains and became a mountain god at the age of 1,908. See Iryŏn, *Samguk yusa* (Seoul: Sŏjŏng Sihak, 2009).

29. Cho Pak memorialized, "Because wŏndan is a sacrificial ritual to Heaven that [only] the Son of Heaven conducts, we request that this ritual be stopped." *T'aejo sillok*, 1-kwŏn, 1-nyŏn (1392), 8/11, second article.

30. According to John Duncan, the capital-based scholar-officials who helped bring Yi Sŏng-gye to power constituted a central aristocracy that had developed a consciousness of themselves as a distinct class toward the end of the Koryŏ period. Using self-identifying terms like *sadaebu*, *sajok*, and *yangban*, this scholar-official class was very conscious of the fact that their power and prestige flowed from their status as officials of the dynastic bureaucracy. The Chosŏn settlement thus dismantled Koryŏ's *hyangni*-based territorial status system by curtailing *hyangni* participation in the central bureaucracy and by putting an end to the Koryŏ monarchic practice of delegating power to foreign retainers, slaves, and eunuchs. John Duncan, *The Origins of the Chosŏn Dynasty* (Seattle: University of Washington Press, 2000).

31. Cho Chun-ha, "Uam Song Si-yŏl ŭi chuch'e ŭisik," *Han'guk sasang kwa munhwa* 42 (2008).

32. On the question of how Song Si-yŏl came to be identified as the central figure behind Punish the Qing, see Im Pu-yŏn. "Yuggyo ŭiryehwa ŭi chŏngchihak: Mandongmyo wa Taebodan ŭr chungsim ŭro," *Chonggyo munhwa pip'yŏng* 15 (2009), 159–84.

33. Adam Clarence Immanuel Bohnet, "Migrant and Border Subjects in Late Chosŏn," Ph.D. dissertation, University of Toronto, 2008, 184–86. As Bohnet points out, this line of argument—that Ming loyalist ritualism aimed to elevate the Chosŏn dynastic state, not China or the defunct Ming dynasty—appears most forcefully in Chŏng Okcha, *Chosŏn hugi Chosŏn Chunghwa sasang yŏn'gu* (Seoul: Ilchisa, 1998).

34. Gari Ledyard, "Hong Taeyong and His Impressions of China in the Year 1766: A Korean Intellectual's Appraisal," lecture given at the University of Michigan, November 2, 2000. Also, Gari Ledyard, "Hong Taeyong and His *Peking Memoir*," *Korean Studies* 6 (1982).

35. James Hevia makes use of the concepts of deterritorialization and reterritorialization to explain how and to what extent British imperialism in nineteenth-century China was above all a pedagogic project. As theorized by Gilles Deleuze and Félix Guattari in *Anti-Oedipus*, deterritorialization refers to how Oedipal capitalism transgresses and destroys territorial limits, the centralizing polity, and feudal hierarchical channels and sets adrift desire. Reterritorialization refers to how production is channeled into commodity form, and desire is concentrated into a neurotic (privatized) father-mother-me. Similarly, from the whipping of Korean criminals (until 1920) to the implementation of bureaucratic rationality, Japanese colonialism was a transgressive and "pedagogic" effort that sought to channel desire and obtain a sufficient degree of acquiescence from the colonized. See James L. Hevia, *English Lessons: The Pedagogy of Imperialism in Nineteenth-Century China* (Durham: Duke University Press, 2003).

36. Kuroda Kiyotaka was the ambassador plenipotentiary at the time, and Inoue Kaoru was the vice envoy. See Martina Deuchler, *Confucian Gentlemen and Barbarian Envoys: The Opening of Korea, 1875–1885* (Seattle: University of Washington Press, 1977).

37. See Yur-bok Lee, "Establishment of a Korean Legation in the United States, 1887–1890," *Illinois Papers in Asian Studies* 3 (1983). In treaties and other legal documents, and as cited here, *sokkuk* or *sokbang* is translated as *dependency*. Elsewhere, I translate *sokkuk* or *sokbang* as *vassal state*.

38. Quoted in Deuchler, *Confucian Gentlemen and Barbarian Envoys*, 119.

39. Alexis Dudden, "Japan's Engagement with International Terms," *Tokens of Exchange: The Problem of Translation in Global Circulations*, ed. Lydia H. Liu (Durham: Duke University Press, 1999). See also Alexis Dudden, *Japan's Colonization of Korea: Discourse and Power* (Honolulu: University of Hawaii Press, 2005).

40. Lewis Lancaster reminds us that "China" of the fourth century CE was dominated by the Han in the south, but northern "China" was dominated by Turkic nomadic kingdoms. Lewis R. Lancaster, introduction to *Buddhism in Koryŏ: A Royal Religion*, ed. Lewis R. Lancaster, Kikun Suh, and Chai-Shin Yu (1996; Fremont, Calif: Asian Humanities Press, 2002).

41. Vermeersch, *The Power of the Buddhas*, 42.

42. Even during the Chosŏn period, when Buddhist institutions not only lost state patronage but were driven from the capital and other urban centers, Buddhism in Korea retained its *hoguk pulgyo* (literally, safeguard-the-state Buddhism) character. See Robert Buswell, "Buddhism in Korea," *Buddhism and Asian History*, ed. Joseph M. Kitagawa and Mark D. Cummings (New York: Macmillan, 1989).

43. Buswell, "Buddhism in Korea." Iryŏn recorded in the *Samguk yusa* (Memorabilia of the Three Kingdoms) that "Hwanin, the Celestial Emperor (Hwanin means Chesŏk), sent down his son, Hwanung, to the peak of T'aebaeksan with three heavenly seals and three thousand followers to rule over the people." In writing the *Samguk yusa*, Iryŏn drew from earlier histories like *Tan'gun kogi*, but those earlier histories are not extant.

44. The inscription was for Kŭngyang (878–956), the founder (*kaesanjo*) of Paengŏm-sa. See "Pongam-sa Chŏngjin taesa pimyŏng (965)," *Yŏkchu namal yŏcho kŭmsŏngmun*, ed. Han'guk yŏksa yŏn'guhoe (Seoul: Hyean, 1996), 270, translated by Sem Vermeersch and cited in *The Power of the Buddhas*, 265.

45. Vermeersch, *The Power of the Buddhas*, 265.

46. My discussion of Confucian ritual and the disavowal of Buddhism in the Chosŏn period is indebted to Martina Deuchler's seminal work *The Confucian Transformation of Korea: A Study of Society and Ideology* (Cambridge: Council on East Asian Studies, Harvard University, 1992). On affective relations, see Jahyun Kim Haboush, "Filial Emotions and Filial Values: Changing Patterns in the Discourse of Filiality in Late Chosŏn Korea," *Harvard Journal of Asiatic Studies* 55, no. 1 (1995).

47. Ledyard, "Hong Taeyong and His Impressions of China in the Year 1766."

48. Andre Schmid, "Tributary Relations and the Qing-Chosŏn Frontier on

Mount Paektu," *The Chinese State at the Borders*, ed. Diana Lary (Vancouver: UBC Press, 2008), 132.

49. Andre Schmid, *Korea between Empires, 1895–1919* (New York: Columbia University Press, 2002), 206–11.

50. Che-ga Pak, "Chonju ron," *Pukhak ŭi, oep'yŏn, Chŏngyugak chŏnjip*, 2 (Seoul: Yŏgang ch'ulp'ansa, 1986), 463–66, translated by Martina Deuchler, *Sources of Korean Tradition*, ed. Yŏngho Ch'oe et al. (New York: Columbia University Press, 2000), 2:102.

51. Si-yŏl Song, *Songja taejŏn*, vol. 5, cited in Tae-yong Huh, "A Critical Review on the Issue of Proto-Nationalism During Late Chosŏn," *International Journal of Korean History* 12 (August 2008), 97.

52. Huh, "A Critical Review on the Issue of Proto-Nationalism during Late Chosŏn," 98.

53. The requisition of boys and girls as tribute was a practice that began with the Yüan.

54. See Peter Yun, "Rethinking the Tribute System: Northeast Asian Interstate Relations, 600–1600," Ph.D. dissertation, UCLA.

55. Widely reported cases of cannibalism indicate the magnitude of human suffering and physical destruction wrought by the Hideyoshi invasions (Imjin Wars, 1592–98) and the extent to which Chosŏn's political and social systems of control had collapsed. With arable land reduced to one-third the area of the pre–Imjin War period, due mostly to conscription of men and the displacement of people from the land, the reduced yields in harvested grain simply could not support the armies and the population. *Sŏnjo sillok* records cases of people eating the flesh of those who had starved to death (including reports of numerous bodies in the streets of the capital with their flesh hacked away) and active cannibalism, "even cases of father and sons, and brothers, killing and eating each other." *Sŏnjo sillok*, 49-kwŏn, 27-nyŏn (1594), 3, cited in Yi Chang-hŭi, "Oeran chung ŭi sahoesang," *Han'guksa* (Seoul: Kuksa p'yŏnchan wiwŏnhoe, 1995), 29:145–47. During the first Hideyoshi invasion, after King Sŏnjo (r. 1567–1608) and his ministers fled the capital to the jeers of the residents, slaves (*nobi*) in the capital seized the opportunity to burn the slave registers (and perhaps the Royal Ancestral Temples too). There were a number of other slave revolts during the Imjin Wars. Moreover many peasants in Kyŏngsang Province who aided the Hideyoshi armies seemed to have agreed with the charge that their king was tyrannical, and the participation of a number of Righteous Army commanders in rebellions led by Song Yu-jin and Yi Mong-hak to overthrow the Chosŏn dynasty suggest how much effort the dynasty had to exert to reestablish control and legitimacy after these wars. The "Confucianization" of Chosŏn society during the seventeenth century must be understood in this context. The denunciation of uxorilocal residence and the reorganization of Chosŏn society on the basis of the patrilineal descent group (that is, the attempt to reestablish masculine identity in the form of Confucian patriarchy) were part and parcel of the frantic but concerted and sustained attempts on the part of the Yi monarchy

and the *yangban* in the countryside to reestablish control over life (and memory), labor, and language — especially discourses that we would recognize as didactic narratives on masculine as well as feminine identity.

56. On the different intellectual reactions to Ming's demise, see JaHyun Kim Haboush, "Constructing the Center: The Ritual Controversy and the Search for a New Identity in Seventeenth-Century Korea," *Culture and the State in Late Chosŏn Korea*, ed. JaHyun Kim Haboush and Martina Deuchler (Cambridge: Harvard University Asia Center, 1999).

57. After the general breakdown of political and social control following the Hideyoshi (late sixteenth century) and Manchu (early seventeenth century) invasions, the literati in the countryside (*sarim*) had to organize local structures that could maintain their own status identity and self-discipline and provide welfare for and moral leadership over both commoners and slaves through the establishment of community compacts (*hyangyak*), communal granaries, rosters of local residents (*hyangan*), and so on.

58. According to Michael Rogers, the concept of Korea as a "Small China" first appeared during the Koryŏ period.

59. Pak Chi-wŏn's *Yŏrha ilgi* is a record of the embassy that Pak accompanied to the seventieth birthday celebrations of the Qianlong emperor in his summer palace. This book is a composite and contains essays on religion, science, and philosophy. See Pak Chi-wŏn, *Yŏrha ilgi*, translated (into contemporary Korean) and edited by Kim Hyŏl-cho (Kyŏnggi-do P'asju-si: Tolbegae, 2009).

60. Although Hong Tae-yong was born into a prestigious *yangban* family at the center of power (Noron), he disputed the orthodox view that science and technology were marginal branches of knowledge. Hong rated Western science and technology superior to anything created during the Tang or Sung periods. He took a deep interest in studies of the earth's rotation, eclipses, and mathematics too. See Hong Tae-yong, *Sinp'yŏn kugyŏk Hong Tae-yong Tamhŏnsŏ* (Kyŏnggi-do Paju-si: Han'guk Haksul Chŏngbo, 2008).

61. In 1876 Inoue was the deputy envoy sent to Chosŏn to negotiate the Kanghwa Treaty, Korea's first "modern" treaty. In 1882, after the *emeute* during which mutinous Korean soldiers killed forty Japanese residents and burned down the Japanese legation, it was Inoue who supervised the conclusion of the Treaty of Chemulp'o that gave Japan the right to station a company of soldiers in the capital. In 1884, after the failure of the Kapsin coup attempt in which Korean "reformers" with ties to Japan tried to seize power, Inoue personally signed the Treaty of Seoul, wherein Korea had to send a letter of apology to Japan for the deaths of Japanese who were killed in the aftermath of the failed coup attempt. Korea was also made to pay 110,000 yen in indemnities. In 1884 Japan was unwilling to go to war with China over Korea, and for ten years, 1885–94, Chinese interference in Korea increased to a level not seen since the early years of the Qing dynasty (1644–1912). Inoue also sponsored the Convention of Tientsin, signed in 1885 by Li Hongzhang and Itō Hirobumi, that became the basis of the Sino-Japanese cooperation for a de-

cade, from 1885 to 1894. It is significant that in the Convention of Tientsin, Li was not able to induce Itō to acknowledge China's suzerainty over the peninsula.

62. See Young Ick Lew, "Minister Inoue Kaoru and the Japanese Reform Attempts in Korea During the Sino-Japanese War, 1894–1895," *Journal of Asiatic Studies* 27, no. 2 (1984).

63. Lew, "Minister Inoue Kaoru and the Japanese Reform Attempts in Korea During the Sino-Japanese War," 163.

64. Yi T'ae-jin argues that in the 1870s, King Kojong adopted a reformist vision exemplified by the concept Kunmin ilch'e (the ruler and his people as one body). Kojong's historical model was King Chŏngjo the Great (1776–1800), and even during the years of Yuan Shikai's dominance (1882–94), Kojong steadily pursued modernizing reforms. See Yi T'ae-jin, *Kojong sidae ŭi chae-chomyŏng* (Seoul: T'aehaksa, 2000).

65. Shin, Yong-ha. "The Revolutionary Movement of the Tonghak Peasant Army of 1894: Seen vis-à-vis the French Revolution," *Korea Journal* 29, no. 10 (1989).

66. Historically, because the *sadaebu* (or *yangban*) checked the power of the monarchy at every turn, Chosŏn monarchs tended to favor more egalitarian policies, policies that would safeguard the throne while weakening the power and privilege of the *yangban* class.

67. It can be argued that the de-centering of China, as described by Andre Schmid, was the denouement of anti-Chinese sentiments that had been accumulating since 1882. See Schmid, *Korea between the Empires*. As for the Sino-Japanese War, Yi T'ae-jin argues that it was at the bidding of Yuan Shikai that King Kojong formally requested military assistance from China to pacify the Tonghak insurgents, allowing prime minister Itō Hirobumi and foreign minister Mutsu Munemitsu to send Japanese troops to Korea. See Yi, *Kojong sidae ŭi chae-chomyŏng*.

68. Yu Kil-chun, *Sŏyu kyŏnmun: Chosŏn chisigin Yu Kil-chun, Sŏyang ŭl pŏnyŏk hada*, translated into contemporary Korean by Hŏ Kyŏng-jin (Seoul: Sŏhae munjip, 2004). In the spring of 1881, at the age of twenty-six, Yu Kil-chun accompanied the Inspection Mission to Japan (*chosa sach'aldan*) and with the permission and support of the Chosŏn court stayed behind to study at Fukuzawa Yukichi's Keio Gijuku. He was, in that sense, the first Korean student in Japan. At Keio Gijuku, Yu read Fukuzawa's *Seiyo jijo* (Conditions in the West, 1867). Returning to Korea in 1883, Yu continued to correspond with Fukuzawa and Inoue Kaoru. He translated Fukuzawa's *Moji no oshie*, a text on *kanji* reform. He helped establish *Hansŏng sunbo*, Korea's first newspaper. In 1884 he accompanied the first diplomatic mission King Kojong sent to the United States. He again stayed behind to study, first with E. S. Morse and then at the Governor Dummer Academy and Boston University. He traveled in Europe, Southeast Asia (Singapore and Hong Kong), and Japan and returned to Korea in December 1885. Under house arrest, he wrote *Sŏyu kyŏnmun* in mixed script. Begun in 1887, the manuscript was completed in 1889; it was published by a Japanese press in 1895. Released from detention in 1892, Yu held a number of high offices during the Kabo reforms, including minister of home affairs. In

1896, after King Kojong took refuge at the Russian Legation, Yu, implicated in the murder of Queen Min, was forced into exile.

69. "Nonsŏ Il-choyak kaejŏngan" (A Proposal for Revising Our Treaty with Japan), saŭi (opinion), *Hanyang chubo*, May 24, 1886.

70. See Joshua John Van Lieu, "Divergent Visions of Serving the Great: The Emergence of Chosŏn-Qing Tributary Relations," Ph.D. dissertation, University of Washington, 2010.

71. In the seventeenth century, even when the Chosŏn court and much of the scholar-official class entertained hopes of "punishing" the Manchus who had overthrown the Ming, they did so with the idea of restoring the Ming to power. Until Japan's victory in the first Sino-Japanese War, the vast majority of Chosŏn scholar-officials would have found it hard to imagine Korea completely separated, politically and culturally, from China.

72. The following day, as was customary, Kojong made the same pledge at the Altars of Land and Harvest. George A. Lensen, in an otherwise carefully documented history of imperialist rivalry in late nineteenth-century Korea, mistakenly states that King Kojong inaugurated the new policy (of independence) on January 7 at the "ancestral tombs," and that he repeated the oaths at the "shrine of his ancestors" the following day. Lensen also describes the January 7 Oath as a "festive declaration" but does not cite his source. See George Alexander Lensen, *Balance of Intrigue: International Rivalry in Korea and Manchuria, 1884–1899* (Tallahassee: University Press of Florida, 1982), 2:522.

73. See Kim To-hyŏng, "Han'guk kŭndaesa ŭi chaju, tongnip ŭi ŭimi," *Yŏksa pip'yŏng* 29 (May 1995), 179. Article 1 of the Treaty of Kanghwa, signed in 1876 by representatives of the Chosŏn and Meiji governments, stated that Korea was an independent state with the same sovereign rights as Japan. But this did not sever Chosŏn's tributary ties to China.

74. In the *Chosŏn wangjo sillok* the word *tongnip* typically referred to a person who stands alone, or is able to stand alone, keeping his own counsel, as in "tongnip pulgu tunse pulmin" (to stand alone without fear, shunning the world without anxiety). See *Sukjong sillok*, 10-kwŏn, 6-nyŏn (1680), 8/14, first article. Sometimes *tongnip* implied being different, or isolated. See, for example *Sŏngjong sillok*, 104-kwŏn, 10-nyŏn (1479), 5/5, third article; *Chungjong sillok*, 21-kwŏn, 9-nyŏn (1514), 10/3, third article; and *Yŏngjo sillok*, 53-kwŏn, 17-nyŏn (1741), 5/22, first article. *Tongnip* could also be used in reference to a local administrative unit, like a county seat, that is, to make it a separate unit. See *Kwanghae'gun ilgi*, 25-kwŏn, 2-nyŏn (1610), 2/7, sixth article.

75. Lew, "Minister Inoue Kaoru and the Japanese Reform Attempts in Korea During the Sino-Japanese War," 163.

76. Having "stolen the jewel" (the Meiji emperor), restoration activists like Ōkubo Toshimichi did not envisage Emperor Meiji's political authority as going beyond the consensus of those who led the struggle against the *bakufu*. The realm (Japan as a whole) belonged to the emperor, but it was to be "publicly admin-

istered" by those who had led the anti-*bakufu* struggle. Participation in politics would be expanded, and yet, as an ethical and sacred duty, all subjects were to submit voluntarily to the will of the emperor. Such an arrangement would provide the leaders of the restoration movement with maximum political authority and justification for suppressing opposition to the new regime. See H. D. Harootunian, *Toward Restoration: The Growth of Political Consciousness in Tokugawa Japan* (Berkeley: University of California Press, 1970).

77. Mutsu Munemitsu, *Kenkenroku: The Memoirs of Count Mutsu Munemitsu*, trans. Gorden M. Berger (Tokyo: University of Tokyo Press, 1982), 29–30.

78. For an English translation of the Oath, see Spencer J. Palmer, ed., *Korean-American Relations: Documents Pertaining to the Far Eastern Diplomacy of the United States*, vol. 2, *The Period of Growing Influence, 1887–1895* (Berkeley: University of California Press, 1963), 350–51.

79. The other public holidays were Sundays, New Year's Eve, and the first three days of the year.

80. Diplomatic practices were largely standardized at the Congress of Vienna (1814–15).

81. F. H. Hinsley, *Sovereignty*, 2nd edition (Cambridge: Cambridge University Press, 1986), 26.

82. Anthony Giddens, *The Nation-State and Violence* (Berkeley: University of California Press, 1987), 263.

83. Stephen D. Krasner, *Sovereignty: Organized Hypocrisy* (Princeton: Princeton University Press, 1999).

84. Krasner, *Sovereignty*, 24.

85. One inequality that irked Western diplomats in Hanyang (especially on rainy days) was not being able to ride in a sedan chair within the walls of the main palace, as the Chinese minister did. Western diplomats again and again demanded that they too be allowed to ride on sedan chairs within the palace walls. Muddy boots notwithstanding, it is safe to say that Western diplomats were obsessed with rituals and symbols of equality among themselves and in relation to China's power over Korea. One of the first Kabo reforms that passed was legislation that allowed Western diplomats to ride in sedan chairs within the palace walls, while discouraging all Koreans from riding in sedan chairs at all.

86. This was a consistent theme in Fukuzawa's *Gakumon no Susume* (An Encouragement of Learning), published in seventeen volumes between 1872 and 1876. See Yukichi Fukuzawa, *An Encouragement of Learning*, trans. David A. Dilworth and Umeyo Hirano (Tokyo: Sophia University Press, 1969).

87. According to Young Ick Lew, Inoue Kaoru probably gave up on this plan to abolish the Korean legation in the United States out of fear that the United States would see this step as a conspiracy, as the first step toward transforming Korea into a Japanese protectorate. See Lew, "Minister Inoue Kaoru and the Japanese Reform Attempts in Korea During the Sino-Japanese War," 165.

88. John M. B. Sill, U.S. legation in Seoul, letter to the secretary of state, Janu-

ary 4, 1895, in *Korean-American Relations: Documents Pertaining to the Far Eastern Diplomacy of the United States*, vol. 2, ed. Spencer J. Palmer (Berkeley: University of California Press, 1963), 259. Maintaining an embassy in Washington, D.C., and having Korean ambassadors received by U.S. officials were more than just hallmarks of sovereign status. King Kojong (and Inoue Kaoru) knew very well that diplomatic practices peculiar to Western diplomacy (for example, ballroom dancing) themselves produce power relations. Like Chosŏn dynastic rituals, maintaining an embassy in Washington and having Chosŏn diplomats recognized as such were indispensable to constituting King Kojong as Korea's sovereign in the nation-state system. On the topic of Western diplomats' fixation on rituals, see James L. Hevia, *Cherishing Men from Afar: Qing Guest Ritual and the Macartney Embassy of 1793* (Durham: Duke University Press, 1995).

89. The British were, at this time, backers of the Qing government. Because they enjoyed paramount influence over the Chinese government, it was logical for the British to support Chinese actions in Korea—and this they did until the outbreak of the Sino-Japanese War, when they stood by watching the Chinese Army and Navy get decimated.

90. See Deuchler, *Confucian Gentlemen and Barbarian Envoys*, 109–27.

91. Commodore Shufeldt saw himself as replicating the feat of Commodore Perry, who "opened up" Japan decades earlier. The treaty itself was signed in Korea at Chemulp'o (now Inch'ŏn).

92. Kwŏn Hyŏk-su, *19-segi mal Han-Chung kwan'gyesa yŏn'gu* (Seoul: Paeksan charyowŏn, 2000).

93. In 1887 King Kojong appointed Pak Chong-yang as minister plenipotentiary to the United States, even in the face of Yuan Shikai and Li Hongzhang's censure. Pak presented his credentials to President Grover Cleveland on January 17, 1888. King Kojong knew well that maintaining a diplomatic presence in Washington would minimize China's claim of suzerainty over Korea and bolster "international" recognition of his sovereign status.

94. See Deuchler, *Confucian Gentlemen and Barbarian Envoys*, 118–19. The Treaty of Amity and Commerce in 1882 granted the United States extraterritoriality, low tariffs, and the right to establish a legation in the capital.

95. In the Taft-Katsura secret protocol, the United States recognized Japan's paramount political, military, and economic interests in Korea, while Japan recognized America's control over the Philippines. Although the American legation was recalled, American missionaries, American investment, and American institutions (hospitals, schools) remained, and according to inclination and circumstance, Americans offered both endorsement and censure of Japanese colonial policies.

96. It is relevant to recall Harry Harootunian's observation about Meiji Japan, that that kind of expertise and competence could do little to mediate the gap between imperial authority and the worlds of communal life, tutelary deities, and ancestors. See Harry Harootunian, *Things Seen and Unseen: Discourse and Ideology in Tokugawa Nativism* (Chicago: University of Chicago Press, 1988), 405–406.

97. Mutsu, *Kenkenroku*, 111.

98. Mutsu wrote *Kenkenroku* in the months immediately following the conclusion of the Sino-Japanese War (1894–95), when the government came under ferocious public criticism that weak diplomacy had lost what was gained on the battlefields of Chosŏn Korea. In *Kenkenroku*, Mutsu defended the government's decision to accept the "advice" of Russia, Germany, and France (the Triple Intervention) to retrocede the Liatung Peninsula.

99. Mutsu, *Kenkenroku*, 111–12.

100. Among other restrictions, King Kojong should have abstained from sex for several days. In that sense, the sacrifice to ancestors involves "giving up," in the form of ritual restrictions, as much as "giving to."

101. The ghosts of dead Chosŏn dynasty kings and queens enter the *chŏngjŏn* through the southern gate (*sinmun*) and proceed up the central stone pathway or stairway. The two stone terraces (*woldae*) are together 150 meters long and 100 meters wide. The two orchestras perform separately. Both orchestras have a set of bells, a set of L-shaped stone chimes, a set of metal chimes, a bamboo flute, a *tangp'iri* (similar to an oboe), a *changgu* (hourglass drum), a *chuk* (wooden box mortar), and a *pak* (wooden clapper). The orchestra on the upper *wŏldae* would also have the *ajaeng* (bowed zither) and *chŏlgo* (drum), while the orchestra on the lower *wŏldae* would have the *t'aepyŏngso*, *haegŭm* (two-string instrument), and *chingo* (a different barrel drum).

102. The central gate in the south wall (*sinmun*) is only for the dead. Not even the king can pass through it.

103. The classic writings of anthropologists like Mary Douglas, Clifford Geertz, and Victor Turner agree on the notion that rituals are communicative and expressive. In his essay on the Balinese cockfight, for example, Geertz stressed that the cockfight is not a depiction of "how things literally are among men, but, what is almost worse, of how, from a particular angle, they imaginatively are." Clifford Geertz, "Notes on the Balinese Cockfight," *The Interpretation of Cultures* (New York: Basic Books, 1973), 446.

104. It should be noted that at the beginning of the Chosŏn period there was widespread resistance to the regulation of domestic ritual life. As part of a concerted attempt to rectify ritual practices among the *sadaebu*, scholar-officials were ordered to establish ancestral shrines in their homes and to eschew Buddhist or shamanistic rituals. See Deuchler, *The Confucian Transformation of Korea*, 182.

105. That is to say, the king and the *sadaebu* sought to monopolize the production of ideas, values, and mores, just as they controlled ritual life in Chosŏn Korea.

106. This insight concerning the ambiguity of authorship in ritual action comes from Caroline Humphrey and James Laidlaw, *The Archetypal Actions of Ritual: A Theory of Ritual Illustrated by the Jain Rite of Worship* (Oxford: Clarendon Press, 1994). Building on Maurice Merleau-Ponty's argument that normal human action is intrinsically intentional (every movement is, indissolubly, movement and consciousness of movement) and that the subject is apprehended as both subject and

object (one "sees," "suffers," and also apprehends oneself as seeing and suffering), Humphrey and Laidlaw argue that actors in ritual are, and are not, the authors of their acts.

107. To make such a momentous oath, tradition dictated that King Kojong visit the dynastic temple on the Winter Solstice, the twenty-fifth day of the eleventh month in the lunar calendar, or December 22, 1894.

108. See *Kojong sillok*, 32-kwŏn, 31-nyŏn (1894), 11/26, first article.

109. This short-lived empire took its name, Han, from the three Han regions (Mahan, Chinhan, and Pyŏnhan) of the pre–Three Kingdoms period, an area roughly coterminous with modern South Korea, on the presumption that these ancestors, organized in small polities ruled by hereditary chiefs, had maintained their independence during the period when Han Chinese commandaries had controlled much of Manchuria and the northern half of the peninsula—Xuantu (K: Hyŏndo), Lelang (K: Nangnang), Lintun (K: Imdun), and Chenfan (K: Chinbŏn).

110. Prasenjit Duara makes a similar argument in *Sovereignty and Authenticity: Manchukuo and the East Asian Modern* (Lanham, Md.: Rowman and Littlefield, 2003).

2. Imperialism and Nationalism

1. The source of this chapter's epigraph is *The Chicago Record's History of the World's Fair* (Chicago: Chicago Daily News Co., 1893), 224.

2. King Kojong's queries were quite interesting: How many countries participated? How large was the Korean pavilion in meters? How did the fairgoers respond to the Korean goods that were displayed, and what was their value in U.S. dollars? Unable to provide the measurements in the metric system, Commissioner Chŏng replied that the Korean pavilion was six to seven *kan* across (that is, about twenty meters across). See *Kojong sillok*, 30-kwŏn, 30-nyŏn (1893), 11/9, first article. The U.S. Treasury Department valued the Korean products at $506. See Youngna Kim, *20th Century Korean Art* (London: Laurence King, 2005), 61n20.

3. Arriving in 1884, Horace Newton Allen was the first American missionary in Korea. In 1887 he accompanied Korea's diplomatic mission to Washington, D.C. For the World's Fair in Chicago, King Kojong asked Allen to help with the arrangements and to escort the Korean Commission. It could well be that Allen was the author (or translator or editor) of the sign over the Korea Exhibit.

4. Sarah Whatmore offers a succinct account of how the autonomous subject came to be privileged in the West: John Locke regarded the individual good as the result of voluntary transactions between independent agents; after Immanuel Kant, the figure of the autonomous subject became central to the social contract tradition of ethics. In this tradition, social institutions of contract (market) and rights (law) formed the basis for establishing universal (impartial) "laws of reason" as the precondition for ethical agency. As Whatmore points out, this autonomous subject constituted as a rights-bearing citizen possessing ethical agency was mas-

culine in conception. Citing Carole Pateman, Whatmore writes, "This has translated at different time-places into the dispossession of women, poor, and black
people of political and ethical agency in their own right, through their 'contractual'
guises as wives, servants, and slaves." Sarah Whatmore, "Dissecting the Autonomous Self: Hybrid Cartographies for a Relational Ethics," *Geographic Thought: A
Praxis Perspective*, ed. George Henderson and Marvin Waterstone (New York: Routledge, 2008), 109–10. As Raymond Williams has pointed out, "Individual originally
meant indivisible." Raymond Williams, "Individual," *Keywords: A Vocabulary of Culture and Society* (London: Fontana, 1983). *Individual* posits distinction from others,
while *indivisibility* is a cornerstone of the notion of sovereignty; thus the relationship between individuality, sovereignty, and ethical agency.

5. See Chong Wha Pyun (Pyŏn Chong-hwa), "The Visit of the Korean Mission
to Boston in 1883 and the Beginning of Scientific and Technological Interactions
between Korea and the United States," *Han'guk kwahak sahakhoeji* 4, no. 1 (1982).
Frederick F. Low served as the American advisor to this goodwill mission. In 1871
Low, as the newly appointed U.S. ambassador to China, along with Rear Admiral
John Rodgers, led five heavily armed warships carrying 1,230 marines and sailors
in what came to be called "America's War with the Hermits." Both Low and Rodgers
staunchly supported the movement to restrict Chinese (Asian) immigration into
the United States. See Gordon H. Chang, "Whose 'Barbarism'? Whose 'Treachery'?
Race and Civilization in the Unknown United States–Korea War of 1871," *Journal of
American History* 89, no. 4 (2003).

6. See Kirk W. Larsen, *Tradition, Treaties, and Trade: Qing Imperialism and Chosŏn
Korea, 1850–1910* (Cambridge: Harvard University Asia Center, Harvard University
Press, 2008), 37, 176–89.

7. Benedict Anderson, *Imagined Communities: Reflections on the Origin and Spread
of Nationalism* (London: Verso, 1983).

8. Lydia Liu, "The Desire for the Sovereign and the Logic of Reciprocity in the
Family of Nations," *Diacritics* 29, no. 4 (1999).

9. Hardt and Negri point out that it was Hegel's conception of sovereignty that
brought together the Hobbes-Rousseau theory of sovereignty and Adam Smith's
theory of value. With that, modern European sovereignty became capitalist sovereignty, "a form of command that overdetermines the relationship between individuality and universality as a function of the development of capital." See Michael
Hardt and Antonio Negri, *Empire* (Cambridge: Harvard University Press, 2000),
83–87.

10. For a concise overview of five centuries of Euro-American colonialism, see
Jürgen Osterhammel, *Colonialism*, trans. Shelley Frisch (Princeton: Markus Wiener,
2005). See also Hardt and Negri, *Empire*, 87; David B. Abernethy, *The Dynamics of
Global Dominance* (New Haven: Yale University Press, 2002), 12–15. According to
Abernethy, at the time of the publication of his book, two-thirds of United Nations
member states were once governed by Euro-Americans, and if China's treaty ports
are included, three-fifths of the world's population.

11. Richard Hughes Seager, *The World's Parliament of Religions: The East/West Encounter, Chicago, 1983* (Bloomington: Indiana University Press, 1995), 11. On December 2, 1893, the *Philadelphia Inquirer* reported that Horace Allen, vice consul general of the United States in Korea, informed the U.S. State Department, "The King of Korea has recently purchased in America an incandescent electric light plant, which is now being installed and will be used for lighting the King's palace and surrounding grounds."

12. William Cronon, *Nature's Metropolis: Chicago and the Great West* (New York: W. W. Norton, 1992), 42.

13. Yun Ch'i-ho seems to have expected the Korean Exhibit to be dismal. About a month before arriving in Chicago he visited the Korean Legation in Washington, D.C. There he saw a photo of the Korean Commission at the World's Fair in Chicago. "On one of the parlor walls there is hung a group picture of the Corean Commission to the World's Fair. I was shocked and disgusted with their looks of supreme stupidity and beastly sensuality. With sad heart I left the room." *Yun Ch'i-ho ilgi* (Seoul: Kuksa py'ŏnchan wiwŏnhoe, 1973–1989), 3:146–47, August 14, 1893.

14. To avoid antagonizing conservatives, the mission was organized and dispatched in secrecy. Twelve midlevel officials and their aides, interpreters, and servants traveled separately to Pusan, and from there took a ship to Nagasaki. Inoue Kaoru arranged their itinerary, which included Kobe, Osaka, Yokohama, and Tokyo. Organizing themselves into different teams, the officials spent seventy days in Japan, met high-ranking officials, inspected government ministries, shipyards, arsenals, schools, industries, hospitals, mints, prisons, and so on, and submitted extensive and detailed reports upon their return.

15. Yun Ch'i-ho had grown up in relative prosperity but with somewhat ambiguous *yangban* status. His father, Yun Ung-ryŏl, was a military official but of *sŏŏl* status (that is, a son of a secondary wife). In 1880 Yun Ung-ryŏl had gone to Japan with Kim Hong-jip to seek advisors to train an elite guard (*pyŏlgigun*) for the palace. Yun Ch'i-ho seems to have been intellectually precocious. According to Lee Kwang-Rin, after six months in Japan Yun Ch'i-ho was able to write freely in Japanese. While studying Japanese at Dōjinsha, he also helped edit *Bungaku zasshi*, a journal that published four of his essays, two written in literary Chinese and two written in Japanese. See Lee Kwang-Rin (Yi Kwang-nin), "Yun Ch'i-ho ŭi Ilbon yuhak," *Tongbang hakji* 59 (1988). Inoue Kaoru, the Japanese foreign minister, had arranged for Yun Ch'i-ho to study at Nakamura Masanao's Dōjinsha.

16. In an essay published in *Tonga ilbo* on January 11, 1930, Yun Ch'i-ho would write that it was Kim Ok-kyun who convinced him to study English because knowledge of English would enable Koreans to "directly import Western civilization." Quoted in Lee Kwang-Rin. "Yun Ch'i-ho ŭi Ilbon yuhak."

17. Minister Foote's full title was American envoy extraordinary and minister plenipotentiary.

18. In hopes of instituting drastic reforms, Kim Ok-kyun, Pak Yŏng-hyo, Hong

Yŏng-sik, Sŏ Kwang-bŏm, and Sŏ Chae-pil staged a coup on December 4, 1884, with support from Japanese troops stationed in the capital. They seized the palace, killed a number of ministers, formed a new government, and proclaimed a reform platform that would abolish class distinctions, restructure the government on the model of Japan's Meiji state, and establish independence for Korea by ending China's interference. The coup ended after three days, when Chinese soldiers intervened. The coup leaders who survived fled to Japan. Yun Ch'i-ho's father, Yun Ung-ryŏl, was banished to Nŭngju.

19. During his year and a half at Vanderbilt, Yun Ch'i-ho read Gibbon, Macaulay, and Carlyle. In 1893 he graduated with a master's degree from Emory College. See Vipan Chandra, *Imperialism, Resistance, and Reform in Late Nineteenth-Century Korea* (Berkeley: Institute of East Asian Studies, University of California, 1988).

20. Tomoko Masuzawa points out that the emergence of the concept of multiple world religions had to do with preserving the status of Christianity as unique and superior. The idea of world religions and the logic of classification it promoted had a determining effect on the study of religion. See Tomoko Masuzawa, *The Invention of World Religions: Or, How European Universalism Was Preserved in the Language of Pluralism* (Chicago: University of Chicago Press, 2005). Though quite inclusive, this World Parliament of Religions did not extend invitations to Sikhs, Native American religious figures, and a host of other religionists.

21. See Judith Snodgrass, *Presenting Japanese Buddhism to the West: Orientalism, Occidentalism, and the Columbian Exposition* (Chapel Hill: University of North Carolina Press, 2003).

22. Yun, *Yun Ch'i-ho ilgi*, entry for September 26, 1893, 3:176.

23. John P. Burris, *Exhibiting Religion: Colonialism and Spectacle at International Expositions* (Charlottesville: University of Virginia Press, 2002), 155.

24. Yun, *Yun Ch'i-ho ilgi*, entry for September 27, 1893, 3:177.

25. Burris, *Exhibiting Religion*, 155.

26. Yun, *Yun Ch'i-ho ilgi*, entry for September 27, 1893, 3:178. Swami Vivekananda introduced Hinduism to the World Parliament of Religions and also spoke on the theme of religious tolerance: "The Christian is not to become a Hindu or a Buddhist, nor a Hindu or a Buddhist to become a Christian. . . . If anybody dreams of the exclusive survival of his own [religion] and the destruction of others, I pity him from the bottom of my heart." Quoted in James Edward Ketelaar, *Of Heretics and Martyrs in Meiji Japan: Buddhism and Its Persecution* (Princeton: Princeton University Press, 1990). Ketelaar cites John Henry Barrows, ed. *The World's Parliament of Religions*, 2 vols. (Chicago: The Parliament Publishing Company, 1893), 1:170–71. Virachand Raghav Gandhi (1864–1901) won the Silver Medal at the World Parliament of Religions. He was a contemporary of Swami Vivekananda and also a friend of Mahatma Gandhi.

27. In his entry of September 24, Yun Ch'i-ho describes, in emotional terms, a joining of hands between John Henry Barrows, chairman of the World Parliament of Religions, and Bishop Benjamin W. Arnett of the African Methodist Episcopal

Church. "Dr. Burrows [sic]. When I saw the eminent Catholic divine join hands with the eloquent Negro Bishop, I could not help saying in my heart 'What God hath joined, let no man part.'" *Yun Ch'i-ho ilgi*, entry for September 24, 1893, 3:170–71.

28. John Henry Barrows (1847–1902) was also head of the First Presbyterian Church of Chicago and a professor of religion at the University of Chicago. Accused of "coquetting with false religions," he noted that the Apostle Paul "was careful to find common ground for himself and his Greek auditors in Athens. . . . [And] as any wise missionary in Bombay or Madras would be glad to gather beneath the shelter of his roof the scholarly and sincere representatives of the Hindu religions, so Christian America invites to the shelter of her hospitable rood, at her grand Festival of Peace, the spiritual leaders of mankind" Barrows, ed. *The World's Parliament of Religions*, 1:3, 27–28. See also Ketelaar, *Of Heretics and Martyrs in Meiji Japan*, 139–41.

29. Yun, *Yun Ch'i-ho ilgi*, entry for October 14, 1893, 3:187–88.

30. My argument here has an affinity with the historical trajectories suggested by Kim Yong-sŏp: relatively more egalitarian and autonomous routes to modernity from below, with peasant rebellions providing the main impetus for progressive change; more exploitative, dependent paths to modernity from above, led by elites like Yun Ch'i-ho, who would ultimately capitulate to imperialist demands. Thus Westernized and Westernizing elites in late nineteenth-century Korea can be located on a historical trajectory that begins in the cultural and political world of the landed class in late Chosŏn, through Westernizing efforts in the late nineteenth century and early twentieth that lead to collaboration and support for the Japanese empire, and then from 1945 onward partnership with the American empire. In other words, I am suggesting a genealogy that connects (Christian) liberal-bourgeois subjectivity in the late nineteenth century with the anticommunist, liberal-bourgeois subjectivity that formed an important political, religious, and class axis around which the South Korean state was established in U.S.-occupied southern Korea. Yun Ch'i-ho first mentions communists in September 1896, while studying French in Paris (*Yun Ch'i-ho ilgi*, 4:291). On Christians and the Korean Production Movement (*mulsan changnyŏ undong*), see Michael E. Robinson, *Cultural Nationalism in Colonial Korea, 1920–1925* (Seattle: University of Washington Press, 1988). See also Pang Kie-chung (Pang Ki-jung), "1930-nyŏndae mulsan changnyŏ undong kwa minjok chabonjuŭi kyŏngje sasang," *Tongbang hakji* 115 (2002). On the Protestant Church, critique of both Marx and the landlord system, and the privileging of small farms (that is, self-cultivating households and capitalist agriculture), see Kie-chung Pang (Pang Ki-jung), "Yi Hun-gu's Agricultural Reform Theory and Nationalist Economic Thought," *Seoul Journal of Korean Studies* 19, no. 1 (2006). On American missionaries and the Protestant denominations' support for the establishment of a separate state in southern Korea, see An Chong-ch'ŏl, "Munmyŏng kaehwa esŏ pan'gong ŭro: Yi Sŭng-man kwa kaesinkyo ŭi kwankye ŭi pyŏnhwa, 1912–1950," *Tongbang hakji* 145 (2009). Regarding Christian anticommunist reaction to the uprising in Taegu in October 1946, see Chŏng T'ae-sik and Yi Ch'ŏl-u,

"Mi'gunchŏnggi wa Taegu 10-wŏl hangjaeng esŏ ŭi kidokkyo chonggyo chidojadŭl ŭi sahoe chŏngch'ijŏk hwaldong kwa yŏkhal ŭi taehan ilkoch'al," *Chiyŏk sahoe yŏn'gu* 14, no. 4 (2006).

31. Robert Rydell, *All the World's a Fair* (Chicago: University of Chicago Press, 1984), 49–50. The Chinese village was built by a private company; Mae Ngai suggests it may have served as an early prototype for Chinese American efforts to develop urban Chinatowns as tourist destinations. Ngai points out that the "marketing of 'Chinese culture' was one of a few spheres of commercial activity available to Chinese Americans during the exclusion era." Mae M. Ngai, "Transnationalism and the Transformation of the 'Other': Response to the Presidential Address," *American Quarterly* 57, no. 1 (2005).

32. The cultural historian Gail Bederman contrasts the spatial configuration of the White City and the Midway Plaisance: "Where the White City spread out in all directions from the Court of Honor, emphasizing the complexity of manly civilization, the Midway's attractions were organized linearly down a broad avenue, providing a lesson in racial hierarchy." Gail Bederman, *Manliness and Civilization: A Cultural History of Gender and Race in the United States, 1880–1917* (Chicago: University of Chicago Press, 1984), 35.

33. Hubert Howe Bancroft, quoted in Rydell, *All the World's a Fair*, 60.

34. Rydell, *All the World's a Fair*, 63, 67.

35. The Meiji government spent about $650,000 to build an exhibit pavilion on the north end of Wooded Island. It seems this high-profile location was set aside for Japan in return for its early and substantial contribution to the Chicago organizers. According to Trumbull White, the Meiji government contributed $630,000, more than any other country. See Trumbull White, *The World's Columbian Exposition, Chicago, 1893* (Philadelphia: P. W. Ziegler, 1893), 542. The exhibit pavilion built on Wooded Island was an imitation of the Phoenix Hall in the Byōdō-in Temple, located in Uji, near Kyōto. The lumber for the wooden structure was prepared in Japan and put together in Chicago. The Japanese pavilion was more than forty times larger than the Korean Exhibit.

36. Louis G. Perez, "Mutsu Munemitsu and the Revision of the 'Unequal' Treaties," Ph.D. dissertation, University of Michigan, 1986, cited in Snodgrass, *Presenting Japanese Buddhism to the West*, 19.

37. See Snodgrass, *Presenting Japanese Buddhism to the West*, 19.

38. Snodgrass, *Presenting Japanese Buddhism to the West*, 19, 179–80.

39. Chicago's population had changed dramatically. In 1890 the number of foreign-born nearly equaled the entire city's population of a decade earlier. In the mid-1890s more Poles, Croatians, Slovakians, Lithuanians, Greeks, Swedes, Norwegians, Dutch, and Danes immigrated to Chicago than to any other U.S. city. The largest percentage of foreign-born remained Irish and German. See Reid Badger, *The Great American Fair: The World's Columbian Exposition and American Culture* (Chicago: N. Hall, 1979), 34.

40. Badger, *The Great American Fair*, 38.

41. Ferdinand L. Barnett, *The Reason Why the Colored American Is Not in the World's Columbian Exposition*, edited by Robert W. Rydell (1893; Chicago: University of Illinois Press, 1999), xlii. Ida B. Wells, the main force behind the publication of this pamphlet, was also the leader of an international campaign against lynching. Barnett and Wells married in 1895, after working together in the boycott and protest against the Columbian Exposition.

42. See Cronon, *Nature's Metropolis*, 42, 349. See also Alan Trachtenberg, *The Incorporation of America: Culture and Society in the Gilded Age* (New York: Hill and Wang, 1982), 213. The Exposition directors took great care in public relations. Photographs of the Exposition do not show farming and working-class families; the crowd is decidedly middle class.

43. Yun, *Yun Ch'i-ho ilgi*, entry for September 24–28, 1893, 3:168–80. Writing about international expositions, Robert Rydell and others have pointed out that these expositions popularized the notion of progress, conceived as "willed national activity to a determined, utopian goal" (*All the World's a Fair*, 2, 46).

44. Euro-American imperialism and the articulation of sovereignty created a complex dynamic within East Asia, ranging from pronouncements of Pan-Asian (racial) solidarity to new forms of racism. After witnessing a white man insulting a Japanese man, Yun Ch'i-ho observed, "The misery is that Japanese and Chinese get maltreated by Americans and Europeans and then go and do likewise to the wretched and slavish Coreans" (*Yun Ch'i-ho ilgi*, entry for October 29, 1893, 3:194).

45. After finishing his studies, Yun Ch'i-ho gave a total of $230 to Warren Candler, president of Emory College, with the request that it be used for missionary work in Korea—the $30 representing one-tenth of his earnings during the summer of 1893.

46. Yun Ch'i-ho fathered twelve children, and they, along with his many nephews, nieces, sons-in-law, and grandchildren, were extraordinarily successful, achieving high-profile careers as politicians, academics, entrepreneurs, artists, and musicians in South Korea (and to some extent in the United States). In Shanghai, while teaching English at the Anglo-Chinese College, Yun married Nora Ma (馬愛芳), an assistant music teacher at the McTyeire Home and School for Girls. With Nora, he had four children: Laura (Pong-hŭi), Allen (Yŏng-sŏn), Candler (Kwang-sŏn), and Helen (Yong-hŭi). When Nora died in 1905, he married Paek Mae-ryŏ, with whom he had eight more children. In 1950, when land reform was to get under way, Allen Yŏng-sŏn Yun was South Korea's minister of agriculture. Yun Po-sŏn, president of South Korea from August 1960 to March 1962, was Yun Ch'i-ho's nephew.

47. On March 28, 1894, Kim Ok-kyun, one of the leaders of the coup attempt in 1884, was assassinated in Shanghai. Yun Ch'i-ho had met him the day before. In his diary entry for March 28, Yun wrote, "As for the why of the thing [Kim Ok-kyun's assassination] it is needless to say that K. O. Q. was baited over here to be gotten rid of." A week later, accompanied by Professor W. B. Bonnell of the Anglo-Chinese College, Yun went to the U.S. Consulate to see if he could be naturalized as a U.S. citizen. He could not. See Yun, *Yun Ch'i-ho ilgi*, 3:302.

48. In April 1896 Yun Ch'i-ho was appointed privy councilor and accompanied

Min Yŏng-hwan to Moscow for the coronation of Tsar Nicholas II. He stayed in Paris for several months and returned to Korea in January 1897.

49. The Anglo-Chinese College was sponsored by the American Methodist Episcopal Church, South. Yun Ch'i-ho converted to Christianity in March 1887.

50. In Shanghai, when Yun Ch'i-ho switched from literary Chinese to Korean, he still dated his entries according to the lunar calendar with the Qing dating system (use of the Qing emperor's reign title) and then an alphabet notation for the Roman weekdays. In Nashville, when Yun switched to English, he also switched his primary dating system to the Gregorian calendar and dropped the Qing dating system. He continued to record lunar dates and notations for the Roman weekdays.

51. As Sidonie Smith and Julia Watson point out, this notion of the sovereign subject emerged from a number of social and philosophical shifts that took place in Europe after the eighteenth century, including the privileging of the liberal-humanist subject, revolutionary movements that pressed for democratization, radical individualism celebrated by Romantic movements, social Darwinism and its emphasis on survival of the fittest, the Industrial Revolution and its myth of the self-made man, history writing centered on the great man, analytical methods used in psychoanalysis to organize self-reflection, and the rise of literacy. Sidonie Smith and Julia Watson, *Reading Autobiography: A Guide for Interpreting Life Narratives*, 2nd edition (Minneapolis: University of Minnesota Press, 2010), 194.

52. William E. Griffis, *A Modern Pioneer in Korea: The Life Story of Henry G. Appenzeller* (New York: Fleming H. Revell, 1912), 189.

53. In 1881 Yu Kil-jun went to Japan, met Fukuzawa Yukichi, and studied for a year at Keio Gijuku. While in Japan, he published an article in Fukuzawa's *Jiji sinpo* on the power of newspapers, and in 1883 he helped with the publication of Korea's first newspaper, *Hansŏng sinbo*. As Ross King points out, Yu is credited with establishing the *kukhanmun* style of writing (mixed Sino-Korean script), drawing on the *ŏnhae-bon* tradition of annotating Confucian and Buddhist texts. Yu also wrote the first grammar of Korean, a work he began in 1895. See Ross King, "Nationalism and Language Reform in Korea: The *Questione della Lingua* in Precolonial Korea," *Nationalism and the Construction of Korean Identity*, ed. Pai Hyung-Il and Timothy R. Tangherlini (Berkeley: Institute of East Asian Studies, University of California, 1998). Yu was also the first Korean to study in the United States; in 1884 he studied at the Governor Dummer Academy and also with Edward Sylvester Morse, who had taught at Tokyo Imperial University from 1887 to 1880.

54. The English name of the newspaper was the *Independent*.

55. Today the Korean alphabet is referred to as *han'gŭl*. But with the installation of the Kabo reform cabinet in 1894, the Korean alphabet came to be designated as Korea's national script: *kungmun*. After 1910, when Japan annexed Korea, the national script in colonial Korea was Japanese. Thus *national script* (*kokubun*) referred to written Japanese during the colonial period, and to avoid confusion Korean intellectuals began to refer to the Korean alphabet as *han'gŭl*.

56. Sŏ Chae-pil actually established *Tongnip sinmun* first. He organized the Inde-

pendence Club in July 1896. Yun Ch'i-ho was at first skeptical of the Independence Club, calling it "a farce." But he soon became an enthusiastic supporter and in 1898 became its president. That same year, when Sŏ returned to the United States, Yun took over management of *Tongnip sinmun*. See Kenneth M. Wells, *New God, New Nation: Protestants and Self-Reconstruction Nationalism in Korea, 1896–1937* (Honolulu: University of Hawaii Press, 1990), 57–58.

57. Sŏ Chae-pil and Yun Ch'i-ho decided to publish the newspaper three times a week in tabloid form: three pages in Korean and one in English. The Korean section was named *Tongnip sinmun*, the English section the *Independent*. Yun left for Russia on April 1, 1896, before the first issue was published. See Chandra, *Imperialism, Resistance, and Reform in Late Nineteenth-Century Korea*, 106.

58. Sŏ Chae-pil [Philip Jaisohn]. "Nonsŏl," *Tongnip sinmun* (April 7, 1896), in *Tongnip sinmun nonsŏljip* (Seoul: Songjae munhwa chaedan ch'ulp'anbu, 1976), 1–2.

59. Sŏ Chae-pil acquired U.S. citizenship in 1888, the first Korean to do so. Sŏ Kwang-bŏm was the second. Like Sŏ Chae-pil, Sŏ Kwang-bŏm sought asylum in the United States after the failed coup attempt in 1884. In 1883 Sŏ Kwang-bŏm had accompanied Min Yŏng-ik's diplomatic mission to the United States. He was the first Korean to travel around the world, returning to Korea in 1884 via Europe on the U.S. naval ship *Trenton*. Sŏ Kwang-bŏm eventually found employment in Washington, D.C., as a translator with the Bureau of Ethnology in the Office of Education (today the U.S. Department of Education). Because of his work with the U.S. government, Sŏ Kwang-bŏm was able to obtain U.S. citizenship in 1892.

60. I am drawing on Paul Ricoeur's discussion of semantic innovation, but not at all in a technical or precise way. I consider semantic innovation simply as a work of synthesis that redescribes reality, creating a new "intelligibility." Productive imagination drives the work of synthesis both at the level of "semantic pertinence" and narrative, but it does not do so willfully, as a writer (translator) pleases. See Paul Ricoeur, *The Rule of Metaphor: Multi-disciplinary Studies of the Creation of Meaning of Language* (Toronto: University of Toronto Press, 1975).

61. I do not think it is necessary to list here all the points of difference between my analysis of how capitalist sovereignty gets articulated in late nineteenth-century Korea and Hardt and Negri's overall argument in *Empire; Multitude: War and Democracy in the Age of Empire* (New York: Penguin Books, 2004); and *Commonwealth* (Cambridge: Belknap Press of Harvard University Press, 2009). Suffice it to say that when I refer to sovereignty as a machine, my analytical focus is on imperialism, the form of rule that preceded empire, that is, capitalist sovereignty rather than imperial sovereignty that is postnational and nonlocalizable. I am sympathetic to Hardt and Negri's deep-rooted belief in the political potentialities of the multitude—thus my focus on "productive imagination," historiography, historical agency, and subject formation—and, I might add, the notion that laughter and happiness in the face of history are appropriate for oppositional politics. The quote is from *Empire*, 87.

62. See note 60 regarding Ricoeur's *The Rule of Metaphor*.

63. I have borrowed this phrase from Yeounsuk Lee, *The Ideology of Kokugo: Na-*

tionalizing Language in Modern Japan, trans. Maki Hirano Hubbard (Honolulu: University of Hawaii Press, 2010), 2.

64. *Ŏnmun* was the Chosŏn literati's designation for vernacular writing using the Korean alphabet created in 1443. They denigrated the Korean alphabet as *ŏnmun* (諺文) because it was used to record what they considered vulgar speech. *Ŏnhanmun* refers to the use of *ŏnmun* and *hanmun* in *ŏnhae-bon* annotations of Confucian and Buddhist texts. *Idumun* refers to the use of certain Chinese characters and their abbreviations to phonetically render Korean words or particles within a basically *hanmun* text. *Hanmun* is Classical Chinese. See King, "Nationalism and Language Reform in Korea," 35–36.

65. *Hyangga* were written down in the Koryŏ period in *hyangch'al*, a vernacular style that used Chinese characters for both their meaning and sound. *Hyangch'al* is considered a subset of *idumun*.

66. Yasuda Hiroshi, "Kindai Nihon ni okeru 'minzoku' kannen no keisei," *Shisō to gendai* 31 (September 1992), cited in Kevin Doak, "Ethnic Nationalism and Romanticism in Early Twentieth-Century Japan," *Journal of Japanese Studies* 22, no. 1 (1996). In this article, Doak also cites Yun Kŏn-ch'a, "Minzoku gensō no satetsu: 'Nihon minzoku' to iu jiko teiji," *Shisō*, no. 834 (December 1993). Contrary to Yasuda, Yun argues that ethnic consciousness (*minzoku ishiki*) was not fully established in Japan until the turn of the twentieth century. For further discussion on national narratives and the ethnic imagination in twentieth-century Japan, see Kevin Doak, "What Is a Nation and Who Belongs?," *American Historical Review* 102, no. 2 (1997).

67. Sin Il-ch'ŏl makes this point: "It must be kept in mind that [the word] 'minjok,' as it is commonly used in our country, is not congruent to either 'nation' or 'race' in English. Rather, it is analogous to 'Volk' or 'Volkschaft' in German." Having attained ethnic homogeneity quite early in its history, Sin argues, the Korean *minjok* or *kyŏre* in premodern times constituted a *chunminjokjŏk kongdongch'e* (a protonational community) comparable to the *Volkschaft*, or to the *narodnosti* as conceptualized in Stalin's later writings on the national question. In an interesting twist, Sin argues that the emergence of modern nationalism (*Gesellschaft*) in Korea was made difficult precisely because traditional society in Korea had such a strong community (*Gemeinschaft*) consciousness. Sin Il-ch'ŏl, "Sin Ch'ae-ho ŭi kŭndae kukkakwan," *Sin Ch'ae-ho*, ed. Kang Man-gil (Seoul: Koryŏ taehakkyo ch'ulp'anbu, 1990), 1–3. See also Joseph Stalin, *Marxism and Linguistics* (New York: International Publishers, 1951).

68. With a similar meaning, *kyŏngje* was also a contraction of *kyŏngguk chese* (經國濟世, manage the state and save mankind). A scholar-official might receive praise for being competent at *kyŏngje*, or statecraft. See, for example, the eulogy for Pak Ŭn in *Sejong sillok*, 18-kwŏn, 4-nyŏn (1422), 10/12, second article. In other words, there was "public" recognition of the fact that the state and its officials were directly involved in the process of surplus extraction—in the form of taxes, tribute in kind, and mobilization of corvée labor—and in rescuing the people.

69. See Wolfgang Lippert, "The Formation and Development of the Term 'Politi-

cal Economy' in Japanese and Chinese," *Mapping Meanings: The Field of New Learning in Late Qing China*, ed. Michael Lackner and Natascha Vittinghoff (Boston: Brill Academic Publishers, 2004).

70. Justin Rosenberg points out that Adam Smith's teacher, Francis Hutcheson, included marital, parental, and master-servant relations under the heading "Principles of Economics." In that sense, Rosenberg argues, "there is nothing in the earlier use of the word (unless it be the hint of a private sphere) which accounts for why it should have come to refer exclusively to market relations. And nothing is explained therefore by using the term 'economic' in its modern sense unless one already assumes (consciously or otherwise) the capitalist relations of production which create its object." Justin Rosenberg, *The Empire of Civil Society: A Critique of the Realist Theory of International Relations* (London: Verso, 1994), 84, 124–26. I thank Monica Kim for referring me to this book.

71. In their memorial to King Sejong, the first objection to ŏnmun raised by Chiphyŏnjŏn (Hall of Worthies) scholars had to do with anxiety about how Chosŏn would be perceived in China once it became known that they had begun using ŏnmun. See *Sejong sillok*, 103-kwŏn, 26-nyŏn (1444), 2/20, first article.

72. The term *national language* (C: *guoyu*, K: *kuk'ŏ*) presents a different case. In King Sejong's *Hunmin chŏngŭm*, language spoken in Chosŏn Korea is referred to as *kukji ŏŭm* (國之語音), the country's speech-sound. *Sejong sillok*, 113-kwŏn, 28-nyŏn (1446), 9/29, fourth article. According to Jerry Norman, during much of the Qing dynasty the term *national language* referred to Manchu and not the Beijing-based *guanhua* (officials' language or Mandarin, 官話): "Historically, the term guoyu seems mainly to have been employed by dynasties whose rulers were not Chinese, but some northern group like the Tabgach, the Jurchens, or the Mongols." In 1909 China's Ministry of Education began to promote the teaching and study of *guanhua*, and in 1910 *guanhua* was designated as *guoyu*: that is, Mandarin as the national language, rendering all other languages nonnational, and eventually "non-Chinese." But in this period, as Norman points out, *guoyu* was seen as a language of school and administration but not of literature. Jerry Norman, *Chinese* (Cambridge: Cambridge University Press, 1988), 133–34.

73. But we should not infer from this that the Korean literati accepted without question the Sinocentric worldview, the world conceptualized as T'ien-hsia, all-under-Heaven, presided over by the emperor of China, the Son of Heaven. The Korean literati de-centered China in many ways, especially when China came to be ruled by "barbarians." When the Ming dynasty was conquered by the Manchus (Ch'ing dynasty) in 1662, the Korean literati imagined Korea to be the last bastion of civilization, and such self-identification continued into the late eighteenth century.

74. Seeking a tributary relationship and investiture from the Ming, Yi Sŏng-gye, the founder of the Chosŏn dynasty, had requested the Ming emperor to choose between Hwaryŏng (和寧) and Chosŏn for the name of the new dynastic state. The Hongwu emperor chose the name Chosŏn for its historical association with China—that is, Chi Tzu (K: Kija) Chosŏn (箕子朝鮮). Chosŏn, of course, also re-

ferred to the "first Korean state" in the Tan'gun narrative. Hwaryŏng was Yi Sŏng-gye's birthplace, but it also evoked Karakorum (喀喇和林), the capital of northern Yuan, its shortened name being 和林 or 和寧. Hwaryŏng suggested that Yi Sŏng-gye could ally with the Mongols if Ming did not support him. In internal documents, Chosŏn officials referred to their country as Tae-Chosŏn'guk, or Great Chosŏn.

75. See Andre Schmid, *Korea between Empires, 1895–1919* (New York: Columbia University Press, 2002). See also Kai-wing Chow, "Narrating Nation, Race, and National Culture: Imagining the Hanzu Identity in Modern China," *Constructing Nationhood in Modern East Asia*, ed. Kai-wing Chow, Kevin M. Doak, and Poshek Fu (Ann Arbor: University of Michigan Press, 2001). By calling Korea semicolonial, I am referring to competing colonialisms in Korea, not just Japanese.

76. Between 1895 and 1936 the British Bible Society distributed 18,079,466 Bibles published in Korean. Between 1910 (when translation of the entire Bible was completed) and 1960, some 30 million Bibles were distributed in Korea, amounting to one Bible per person. See Kim Yun-gyŏng, *Han'guk muncha kŭp ŏhaksa* (1934; Seoul: Kyŏngin munhwasa, 1987) and Ch'oe Hyŏn-bae, "Kidokkyo wa Han'gŭl," *Sinhak nondan*, 7 (1962). Both are cited in Ross King, "Western Protestant Missionaries and the Origins of Korean Language Modernization," *Journal of International and Area Studies* 11, no. 3 (2004). Standardizing the writing system to produce what is today called *han'gŭl* (in South Korea) is still ongoing, and as King points out, until 1910 the role and contributions of Western missionaries in Korea (especially Anglophone Protestant missionaries from Britain, Canada, and the United States) cannot be dismissed.

77. Rey Chow, *Women and Modernity: The Politics of Reading between East and West* (Minneapolis: University of Minnesota Press, 1991), xv.

78. This is drawn from Naoki Sakai's critique of such presumed unity: "As long as we consider 'Japanese people,' 'Japanese language,' and 'Japanese culture' as the three inherent attributes of a unity, we are not able to imagine any different way a society can exist." Sakai Naoki (1996), cited in Lee, *The Ideology of Kokugo*, xvi.

79. Initially only three hundred copies of *Tongnip sinmun* were printed. By 1898 circulation had increased to three thousand copies, published six days per week rather than three. See Wells, *New God, New Nation*, 57–58. Aside from "print capitalism," the clock, telegraph, electric street lights, the Gregorian calendar, the creation of new public spaces—all these have to be considered. See Min Suh Son, "Enlightenment and Electrification: The Introduction of Electric Light, Telegraph and Streetcars in Late Nineteenth Century Korea," *Reform and Modernity in the Taehan Empire*, ed. Kim Dong-no, John B. Duncan, and Kim Do-hyung (Seoul: Jimoondang, 2006). For comparison, see also Stefan Tanaka, *New Times in Modern Japan* (Princeton: Princeton University Press, 2006).

80. Rebecca Karl makes the important point that nationalism in places like China at the turn of the twentieth century "must be seen as part of the general global problematic in which it was embedded, lest the inquiry become . . . merely a catalog of the reactive replication in China of globally existing institutional forms

and ideologies." While I mostly agree with this point, it seems to me that the phrase "the general global problematic" is not too different from how I see sovereignty functioning globally as both political power and police power. At this historical juncture, what *Tongnip sinmun* helped establish is a logic of equivalence based on a racial geography of the world. While this logic would later enable articulation of political solidarity with other colonized peoples, I do not think it is useful to refer to "a non-Euro-American consciousness of globality." See Rebecca Karl, *Staging the World: Chinese Nationalism at the Turn of the Twentieth Century* (Durham: Duke University Press, 2002), 5–7.

81. Philip Jaisohn's later editorials deriding the barbarism of the Chinese, including Chinese in America, illustrate another of the ways he articulated this civilizational and racial hierarchy. See Schmid's chapter "Decentering the Middle Kingdom" in *Korea between Empires*. A decade later, Sin Ch'ae-ho explained the "sudden respect" given to *kungmun* quite simply: literary Chinese (*hanmun*) had perpetrated a great deal of harm; *kungmun* had not. Sin Ch'ae-ho, "Kukhanmun ŭi kyŏngjung," reprinted in *Sin Ch'ae-ho yŏksa nonsŏljip*, translated into contemporary Korean by Chŏng Hae-yŏm (Seoul: Hyŏndae silhaksa, 1995), 278.

82. In terms of law, formal political inequality was significantly reduced by the reform legislation of 1894. The Kabo reforms of 1894 abolished slavery and the social status system. In the recruitment of officials (men), the distinction between *yangban* and commoner was dropped and the civil examination system abolished. Widows were allowed to remarry; Buddhist monks were allowed to enter the capital. In the economic realm, the Independence Club and *Tongnip sinmun* supported free trade; that is, they opposed higher tariffs that would have protected native producers and industries. They also sought to maintain Korea's sovereignty through the granting of concessions to different imperial powers, hoping that balancing competing interests among the imperial powers would allow for Korean neutrality and protection from becoming colonized by one of the imperial powers. They also did not call for renegotiation of unequal treaties or an end to extraterritoriality, judging such demands to be premature.

83. Rhee Syngman, *Tongnip chŏngsin*, in *Ihwajang sojang Unam Yi Sŭngman munsŏ* (Seoul: Kukhak charyowŏn, 1998), 1:7–8. I have referred to the English translation in *The Spirit of Independence: A Primer of Korean Modernization and Reform*, translated, annotated, and with an introduction by Han-kyo Kim (Honolulu: University of Hawaii Press, 2001). But the translation here is my own, based on the version of *Tongnip chŏngsin* published in *Unam Yi Sŭngman munsŏ*. According to Robert T. Oliver, the first thirty-four "chapters" were written while Rhee was in prison, and the last eighteen chapters were written later. *Tongnip chŏngsin* was published in Los Angeles in 1910. See *The Spirit of Independence*, 11; Robert T. Oliver, *Syngman Rhee: The Man behind the Myth* (New York: Dodd, Mead, 1954), 56, 339. The meaning of *chŏngsin* in *Tongnip chŏngsin* (獨立精神), translated as *spirit*, is closer to the meaning of the German word *Geist*.

84. Rhee Syngman, 立國以敎化爲本, *Okjung chapki*, cited in *Yi Sŭng-man yŏn'gu*, ed. Lew Young-Ick (Yu Yŏng-ik) (Seoul: Yonsei University Press, 2000), 37.

85. Rhee argues against the notion that political dissent weakens the state.

86. *Tongnip sinmun*, editorial, March 9, 1897, in *Tongnip sinmun nonsŏljip, 1896.4–1899.12* (Seoul: Songjae munhwa chaedan, 1976), 184.

87. Rhee, *Tongnip chŏngsin*, 1:8.

88. Rhee, *Tongnip chŏngsin*, 1:45.

89. The first assembly on March 10, on Chongno, a main thoroughfare, drew a crowd of about eight thousand people. A speech by Rhee Syngman was impressive and well received. See Chandra, *Imperialism, Resistance, and Reform in Late Nineteenth-Century Korea*, 167. The topic set for discussion in the assembly in April 1898 was whether a parliament (*ŭihoewŏn*) should be established. When Philip Jaisohn was pressured to return to the United States in May, Yun Ch'i-ho became president of the Independence Club. As these assemblies drew thousands of people from all the social classes, Yun became wary. One of the ways he tried to maintain control over the proceedings was by translating and disseminating Henry M. Robert's *Pocket Manual of Rules of Order for Deliberative Assemblies*, published in 1894. See Yi Hwang-jik, "Kŭndae Han'guk ŭi ch'ogi kongnonjang hyŏngsŏng mit pyŏnhwa e kwanhan yŏn'gu," *Sahoe iron* 32 (2007).

90. The October assembly was a two-day meeting. Cosponsorship and participation by reformist officials in the Manmin kongdonghoe was led by Pak Chŏng-yang. The first speaker to address the assembly was Pak Sŏng-ch'un, a person of *paekjŏng* (白丁) status, the lowest status group.

91. As Kenneth Wells points out, Yun Ch'i-ho "opposed the demands of the 'radicals' like Syngman Rhee for direct political confrontation." Both Philip Jaisohn and Yun were unwilling to foment a coup against the monarchy. Wells, *New God, New Nation*, 60.

92. In October 1897, to claim equivalence with the imperial powers, including China and Japan, King Kojong proclaimed Korea to be an empire, and himself an emperor. Pak Yŏng-hyo had been involved in the coup attempt in 1884, and in 1894 he had been the home minister until he was forced into exile for plotting against Queen Min.

93. While in prison from 1899 until 1904, Rhee was able to convince the director of the prison to establish a small library there, and he began a school for the inmates. Rhee also translated a number of texts, including books and essays on the history of the Sino-Japanese War, world history, Methodism, and English grammar. He translated the Waeber-Komura memorandum signed in 1896, the Lobanov-Yamagata protocol in the same year, and the Treaty of Alliance between Britain and Japan signed in London in 1902. Rhee also began working on an English-Korean dictionary but stopped after completing one-third of the project to write *Tongnip chŏngsin*. While a student at Paejae Boys' High School, he had come under the influence of Sŏ Chae-pil (Philip Jaisohn). It has been suggested that many of the topics taken up in *Tongnip chŏngsin* Rhee first learned from Sŏ's lectures on history and geography.

94. President Theodore Roosevelt was awarded the Nobel Peace Prize in 1906 for his role in negotiations that led to the Treaty of Portsmouth.

95. For Rhee Syngman's political activism in relation to other independence activists in the United States, see Bong-Youn Choy, *Koreans in America* (Chicago: Nelson-Hall, 1979). See also Richard Kim, *The Quest for Statehood: Korean Immigrant Nationalism and U.S. Sovereignty, 1905–1945* (New York: Oxford University Press, 2011).

96. Rhee, *Tongnip chŏngsin*, 1:73–74.

97. See Uday Mehta's discussion of John Locke's *Thoughts Concerning Education* and *Second Treatise*. Uday Mehta, *Liberalism and Empire: A Study in Nineteenth Century British Liberal Thought* (Chicago: University of Chicago Press, 1999), 46–76. See also Locke, *Some Thoughts Concerning Education*, ed. John W. and Jean S. Yolton (New York: Oxford University Press, 1989); and *Second Treatise of Government*, ed. C. B. Macpherson (Indianapolis, Ind.: Hackett Pub. Co., 1980).

98. As Prasenjit Duara points out, understanding the process by which narratives get transmitted over time requires that we understand how narratives break down over time: "Transmission of a trace or a narrative is premised upon repression, contestation, and negotiation of other, dispersed traces and narratives. For the historian, it is methodologically necessary to grasp this bifurcation of history as linear transmission and dispersion; only then can we keep in view the heterogeneity of the past upon which both our historical narratives and the representations from the past—the traces, our sources—have been constructed." Prasenjit Duara, "Bifurcating Linear History: Nation and Histories in China and India," *positions* 1, no. 3 (1993). In other words, it is only through the violence of historiography (both premodern and modern) that "Korean history" (or any other national history) can be understood as a single coherent narrative.

99. Depending on the context, I will translate *minjok* as *people*, as *Koreans*, or as an ethnically defined *nation*. In those cases in which I employ the word *nation* for *minjok*, I *do* mean to convey the idea of common blood ties as suggested in the Latin noun *natio* (from which the word *nation* is derived). On the etymology of words like *nation* and *ethnicity*, and the conflation of the words *state* and *nation*, see Walker Conner, "A Nation Is a Nation, Is a State, Is an Ethnic Group, Is a. . . . ," *Ethnic and Racial Studies* 1, no. 4 (1978), 379–88.

100. Andre Schmid, "Rediscovering Manchuria: Sin Ch'aeho and the Politics of Territorial History in Korea," *Journal of Asian Studies* 56, no. 1 (1997). Schmid cites two sources on how the term *minzoku* was appropriated by Chinese intellectuals in the early years of the twentieth century: Han Jinchun and Li Yinfun, "Hanwen 'minzu' yici chuxian ji qi chuji shiyong qingkuang," *Minzu yanjiu*, no. 2 (1984), 36–43; and Peng Yingming, "Guanyu woguo minzu gainian lishi de chubu kaocha," *Minzu Yanjiu*, no. 2 (1985), 5–11.

101. Such a model—which implies that "a word in language A must equal a word or a phrase in language B; otherwise one of the languages is lacking"—will lead the observer to form mistaken opinions about other peoples and, conversely, about the observer's own totalized identity. See Lydia H. Liu, *Translingual Practice: Literature, National Culture, and Translated Modernity, China, 1900–1937* (Stanford: Stanford University Press, 1995), 4.

102. Son Chin-t'ae, *Chosŏn minjoksa kaeron* (Seoul: Ŭryu munhwasa, 1948). The quotation is from his introduction and can be found in *Yŏkdae Han'guksa nonsŏn*, compiled by Yi Ki-baek (Seoul: Saemunsa, 1993), 241. Son's introduction to *Chosŏn minjoksa kaeron* (Outline of Korean National History) was written in the postliberation context of divided occupation (Soviet forces north of the 38th parallel, U.S. forces to the south) and the violent struggle between the Left and the Right that led to the establishment of separate states (DPRK and ROK) in 1948. As an anticommunist, Son nonetheless extended high praise to the Marxist historiography of Paek Nam-un, but then criticized him for discovering only a part of "ourselves" (*uri chasin*). Son's privileging of the *minjok* as the totality of "ourselves" that transcends class divisions attests to how the category of *minjok* was implicated in ideological struggles during and after the colonial period. Son became South Korea's vice minister of education in 1950, and he was forcibly taken to North Korea during the Korean War.

103. Cho Tong-gŏl, "Kŭndae ch'ogi ŭi yŏksa insik," *Han'guk ŭi yŏksaga wa yŏksa insik*, ed. Cho Tong-gŏl, Han Yŏng-u, and Pak Ch'an-sŭng (Seoul: Ch'angjak kwa pip'yŏngsa, 1994), 2, 19.

104. Eugen Weber, *Peasants into Frenchmen: The Modernization of Rural France, 1870–1914* (Stanford: Stanford University Press, 1976). Ernest Gellner makes a similar argument: "[Nationalism] claims to defend folk culture while in fact it is forging a high [i.e., *yangban*] culture; it claims to protect an old folk society while in fact helping to build up an anonymous mass society; . . . it preaches and defends continuity, but owes everything to a decisive and unutterably profound break in human history [the development of industrial society]." Ernest Gellner, *Nations and Nationalism* (Ithaca: Cornell University Press, 1983), 124–25.

105. As Fujiya Kawashima has shown, by the eighteenth century the *yangban* elite in the countryside had succeeded in constructing diverse local cultures based on Confucian ethics, a culture that structured the daily lives of not just *yangban* but also *chungin*, commoners, and slaves. This "cultural localism" was upheld as being universal in that Confucian ethics and morality were applicable to everyone everywhere, even as it accentuated a shared sense of self-discipline, self-rule, and self-sufficiency. But this shared local culture did not transgress status distinctions. This culture assumed that the social hierarchy separating the different status groups (*myŏngbun*) was natural and commonsensical. Fujiya Kawashima, "Cultural Localism in the Late Chosŏn Dynasty and Its Significance in Modern Korea," *Bulletin of Hiroshima Jogakuin University*, no. 45 (December 1995).

106. Carter Eckert, *Offspring of Empire: The Koch'ang Kims and the Colonial Origins of Korean Capitalism, 1876–1945* (Seattle: University of Washington Press, 1991), 226–27.

107. Although Chinese dynasties viewed their interaction with peoples and kingdoms beyond their borders in terms of the "tribute system," Peter Yun points out that this system encompassed a wide range of political relationships, from total subjugation to virtual equality. Yun argues that from the fourth century until the Mongol conquest of the whole region in the thirteenth century, a triangular bal-

ance of power among China, Manchuria, and Korea prevailed in Northeast Asia. By destroying this triangular balance of power, the Mongols for the first time forced Korea (Koryŏ) to perform all the duties of a "model tributary." It was not until the sixteenth century, however, that Korean Confucian elites developed a strong ideological commitment to the moral correctness of the tribute system. See Peter Yun, "Rethinking the Tribute System: Northeast Asian Interstate Relations, 600–1600." Ph.D. dissertation, UCLA, 1998.

108. There are, of course, other factors behind Chosŏn's remarkable longevity. See, for example, James Palais, "Stability in Chosŏn Dynasty Korea," *Occasional Papers on Korea* 3 (June 1975), 1–18.

109. Anderson, *Imagined Communities*, 1–18.

110. As commonly defined in present-day South Korea, the categories of "nationalist historians" and "nationalist historiography" for the colonial period encompass a wide range of historical writing by writers who embraced quite different, sometimes opposing philosophical, political, and methodological positions. By nationalist historiography, I mean histories written as a narrative of resistance to colonial rule, devoted to countering the pernicious effects of colonialist historiography and to empowering Koreans to join the struggle for Korea's independence, by historians such as Sin Ch'ae-ho, Pak Ŭn-sik, An Chae-hong, Mun Il-p'yŏng, and Chŏng In-bo. We should be careful to distinguish between national historiography (*minjok sahak*) and nationalist historiography (*minjokjuŭi yŏksahak*). Almost all histories written today are national histories (for example, histories of Korean women, religion, literature, music, art—not to mention politics), but not all histories are nationalist histories.

111. Sin Ch'ae-ho was born in 1880 in South Ch'ungch'ŏng Province. He received a classical education from his grandfather and at the age of eighteen entered the Sŏnggyun'gwan, the government-run Confucian academy. In 1905 Sin received his *paksa* degree and at the invitation of Chang Chi-yŏn joined the editorial staff of the *Hwangsŏng sinmun* (Capital Gazette). When the Japanese authorities forced the *Hwangsŏng sinmun* to close, he moved to the *Taehan maeil sinbo* (Korea Daily News) and became its editor in chief. In 1907, with the intention of inspiring Korean youth to become heroes themselves, Sin translated Liang Qichao's (Liang Ch'i-ch'ao) biographical sketches of Mazzini, Garibaldi, and Cavour (*Itali kŏn'guk samgŏljŏn*) and in the following year wrote biographic sketches of the Koguryŏ general Ŭlchi Mundŏk and Chosŏn admiral Yi Sun-sin. In 1907 he also helped organize the Sinminhoe (New People's Association, a clandestine nationalist organization), and in his editorials publicized Sinminhoe views. Until annexation in 1910, Sin published *Kajŏng chapchi* (Family Magazine), a magazine for women, and wrote essays on nationalism, Korean linguistics, Korean history, and poetry. He left Korea just before annexation to continue his nationalist activities abroad, and with the exception of a brief trip home in 1916, he never set foot in Korea again. In 1919, when the March First Movement erupted in Korea, Sin took part in organizing the Korean provisional government (KPG) in Shanghai. By 1920, however, he was so disgusted

with the diplomatic and gradualist strategies advocated by Rhee Syngman and An Ch'ang-ho that he turned his back on the KPG. Although active in revolutionary nationalist politics, Sin also immersed himself in historical study. His writings in the early twentieth century were influenced by Liang Qichao's historical methodology and by Chinese anarchist intellectuals. In 1923 he wrote "Declaration of Korean Revolution" for the Korean revolutionary organization Ŭiyŏldan. By 1925 he had become an anarchist. In 1927 he joined the Eastern Anarchist Association, and in the following year he was arrested by the Japanese military in connection with a forgery scheme to raise funds for anarchist activities. In 1936 he died in a Japanese prison in Port Arthur.

112. The Tan'gun legend is a prototypical foundation myth which explains the creation of the people, the state, and the culture of ancient Chosŏn. As narrated by Iryŏn in the *Samguk yusa*, Hwanin, the Supreme Spirit, sent down his son, Hwanung, to the peak of T'aebaeksan. A bear and a tiger, which lived together in a cave, prayed to Hwanung to be transformed into human form. Hwanin then gave them mugwort and garlic to eat and told them not to see light for one hundred days. The tiger could not endure the ordeal; the bear persevered and became a woman. Hwanung married her, and she bore a son who was called Tan'gun wanggŏm. Iryŏn goes on to say that in the fiftieth year of the Emperor Yao, Tan'gun established a city at Pyongyang and called his country Chosŏn. This would date the establishment of Ancient Chosŏn to 2306 BCE, but the Tan'gun calendar traditionally begins with Tan'gun's birth, which is said to have occurred in 2333 BCE. See *Samguk yusa*, trans. Tae-Hung Ha and Grafton K. Mintz (1972; Seoul: Yonsei University Press, 2004).

113. Homer B. Hulbert, "Introductory Note," *Korea Review* (1901).

114. Starting in the 1920s, with more sophisticated approaches to the study of religion and ways of reading myth, new semantic value was given to the term *myth*, as fable but also as sacred tradition and revelation of beginnings. In Korea today the Tan'gun myth holds both of these aspects: as fiction that nevertheless narrates Korea's origin in the time of beginnings.

115. Although no longer extant, state histories were compiled by each of the Three Kingdoms: Yi Mun-jin for Koguryŏ (600); Kohŭng for Paekche (375; and as noted by Peter Lee, judging from quotations in the *Nihon shoki*, other Paekche histories must have existed); and Kŏch'ilbu (fl. 545–76) for Silla. Peter Lee et al., eds., *Sourcebook of Korean Civilization*: vol. 1, *From Early Times to the Sixteenth Century* (New York: Columbia University Press, 1993), 119. It is thought that *Samguksa* (History of the Three Kingdoms), written at the beginning of the Koryŏ period but no longer extant, did mention the Tan'gun legend. But according to Han Yŏng-u, the *Samguksa* probably was not a sophisticated Confucian history and was probably not written in the annal biography (*kijŏnch'e*) style. See Han Young-Woo (Han Yŏng-u), "Uri nara yŏksahak ŭi hŭrŭm," *Han'guk ŭi yŏksaga wa yŏksahak*, ed. Cho Tong-gŏl et al. (Seoul: Ch'angjak kwa pip'yŏngsa, 1994), 1:15.

116. A Buddhist monk versed in geomancy, Myoch'ŏng (?–1135) contended that

the topographical vigor of Kaegyŏng (Kaesŏng, the capital of Koryŏ) was depleted. Myoch'ŏng's proposal to move the capital to Sŏgyŏng (Pyongyang) would have weakened the power of aristocratic families entrenched in Kaegyŏng and would have instated a more aggressive policy toward the Jurchen Jin in the north. Conservatives like Kim Pu-sik opposed Myoch'ŏng's plan because moving the capital to a more "propitious" area would have also sanctioned an extensive (and expansive) program of reconstructing the physical and social order. In 1135, after years of fruitless polemic, Myoch'ŏng raised an army in revolt, which ended in defeat to forces led by Kim Pu-sik. According to Song Ki-ho, the core of Parhae's ruling class was made up of Koguryŏ émigrés and the subject population was mostly Malgal people. "Unified" Silla regarded Parhae as a state founded by the descendents of Koguryŏ, and, in its dealings with "Japan," Parhae referred to itself as Koryŏ (that is, Koguryŏ). There are passages in the *Samguk sagi* and in Ch'oe Ch'i-wŏn's writings (857–?; a scholar-official of late Silla) which refer to Parhae as "the Northern State" (*pukguk*), and Song infers that Parhae might have regarded Silla as "the Southern State" (*namguk*). Song then reasons that Parhae and Silla saw themselves as forming a single ethnic group. See Song Ki-ho, "Silla chungdae sahoe wa Parhae," *Han'guksa t'ŭkgang*, ed. Han'guksa t'ŭkgang p'yŏnchan wiwŏnhoe (Seoul: Sŏul taehakkyo ch'ulp'anbu, 1990), 67–81. I think it is entirely possible that, when convenient, that is, for political reasons (to seek asylum, or as justification for territorial ambitions), the ruling classes of Parhae and Silla might have articulated their relationship to one another in terms of clientship and kinship ties. But I think it is doubtful that they even thought about their own subjects (people from whom they extracted tribute and labor) in terms of a deep, horizontal comradeship that is the hallmark of the ethnic nation.

117. Traditional dates: Koguryŏ, 37 BCE–668 CE; Paekche, 18 BCE–660 CE; and Silla, 57 BCE–935 CE. "Unified" Silla is 668–935.

118. Han, "Uri nara yŏksahak ŭi hŭrŭm," 14–17.

119. The Tan'gun legend in *Samguk yusa* might have been based on much earlier sources, such as the *Wei shu* and *Tan'gun kogi*. The Tan'gun legend also appears in later (Chosŏn) court-sponsored works like the *Ŭngjesi chu* (Commentary on Poems Written at Royal Command) by Kwŏn Nam (1416–65), the monograph on geography in the *Sejong sillok*, and the *Tongguk yŏji sŭngnam* (1481).

120. Ki-baik Lee (Yi Ki-baek), *A New History of Korea*, trans. Edward W. Wagner (Cambridge: Harvard-Yenching Institute, 1984), 167.

121. As Peter Yun ("Rethinking the Tribute System") points out, successive Koryŏ kings had princesses of the Yüan imperial house as their primary consorts, and the throne was reserved for the princes born to Mongol queens.

122. Iryŏn writes, "It is written in an old book, 'In ancient times, Hwanung, the son of Hwanin (this means Chesŏk), desired to descend from Heaven and to live amongst men. . . . Together with his ministers of wind, rain, and cloud, Hwanung instructed mankind about agriculture, the preservation of life, the curing of disease, punishments, the difference between right and wrong.'" This translation by

James H. Grayson can be found in *Korea: A Religious History* (New York: Oxford University Press, 1989), 282. See also Peter Lee's translation in *Sourcebook of Korean Civilization*, 1:4–7. For Iryŏn, Koryŏ was the land wherein the Buddha dwells (thus culturally superior to the Mongols), and it was Buddhism that could safeguard the land and the people. This was why he equated Hwanin, the Ruler of Heaven, with Chesŏk, a rendering of Indra, one of the three great deities of Vedic Hinduism.

123. There were histories written in the epic style, most notably the vernacular translation of the *Sanguozhi tongsu yanyi* (Romance of the Three Kingdoms; K: *Samgukji t'ongsok yŏnŭi*). Confucian historians considered such popular histories fiction rather than history proper. But much to their dismay, *Samgukji t'ongsok yŏnŭi* was widely read in late Chosŏn. As Emanuel Pastreich points out, Yi Ik (1681–1763), for example, lamented the fact that the *Samgukji t'ongsok yŏnŭi* was being read aloud in every home and even quoted in the civil service examination questions. The earliest complaint on record seems to be a memorial written by the scholar Ki Taesŭng to King Sŏnjo in 1569 in which he rebukes the king for drawing a reference from *Samgukji t'ongsok yŏnŭi*. Without having to read it, Ki was able to compare its extreme ludicrousness to books on astrology. Pastreich argues that the literary style of *Samgukji t'ongsok yŏnŭi* set some of the basic conventions for the vernacular novel in late Chosŏn. See Emanuel Pastreich, "The Reception of Chinese Vernacular Narrative in Korea and Japan," Ph.D. dissertation, Harvard University, 1997, 49–52. But it is not clear what influence, if any, literary conventions in late Chosŏn vernacular literature had on history writing in the modern period. In the case of Sin Ch'ae-ho, Thomas Carlyle's *On Heroes, Hero-Worship, and the Heroic in History* and Liang Qichao's biographical sketches of Mazzini, Garibaldi, and Cavour (which Sin translated in 1907 as *Itali kŏn'guk samgŏljŏn*) stimulated him to write biographic sketches of the Koguryŏ general Ŭlchi Mundŏk (mid-sixth century to early seventh century) and Yi Sun-sin (1545–98). (*Ŭlchi Mundŏk* was published as a booklet in 1908 and *Yi Sunsin-jŏn* was serialized in the *Taehan maeil sinbo* in the same year.) As Michael Robinson points out, Sin's motives for writing these biographies was to exhort Korean youth to emulate the purity of spirit and patriotic example of these military heroes in Korean history. Michael Robinson, "National Identity and the Thought of Sin Ch'aeho," *Journal of Korean Studies* 5 (1984), 134.

124. Private histories were sometimes free of some of the restraints that inhibited official historiography. However, because the authors were either potential or actual officeholders, there was a strong similarity in outlook between private historiography and official historiography.

125. In an interview in 1984, Yi Pyŏng-do (1896–1989) recalled how he saw the *Chosŏn wangjo sillok* for the first time in the home of Ikeuchi Hiroshi, a professor of Korean history at Tokyo Imperial University. This was during his student days at Waseda University (1916–19). During the Chosŏn period, copies of the *Sillok* were kept at four separate archives in remote mountainous areas in addition to the central archive in Seoul. The *Sillok* kept by Ikeuchi was destroyed during the Tokyo earthquake of 1923. During the colonial period, Yi Pyŏng-do worked on and off for

the Chōsenshi henshūkai (Society for the Compilation of Korean History), and after liberation he taught in the History Department at Seoul National University. Among Korean historians, Yi was the most influential in the positivist school (*silchŭng sahak*). The interview, conducted by Chŏng Hong-jun, appears in Chindan hakhoe, ed., *Yŏksaga ŭi yuhyang* (Seoul: Ilchogak, 1991), 264–76.

126. Sinminhoe was a secret society organized in 1907 by An Ch'ang-ho, with Yi Tong-hwi, Yang Ki-t'ak, Yi Kap, Yi Sung-hun, Chŏn Tŏk-ki, An T'ae-guk, Yi Tong-nyŏng, Sin Ch'ae-ho, and others (Sin Ch'ae wrote its prospectus, "Chwijimun"). It consisted of patriots, each of whom committed his life and property to the organization in the cause of promoting nationalist consciousness, Korean independence, and popular sovereignty. At one point the membership grew to about eight hundred men, many of whom were journalists, religious leaders, military men, and businessmen. To promote education, the Sinminhoe founded schools in Pyongyang and Chŏngju; to promote modern industry, it established a ceramics factory in Pyongyang; and to promote nationalist politics in the public sphere, it established the bilingual newspaper *Taehan maeil sinbo* (Korea Daily News).

127. This parallels historical trends among Western imperial powers, where the maintenance and expansion of imperial structures required, among and for its own citizens, greater participatory democracy, higher levels of education, and more attention paid to health and welfare.

128. Han Young-Woo identifies Sin Ch'ae-ho as the initiator (*sŏnch'angja*) of modern nationalist historiography in Korea. According to Han, Sin Ch'ae-ho's "Toksa sillon," written in 1908, was a pioneering work in modern nationalist historiography because its epistemology was informed by three tenets: nation (*minjok*), democracy (*minju*), and science (*kwahak*). Han Young-Woo (Han Yŏng-u), *Han'guk minjokjuŭi yŏksahak* (Seoul: Ilchogak, 1994), 4, 6.

129. Sin Ch'ae-ho, "Chosŏn yŏksasang ilch'ŏnnyŏnlae cheil taesakkŏn" (The Most Disastrous Event in the Past One Thousand Years of Korean History), *Tonga Ilbo* (October 1924 through March 1925). The historical context for this polemic had to do with Sin's denunciation of those Koreans who were lobbying for an "independent domestic administration" (*naejŏng tongnip*), "participatory government" (*ch'am chŏngkwŏn*), or "self-rule" (*chach'i*) within colonial Korea. Sin understood these moves as capitulation to Japan's claim over Korea, a capitulation that emanated from the mentality of subservience begun by Kim Pu-sik.

130. I thank Christine Hong for this formulation and her reading of Yun Ch'i-ho's narrative about his experiences in the United States as a narrative of disavowal through a temporal displacement.

3. Nationalizing Korea's Past

1. Sin Ch'ae-ho, "Toksa sillon," *Tanjae Sin Ch'ae-ho chŏnjip* (Seoul: Tanjae Sin Ch'ae-ho sŏnsaeng kinyŏm saŏphoe, 1987), 1:471–72.

2. Yanagi Sōetsu's first long essay on an Asian artwork was about the Sŏkkuram

Grotto, published in 1919 just after the March First Uprising. For Yanagi, the glory of the Silla capital of Kyŏngju was comparable to the golden age of Tang China and Tenpyō Japan. See Janet Poole, chapter 3 of "Colonial Interiors: Modernist Fiction of Korea," Ph.D. dissertation, Columbia University, 2004.

3. Kim Tae-sik, "Ilje kangjŏmgi Kyŏngju chiŏk munhwaje ŭi suri pokwŏn sare," *Kyŏngju Silla yujŏk ŭi ŏje wa onŭl: Sŏkkuram, Pulguksa, Namsan* (Seoul: Sungkyun-kwan taehakkyo pangmulkwan kihoeg chŏnsisil, 2007). Sekino Tadashi's field of expertise was Buddhist architecture, and in 1902 he had already conducted a study of Pulguksa.

4. The photos were taken by Tokio Shunzo, probably in the fall of 1909 when Resident General Sone went to view Sŏkkuram. There were two photos of Sŏk-kuram, and these were published in a book on Korean art titled *Chōsen bijutsu tai-kan* (Keijō [Seoul]: Chōsen kosho kankōkai, 1910). Under the direction of Sekino Tadashi, the Office of the Governor General of Chōsen (Chōsen Sotokufu) began in 1915 to publish the results of excavating, identifying, photographing, and classi-fying significant sites and artifacts throughout Korea. See *Chōsen koseki zufu* (Ar-chaeological Survey of Korea), 15 vols. (Seoul: Chōsen Sotokufu, 1915–35).

5. Su-young Hwang, "Sŏkkuram Grotto Shrine," *Koreana* 6, no. 4 (1992).

6. There may have been ten "windows," invisible from within, that allowed air and indirect light into the rotunda. See Chun-woo Nahm, "Discoveries of Hitherto Forgotten Sciences in Sŏkkuram Temple," *Chindan hakbo* 32 (1969).

7. Several efforts were made to fix the problem, but without success.

8. *Mail sinbo*, September 12, 1913.

9. In Meiji Japan, along with preservation guidelines, the Ministry of Interior also regulated the appointment of chief abbots and required the reporting of all temple affairs, including the issuance of permits to hold public religious events. See Hyung Il Pai, "The Creation of National Treasures and Monuments: The 1916 Japanese Laws on the Preservation of Korean Remains and Relics and Their Colo-nial Legacies," *Korean Studies* 25, no. 1 (2001), 79.

10. See Stefan Tanaka, "Imaging History: Inscribing Belief in the Nation," *Journal of Asian Studies* 53, no. 1 (1994).

11. Ernest Fenollosa began teaching at Tokyo Imperial University in 1878. He was hired to teach philosophy, but he soon developed a passion for Japanese art, and in 1887 he was appointed professor of esthetics and art history. The following year, both Fenollosa and Okakura were appointed to the Tokyo Imperial Museum, Fenollosa serving on the administrative board and Okakura as head of the art sec-tion. See F. G. Notehelfer, "On Idealism and Realism in the Thought of Okakura Tenshin," *Journal of Japanese Studies* 16, no. 2 (1990), 320, 326. In 1890 Fenollosa became the curator of the Department of Oriental Art of the Boston Museum of Fine Arts. He helped select art pieces for the Japanese Exhibit at the Columbian Exposition in Chicago in 1893.

12. This hall came to be referred to as Yumedono (Hall of Dreams) starting in the Heian period, with the veneration of Prince Shōtoku, based on the claim that

Nichira, a nobleman from Paekche, had worshipped the prince as early as 583. According to the Kamakura-period text *Shōtoku taishi den shiki* (1238), Shōtoku studied Buddhist scripture with the Korean monk Hyeja. See Lucie R. Weinstein, "The Yumedono Kannon: Problems in Seventh-Century Sculpture," *Archives of Asian Art* 42 (1989).

13. Suiko refers to Empress Suiko (554–628). The Guze Kannon is said to be a representation of Prince Shōtoku. Ernest F. Fenollosa, *Epochs of Chinese and Japanese Art: An Outline History of East Asiatic Design* (New York: Frederick A. Stokes, 1911), 501–51. The bulk of the text quoted here is also quoted in Tanaka, "Imaging History."

14. The Kannon sees and hears the suffering of the world, thus the compassionate Bodhisattva. The Guze Kannon was locked away within the octagonal hall as a *hibutsu*, an image too sacred to view. According to Lucie Weinstein, from the thirteenth century until 1884 there is little indication that the Kannon was ever on view ("The Yumedono Kannon," 29).

15. Okakura graduated from Tokyo Imperial University in 1880. Starting in the fall of 1881, he worked in the art section of the Ministry of Education. The first tour of imperial art commissioners occurred in 1882, when Okakura and Fenollosa joined Kuki Ryūichi on a trip to the Kyoto-Nara area. Thereafter Okakura and Fenollosa went on a series of trips to search out and identify Japan's national treasures. See Notehelfer, "On Idealism and Realism in the Thought of Okakura Tenshin," 324.

16. Kakuzō Okakura, *The Awakening of the East* (1938; Tokyo: Seibun-kaku, 1940), 54–55. According to F. G. Notehelfer, Okakura wrote *The Awakening of the East* during his stay in India from November 1901 to October 1902. In 1906 he became curator of the Chinese and Japanese Department of the Boston Museum, and until his death in 1913 he spent half the year in the United States and half the year in Japan. Notehelfer comments that Okakura "never wrote as powerfully or as beautifully in Japanese as he wrote in English. No doubt this was the reason why all of his important books were written in English" ("On Idealism and Realism in the Thought of Okakura Tenshin," 317, 330, 347).

17. During his stay in India from 1901 to 1902, Okakura formed a deep friendship with Rabindranath Tagore. On their friendship, see Rustom Bharucha, *Another Asia: Rabindranath Tagore and Okakura Tenshin* (New Delhi: Oxford University Press, 2009). Bharucha sums up the difference between Okakura and Tagore this way: while both were cosmopolitan, Okakura lived halfway between East and West; Tagore, on the other hand, thought of Bengal as his home, the place "where the world finds its home in one nest" (126).

18. Kakuzō Okakura, *Ideals of the East with Special Reference to the Art of Japan* (London: John Murray, 1903), 5, 7.

19. Okakura, *Ideals of the East*, 235.

20. Okakura, *Ideals of the East*, 7–8, 207.

21. Sekino Tadashi. *Chōsen bijutsushi* (Keijō: Chōsen shigakkai, 1932).

22. Song Ch'an-sŏp, "Ilje ŭi singmin sahak," *Han'guk ŭi yŏksaga wa yŏksahak*, 2, ed. Cho Tong-gŏl et al. (Seoul: Ch'angjak kwa pip'yŏngsa, 1994).

23. Shigeno Yasutsugu, Kume Kunitake, and Hoshino Hisashi were all on the faculty of Tokyo Imperial University. Numata Jirō, "Shigeno Yasutsugu and the Modern Tokyo Tradition of Historical Writing," *Historians of Japan and China*, ed. W. G. Beasley and E. G. Pulleyblank (London: Oxford University Press, 1961), 281. It can be argued that this "tradition" was reproduced in colonial Korea by historians like Yi Pyŏng-do and the positivist school (*silchŭng sahak*).

24. Hatada Takashi, *Nihonjin no chōsenkan* (Tokyo: Chikuma Shobō, 1969).

25. Archaeological evidence suggests a complex dynamic between "Japan" and "Korea" during the Three Kingdoms period. Émigrés from Koguryŏ, Paekche, and Silla played decisive roles (cultural and political) in the formative period of "Japanese" history; for example, one of the early emperors, Ōjin, was probably a member of the Puyŏ ruling house of Paekche.

26. As Andre Schmid has pointed out, Hyŏn Ch'ae's "translation" never raised the issue of whether Japanese garrisons were established on the Korean peninsula, or whether Korean kingdoms sent tribute to Japan. Andre Schmid, *Korea between Empires, 1895–1919* (New York: Columbia University Press, 2002), 154.

27. Besides Hyŏn Ch'ae, Kim T'ae-yŏng's *Tongsa chipnyak* (1902) and even Chang Chi-yŏn in his *Taehan kangyŏk-ko* repeated the colonialist claims about Mimana (Kaya). In 1901 Hayashi published the sequel *Chōsen kinseishi*, which covered Korean history up to 1895. This work more explicitly advocated Japan's control of Korea.

28. When Paek Nam-un wrote *Chōsen shakai keizaishi* (The Social Economic History of Korea, 1933), his polemical target was Fukuda Tokuzō and the "stagnation theory" then prevalent in Japanese historiography on Korea. Paek studied at the Tokyo College of Commerce (today Hitotsubashi University) from 1919 to 1924, where Fukuda had previously taught economics.

29. Stefan Tanaka, *Japan's Orient: Rendering Pasts into History* (Berkeley: University of California Press, 1993), 4.

30. Shiratori Kurakichi was a professor at Tokyo Imperial University from 1904 to 1925 and the scholar primarily responsible for the formation and formulation of *tōyōshi* as an academic field of study. See Tanaka, *Japan's Orient*, 4.

31. Cited in Andre Schmid, *Korea between Empires*, 57.

32. One could perhaps locate the emergence of Japan's Orientalism in the early years of the Meiji period, when Fukuzawa Yukichi argued that Japan must "leave Asia" (*Datsu-A*). But this ideological system really established itself in Japanese popular discourse around the turn of the century—especially after Japan's victory over Russia—when an army of cartoonists, novelists, and pundits conceptualized East Asia as Tōyō, and China not as Chūgoku but as Shina, a name now connoting backwardness and corruption.

33. Tanaka, *Japan's Orient*, 47.

34. Tanaka, *Japan's Orient*, 17.

35. For the list of history textbooks used in this period, see Han Young-Woo (Han Yŏng-u), *Han'guk minjokjuŭi yŏksahak* (Seoul: Ilchogak, 1994), 43. It is not clear to what extent Sin Ch'ae-ho had direct access to Japanese writings on Korea. But in other essays, he does cite a number of Japanese texts, for example, *Chōsen no ichi* (Korea's Position). See "Tongyang itaeli (The Italy of the Orient)," *Tanjae Sin Ch'ae-ho chŏnjip*, 4:184.

36. Kim Han-kyo's translation of this sentence reads, "If this were true, our relatively small land would be a pandemonium with barbarians from north and south milling around, and the accomplishments of four thousand years would be what various foreign nations had offered at auction." But according to the Kug-hanmun text in *Tanjae Sin Ch'ae-ho chŏnjip*, vol. 1, the geographic size of Korea is depicted as "our land which encompasses several tens of thousands of *li*" (that is, not just the Korean peninsula) and should not be translated as "our relatively small land." See the English translation in Lee et al., *Sourcebook of Korean Civilization*, 2:424. Several tens of thousands of *li* would encompass not just the Korean peninsula, but much of Manchuria—which is exactly what Sin Ch'ae-ho is arguing for in "Toksa sillon." Liang and Ch'u were "Chinese" states in the Warring States period.

37. Sin, "Toksa sillon," *Tanjae Sin Ch'ae-ho chŏnjip*, 1:482.

38. Vipan Chandra contrasts this with the situation in China and Japan: "Unlike China, where revolutionists could draw on 'Han nationalism' against 'alien' Manchu rule, or Japan, where the Meiji Restorationists . . . could paint the shogunate as a usurper of imperial sovereignty, Korea offered no such rationale for radical activists." Vipan Chandra, *Imperialism, Resistance, and Reform in Late Nineteenth-Century Korea: Enlightenment and the Independence Club* (Berkeley: Institute of East Asian Studies, 1988), 215.

39. See the preface in Kang Man-gil, "Ilje sidae ŭi pan-sigmin sahaknon," *Han'guk sahaksa ŭi yŏn'gu*, ed. Han'guksa yŏn'guhoe (Seoul: Ŭlyu munhwasa, 1985), 231–32.

40. But as noted in chapter 1, Yu Tŭk-kong wrote *Palhaego* to reinforce the notion of Chosŏn as the last bastion of civilization, that is, for cultural and political aims quite different from that of Sin Ch'ae-ho in the early twentieth century. See Tae-yong Huh, "A Critical Review on the Issue of Proto-Nationalism during Late Chosŏn," *International Journal of Korean History* 12 (August 2008).

41. In South Korea, Yi U-sŏng has been the strongest promoter of this term. For an overview of historiographical issues surrounding Parhae, see Song Ki-ho, "Silla chungdae sahoe wa Parhae," *Han'guksa t'ŭkgang*, ed. Cho Tong-gŏl et al. (Seoul: Sŏul taehakkyo ch'ulp'anbu, 1990), 67–81; and his essay on Yu Tŭk-kong in *Han'guk ŭi yŏksaga wa yŏksahak*, ed. Cho Tong-gŏl et al. (Seoul: Ch'angjak kwa pip'yŏngsa, 1994), 2:296–309.

42. See Andre Schmid, "Rediscovering Manchuria: Sin Ch'aeho and the Politics of Territorial History in Korea," *Journal of Asian Studies* 56, no. 1 (1997), 27.

43. The reference is to Kume Kunitake, "Nihon fukuin no enkaku," *Shigakkai zasshi* 1 (December 1889–February 1890). According to Stefan Tanaka, in making the argument that Japan before Jinmu (the mythical first emperor) was a sort of

thalassocracy encompassing Kyūshū, Korea, and southeastern China, Kume used passages from the *Nihon shoki* and *Kojiki* not as actual facts but as allegorical data that describe historical events. See Tanaka, *Japan's Orient*, 71–75.

44. That is, two years after his "Nihon fukuin no enkaku" essay. See Numata, "Shigeno Yasutsugu and the Modern Tokyo Tradition of Historical Writing," 272.

45. As Schmid points out, the depiction of Korea as encompassing nearly all of Manchuria reveals an irredentism in Sin Ch'ae-ho's thought that has not been adequately addressed—especially since irredentism looms large in present-day imaginations of right-wing nationalists in South Korea who dream about reclaiming Korea's "ancestral lands" (*kut'o hoebok*). See Schmid, "Rediscovering Manchuria."

46. Partha Chatterjee, *Nationalist Thought and the Colonial World: A Derivative Discourse* (Minneapolis: University of Minnesota Press, 1986).

47. I thank Suzy Kim for this insight.

48. Elie Kedourie, *Nationalism* (London: Hutchinson, 1960), 71–81.

49. Prasenjit Duara, *Rescuing History from the Nation* (Chicago: University of Chicago, 1995), 4.

50. By the mid-Koryŏ period, however, Duncan argues that the formation of a homogeneous, kingdomwide elite class was well under way. Moreover he argues that we should not rule out the possibility that state-organized corvée and military service could have created a wider sense of identification with the state, "however negative that may have been at times," and a certain homogenizing of the populace. John B. Duncan, "Hyanghwain: Migration and Assimilation in Chosŏn Korea," *Acta Koreana* 3 (July 2000).

51. See Etienne Balibar, "The Nation Form: History and Ideology," *Race, Nation, Class: Ambiguous Identities*, ed. Etienne Balibar and Immanuel Wallerstein (New York: Verso, 1991), 86.

52. The reason for the discrepancy is quite simple: the kingdom of Koguryŏ, and subsequently Parhae, encompassed northern Korea and southern Manchuria, whereas "Unified" Silla (after causing Koguryŏ's collapse with the aid of Tang China) encompassed the southern two-thirds of the Korean peninsula. "Unified" Silla's northern boundary with Parhae ran east along the Taedong River to the Bay of Wŏnsan.

53. See Balibar, "The Nation Form," 88.

54. In *Han'guk kodaesa sanch'aek*, the authors begin their narrative with an admission of uncertainty: "When did people begin to live in the Korean peninsula? And who are our ancestors? These questions engross many people, but the reader cannot expect clear-cut answers. And this situation will remain the same. Clear-cut answers will not be forthcoming because it was so long ago, and because there is such a dearth of historical evidence. . . . Habitually calling ourselves a homogeneous nation [*tanil minjok*], there is a tendency to stress the purity of our bloodline. But the bloodline of contemporary Koreans was not homogeneous nor constant from the beginning." See Han'guk Yŏksa Yŏn'guhoe Kodaesa Punkwa, *Mundap*

ŭro yŏkkŭn Han'guk kodaesa sanch'aek (Seoul: Yŏksa pip'yŏngsa, 1994), 11, 15. As this book suggests, the essentialist, totalizing strategy does get problematized by Korean historians. But it seems to me that this undertaking needs to be theorized in a more rigorous way.

55. See Prasenjit Duara, "Rescuing History from the Nation-State," *Working Papers and Proceedings of the Center for Psychosocial Studies* (Chicago: Center for Psychosocial Studies, 1991), 7.

56. Kuksa kyojae p'yŏnch'an wiwŏnhoe, *Han'guksa kaesŏl* (Seoul: T'amgudang, 1983), 15.

57. See Son Yŏng-jong et al., *Chosŏn t'ongsa* (Pyongyang: Sahoe kwahak ch'ulp'ansa, 1991), 1:2.

58. I am indebted to Theodore Hughes for his discussion of Naisen Ittai. Hughes writes, "Japan as 'inside' (*nae* [J: *nai*]) reveals its ambivalent position as subject in relation to a colonial other (*sŏn* [J: *sen*]). *Sŏn* becomes a particularized, geographically marked supplement that enables a universalist inside (*nae* [J: *nai*]) even as the phrase equates *nae* and *sŏn* (as one body)." See Theodore Hughes, *Literature and Film in Cold War South Korea: Freedom's Frontier* (New York: Columbia University Press, 2012), 51. For a discussion of racism not as an "expression" of nationalism but as its "supplement," see Etienne Balibar, "Racism and Nationalism," in Balibar and Wallerstein, *Race, Nation, Class*.

59. Contemporary South Korean historians usually divide historiography in the colonial period into four different categories. (1) The ultimate political aim of colonialist historiography was to justify Japan's annexation of Korea; it portrayed Korean history as being stagnant and determined by external forces. (2) Nationalist historiography was a narrative of resistance, devoted to countering the pernicious effects of colonialist historiography and to empowering Koreans to join the struggle for Korea's independence; representative historians are Sin Ch'ae-ho, Pak Ŭn-sik, An Chae-hong, Mun Il-p'yŏng, and Chŏng In-bo. (3) Empiricist historiography claimed to take an objective, positivist approach to historiography, but its chief practitioners were usually employed by the colonial state—Yi Pyŏng-do, for example. (4) Marxist historiography sought to narrate Korean history as part of world history, unfolding in accordance with historical laws and by way of universal stages of development; representative historians are Paek Nam-un and Yi Ch'ŏng-wŏn. There are problems with creating a typology such as this, a basic shortcoming being that a number of historians and their work do not fit into any of these categories, for example, Hae Wŏn, Hwang Ŭi-don, Ch'oe Nam-sŏn, An Hwak, Kwŏn Tŏk-kyu, and Chang To-bin.

60. By this I mean starvation alongside plenty, brutal oppression alongside new forms of pleasure and new objects of desire (made possible by a new popular and consumer culture). These contradictions, experienced in radically different ways by Koreans and Japanese residents of Korea, endlessly reproduced the politics of identity and difference.

61. Military advantage, conventionally thought to be crucial to hegemony,

merely locks in hegemony for a limited period. Rather than military advantage, the critical element in maintaining hegemony is productive advantage, which conditions the other two elements — commerce and finance. But productive advantage is ephemeral — thus the rise and fall of the British (and American) Empire. See Terence K. Hopkins and Immanuel Wallerstein, "Patterns of Development of the Modern World-System," *Review* 1, no. 2 (1977), 120–21, cited in Bruce Cumings, "Archaeology, Descent, Emergence: Japan in British/American Hegemony, 1900–1950," *Japan in the World*, ed. Masao Miyoshi and H. D. Harootunian (Durham: Duke University Press, 1993), 102.

62. See his essay "The Construction of Peoplehood," in Balibar and Wallerstein, *Race, Nation, Class*.

63. Cumings, *Japan in the World*, 87.

64. Cumings, *Japan in the World*, 86.

65. Balibar and Wallerstein, *Race, Nation, Class*, 89.

66. Balibar and Wallerstein, *Race, Nation, Class*, 90.

67. Balibar and Wallerstein, *Race, Nation, Class*, 84.

68. Robert Young suggests that if poststructuralism was the product of a single historical moment, then that moment was probably not May 1968 but rather the Algerian War of Independence. That is to say, there is a link between subversive tendencies in poststructuralism and resistance to colonialism in the periphery (Algeria). Young notes that Sartre, Althusser, Derrida, and Lyotard, among others, were all either born in Algeria or personally involved with the events of the war. See Robert Young, *White Mythologies: Writing History and the West* (New York: Routledge, 1990), 1.

69. Chōsenshi henshūkai began as Chōsenshi hensan iinkai and was renamed in 1925. See Yi Man-yŏl's chapter on "colonialist historiography" in his *Han'guk kŭndae yŏksahak ŭi ihae* (Seoul: Ch'angjak kwa pip'yŏngsa, 1981).

70. The series began in June 1931 and ended in October of the same year. Sin Ch'ae-ho probably wrote the introduction to *Chosŏn sanggosa* in Beijing around 1924. When *Chosŏn sanggosa* was published in the *Chosŏn ilbo*, it was entitled "Chosŏnsa." After Liberation, it was republished as a monograph (in 1948).

71. Before graduating from Waseda University in 1914, An Chae-hong traveled to China and met Sin Ch'ae-ho in Shanghai. The powerlessness of the Korean independence movement in China (especially its weak financial base) in the early twentieth century seems to have persuaded him not to go into exile. After returning to Korea, An served as the vice principal of Chungang Middle School and organized the Taehan ch'ŏngnyŏn oegyodan (Korean Youth Diplomatic Corps), for which he spent three years in jail. In 1924 he became the chief editor of *Chosŏn ilbo*. When the Sin'ganhoe was organized in 1927, he became its secretary and was jailed for eight months. In 1931 he opposed the socialists' call for the dissolution of the Sin'ganhoe, and after its breakup he aligned himself with moderate and conservative nationalists. After liberation, An tried to create a left-right coalition, but when this effort failed, he accepted the position of chief civil administrator in the U.S.

Army Military Government in Korea. Thereafter he allied himself with anticommunist forces who argued for the creation of a separate state in southern Korea. During the Korean War, An was taken to North Korea, and he died in Pyongyang in 1965.

72. In translating these paragraphs, I have consulted J. Michael Allen's translation in "In the Beginning: National Origins and National Identity in Korea," a paper he presented at the conference Korea's Minjung Movement in Bloomington, Indiana (November 1989). Sin Ch'ae-ho, *Chosŏn sanggosa, Tanjae Sin Ch'ae-ho chŏnjip,* 1:31–32.

73. Sin Ch'ae-ho writes, "Neither individuals nor societies possess an intrinsic self-identity [*chasŏng*: inner essence, true nature]. . . . Self-identity comes to be constituted by way of the environment [*hwankyŏng*] and the epoch [*sidae*]." Introduction to *Chosŏn sanggosa, Tanjae Sin Ch'ae-ho chŏnjip,* 1:70.

74. Young, *White Mythologies,* 3.

75. According to Shin Yong-ha, Yu Cha-myŏng's anarchist ideas were influenced by Li Shizeng and Wu Zhihui. See Shin Yong-ha, "Sin Ch'ae-ho ŭi mujŏngbujuŭi tongnip sasang," *Sin Ch'ae-ho,* ed. Kang Man-gil (Seoul: Koryŏ taehakkyo ch'ulp'anbu, 1990), 106. Li Shizeng and Wu Zhihui were among the doyens of Chinese anarchism. They were important members of the Guomindang, and according to Arif Dirlik, both played important roles in anarchist anticommunism in the early 1920s. Arif Dirlik, *Anarchism in the Chinese Revolution* (Berkeley: University of California Press, 1991), 12–14. Although I don't know of any evidence of a direct relationship between Sin Ch'ae-ho and the Chinese anarchist thinkers Li Shizeng and Wu Zhihui, it is clear that anarchist ideals were broadly diffused in radical circles in Beijing and Shanghai in the early 1920s. One very apparent commonality between Li, Wu, and Sin was their admiration of Pyotr Kropotkin. In his essay "Nanggaek ŭi sinnyŏn manp'il" (1925), Sin called on Korean youth to "become baptized" with Kropotkin's essay "An Appeal to the Young." See *Sin Ch'ae-ho yŏksa nonsŏljip* (Seoul: Hyŏndae silhaksa, 1995), 350.

76. Sin Ch'ae-ho, Introduction to *Chosŏn sanggosa, Tanjae Sin Ch'ae-ho chŏnjip,* 1:31–32.

77. Sin Ch'ae-ho, "Chosŏn hyŏngmyŏng sŏnŏn," *Tanjae Sin Ch'ae-ho chŏnjip,* 3:35–46. See also the *han'gŭl* text in *Sin Ch'ae-ho yŏksa nonsŏljip,* 329–39.

78. Unlike other conservative nationalist intellectuals, Shin Yong-ha acknowledges Sin Ch'ae-ho's turn toward anarchism. According to Shin Yong-ha [Sin Yong-ha], Sin Ch'ae-ho turned to anarchism because of his estrangement from the nationalists in the Korean Provisional Government and because he was persuaded by Kropotkin's critique of social Darwinism. For Kropotkin, mutual aid (that is, cooperation) was as central to animal and human evolution as the struggle of the fittest. In Sin Ch'ae-ho's earlier nationalist writings, there was a tension between his program of strengthening national power and his critique of Japanese imperialism. That is, if survival depended on national power, what could be the ethical basis for criticizing imperialism? As Shin Yong-ha notes, this tension emanated from

social Darwinist assumptions that emphasized competition but not mutual aid. In Kropotkin, then, Sin Ch'ae-ho found a more ethical way to understand human evolution. Repelled by the antics of nationalist politicians, he turned to anarchism, which placed so much faith on the cooperative spirit of the *minjung* while at the same time taking direct action against imperialism. Shin Yong-ha, "Sin Ch'ae-ho ŭi mujŏngbujuŭi tongnip sasang," 78–147.

79. In a later declaration ("Sŏnŏnmun," *Tanjae Sin Ch'ae-ho chŏnjip*, 3:47–50), Sin Ch'ae-ho uses "propertyless masses" (*musan taejung*), "propertyless *minjung*" (*musan minjung*), and *minjung* interchangeably.

80. Sin Ch'ae-ho, "Chosŏn hyŏngmyŏng sŏnŏn," 3:44.

81. Sin Il-chŏl suggests that anarchism was a mere tool for Sin Ch'ae-ho's nationalist goals; see his *Sin Ch'ae-ho ŭi sahoe sasang yŏn'gu* (Seoul: Han'gilsa, 1984), 328. The dismissal of Sin Ch'ae-ho's anarchism is difficult to fathom in light of the textual evidence. Shin Yong-ha, who acknowledges Sin Ch'ae-ho's turn to anarchism in the mid-1920s, argues that Sin would have abandoned his anarchism after Korea's liberation from Japanese colonial rule. But this is just another way of erasing the tension between Sin Ch'ae-ho's earlier writings on *minjok* and his later emphasis on *minjung*. By erasing this tension, what is being repressed is the radically egalitarian, anti-authoritarian, and open-ended character of his later writings.

82. Sin Ch'ae-ho, "Chosŏn hyŏngmyŏng sŏnŏn," 3:43–44.

4. Universalizing Korea's Past

1. Paek Nam-un, "*Chosŏn sahoe kyŏngjesa* ch'ulp'an e taehan sogam," *Chungang* (November 1933), *Paek Nam-un chŏnjip*, trans. Ha Il-sik (Seoul: Iron kwa silch'ŏn, 1994), 4:87. See also Pang Kie-chung, *Han'guk hyŏndae sasangsa yŏn'gu* (Seoul: Yŏksa pip'yŏngsa, 1992).

2. Vigilantes looked for certain physical features that Japanese associated with Korean physiognomy—for example, a flat back of the head. Those suspected of being Korean were made to say Japanese words that many Koreans had difficulty pronouncing. Some Japanese students from Kyūshū had difficulty convincing the vigilantes that they were Japanese, and were also killed. See Jinhee Lee, "The Enemy Within: Earthquake, Rumours and Massacre in the Japanese Empire," *Violence: "Mercurial Gestalt*," ed. Tobe Levin (New York: Rodopi, 2008). See also Lee Jinhee, "Kwandong taejijin ŭl ch'udoham: Ilbon cheguk ŭi 'pulyŏng sŏnin' kwa ch'udo ŭi chŏngch'ihak," *Asea yŏn'gu* 51, no. 1 (2008).

3. See Robert A. Scalapino and Chong-sik Lee, *Communism in Korea*: vol. 1, *The Movement* (Berkeley: University of California Press, 1972), 51–93.

4. Regarding the role of the police in colonial Korea, see Chulwoo Lee, "Modernity, Legality, and Power in Korea under Japanese Rule," *Colonial Modernity in Korea*, ed. Gi-Wook Shin and Michael Robinson (Cambridge: Harvard University Asia Center, 1999), 34–35.

5. See Micah Auerback, "'Ch'in-Il pulgyo' yŏksahak ŭi chaego: Chosŏn Pulgyo-

dan kwa 1920-nyŏndae Chosŏn esŏ ŭi sŭngnyŏ kyŏlhon e taehan nonjaeng," *Asea yŏn'gu* 51, no. 3 (2008).

6. According to Chulwoo Lee, during the first decade after annexation in 1910, the colonial effort to discipline and transform Koreans into "docile bodies" focused on coercive measures ranging from flogging to military action. The flogging took place in a closed cell, ostensibly in the presence of a physician and a number of officials. The colonial government justified this "rationalized" form of flogging on the grounds that many Koreans lacked the capacity to reason, and anyway destitute Koreans would not feel any pain from imprisonment. A year after the March First demonstrations of 1919, flogging was abolished. Lee, "Modernity, Legality, and Power in Korea under Japanese Rule." On the reasons for abolishing the Corporation Law and the political calculus behind that decision, see Carter Eckert, *Offspring of Empire: The Koch'ang Kims and the Colonial Origins of Korean Capitalism, 1876–1945* (Seattle: University of Washington Press, 1991).

7. *Sinsaenghwal* and *Shinch'ŏnji* were shut down in November 1922; *Kaebyŏk*, the leading intellectual magazine of the day, was shut down in July 1926. Korean materials that were confiscated became the property of the colonial state, while Japanese materials were returned to the publisher. Japanese publishers could sell magazines on a subscription basis, but Korean publishers could not. See Michael Robinson, "Colonial Publication Policy and the Korean Nationalist Movement," *The Japanese Colonial Empire, 1895–1945*, ed. Ramon H. Myers and Mark R. Peattie (Princeton: Princeton University Press, 1984).

8. It has to be said that between 1924 and 1931, *Tonga ilbo*, and especially *Chosŏn ilbo*, devoted significant space to socialist and communist ideas. See Robinson, "Colonial Publication Policy and the Korean Nationalist Movement."

9. Born in 1891, Kim Sŏng-su graduated from Waseda University in 1914. In 1919 he founded the Kyŏngsŏng Spinning and Weaving Company, and in 1920 the *Tonga ilbo*, with Song Chin-u as its president. In many ways, Kim was the power behind Song. Two years older, Song also studied in Japan (at Waseda and Meiji). In 1919 Song was imprisoned for a year in connection with the March First Movement and upon his release became the president of *Tonga ilbo*, a post he kept until the Japanese closed the newspaper in 1940. After liberation, Song opposed Yŏ Un-hyŏng and rallied the conservative forces in southern Korea, but he was assassinated by Kim Ku's men for supporting American plans for placing Korea under a trusteeship. On Kim Sŏng-su, see Eckert, *Offspring of Empire*.

10. For a concise overview of how a nascent home rule movement prompted the formation of the Sin'ganhoe, see Park Chan-seung (Pak Ch'an-sŭng), *Han'guk chŏngch'i sasangsa yŏn'gu* (Seoul: Yŏksa pip'yŏngsa, 1992), 330–55.

11. An Chae-hong studied at Waseda, graduating in 1914 from the College of Political Science and Economy. In 1913 he went to Shanghai and met Sin Ch'ae-ho. Disheartened by the weakness of the Korean independence movement in China at the time, especially its weak financial base, An chose not to join the independence struggle in exile and returned to Korea after finishing his studies. Beginning

in 1919, when he was first imprisoned for underground activities in support of the Korean provisional government in Shanghai, An was imprisoned nine times over the course of the colonial period for a total of seven years and three months.

12. As Scalapino and Lee succinctly put it, in practice the "correct position" could be defined only after the event: to steer between the Scylla of right-wing opportunism and the Charybdis of left-wing extremism was tremendously difficult (*Communism in Korea*, 1:62).

13. See the chapter "The Canton Commune," in Nym Wales and Kim San, *Song of Ariran: A Korean Communist in the Chinese Revolution* (1941; San Francisco: Ramparts Press, 1972).

14. See Park, *Han'guk kŭndae chŏngch'i sasangsa yŏn'gu*, 305–65.

15. From 1919 to 1924 Paek Nam-un studied in Japan at Tōkyō Kōshō (today, Hitotsubashi University) and returned to Korea to teach at Yŏnhŭi chŏnmun (today, Yonsei University). He wrote *Chōsen shakai keizaishi* (1933) and *Chōsen hōken shakai keizaishi* (1937) in Japanese and had them published in Japan to avoid the more stringent censorship laws in colonial Korea.

16. From 1898 to 1901 Fukuda Tokuzō studied under K. Bücher in Leipzig and L. Brentano in Munich. Fukuda Tokuzō, "Kankoku no keizai soshiki to keizai tani," *Keizaigaku kenkyū* (Tokyo: Dōbunkan, 1904).

17. Paek Nam-un took some liberties in this polemic. By the mid-1920s Sin Ch'ae-ho had become an anarchist, and while he may have referred to Ancient Chosŏn as if it formed a unique "mikrokosmus," he no longer wrote about the ethnic nation (*minjok*) as an undifferentiated transhistorical subject. Instead his focus had turned to the exploited masses (*minjung*). As for Ch'oe Nam-sŏn, he had joined the colonial government organ Chōsenshi henshūkai (Society for the Compilation of Korean History) in 1928, and he often did treat what he called the Korea-centered *Purham* cultural sphere as if it formed a unique "mikrokosmus." But Ch'oe also made a distinction between culture which was "global" from the start (but actually regional, as in cultural spheres), and ethnic-national origins which are particular. Thus, for Ch'oe, Korea and Japan could share a common (shamanistic) culture, and yet have distinct ethnic-national origins. See Ryu Si-hyun, *Ch'oe Nam-sŏn yŏn'gu: cheguk ŭi kŭndae wa singminji ŭi munhwa* (Seoul: Yŏksa pip'yŏngsa, 2009), 221–23.

18. Cited in Cho Hyŏn-sŏl, "Kŭndae kyemonggi Tan'gun sinhwa ŭi tal-sinhwa wa chaeinhwahwa," *Minjok munhaksa yŏn'gu* 32 (2006).

19. Roger L. Janelli, "The Origins of Korean Folklore Scholarship," *The Journal of American Folklore* 99, no. 391 (1986).

20. See Chizuko T. Allen, "Northeast Asia Centered around Korea: Ch'oe Nam-sŏn's View of History," *Journal of Asian Studies* 49, no. 4 (1990); "Ch'oe Namsŏn at the Height of Japanese Imperialism," *Sungkyun Journal of East Asian Studies* 5, no. 1 (2005); and "Early Migrations, Conquests, and Common Ancestry: Theorizing Japanese Origins in Relation with Korea," *Sungkyun Journal of East Asian Studies* 8, no. 1 (2008). For Ch'oe Nam-sŏn, the study of Tan'gun was the central, most important topic of research. Throughout the 1920s and up until the Korean

War, he continued to research and write about Tan'gun. See Yi P'il-yŏng. "Tan'gun yŏn'gusa," *Tan'gun*, ed. Yun I-hum et al. (Seoul: Seoul taehakkyo ch'ulp'anbu, 1994). For a full-length study of Ch'oe Nam-sŏn's life and work see Ryu Si-hyun, *Ch'oe Nam-sŏn yŏn'gu.*

21. Paek, *Chōsen shakai keizaishi*, 1:33. Paek Nam-un might also have been thinking about Taejonggyo (Religion of the Great Progenitor), a new religion organized in 1909 as a revival of a religious practice that Taejonggyo adherents traced back to the time of Tan'gun. In 1915 the Japanese colonial government forced Taejonggyo to disband, charging it as an anti-Japanese organization operating under the guise of a religion. For Taejonggyo adherents the story of Tan'gun was not a myth. As a nationalist church, Taejonggyo professed Hanin (Hwanin, God as creator), Hanung (Hwanung, God as educator), and Han'gŏm (Tan'gun, God as ruler) as a Trinity.

22. For a refutation of Morgan's claims about the consanguineous collective, communal family sex relations in Polynesia, see E. S. Craighill Handy and Mary Kawena Pukui, *The Polynesian Family System in Ka-u, Hawai'i* (Rutland, Vt.: Charles E. Tuttle, 1972). See also Thomas Trautmann, *Lewis Henry Morgan and the Invention of Kinship* (Berkeley: University of California Press, 1987); Paul Van der Grijp, "Pioneer of Untaught Anthropology: Recontextualizing Lewis H. Morgan and His Kinship Perspective," *Dialectical Anthropology* 22 (1997), 103–36.

23. Paek, *Chōsen shakai keizaishi*, 1:56, 67.

24. Lewis Henry Morgan, *Ancient Society* (New York: Henry Holt, 1878), 7–8, 3.

25. Frederick Engels, *The Origin of the Family, Private Property and the State: In the Light of the Researches of Lewis H. Morgan* (1884; New York: International Publishers, 1942).

26. There were Marxist critics too. Yi Ch'ŏng-wŏn, for example, attacked *Chōsen shakai keizaishi* as a mechanical application of Japanese Marxist (*Kōza-ha*) historiography to Korean history.

27. Paek Nam-un, "Chosŏn t'ŭkyu ŭi sahoe chedo" (1934), *Paek Nam-un chŏnjip*, 4:98.

28. A campaign led by the *Tonga ilbo* successfully prevented a bank auction of Yi Sun-sin's gravesite. See Yi Chi-wŏn, "1930-nyŏndae minjokjuŭi kyeyŏl ŭi kojŏk pojŏn undong," *Tongbang hakchi*, June 1993.

29. Yi Kwang-su, *Tonga Ilbo.*

30. Yi Kwang-su, *Tonga Ilbo.*

31. Paek, *Chōsen shakai keizaishi*, 1:20–21.

32. See Serk-Bae Suh, "The Wanpaoshan Incident and the Anti-Chinese Riots in Colonial Korea," unpublished paper, 7, 10.

33. Until the establishment of Manchukuo in 1932, the question of citizenship for Koreans (that is, jurisdiction over Koreans) in Manchuria remained an important issue in Sino-Japanese rivalry.

34. Anti-Chinese feelings can be traced to a number of sources: the success of Chinese merchants in colonial Korea, competition between unskilled Korean and

Chinese workers, and the operation of racial and ethnic hierarchies in colonial and imperial cultures. After the riots, *Chosŏn ilbo* published editorials urging Koreans not to resort to violence to protest the Chinese oppression of Koreans in Manchuria.

35. An Chae-hong was jailed on charges of diverting public funds and could not return to his position at *Chosŏn ilbo*.

36. *T'aejo sillok*, in the founding year of the Chosŏn dynasty, records a memorial submitted by Cho Pak of the Board of Rites defining the distinctive status to be accorded to Tan'gun and Kija in state rituals. Because Tan'gun was the first ruler to receive the Mandate of Heaven in Korea (*tongbang*) and Kija was the first ruler to bring civilization to fruition in Korea, the magistrate in Pyongyang was instructed to conduct sacrifices to them at appropriate times. *T'aejo sillok*, 1-kwŏn, 1-nyŏn (1392), 8/11, second article.

37. Shim Jae-hoon has argued that Kija should not be associated with Chosŏn at all. According to Shim, Kija does seem to be a nobleman of Shang and did go east. But a political entity called Chosŏn should be dated much later: it was not until the Han dynasty that sources clearly associated Kija with Chosŏn. Shim Jae-Hoon, "A New Understanding of Kija Chosŏn as a Historical Anachronism," *Harvard Journal of Asiatic Studies* 62, no. 2 (2002).

38. Korean historians critical of positivist and critical-textual historiography in twentieth-century Korea posit a break between the *munhŏn kojŭng sahak* (文獻考 證史學) of the Chosŏn period and the practice of critical-textual historiography in the colonial period. These historians, for reasons that are at least partially political, readily concur with Japanese historians' claim that critical-textual historiography in twentieth-century Japan developed out of the *kōshōgaku* tradition of the Tokugawa period, transitioning to "modern" historiography through the influence of Rankean historiography. Such a genealogy highlights critical-textual historiography's intellectual and institutional origins to Japanese imperialist politics and colonial institutions.

39. There were other, smaller academic associations organized around disciplines: the Society of Korean Language Research (Chosŏnŏ hakhoe, established in 1931), the Korean Language and Literature Society (Chosŏnŏ munhakhoe, organized in 1931 by Cho Yun-jae and other graduates of the Department of Korean Language and Literature, Keijō Imperial University), the Korean Folklore Society (Chosŏn minsok hakhoe, established formally in 1933 by Son Chin-tae), and the Society for Korean Economic History Research (Chosŏn kyŏngje hakhoe, established in 1933). Membership in Chosŏn minsok hakhoe included such prominent Japanese scholars as Akiba Takashi, a member of the faculty at Keijō Imperial University whose studies on Korean shamanism were enormously influential.

40. The Chindan Society published the first issue of its journal, *Chindan hakbo*, in November 1934. Until pressured to stop publication in 1943, the Chindan Society published fourteen issues of *Chindan hakbo* during the colonial period. From October 1942 to March 1943, as the momentum of the war in the Pacific swung

toward the United States, dozens of people were arrested and tortured in connection with the Korean Linguists Association incident, including several Chindan hakhoe members. Until 1943 Yi Pyŏng-do had contributed an article for every issue of *Chindan hakbo*, including essays on Samhan in the pre–Three Kingdoms period, geomantic thought during the Koryŏ period, and Confucianism in the Chosŏn period.

41. Remco E. Breuker, "Contested Objectivities: Ikeuchi Hiroshi, Kim Sanggi and the Tradition of Oriental History (Tōyōshigaku) in Japan and Korea," *East Asian History* 29 (2005).

42. Ch'oe Nam-sŏn was the first to study history in Japan, but the time he spent at Waseda was relatively short. Yi Pyŏng-do is thus considered the first Korean historian to be trained in historiography at a Japanese university. In 1932, after ten years of work, Chōsenshi henshūkai published the first five volumes of what became the thirty-eight-volume *Chōsenshi* (Korean History), along with the three-volume *Chōsen shiryō shushin* (Collection of Korean Documents) and the twenty-one-volume *Chōsen shiryō sōkan* (Archive of Korean Documents).

43. See Stefan Tanaka, *Japan's Orient: Rendering Pasts into History* (Berkeley: University of California Press, 1993).

44. See Han Young-Woo (Han Yŏng-u), "Yi Pyŏng-do," *Han'guk ŭi yŏksaga wa yŏksahak*, ed. Cho Tong-gŏl et al. (Seoul: Ch'angjak kwa pip'yŏngsa, 1994), 2:255.

45. See Cho Tong-gŏl, *Hyŏndae Han'guk sahaksa* (Seoul: Nanam ch'ulpan, 1998), 219.

46. Kim T'ae-jun was a member of the Central Committee of the South Korean Workers' Party.

47. An Chae-hong and others would have preferred *kukhak* (national studies) over *Chosŏnhak* (Korean studies), but *kukhak* (J: *kokugaku*) would have been confused with "Japanese studies."

48. Paek Nam-un, "Chŏng Tasan ŭi sasang," *Paek Nam-un chŏnjip*, 4:113–21.

49. Paek, *Chōsen shakai keizaishi*, 1:22.

50. In China too Marxist intellectuals were hostile to the concept of an Asiatic mode of production and attracted to the idea that all societies travel the same road.

51. The most well-known cases are Yi Kwang-su and Ch'oe Nam-sŏn. It should be noted, however, that An Chae-hong and Chŏng In-bo did not compromise their nationalist stance. The same cannot be said of Kim Sŏng-su. See Carter Eckert, *Offspring of Empire*.

52. The influence of Kōza-ha theory is clearly evident in Paek's economic historiography. According to Pang Ki-jung, Paek also benefited from reading Guo Moruo's *Zhongguo guudai shehui yaniu* (Research on Ancient Chinese Society); the first edition was published in 1929. Pang Kie-chung (Pang Ki-jung), "Paek Nam-un yŏn'gu I," *Yŏksa pip'yŏng* 7 (Summer 1989), 198.

53. Yi Ch'ŏng-wŏn, *Chosŏn sahoesa tokbon* (Tokyo: Paekyangsa, 1936), 1–2.

54. In the preface to *Chōsen shakai keizaishi* Paek expressed warm gratitude to Chŏng In-bo. After liberation and the establishment of North and South Korea

in 1948, Chŏng became South Korea's first inspector general, while Paek went to North Korea.

55. Paek, "Chosŏn t'ŭkyu ŭi sahoe chedo," 4:95.

56. Paek, "Chōsen shakai keizaishi ch'ulp'an e taehan sogam," 4:87.

57. Paek, Chōsen shakai keizaishi, 1:373.

5. Divided Sovereignty

1. The writers met at Ponghwanggak in Ui-dong, built by Son Pyŏng-hŭi in 1912 as a training center for Ch'ŏndogyo (and independence) activists. As the third leader of the Tonghak faith, Son had changed the name of the religion to Ch'ŏndogyo (Religion of the Heavenly Way). Son was one of the thirty-three signers of the declaration of independence in 1919, and thus Ponghwanggak had some association with the independence movement. The source for this chapter's epigraph is *Inmin yesul* 2 (October 1946), reprinted in *Haebang 3-nyŏn ŭi pip'yŏng munhak*, ed. Sin Hyŏng-gi (Seoul: Segye, 1988), 79–85.

2. In what came to be known as the August Thesis, which became the platform of the Korean Communist Party when it was reconstituted soon after liberation, Pak Hŏn-yŏng also referred to Koreans as "having arrived at the moment when they have to engage in self-criticism." Park Tae Gyun (Pak T'ae-gyun), "Haebang chŏnggaek Pak Hŏn-yŏng kwa 8-wŏl t'eje," *Obsŏbŏ* 8 (2002).

3. Kim Yun-sik, "Haebang gonggan ŭi munhak," *Haebang chŏnhusa ŭi insik*, ed. Kang Man-gil et al. (Seoul: Han'gilsa, 1985), 2:449.

4. The Korean Communist Party was reconstituted in Seoul in September 1945 under the leadership of Pak Hŏn-yŏng. In Seoul in December 1946, the KCP in the South merged with the South Korean New Democracy Party (Nam-Chosŏn sinmindang), which included Paek Nam-un in its leadership, and the Korean People's Party (Chosŏn inmindang), led by Yŏ Un-hyŏng, to form the South Korean Workers' Party (Nam-Chosŏn nodongdang). In September 1945 Kim Nam-ch'ŏn and Im Hwa organized the Chosŏn munhak kŏnsŏl ponbu (Headquarters for Construction of Korean Literature), and Han Sŏl-ya and Yi Ki-yŏng organized the Chosŏn p'ŭlollaetaeria munhak tongmaeng (Korean Federation for Proletarian Literature), explicitly committed to, as suggested by the organization's name, proletarian literature. Hong Hyo-min traces the reason for the formation of two separate groups immediately after liberation to political differences that go back to the colonial period and the Korea Artista Proleta Federatio (1925–1935). Hong Hyo-min, "Yesul yŏn'gam," 1947, cited in Pak Ch'an-mo, "Haebang chikhu ŭi Han Hyo ŭi munhak pip'yŏng koch'al," *Hyŏndae munhak iron yŏn'gu* 27 (2006). According to Pak, one explanation for why Han Sŏl-ya and Yi Ki-yŏng went north had to do with this merger, as the Chosŏn munhakga tongmaeng adopted the platform of Munhak kŏnsŏl ponbu and, more broadly, that of Pak Hŏn-yŏng's (Korean Communist Party) bourgeois democratic revolution.

5. Lawyers for the USAMGIK put it this way: the USAMGIK did not claim sover-

eignty over (southern) Korea but did take unto itself all sovereign powers formerly held by the Japanese colonial government, until sovereignty could be assumed by a legally constituted Korean government. See United States, Office of the Provost Marshal General, "Introduction and Orientation," *History of Military Government Training*, vol. 1, 1945 (microfilm). The establishment of a military government is predicated on a state of exception, to restore order over a hostile population to secure areas behind (an advancing) front line. The U.S. Army Military Government would decide when and how a "legally constituted government" took its place.

6. Kim Sa-ryang entered the Department of German Literature at Tokyo Imperial University in 1936 and finished "Hikari no naka ni" soon after graduating in 1939. "Hikari no naka ni" was published in *Bungei shuto* in 1939. In addition to the reprint published by Kodansha in 1999, I also consulted the Korean translation *Kim Saryang chakp'umjip*, ed. Im Hŏn-yŏng (Seoul: Chisik ŭl mandŭnŭn chisik, 2008).

7. Kim Sa-ryang's name was pronounced Kin Shiryō.

8. This forum and an earlier one on December 12 served, in part, as preparation and consolidation work, including qualification for membership, for the merger that formally took place on December 13, 1945, to form the Chosŏn munhakga tongmaeng (Federation of Korean Writers). Kim Nam-ch'ŏn, who also headed the Communist Youth League, played a central role in the merger.

9. See "Munhakja ŭi chaki pip'an," *Inmin yesul*, October 1946, reprinted in Sin, *Haebang 3-nyŏn ŭi pip'yŏng munhak*, 79–85.

10. Among positivist historians Yi Sang-baek perhaps took the most interest in theoretical questions. Embracing the idealist underpinnings of Ranke's positivist historiography, Yi understood historiography's aim to be comprehension of the universal meaning immanent in particular historical facts. See Kim P'il-dong, "Yi Sang-baek," *Han'guk ŭi yŏksaga wa yŏksahak*, vol. 2, ed. Cho Tong-gŏl et al. (Seoul: Ch'angjak kwa pip'yŏngsa, 1994).

11. A representative historian would be Yi Sŏn-gŭn, a virulent anticommunist who taught Korean history to President Park Chung Hee and became the first president of Chŏngsin munhwa yŏn'guwŏn, today the Academy of Korean Studies.

12. There was some precedent for this. Aside from Paek Nam-un's stature as a historian and intellectual, he had attempted something of this kind in 1936, when he set out to organize a chungang akademi (central academy). The Chosŏn haksul-wŏn Paek established in 1945 was heavily tilted toward scholars in the social sciences and the natural sciences. See Cho Tong-gŏl, *Hyŏndae Han'guk sahaksa* (Seoul: Nanam ch'ulp'an, 1998), 323.

13. See Pang Kie-chung (Pang Ki-jung), "Haebanghu kukka kŏnsŏl munje wa yŏksahak," *Han'guksa insik kwa yŏksa iron* (Seoul: Chisik sanŏpsa, 1997), 84.

14. Chindan hakhoe was formally reconstituted on August 31, 1945.

15. Organized on Christmas Day 1945, the Korean Historical Association (Yŏksa hakhoe) included historians across the political spectrum, in the fields of art history as well as European, Asian, and Korean history. It was organized with the specific intent of bridging the Left-Right divide. During the Korean War another

organization with the same name was established, but the association established in 1952 did not claim any link to the earlier association, perhaps because the earlier one had included many leftist scholars. In 1946 a student group with the same name was formed under the sponsorship of Yi In-yŏng, then a faculty member of the Department of History at Kyŏngsŏng University (Seoul National University). See Cho, *Hyŏndae Han'guk sahaksa*, 328–29.

16. Hannah Arendt, *The Origins of Totalitarianism* (1968; Oxford: Benediction Classics, 2009), 4–5. See also Alexis de Tocqueville, *The Old Regime and the French Revolution*, trans. John Bonner (New York: Harper and Brothers, 1856), 39–49.

17. According to Pang Kie-chung, it was probably Yi Sang-baek who led the initiative to join the Committee on Science (chŏnmun wiwŏnhoe) within the Democratic National Front. Pang, "Haebanghu kukka kŏnsŏl munje wa yŏksahak," 87.

18. Pang Kie-chung suggests that, immediately after liberation and until just prior to the second U.S.-Soviet Joint Commission talks in 1947, there was close coordination between Son Chin-t'ae, Cho Yun-jae, and others with An Chae-hong. Pang, "Haebanghu kukka kŏnsŏl munje wa yŏksahak." See note 57 below, and works cited in note 2.

19. Yi Pyŏng-do's work on *Chōsenshi* had to do with the compilation of volumes that dealt with "Unified" Silla and Koryŏ periods.

20. Yi Pyŏng-do's self-defense did not nearly match the intricacy and ambivalence of Yi Kwang-su's self-defense and self-critique: Yi Kwang-su did not think Japan would lose, and what he did he did for the welfare of the Korean people.

21. See Shin Ju Baek (Sin Chu-baek), "Perception of August 15 Remembered in and Forgotten from Korean Textbooks," *Review of Korean Studies* 8, no. 1 (2005), 51–84.

22. This level of university autonomy came on the heels of a case in 1914, when the faculty of the School of Law at Kyoto Imperial University successfully resisted the attempt by the university president, at that time appointed by the Ministry of Education, to fire seven faculty members. It should be said, of course, that institutionalization of academic self-governance in the 1920s did not ensure academic freedom, especially in the 1930s. Byron K. Marshall, "The Tradition of Conflict in the Governance of Japanese Imperial Universities," *History of Education Quarterly* 17, no. 4 (1977).

23. These included Kim Sang-gi, Yi Sang-baek, Son Chin-t'ae, Yi In-yŏng, and Yu Hong-ryŏl. Following liberation there were calls within Chindan hakhoe to expel "pro-Japanese" scholars. It was not until 1954, when extreme anticommunism suppressed all talk of collaboration during the colonial period, that Yi Pyŏng-do again took over leadership of Chindan hakhoe.

24. It is likely that An Chae-hong's withdrawal of support for the KPR was also influenced by the USAMGIK's refusal to recognize the KPR as a government.

25. During the Korean War, nationalist historians like An Chae-hong, Son Chin-t'ae, and Yi In-yŏng were taken to the North. See Cho, *Hyŏndae Han'guk sahaksa*.

26. See Kim Dong-Choon, chapter on massacres, *Chŏnjaeng kwa sahoe: uri ege*

Han'guk chŏnjaeng ŭn muŏt iŏnna (Seoul: Tolbaegae, 2000), or the English-language publication *The Unending Korean War: A Social History* (Larkspur, Calif: Tamal Vista Publications, 2009). See also Hee-Kyung Suh, "Atrocities Before and During the Korean War," *Critical Asian Studies* 42, no. 4 (2010).

27. Born in 1924, Yi Ki-baek graduated from Osan Middle School, where he read Sin Ch'ae-ho's *Chosŏnsa yŏn'gu ch'o*. In early 1945 Yi was a student in the History Department at Waseda when he was drafted into the Kwantung Army. He was captured by the Soviet Red Army and held as a prisoner for a short time. He entered Seoul National University's (previously Keijō Imperial University) Department of History in 1946 and graduated in one year. At SNU, he studied under Yi Pyŏng-do.

28. Yi Ki-baek attributed historical transformation and dynastic change to the emergence of a new (ruling) class or group. Narrating historical progress in terms of newly emerging forces, he argued that, over time, the aristocratic class in Korea transformed itself from a small elite minority to a ubiquitous force in society.

29. Yi Ki-baek, "Sahoe kyŏngje sahak kwa silchŭng sahak ŭi munje," 1971, *Yŏksa wa minjok* (Seoul: Ilchogak, 1997), 34.

30. Kim Yong-sŏp's thesis regarding two paths to modernity rested on a more general argument about the breakdown of feudal structures in late Chosŏn. He drew attention to the emergence of what he called wealthy managerial farmers (*kyŏngyŏnghyŏng pu'nong*), eighteenth- and nineteenth-century Chosŏn's equivalent of the English yeoman farmer, who leased a substantial amount of land, employed wage laborers, engaged in commodity trade, accumulated surpluses, and established a capitalist way of farming. According to Kim, this kind of large-scale commercial farming and differentiation of the peasant class gave evidence of feudal structures breaking down in late Chosŏn.

31. The first volume of *Haebang chŏnhusa ŭi insik* was published in 1979, the sixth volume in 1989. Each volume was organized around one or more themes, with the author of the lead essay making the central historiographic arguments which gave each volume its distinctiveness.

32. As Song Kŏn-ho points out, enormous consequences resulted from Japan's surrendering only to the United States. Because it was not Koreans who had defeated the Japanese but American blood, treasure, and technology, the United States could divide Korea into two, with Soviet agreement, and refuse to recognize either the Korean Provisional Government based in China or the Korean People's Republic (Chosŏn Inmin Konghwaguk) that had formed just before the arrival of U.S. troops in 1945. Song Kŏn-ho, *Haebang chŏnhusa ŭi insik*, vol. 1, revised edition (Seoul: Han'gilsa, 1989).

33. In collaboration and South Korean historiography, see Koen de Ceuster, "The Nation Exorcised," *Korean Studies* 25, no. 2 (2001).

34. For a history of the democracy movement, see Namhee Lee, *The Making of Minjung: Democracy and the Politics of Representation in South Korea* (Ithaca: Cornell University Press, 2007).

35. *Haebang chŏnhusa ŭi insik*, along with dozens of other books, was banned dur-

ing the martial law period following the assassination of Park Chung Hee in 1979 by the director of the Korean Central Intelligence Agency. When the ban was lifted in the early 1980s, *Haebang chŏnhusa ŭi insik* became the preeminent best-seller among social science books.

36. On May 17, the martial law command led by Chun Doo-hwan induced President Choi Kyu-hwa to extend martial law throughout South Korea. All political activities and strikes were to cease, all news organizations were to be censored, and universities were to go into recess. When the students in Kwangju continued their protest against martial law, paratroopers were sent in to put a stop to the demonstrations. The brutality of the paratroopers enraged the entire city, and on May 20 bus and taxi drivers blocked the main thoroughfares, the city hall was taken over, and a citizen's army organized. On May 27 ROK government troops, released by General John Wickham from the Joint Command structure, retook the city. The exact number of people killed by the military has yet to be established; estimates range from several hundred to nearly a thousand.

37. After the bloody experience of Kwangju there was a decisive shift toward reconstituting the movement as a revolutionary movement on the basis of Marxism as a science. In one wing of the student movement familiarity with DPRK's Chuch'e Thought became de rigueur, while dozens of master's theses were being written on the revolutionary nationalist (communist) movement before and during the liberation period, theses which were almost unanimously critical of the American role in the liberation period.

38. It took courage to write critically about history after 1945. In 1980 Kang Man-gil was forced to resign from the faculty at Korea University. (He was able to return to his position the following year.) When Choi Sang-ryong (Ch'oe Sangyŏng), Kang's colleague in the Political Science Department, returned to Korea in the early 1970s, the Korean CIA read out loud passages from his Tokyo University Ph.D. dissertation while torturing him. See Bruce Cumings, "The Korea War: What Is It That We Are Remembering to Forget?," *Ruptured Histories: War, Memory, and the Post-Cold War in Asia*, ed. Sheila Miyoshi Jager and Rana Mitter (Cambridge: Harvard University Press, 2007).

39. Choi Jang-jip and Chŏng Hae-gu, "Haebang 8-nyŏnsa ŭi ch'ongch'ejŏk insik," *Haebang chŏnhusa ŭi insik*, vol. 4, ed. Choi Jang-jip and Chŏng Hae-gu (Seoul: Han'gilsa, 1989).

40. According to a public opinion poll of eight thousand people taken in 1946 by the USAMGIK, in southern Korea 70 percent supported socialism, 10 percent communism, and 13 percent capitalism. See Tae-Gyun Park, "Different Roads, Common Destination: Economic Discourses in South Korea During the 1950s," *Modern Asian Studies* 39, no. 3 (2005), 661–82.

41. Bruce Cumings's *Origins of the Korean War*, vol. 1, first made an impact after underground translations circulated in the mid-1980s. According to Pak Myŏnglim, "In the 1980s, Professor Cumings was for young intellectuals in South Korea both intellectual guide and inspiration for committed scholarship; at the same

time, his work was an intellectual hurdle to be overcome by scholars trained in Korea." Pak Myŏng-lim, "Bruce Cumings ŭi Han'guk chŏnjaeng ŭi kiwŏn e taehan hana ŭi nonp'yŏng," unpublished paper, 1992. See Bruce Cumings, *The Origins of the Korean War*: vol. 1, *Liberation and the Emergence of Separate Regimes, 1945–1947* (Princeton: Princeton University Press, 1981).

42. Chong-Sik Lee (Yi Chŏng-sik) made a similar argument in *Korean Workers' Party: A Short History* (Stanford: Hoover Institution Press, 1978), 73–75.

43. On January 12, 1950, in a speech at the National Press Club, Secretary of State Dean Acheson included Japan in the U.S. defense perimeter but left South Korea and Taiwan outside of that perimeter. Referring obliquely to South Korea, Acheson added, "the initial reliance must be on the people attacked to resist it and then upon the commitments of the entire civilized world under the Charter of the United Nations which so far has not proved a weak reed." Dean Acheson, *Present at the Creation: My Years in the State Department* (New York: Norton, 1969), 354–58. Acheson had not said that the United States would not come to South Korea's defense. Nevertheless, with South Korea placed outside of the American line of defense, the entrapment thesis argues that North Korea invaded South Korea, gambling that the United States would not intervene. Acheson's strategic thinking was not fixated on Korea; Europe was his primary concern. But when North Korea launched a general military offensive across the 38th parallel, Acheson did not hesitate in committing U.S. forces. NSC 68, completed on April 14, 1950, was a comprehensive statement of what United States national security policy should be. Until the outbreak of the Korean War on June 25, top officials in Washington debated NSC 68's call for more than a three-fold increase in the U.S. military budget. In his 1948 Presidential campaign, President Truman had stated categorically that the U.S. economy could not afford military spending in excess of $15 billion a year. See Samuel F. Wells, Jr., "Sounding the Tocsin: NSC 68 and the Soviet Threat," *International Security* 4, no. 2 (1979), 123. The military appropriation for 1950 had been $13 billion, and supporters of NSC 68 thought they could realistically expect an additional $3 billion. After the outbreak of the Korean War, however, President Truman approved NSC 68 and by May 1951 the U.S. military budget swelled to $48 billion. See David T. Fautua, "The 'Long Pull' Army: NSC 68, the Korean War, and the Creation of the Cold War U.S. Army," *The Journal of Military History* 61, no. 1 (1997). There can be no disagreement that the Korean War convinced President Truman to sign NSC 68 (on September 30, 1950) and Congress to approve the massive increase in the military budget. As NSC 68 pointed out, "It goes without saying that the idea of 'preventive' war—in the sense of a military attack not provoked by a military attack upon us or our allies—is generally unacceptable to Americans." United States Department of State, *Foreign Relations of the United States, 1950*, vol. 1, p. 281. According to the entrapment thesis, North Korea walked into a trap in the sense that its attack across the 38th parallel provided the occasion for rallying the American people, and for NSC 68 to become the foundation for U.S. national security policy.

44. For a more comprehensive discussion of the multivolume *Haebang chŏnhusa ŭi insik*, see Henry Em, "'Overcoming' Korea's Division: Narrative Strategies in Recent South Korean Historiography," *positions: east asia cultures critique* 1, no. 2 (1993).

45. Writing in 2000, Kang Man-gil wryly notes that, from 1960 through the end of the 1980s, people referred to as "conservatives" in the 1990s used to be called antidemocrats (*pan-minju insa*). "Posup'a chach'ŏ hannŭn Kim sŏnsaeng kke," *Hankyŏre sinmun*, January 23, 2000, 8.

46. Pak Chi-hyang et al., eds., *Haebang chŏnhusa ŭi chaeinsik* (Reconsideration of Liberation History), vols. 1 and 2 (Seoul: Chaek sesang, 2006). Roh Moo-hyun (No Mu-hyŏn) became president in February 2003; his term ended in February 2008. During his inaugural speech, President Roh referred to justice being defeated and opportunism having prevailed in modern Korean history. The editors of *Haebang chŏnhusa ŭi chaeinsik* interpreted this as Roh's disavowing the very legitimacy of South Korea. Yi Yŏng-hun notes that the generation that studied *Haebang chŏnhusa ŭi insik* now form Roh's core advisors. See the lead article by Yi Yŏng-hun, "Wae tasi haebang chŏnhusa in'ga," *Haebang chŏnhusa ŭi chaeinsik*, vol. 1.

47. See Cumings, "The Korea War: What Is It That We Are Remembering to Forget?," 283–84.

48. A number of contributors to *Haebang chŏnhusa ŭi chaeinsik* were taken aback by how their work was framed in the introduction and distanced themselves from the editors' polemical stance.

49. Yu In-ho's essay in *Haebang chŏnhusa ŭi insik* was critical of the impact of land reform that finally got under way in 1950. Of the 1.4 million hectares in wet paddies and dry fields, up to 874,000 hectares (61 percent) of land that should have been targeted for land reform was sold to tenant farmers, its ownership was transferred to family members, or it was flooded (to evade compliance) prior to implementation of land reform. Yu In-ho, "Haebang-hu nongji kaehyŏk ŭi chŏn'gaekwajŏng kwa sŏnggyŏk," *Haebang chŏnhusa ŭi insik*, vol. 1. Chang Si-wŏn's essay in *Haebang chŏnhusa ŭi chaeinsik*, originally published in 1995, argues that the average sale price of those lands sold to tenant farmers before 1950 was roughly equivalent to prices mandated by the land reform law. Landlords, anticipating the passage of the land reform bill, sold their land to tenant farmers at prices the tenant farmers would have had to pay anyway. See Chang Si-wŏn, "Nongji kaehyŏk: chijuje haech'e wa chagaknongcheje ŭi sŏngnip," *Haebang chŏnhusa ŭi chaeinsik*, vol. 2.

50. Lee Chong-Sik (Yi Chŏng-sik), "Naengjŏn ŭi chŏn'gae kwajŏng kwa Hanbando pundan ŭi koch'akhwa," *Haebang chŏnhusa ŭi chaeinsik*, vol. 2.

51. Pak Chi-hyang, Kim Chŏl, Kim Il-yŏng, and Yi Yŏng-hun, "Taedam," *Haebang chŏnhusa ŭi chaeinsik*, vol. 2.

52. On August 15, 2004, a year before the fiftieth year marking Korea's liberation from Japanese colonial rule, President Roh Moo-hyun had spoken of the necessity for a comprehensive settlement of past wrongs. In 2005 the South Korean National Assembly passed the Framework Act that established the Truth and Reconcilia-

tion Commission, Republic of Korea (TRCK). TRCK's mandate was broad enough to encompass most wrongdoings committed by the South Korean state prior to 1992. But it did not have prosecutorial authority: it could not punish perpetrators even when they were identified. The TRCK's investigative authority was also curtailed in that state institutions like the Bureau of Police, the Ministry of Defense, and the National Intelligence Service (formerly the KCIA) could refuse TRCK's demands for documents if they deemed those documents to be potentially damaging to national security. The TRCK was established with such limitations because the stated goal of reconciliation made it necessary for the Framework Act of 2005 to be passed by the National Assembly with support from both the liberal and conservative parties. In spite of such limitations, during the two years that the TRCK pursued its investigations under the Roh Moo-hyun administration, the TRCK presented an impressive range of findings and recommendations that threatened conservatives. For example, TRCK findings included facts about massacres of civilians, in South Korea, committed by United States and South Korean forces during the Korean War, and findings that controverted judicial rulings involving momentous national security cases. For example, TRCK recommended that the government issue an official apology in the case of Cho Pong-am. See Dong-Choon Kim [Kim Tong-ch'un], "The Long Road Toward Truth and Reconciliation: Unwavering Attempts to Achieve Justice in South Korea," *Critical Asian Studies* 42, no. 4 (2010). In the same volume, see also Jae-Jung Suh, "Truth and Reconciliation in South Korea." In 1956, Cho Pong-am had organized the Progressive Party (Chinbodang) and ran as a Presidential candidate on a platform that called for responsible reform, a non-exploitative planned economy, and democratic peaceful reunification with North Korea. He received 30 percent of the vote in that election. In January 1958, a few months before the National Assembly elections, Cho Pong-am was arrested on charges of spying for North Korea, receiving funds from North Korea during the 1956 Presidential election, and fomenting subversion. He was executed on July 31, 1959. On January 20, 2011, the South Korean Supreme Court found Cho Pong-am innocent of the charges.

53. See Yi Yŏng-hun, *Taehan Min'guk iyagi* (Seoul: Kip'arang, 2007).

54. According to Kang Man-gil in a seminar at Korea University in 1998, historians should look forward to the day when nationalism can be dispensed with. But so long as Korea remains divided, nationalist historiography is necessary.

55. In this question, see the two-volume anthology *Kŭndae rŭl tasi ignŭnda*, ed. Yun Hae-dong et al. (Seoul: Yŏksa pip'yŏngsa, 2006). See also essays in *Kuksa ŭi sinhwa rŭl nŏmŏsŏ*, ed. Lim Jie-Hyun (Im Chi-hyŏn) et al. (Seoul: Humŏnistŭ, 2004).

56. See Alain Badiou, *Ethics: an Essay on the Understanding of Evil*, translated by Peter Hallward (New York: Verso, 2001).

57. See Lauren Berlant's Introduction, in *Cruel Optimism* (Durham: Duke University Press, 2011).

BIBLIOGRAPHY

Sources in Japanese and Korean

An Chae-hong. *Minse An Chae-hong sŏnjip*. 8 vols. Seoul: Chisik sanŏpsa, 1981–2004.

An Chong-ch'ŏl. "Munmyŏng kaehwa esŏ pan'gong ŭro: Yi Sŭng-man kwa kaesinkyo ŭi kwankye ŭi pyŏnhwa, 1912–1950." *Tongbang hakji* 145 (2009).

Auerback, Micah. "'Ch'in-Il Pulgyo' yŏksahak ŭi chae'go: Chosŏn Pulgyodan kwa 1920-nyŏndae Chosŏn esŏ ŭi sŭngryŏ kyŏlhon e taehan nonjaeng." *Asea yŏn'gu* 51, no. 3 (2008).

Chang Si-wŏn. "Nongji kaehyŏk: Chijuje haech'e wa chagaknongcheje ŭi sŏngnip." *Haebang chŏnhusa ŭi chaeinsik*, vol. 2. Seoul: Chaek sesang, 2006.

Chindan hakhoe, ed. *Yŏksaga ŭi yuhyang*. Seoul: Ilchogak, 1991.

Cho Chun-ha. "Uam Song Si-yŏl ŭi chuch'e ŭisik." *Han'guk sasang kwa munhwa* 42 (2008).

———. "Uri nara ŭi chesa munhwa wa chongmyo taeje." *Han'guk sasang kwa munhwa* 12 (2001).

Cho Hyŏn-sŏl. "Kŭndae kyemonggi Tan'gun sinhwa ŭi t'al-sinhwa wa chaesinhwahwa." *Minjok munhaksa yŏn'gu* 32 (2006).

Cho Tong-gŏl. *Hyŏndae Han'guk sahaksa*. Seoul: Nanam ch'ulpan, 1998.

———. "Kŭndae ch'ogi ŭi yŏksa insik." *Han'guk ŭi yŏksaga wa yŏksa insik*, vol. 2, ed. Cho Tong-gŏl et al. Seoul: Ch'angjak kwa pip'yŏngsa, 1994.

Cho Tong-gŏl et al. *Han'guk ŭi yŏksaga wa yŏksahak*, vols. 1 (*sang*) and 2 (*ha*). Seoul: Ch'angjak kwa pip'yŏngsa, 1994.

Ch'oe Hyŏn-bae, "Kidokkyo wa Han'gŭl," *Sinhak nondan*, 7 (1962).

Ch'oe Nam-sŏn. *Yuktang Ch'oe Nam-sŏn chŏnjip*. 15 vols. Seoul: Hyŏnamsa, 1973–75.

———. *Yuktang Ch'oe Nam-sŏn chŏnjip*. 14 vols. Seoul: Yŏngnak, 2003.

Choi Jang-jip and Chŏng Hae-gu. "Haebang 8-nyŏnsa ŭi ch'ongch'ejŏk insik." *Haebang chŏnhusa ŭi insik*, vol. 4, ed. Choi Jang-jip et al. Seoul: Han'gilsa, 1989.

Chŏn Sŏk-dam. *Chosŏn kyŏngjesa t'amgu*. Seoul: Pŏmusa, 1990.

Chŏng Okcha. *Chosŏn hugi Chosŏn Chunghwa sasang yŏn'gu*. Seoul: Ilchisa, 1998.

Chŏng T'ae-sik and Yi Ch'ŏl-u. "Mi'gunjŏnggi wa Taegu 10-wŏl hangjaeng esŏ ŭi kidokkyo chonggyo chidojadŭl ŭi sahoe chŏngch'ijŏk hwaldong kwa yŏkhal ŭi taehan ilkoch'al." *Chiyŏk sahoe yŏn'gu* 14, no. 4 (2006).

Chōsen Sotokufu . *Chōsen koseki zufu*, 15 vols. Seoul: Chōsen Sotokufu, 1915–35.

Ch'u Myŏng-yŏp, *Han'guksa yŏn'gu*, no. 129 (2005).

Fukuda Tokuzō. "Kankoku no keizai soshiki to keizai tani." *Keizaigaku kenkyū*. Tokyo: Dōbunkan, 1904.

Han Young-Woo [Han Yŏng-u]. *Han'guk minjokjuŭi yŏksahak.* Seoul: Ilchogak, 1994.

———. "Uri nara yŏksahak ŭi hŭrŭm." *Han'guk ŭi yŏksaga wa yŏksahak*, vol. 1, ed. Cho Tong-gŏl et al. Seoul: Ch'angjak kwa pip'yŏngsa, 1994.

———. "Yi Pyŏng-do." *Han'guk ŭi yŏksaga wa yŏksahak*, vol. 2, ed. Cho Tong-gŏl et al. Seoul: Ch'angjak kwa pip'yŏngsa, 1994.

Han'guk Yŏksa Yŏn'guhoe Kodaesa Punkwa. *Mundap ŭro yŏkkŭn Han'guk kodaesa sanch'aek.* Seoul: Yŏksa pip'yŏngsa, 1994.

Han'guksa yŏn'guhoe, ed. *Han'guk sahaksa ŭi yŏn'gu.* Seoul: Ŭryu munhwasa, 1985.

Hatada Takashi. *Nihonjin no chōsenkan.* Tokyo: Chikuma Shobō, 1969.

Hong Tae-yong. *Sinp'yŏn kugyŏk Hong Tae-yong Tamhŏnsŏ.* Kyŏnggi-do Paju-si: Han'guk Haksul Chŏngbo, 2008.

Im Chong-guk. *Sillok ch'inilp'a.* Seoul: Tolbegae, 1991.

Im Pu-yŏn. "Yuggyo ŭiryehwa ŭi chŏngchihak: Mandongmyo wa Taebodan ŭr chungsim ŭro."*Chonggyo munhwa pip'yŏng* 15 (2009).

Iryŏn. *Samguk yusa.* Seoul: Sŏjŏng Sihak, 2009.

Kang Man-gil. "Ilje sidae ŭi pansigmin sahaknon." *Han'guk sahaksa ui*, ed. Han'guksa yŏn'guhoe. Seoul: Ŭryu munhwasa, 1985.

———. "Posup'a chach'ŏ hannŭn Kim sŏnsaeng kke," *Hankyŏre sinmun*, January 23, 2000, 8.

———. *Pundan sidae ŭi yŏksa insik.* Seoul: Ch'angjak kwa Pip'yŏngsa, 1978.

———, ed. *Sin Ch'ae-ho.* Seoul: Koryŏ taehakkyo ch'ulp'anbu, 1990.

Kang Man-gil et al. *Haebang chŏnhusa ŭi insik*, vol. 2. Seoul: Han'gilsa, 1985.

Kang Tong-il. *NamHan eso ŭi chuch'e sasang.* Seoul: Palgun'gul, 1989.

Kim Dong-Choon [Kim Tong-chun]. *Chŏnjaeng kwa sahoe: uri ege Han'guk chŏnjaeng ŭn muŏt iŏnna.* Seoul: Tolbaegae, 2000.

Kim Hwal-lan. "Na nŭn tanbal ŭl irrŏkkye ponda." *Tongkwang*, no. 37 (September 1932).

Kim Ki-rim. "'Missŭ Koria' tanbal hasio." *Tongkwang* no. 37 (September 1932).

Kim Nam-sik et al. *Haebang chŏnhusa ŭi insik*, vol. 5. Seoul: Han'gilsa, 1989.

Kim P'il-dong, "Yi Sang-baek," *Han'guk ŭi yŏksaga wa yŏksahak*, vol. 2, ed. Cho Tong-gŏl et al. Seoul: Ch'angjak kwa pip'yŏngsa, 1994.

Kim Sa-ryang. *Kim Saryang chakp'umjip*, ed. Im Hŏn-yŏng. Seoul: Chisik ŭl mandŭnŭn chisik, 2008.

Kim Tae-sik. "Ilje kangjŏmgi Kyŏngju chiŏk munhwaje ŭi suri pokwŏn sare." *Kyŏngju Silla yujŏk ŭi ŏje wa onŭl: Sŏkkuram, Pulguksa, Namsan.* Seoul: Sungkyunkwan taehakkyo pangmulkwan kihoeg chŏnsisil, 2007.

Kim To-hyŏng. "Han'guk kŭndaesa ŭi chaju, tongnip ŭi ŭimi." *Yŏksa pip'yŏng* 29 (May 1995).

———. *Taehan Chegukki ŭi chŏngch'i sasang yŏn'gu.* Seoul: Chisik Sanŏpsa, 1994.

Kim Yong-min. *Han'guk munhak pip'yŏng nonjaengsa.* Seoul: Han'gilsa, 1992.

Kim Yong-sŏp. *Chosŏnhugi nongŏpsa yŏn'gu.* 2 vols. Seoul: Ilchogak, 1970–71.

Kim Yun-gyŏng, *Han'guk muncha kŭp ŏhaksa*. 1934. Seoul: Kyŏngin munhwasa, 1987.

Kim Yun-sik. "Haebang gonggan ŭi munhak." *Haebang chŏnhusa ŭi insik*, vol. 2, ed. Kang Man-gil et al. Seoul: Han'gilsa, 1985.

———. *Han'guk hyondae munhaksaron*. Seoul: Hansem, 1988.

———. *Han'guk kundae munhak sasangsa*. Seoul: Han'gilsa, 1984.

Kim Yun-sik et al. *Haebang konggan ŭi munhak undong kwa munhak ŭi hyonsil insik*. Seoul: Han'ul, 1989.

Kuksa kyojae p'yŏnch'an wiwŏnhoe. *Han'guksa kaesŏl*. Seoul: T'amgudang, 1983.

Kuksa p'yŏnch'an wiwŏnhoe. *Chungjong sillok*. http://sillok.history.go.kr

———. *Kojong sillok*. http://sillok.history.go.kr

———. *Koryŏsa*. http://db.history.go.kr/KOREA/

———. *Kwanghae'gun ilgi*. http://silok.history.go.kr

———. *Sejong sillok*. http://sillok.history.go.kr

———. *Sŏngjong sillok*. http://sillok.history.go.kr

———. *Sŏnjo sillok*. http://sillok.history.go.kr

———. *Sukjong sillok*. http://sillok.history.go.kr

———. *T'aejo sillok*. http://sillok.history.go.kr

———. *Yŏngjo sillok*. http://sillok.history.go.kr

Kŭm Chang-t'ae. "Tasan ŭi sajikje wa ch'eje kojŭng." *Chongkyohak yŏn'gu* 16 (1997).

Kume, Kunitake. "Nihon fukuin no enkaku." *Shigakkai zasshi* 1 (December 1889– February 1890).

Kwŏn Hyŏk-su. *19-segi mal Han-Chung kwan'gyesa yŏn'gu*. Paeksan charyowŏn, 2000.

K. Y. "Tanbalhan kamsang." *Tongkwang*, no. 37 (September 1932).

Lee Chong-Sik [Yi Chŏng-sik]. "Naengjŏn ŭi chŏn'gae kwajŏng kwa Hanbando pundan ŭi koch'akhwa." *Haebang chŏnhusa ŭi chaeinsik*, vol. 2. Seoul: Chaek sesang, 2006.

Lee Jinhee. "Kwandong taejijin ŭl ch'udoham: Ilbon cheguk ŭi 'pulyŏng sŏnin' kwa ch'udo ŭi chŏngch'ihak." *Asea yŏn'gu* 51, no. 1 (2008).

Lee Kwang-Rin [Yi Kwang-nin]. *Yu Kil-chun*. Seoul: Tonga ilbosa, 1992.

———. "Yun Ch'i-ho ŭi Ilbon yuhak." *Tongbang hakji* 59 (1988).

Lew Young-Ick [Yu Yŏng-ik], ed. *Yi Sŭng-man yŏn'gu*. Seoul: Yonsei University Press, 2000.

Lim Jie-Hyun [Im Chi-hyŏn] et al. *Kuksa ŭi sinhwa rŭl nŏmŏsŏ*. Seoul: Humŏnistŭ, 2004.

Paek Nam-un. *Chōsen hōken shakai keizaishi*. Tokyo: Kaizōsha, 1937.

———. *Chōsen shakai keizaishi*. Tōkyō: Kaizōsha, 1933.

———. "Chosŏn sahoe kyŏngjesa ch'ulp'an e taehan sogam," *Chungang* (November 1933).

———. *Paek Nam-un chŏnjip*, trans. Ha Il-sik. Seoul: Iron kwa silch'ŏn, 1991–94.

Pak Ch'an-mo. "Haebang chikhu Han Hyo ŭi munhakpip'yŏng koch'al." *Hyŏndae munhak iron yŏn'gu* 27 (2006).

Pak Chi-hyang et al., eds. *Haebang chŏnhusa ŭi chaeinsik*, vols. 1 and 2. Seoul: Ch'aek Sesang, 2006.

——— et al., "Taedam," *Haebang chŏnhusa ŭi chaeinsik*, vol. 2. Seoul: Ch'aek Sesang, 2006.

Pak Chi-wŏn, *Yŏrha ilgi*, trans. and ed. Kim Hyŏl-cho. Kyŏnggi-do P'aju-si: Tolbegae, 2009.

Pang Kie-chung [Pang Ki-jung]. "1930-nyŏndae mulsan changnyŏ undong kwa minjok chabonjuŭi kyŏngje sasang." *Tongbang hakji* 115 (2002).

———. "Haebanghu kukka kŏnsŏl munje wa yŏksahak." *Han'guksa insik kwa yŏksa iron*. Seoul: Chisik sanŏpsa, 1997.

———. *Han'guk hyŏndae sasangsa yŏn'gu*. Seoul: Yŏksa pip'yŏngsa, 1992.

———. "Paek Nam-un yŏn'gu I." *Yŏksa pip'yŏng* 7 (summer 1989).

Park Chan-seung [Pak Ch'an-sŭng]. *Han'guk chŏngch'i sasangsa yŏn'gu*. Seoul: Yŏksa pip'yŏngsa, 1992.

Park Hyon-ch'ae et al. *Haebang chŏnhusa ŭi insik*, vol. 3. Seoul: Han'gilsa, 1987.

Park Tae Gyun [Pak T'ae-gyun]. "Haebang chŏnggaek Pak Hŏn-yŏng kwa 8-wŏl t'eje." *Obsŏbŏ* 8 (2002).

Rhee Syngman [Yi Sung-man]. *Ilminjuui kaesol*. Seoul: Ilminjuui poguphoe, 1949.

———. *Tongnip chŏngsin*, in *Ihwajang sojang Unam Yi Sŭngman munsŏ*. Seoul: Kukhak charyowŏn, 1998.

———. *Yi Sŭng-man yŏn'gu*, ed. Lew Young-Ick. Seoul: Yonsei University Press, 2000.

Ro Myoung-ho [No Myŏng-ho]. "Koryŏ sidae ŭi tawŏnjŏk ch'ŏnhakwan kwa Haedong Ch'ŏnja." *Han'guksa yŏn'gu*, no. 105 (1999).

———. "Tongmyŏng Wangpyŏn kwa Yi Kyu-bo ŭi tawŏnjŏk ch'ŏnhakwan." *Chindan hakbo* 83 (1997).

Ryu Si-hyun, *Ch'oe Nam-sŏn yŏn'gu: cheguk ŭi kŭndae wa singminji ŭi munhwa*. Seoul: Yŏksa pip'yŏngsa, 2009.

Sekino Tadashi. *Chōsen bijutsushi*. Keijō: Chōsen shigakkai, 1932.

Shim Ji-yon, ed. *Haebang chŏngguk nonjaengsa*. Seoul: Han'ul, 1986.

Shin Yong-ha [Sin Yong-ha]. "Sin Ch'ae-ho ŭi mujŏngbujuŭi tongnip sasang," *Sin Ch'ae-ho*, ed. Kang Man-gil. Seoul: Koryŏ taehakkyo ch'ulp'anbu, 1990.

Sin Ch'ae-ho. *Sin Ch'ae-ho yŏksa nonsŏljip*, trans. Chŏng Hae-yŏm. Seoul: Hyŏndae silhaksa, 1995.

———. *Tanjae Sin Ch'ae-ho chŏnjip*, vols. 1–4. Seoul: Tanjae Sin Ch'ae-ho sŏnsaeng kinyŏm saŏphoe, 1987.

———. *Tanje Sin Ch'ae-ho chŏnjip*. 10 vols. Chungnam Chŏnan-si: Tongnip Kinyŏmgwan Han'guk Tongnip Undongsa Yŏn'guso, 2007.

Sin Hyŏng-gi, ed. *Haebang 3-nyŏn ŭi pip'yŏng munhak*. Seoul: Segye, 1988.

Sin Il-ch'ŏl. "Sin Ch'ae-ho ŭi kŭndae kukkakwan." *Sin Ch'ae-ho*, ed. Kang Man-gil. Seoul: Koryŏ taehakkyo ch'ulp'anbu, 1990.

———. *Sin Ch'ae-ho ŭi sahoe sasang yŏn'gu*. Seoul: Han'gilsa, 1984.

Sŏ Chae-p'il [Philip Jaisohn]. "Nonsŏl," *Tongnip sinmun* (April 7, 1896), in *Tongnip sinmun nonsŏljip*. Seoul: Songjae munhwa chaedan ch'ulp'anbu, 1976.

Son Chin-t'ae. *Chosŏn minjoksa kaeron*. 1948. *Yŏkdae Han'guksa nonsŏn*, ed. Yi Ki-baek. Seoul: Saemunsa, 1993.

———. *Son Chin-tae sŏnsaeng chŏnjip*. 6 vols. Seoul: T'aehaksa, 1981.

Son Yŏng-jong et al. *Chosŏn t'ongsa*. P'yŏngyang: Sahoe kwahak ch'ulp'ansa, 1991.

Song Ch'an-sŏp. "Ilje ŭi singmin sahak." *Han'guk ŭi yŏksaga wa yŏksahak*, vol. 2, ed. Cho Tong-gŏl et al. Seoul: Ch'angjak kwa pip'yŏngsa, 1994.

Song Ki-ho. "Silla chungdae sahoe wa Parhae." *Han'guksa t'ŭkgang*. Seoul: Sŏul taehakkyo ch'ulp'anbu, 1990.

———. "Yu Tŭk-kong." *Han'guk ŭi yŏksaga wa yŏksahak*, vol. 2, ed. Cho Tong-gŏl et al. Seoul: Ch'angjak kwa pip'yŏngsa, 1994.

Song Kŏn-ho and Kang Man-gil, eds. *Han'guk minjokjuuiron*. Seoul: Ch'angjak kwa pip'yŏngsa, 1982.

Song Kŏn-ho et al. *Haebang chŏnhusa ŭi insik*, vol. 1. Revised edition. Seoul: Han'gilsa, 1989.

———. *Han'guk hyondae inmulsa ron*. Seoul: Han'gilsa, 1974.

Sŏul taehakkyo inmun taehak Han'guk hyŏndaesa yŏn'guhoe. *Haebang chŏngguk kwa minjok t'ongil chŏnsŏn*. Seoul: Segye, 1987.

Tongnip sinmun. http://www.kinds.or.kr/ (Han'guk ŏllon chinhŭng chaedan).

Tongnip sinmun nonsŏljip. Seoul: Songjae munhwa jedan, 1976.

Uchida Jun. "Ch'ongnyŏkjŏn sigi chae-Chosŏn Ilbonin ŭi 'NaeSŏn Ilch'e' chŏngchaek e taehan hyŏmnyŏk." *Asea yŏn'gu* 51, no. 1 (2008).

Yasuda, Hiroshi. "Kindai Nihon ni okeru 'minzoku' kannen no keisei," *Shisō to gendai* 31 (September 1992).

Yi Chang-hŭi. "Oeran chung ŭi sahoesang." *Han'guksa*, vol. 29. Seoul: Kuksa p'yŏnchan wiwŏnhoe, 1995.

Yi Chi-wŏn. "1930-nyŏndae minjokjuŭi kyeyŏl ŭi kojŏk pojŏn undong." *Tongbang hakchi*, June 1993.

———. "An Chae-hong." *Han'guk ŭi yŏksaga wa yŏksahak*, vol. 2, ed. Cho Tong-gŏl et al. Seoul: Ch'angjak kwa Pip'yŏngsa, 1994.

Yi Ch'ŏl-sŏng. "Singminjisigi yŏksainsik kwa yŏksasŏsul," *Han'guksa* 23. Seoul: Han'gilsa, 1994.

Yi Ch'ŏng-wŏn, *Chosŏn sahoesa tokbon*. Tokyo: Paekyangsa, 1936.

Yi Hwang-jik. "Kŭndae Han'guk ŭi ch'ogi kongnonjang hyŏngsŏng mit pyŏnhwa e kwanhan yŏn'gu." *Sahoe iron* 32 (2007).

Yi Ki-baek. *Han'guk sahak ŭi panghyang*. Seoul, Ilchogak, 1978.

———. *Han'guksa sillon*. Seoul: Ilchogak, 1967.

———. *Kuksa sillon*. Seoul: T'aesŏngsa, 1961.

———. "Sahoe kyŏngje sahak kwa silchŭng sahak ŭi munje." 1971. *Yŏksa wa minjok*. Seoul: Ilchogak, 1997.

Yi Ki-mun. "Han'gul ŭi yŏn'gu wa pogup." *Han minjok tongnip undongsa*, vol. 2. Seoul: Kuksa p'yŏnch'an wiwŏnhoe, 1987.

Yi Kyun-yong. *Singanhoe yŏn'gu*. Seoul: Yoksa pip'yŏngsa, 1993.

Yi Man-yŏl. *Han'guk kŭndae yŏksahak ŭi ihae*. Seoul: Ch'angjak kwa pip'yŏngsa, 1981.

Yi P'il-yŏng. "Tan'gun yŏn'gusa." *Tan'gun*, ed. Yun I-hum et al. Seoul: Seoul taehak-kyo ch'ulp'anbu, 1994.

Yi Puk-man. *Yijo sahoe kyongjesa*. Seoul: Taesang Ch'ulp'ansa, 1948.

Yi Pyong-ch'on, ed. *Pukhan hakgye ŭi Han'guk kundaesa nonjaeng: Sahoe sŏngkyŏk kwa sidae kupun*. Seoul: Ch'angjak kwa pip'yŏngsa, 1989.

Yi Pyŏng-do. *Chosŏnsa taegwan*. Seoul: Tongjisa, 1948.

———. *Koryŏ sidae ŭi yŏn'gu: T'ŭkhi chiri toch'am sasang ŭi palchŏn ŭl chungsim ŭro*. 1954. Seoul: Asea munhwasa, 1980.

———. *Yŏksaga ŭi yuhyang*, ed. Chindan hakhoe. Seoul: Ilchogak, 1991.

Yi T'ae-jin. *Kojong sidae ŭi chae-chomyŏng*. Seoul: T'aehaksa, 2000.

Yi U-song and Kang Man-gil, eds. *Han'guk ŭi yoksa insik*. Seoul: Ch'angjak kwa pip'yŏngsa, 1976.

Yi Yŏng-hun. *Taehan Min'guk iyagi*. Seoul: Kip'arang, 2007.

———. "Wae tasi haebang chŏnhusa inga." *Haebang chŏnhusa ŭi chaeinsik*, vol. 1. Seoul: Chaek sesang, 2006.

Yu In-ho. "Haebang-hu nongji kaehyŏk ŭi chŏn'gaekwajŏng kwa sŏnggyŏk." *Haebang chŏnhusa ŭi insik*, vol. 1, ed. Song Kŏn-ho et al. Seoul: Han'gilsa, 1979.

Yu Kil-chun. *Sŏyu kyŏnmun: Chosŏn chisigin Yu Kil-chun, Sŏyang ŭl pŏnyŏk hada*, trans. and ed. Hŏ Kyŏng-jin. Seoul: Sŏhae munjip, 2004.

Yun Ch'i-ho. *Yun Ch'i-ho ilgi*. Seoul: Kuksa py'ŏnchan wiwŏnhoe, 1973–1989.

Yun Hae-dong et al. *Kŭndae rŭl tasi ignŭnda: Han'guk kŭndae insik ŭi saeroun p'aerŏdaim ŭl wihayŏ*. Seoul: Yŏksa pip'yŏngsa, 2006.

Yun Kŏn-ch'a, "Minzoku gensŏ no satetsu: 'Nihon minzoku' to iu jiko teiji," *Shisō*, no. 834 (December 1993).

Sources in English

Abernethy, David B. *The Dynamics of Global Dominance*. New Haven: Yale University Press, 2002.

Allen, Chizuko T. "Ch'oe Namsŏn at the Height of Japanese Imperialism," *Sungkyun Journal of East Asian Studies* 5, no. 1 (2005).

———. "Early Migrations, Conquests, and Common Ancestry: Theorizing Japanese Origins in Relation with Korea," *Sungkyun Journal of East Asian Studies* 8, no. 1 (2008).

———. "Northeast Asia Centered around Korea: Ch'oe Namsŏn's View of History." *Journal of Asian Studies* 49, no. 4 (1990).

Anderson, Benedict. *Imagined Communities: Reflections on the Origin and Spread of Nationalism*. London: Verso, 1983.

Anghie, Antony. *Imperialism, Sovereignty, and the Making of International Law*. Cambridge: Cambridge University Press, 2004.

Arendt, Hannah. *The Origins of Totalitarianism*. 1968. Oxford: Benediction Classics, 2009.

Armstrong, Charles. *The North Korean Revolution, 1945–1950*. Ithaca: Cornell University Press, 2003.

Badger, Reid. *The Great American Fair: The World's Columbian Exposition and American Culture*. Chicago: N. Hall, 1979.

Badiou, Alain. *Ethics: An Essay on the Understanding of Evil*, translated by Peter Hallward. New York: Verso, 2001.

Bailey, Anne M., and Josep R. Llobera, eds. *The Asiatic Mode of Production: Science and Politics*. London: Routledge, 1981.

Balibar, Etienne, and Immanuel Wallerstein, eds. *Race, Nation, Class: Ambiguous Identities*. New York: Verso, 1991.

Barnett, Ferdinand L. *The Reason Why the Colored American Is Not in the World's Columbian Exposition*, ed. Robert W. Rydell. 1893. Chicago: University of Illinois Press, 1999.

Barrows, John Henry, ed. *The World's Parliament of Religions*. Vol. 1. Chicago: The Parliament Publishing Company, 1893.

Beasley, W. G., and Edwin G. Pulleyblank. *Historians of China and Japan*. London: Oxford University Press, 1961.

Bederman, Gail. *Manliness and Civilization: A Cultural History of Gender and Race in the United States, 1880–1917*. Chicago: University of Chicago Press, 1984.

Berlant, Lauren. *Cruel Optimism*. Durham: Duke University Press, 2011.

Bernstein, Gail Lee. *Japanese Marxist: A Portrait of Kawakami Hajime, 1879–1946*. Harvard East Asian Series, no. 86. Cambridge: Harvard University Press, 1976.

Bharucha, Rustom. *Another Asia: Rabindranath Tagore and Okakura Tenshin*. New Delhi and New York: Oxford University Press, 2009.

Bird, Isabella L. *Korea and Her Neighbors*. Boston: KPI, 1985. (1897)

Bohnet, Adam Clarence Immanuel. "Migrant and Border Subjects in Late Chosŏn." Ph.D. dissertation, University of Toronto, 2008.

Breuker, Remco E. "Contested Objectivities: Ikeuchi Hiroshi, Kim Sanggi and the Tradition of Oriental History (Tōyōshigaku) in Japan and Korea." *East Asian History* 29 (2005).

———. "Koryŏ as an Independent Realm: The Emperor's Clothes?" *Korean Studies* 27 (2004).

Burris, John P. *Exhibiting Religion: Colonialism and Spectacle at International Expositions*. Charlottesville: University of Virginia Press, 2002.

Buswell, Robert. "Buddhism in Korea." *Buddhism and Asian History*, ed. Joseph M. Kitagawa and Mark D. Cummings. New York: Macmillan, 1989.

Ceuster, Koen de. "The Nation Exorcised." *Korean Studies* 25, no. 2 (2001).

Chandra, Vipan. *Imperialism, Resistance, and Reform in Late Nineteenth-Century Korea*. Berkeley: Institute of East Asian Studies, University of California, 1988.

Chang, Gordon H. "Whose 'Barbarism'? Whose 'Treachery'? Race and Civilization in the Unknown United States–Korea War of 1871." *Journal of American History* 89, no. 4 (2003).

Chatterjee, Partha. *The Nation and Its Fragments: Colonial and Postcolonial Histories*. Princeton: Princeton University Press, 1993.

———. *Nationalist Thought and the Colonial World: A Derivative Discourse*. Minneapolis: University of Minnesota Press, 1986.

Chicago Daily News, *The Chicago Record's History of the World's Fair*. Chicago: Chicago Daily News Co., 1893.

Choe, Yŏngho, et al., eds. *Sources of Korean Tradition*, vol. 2. New York: Columbia University Press, 2000.

Choi, Jang-jip. "Political Cleavages in South Korea." *State and Society in Contemporary Korea*, ed. Hagen Koo. Ithaca: Cornell University Press, 1993.

Chou, Evan Shan. "'A Story about Hair': A Curious Mirror of Lu Xun's Pre-Republican Years." *Journal of Asian Studies* 66, no. 2 (2007).

Chow, Kai-wing. "Narrating Nation, Race, and National Culture: Imagining the Hanzu Identity in Modern China." *Constructing Nationhood in Modern East Asia*, ed. Kai-wing Chow, Kevin M. Doak, and Poshek Fu. Ann Arbor: University of Michigan Press, 2001.

Chow, Rey. *Women and Modernity: The Politics of Reading between East and West*. Minneapolis: University of Minnesota Press, 1991.

Choy, Bong-Youn. *Koreans in America*. Chicago: Nelson-Hall, 1979.

Clark, Donald N. "Sino-Korean Tributary Relations under the Ming." *The Ming Dynasty, 1398–1644*, part 2, ed. Denis Twitchett and Frederick W. Mote. *The Cambridge History of China*, vol. 8. Cambridge: Cambridge University Press, 1998.

Conner, Walker. "A Nation Is a Nation, Is a State, Is an Ethnic Group, Is a. . . ." *Ethnic and Racial Studies* 1, no. 4 (1978).

Cronon, William. *Nature's Metropolis: Chicago and the Great West*. New York: W. W. Norton, 1992.

Cumings, Bruce. "Archaeology, Descent, Emergence: Japan in British/American Hegemony, 1900–1950." *Japan in the World*, ed. Masao Miyoshi and H. D. Harootunian. Durham: Duke University Press, 1993.

———. "The Korea War: What Is It That We Are Remembering to Forget?" *Ruptured Histories: War, Memory, and the Post–Cold War in Asia*, ed. Sheila Miyoshi Jager and Rana Mitter. Cambridge: Harvard University Press, 2007.

———. *The Origins of the Korean War*: Vol. 1, *Liberation and the Emergence of Separate Regimes, 1945–1947*. Princeton: Princeton University Press, 1981.

———. *The Origins of the Korean War*: Vol. 2, *The Roaring of the Cataract, 1947–1950*. Princeton: Princeton University Press, 1990.

De Bary, W. M. Theodore, and Jahyun Haboush Kim. *The Rise of Neo-Confucianism in Korea*. New York: Columbia University Press, 1985.

Degras, Jane. *The Communist International, 1919–1943*. 3 vols. London: Oxford University Press, 1956–65.

Deleuze, Gilles and Felix Guattari. *Anti-Oedipus: Capitalism and Schizophrenia*. 1977. Minneapolis: University of Minnesota Press, 1983.

Deuchler, Martina. *Confucian Gentlemen and Barbarian Envoys: The Opening of Korea, 1875–1885*. Seattle: University of Washington Press, 1977.

———. *The Confucian Transformation of Korea: A Study of Society and Ideology*. Cambridge: Council on East Asian Studies, Harvard University, 1992.

————. "The Practice of Confucianism: Ritual and Order in Chosŏn Dynasty Korea." *Rethinking Confucianism: Past and Present in China, Japan, Korea, and Vietnam*, ed. Benjamin A. Elman, John B. Duncan, and Herman Ooms. Los Angeles: UCLA Asian Pacific Monograph Series, 2002.

Dirlik, Arif. *Anarchism in the Chinese Revolution*. Berkeley: University of California Press, 1991.

Doak, Kevin. "Ethnic Nationalism and Romanticism in Early Twentieth-Century Japan." *Journal of Japanese Studies* 22, no. 1 (1996).

————. "What Is a Nation and Who Belongs?" *American Historical Review* 102, no. 2 (1997).

Duara, Prasenjit. "Bifurcating Linear History: Nation and Histories in China and India." *positions* 1, no. 3 (1993).

————. *Rescuing History from the Nation*. Chicago: University of Chicago Press, 1995.

————. *Sovereignty and Authenticity: Manchukuo and the East Asian Modern*. Lanham, Md.: Rowman and Littlefield, 2003.

Dudden, Alexis. *Japan's Colonization of Korea: Discourse and Power*. Honolulu: University of Hawaii Press, 2004.

————. "Japan's Engagement with International Terms." *Tokens of Exchange: The Problem of Translation in Global Circulations*, ed. Lydia H. Liu. Durham: Duke University Press, 1999.

Duncan, John B. "Hyanghwain: Migration and Assimilation in Chosŏn Korea." *Acta Koreana* 3 (July 2000).

————. *The Origins of the Chosŏn Dynasty*. Seattle: University of Washington Press, 2000.

Eckert, Carter. *Offspring of Empire: The Koch'ang Kims and the Colonial Origins of Korean Capitalism, 1876–1945*. Seattle: University of Washington Press, 1991.

Eckert, Carter, et al. *Korea, Old and New: A History*. Cambridge: Korea Institute, Harvard University, 1990.

Em, Henry. "Civil Affairs Training and the U.S. Military Government in Korea." *Chicago Occasional Papers on Korea*, ed. Bruce Cumings. Chicago: Select Papers No. 6, Center for East Asian Studies, University of Chicago, 1991.

————. "Historians and History Writing in Modern Korea." *Oxford History of Historical Writing*: Vol. 5, *Historical Writing Since 1945*, ed. Axel Schneider and Daniel Woolf. New York: Oxford University Press, 2011.

————. "Minjok as a Modern and Democratic Construct: Sin Ch'ae-ho's Historiography." *Colonial Modernity in Korea*, ed. Gi-Wook Shin and Michael E. Robinson. Cambridge: Harvard University Asia Center, 1999.

————. "'Overcoming' Korea's Division: Narrative Strategies in Recent South Korean Historiography." *positions: east asia cultures critique* 1, no. 2 (1993).

Engels, Frederick. *The Origin of the Family, Private Property and the State: In the Light of the Researches of Lewis H. Morgan*. 1884. New York: International Publishers, 1942.

Ernest F. Fenollosa. *Epochs of Chinese and Japanese Art: an Outline History of East Asiatic Design.* New York: Frederick A. Stokes, 1911.

Fogel, Johua A. "The Debates over the Asiatic Mode of Production in Soviet Russia, China, and Japan." *American Historical Review* 93, no. 1 (1988).

Fukuzawa, Yukichi. *An Encouragement of Learning,* trans. David A. Dilworth and Umeyo Hirano. Tokyo: Sophia University Press, 1969.

Geertz, Clifford. "Notes on the Balinese Cockfight," *The Interpretation of Cultures.* New York: Basic Books, 1973.

Gellner, Ernest. *Nations and Nationalism.* Ithaca: Cornell University Press, 1983.

Giddens, Anthony. *The Nation-State and Violence.* Berkeley: University of California Press, 1987.

Grayson, James H. *Korea: A Religious History.* New York: Oxford University Press, 1989.

Griffis, William E. *A Modern Pioneer in Korea: The Life Story of Henry G. Appenzeller.* New York: Fleming H. Revell, 1912.

Haboush, JaHyun Kim. "Constructing the Center: The Ritual Controversy and the Search for a New Identity in Seventeenth-Century Korea." *Culture and the State in Late Chosŏn Korea,* ed. JaHyun Kim Haboush and Martina Deuchler. Cambridge: Harvard University Asia Center, 1999.

———. "Filial Emotions and Filial Values: Changing Patterns in the Discourse of Filiality in Late Chosŏn Korea." *Harvard Journal of Asiatic Studies* 55, no. 1 (1995).

Han, Hong-koo. "Wounded Nationalism: The Minsaengdan Incident and Kim Il Sung in Manchuria." Ph.D. dissertation, University of Washington, 1999.

Han, Young-woo. "Kija Worship in the Koryŏ and Early Yi Dynasties: A Cultural Symbol in the Relationship between Korea and China," *The Rise of Neo-Confucianism in Korea,* ed. W. M. Theodore de Bary and JaHyun Kim Haboush. New York: Columbia University Press, 1985.

Handy, E. S. Craighill, and Mary Kawena Pukui. *The Polynesian Family System in Ka-u, Hawai'i.* Rutland, Vt.: Charles E. Tuttle, 1972.

Hardt, Michael, and Antonio Negri. *Commonwealth.* Cambridge, Mass.: Belknap Press of Harvard University, 2009.

———. *Empire.* Cambridge: Harvard University Press, 2000.

———. *Multitude: War and Democracy in the Age of Empire.* New York: Penguin Books, 2004.

Harootunian, Harry D. *Things Seen and Unseen: Discourse and Ideology in Tokugawa Nativism.* Chicago: University of Chicago Press, 1988.

———. *Toward Restoration: The Growth of Political Consciousness in Tokugawa Japan.* Berkeley: University of California Press, 1970.

Harootunian, Harry D., and Tetsuo Najita. "Japanese Revolt against the West." *The Cambridge History of Japan,* vol. 6, ed. Peter Duus. Cambridge: Cambridge University Press, 1988.

Hevia, James L. *Cherishing Men from Afar: Qing Guest Ritual and the Macartney Embassy of 1793.* Durham: Duke University Press, 1995.

———. *English Lessons: The Pedagogy of Imperialism in Nineteenth-Century China*. Durham: Duke University Press, 2003.

Hinsley, F. H. *Sovereignty*. 2nd edition. Cambridge: Cambridge University Press, 1986.

Hobsbawm, E. J. *Nations and Nationalism since 1780: Programme, Myth, Reality*. Cambridge: Cambridge University Press, 1990.

Homer B. Hulbert. "Introductory Note," *Korea Review* (1901).

Hopkins, Terence K., and Immanuel Wallerstein. "Patterns of Development of the Modern World-System." *Review* 1, no. 2 (1977).

Hughes, Theodore. *Literature and Film in Cold War South Korea: Freedom's Frontier*. New York: Columbia University Press, 2012.

Huh, Tae-yong. "A Critical Review on the Issue of Proto-Nationalism during Late Chosŏn." *International Journal of Korean History* 12 (August 2008).

Humphrey, Caroline, and James Laidlaw. *The Archetypal Actions of Ritual: A Theory of Ritual Illustrated by the Jain Rite of Worship*. Oxford: Clarendon Press, 1994.

Hwang, Su-young. "Sŏkkuram Grotto Shrine." *Koreana* 6, no. 4 (1992).

Ihwa Yŏksagwan. *Ewha Old and New: 110 Years of History (1886–1996)*. Seoul: Ewha Woman's University Press, 2005.

Iryŏn. *Samguk yusa*, trans. Tae-Hung Ha and Grafton K. Mintz. Seoul: Yonsei University Press, 2004.

Jaisohn, Philip. *My Days in Korea and Other Essays*. Seoul: Yonsei University Press, 1999.

Jameson, Fredric. *The Political Unconscious: Narrative as a Socially Symbolic Act*. Ithaca: Cornell University Press, 1981.

Karl, Rebecca. *Staging the World: Chinese Nationalism at the Turn of the Twentieth Century*. Durham: Duke University Press, 2002.

Kawashima, Fujiya. "Cultural Localism in the Late Chosŏn Dynasty and Its Significance in Modern Korea." *Bulletin of Hiroshima Jogakuin University*, no. 45 (December 1995).

Kedourie, Elie. *Nationalism*. London: Hutchinson, 1960.

Ketelaar, James Edward. *Of Heretics and Martyrs in Meiji Japan: Buddhism and Its Persecution*. Princeton: Princeton University Press, 1990.

Kim, Dong-Choon [Kim Tong-chun]. "The Long Road Toward Truth and Reconciliation: Unwavering Attempts to Achieve Justice in South Korea," *Critical Asian Studies* 42, no. 4 (2010).

———. *The Unending Korean War: A Social History*. Larkspur, Calif.: Tamal Vista Publications, 2009.

Kim, Dong-Uk. "Chongmyo." *Korea Journal* 40, no. 3 (2000).

Kim, Key-Hiuk. "The Aims of Li's Policies towards Japan and Korea, 1870–1882." *Chinese Studies in History* 24, no. 4 (1991).

———. *The Last Phase of the East Asian World Order: Korea, Japan, and the Chinese Empire, 1860–1882*. Berkeley: University of California Press, 1980.

Kim, Kyu Hyun. "Reflections on the Problems of Colonial Modernity and 'Collaboration' in Modern Korean History." *Journal of International and Area Studies* 11, no. 3 (2004).

Kim, Richard. *The Quest for Statehood: Korean Immigrant Nationalism and U.S. Sovereignty, 1905–1945*. New York: Oxford University Press, 2011.

Kim, Youngna. *20th Century Korean Art*. London: Laurence King, 2005.

King, Ross. "Nationalism and Language Reform in Korea: The *Questione della Lingua* in Precolonial Korea." *Nationalism and the Construction of Korean Identity*, ed. Pai Hyung-Il and Timothy R. Tangherlini. Berkeley: Institute of East Asian Studies, University of California, 1998.

———. "Western Protestant Missionaries and the Origins of Korean Language Modernization." *Journal of International and Area Studies* 11, no. 3 (2004).

Koselleck, Reinhart. *Futures Past: On the Semantics of Historical Time*, trans. Keith Tribe. Cambridge: MIT Press, 1985.

Koskenniemi, Martti. *The Gentle Civilizer of Nations: The Rise and Fall of International Law, 1870–1960*. Cambridge: Cambridge University Press, 2001.

Krasner, Stephen D. *Sovereignty: Organized Hypocrisy*. Princeton: Princeton University Press, 1999.

Kwon, Insook. "Feminists Navigating the Shoals of Nationalism and Collaboration: The Post-Colonial Korean Debate over How to Remember Kim Hwallan." *Frontiers: A Journal of Women Studies* 27, no. 1 (2006).

Laclau, Ernesto, and Chantal Mouffe. *Hegemony and Socialist Strategy: Towards a Radical Democratic Politics*. London: Verso, 1985.

Lancaster, Lewis R. Introduction to *Buddhism in Koryŏ: A Royal Religion*, ed. Lewis R. Lancaster, Kikun Suh, and Chai-Shin Yu. 1996; Fremont, Calif.: Asian Humanities Press, 2002.

Larsen, Kirk W. *Tradition, Treaties, and Trade: Qing Imperialism and Chosŏn Korea, 1850–1910*. Cambridge: Harvard University Asia Center, Harvard University Press, 2008.

Ledyard, Gari. "Hong Taeyong and His *Peking Memoir*," *Korean Studies* 6 (1982).

Lee, Chong-Sik. *Korean Workers' Party: A Short History*. Stanford: Hoover Institution Press, 1978.

———. *Revolutionary Struggle in Manchuria*. Berkeley: University of California Press, 1983.

Lee, Chulwoo. "Modernity, Legality, and Power in Korea under Japanese Rule." *Colonial Modernity in Korea*, ed. Gi-Wook Shin and Michael Robinson. Cambridge: Harvard University Asia Center, 1999.

Lee, Jinhee. "The Enemy Within: Earthquake, Rumours and Massacre in the Japanese Empire." *Violence: "Mercurial Gestalt,"* ed. Tobe Levin. New York: Rodopi, 2008.

Lee, Ki-baik [Yi Ki-baek]. *A New History of Korea*, trans. Edward W. Wagner. Cambridge: Harvard-Yenching Institute, 1984.

Lee, Namhee. *The Making of Minjung: Democracy and the Politics of Representation in South Korea*. Ithaca: Cornell University Press, 2007.

Lee, Peter, et al., eds. *Sourcebook of Korean Civilization*: vol. 1, *From Early Times to the Sixteenth Century*. New York: Columbia University Press, 1993.

——— et al., eds. *Sourcebook of Korean Civilization*: vol. 2, *From the Seventeenth Century to the Modern Period*. New York: Columbia University Press, 1996.

Lee, Yeounsuk. *The Ideology of Kokugo: Nationalizing Language in Modern Japan*, trans. Maki Hirano Hubbard. Honolulu: University of Hawaii Press, 2010.

Lee, Yur-bok. "Establishment of a Korean Legation in the United States, 1887–1890." *Illinois Papers in Asian Studies* 3 (1983).

Lensen, George Alexander. *Balance of Intrigue: International Rivalry in Korea and Manchuria, 1884–1899*, vol. 2. Tallahassee: University Presses of Florida, 1982.

Lew, Young Ick. "An Analysis of the Reform Documents of the Kabo Reform Movement, 1894." *Journal of Social Sciences and Humanities* 40 (December 1974).

———. "The Conservative Character of the 1894 Tonghak Peasant Uprising: A Reappraisal with Emphasis on Chon Pong-Jun's Background and Motivation." *Journal of Korean Studies* 7 (1990).

———. "Korean-Japanese Politics behind the Kabo-Ŭlmi Reform Movement." *Journal of Korean Studies* 3 (1981).

———. "Minister Inoue Kaoru and the Japanese Reform Attempts in Korea During the Sino-Japanese War, 1894–1895." *Journal of Asiatic Studies* 27, no. 2 (1984).

———. "On Two English Documents Related to Pak Yong-hyo's Reforms, 1895." *Journal of Social Sciences and Humanities* 42 (December 1975).

———. "The Reform Efforts and Ideas of Pak Yong-hyo, 1894–1895." *Korean Studies* 1 (1977).

———. "Yuan Shih-k'ai's Residency and the Korean Enlightenment Movement, 1885–94." *Journal of Korean Studies* 5 (1984).

Lippert, Wolfgang. "The Formation and Development of the Term 'Political Economy' in Japanese and Chinese." *Mapping Meanings: The Field of New Learning in Late Qing China*, ed. Michael Lackner and Natascha Vittinghoff. Boston: Brill Academic Publishers, 2004.

Liu, Lydia. "The Desire for the Sovereign and the Logic of Reciprocity in the Family of Nations." *Diacritics* 29, no. 4 (1999).

———. *Translingual Practice: Literature, National Culture, and Translated Modernity. China, 1900–1937*. Stanford: Stanford University Press, 1995.

Locke, John. *Second Treatise of Government*, ed. C. B. Macpherson. Indianapolis, Ind.: Hackett, 1980.

———. *Some Thoughts Concerning Education*, ed. John W. and Jean S. Yolton. New York: Oxford University Press, 1989.

Marshall, Byron K. "The Tradition of Conflict in the Governance of Japanese Imperial Universities." *History of Education Quarterly* 17, no. 4 (1977).

Masuzawa, Tomoko. *The Invention of World Religions: Or, How European Universal-*

ism Was Preserved in the Language of Pluralism. Chicago: University of Chicago Press, 2005.

Mbembe, Achille. "Necropolitics," *Public Culture* 15, no. 1 (2003).

Mehta, Uday Singh. *Liberalism and Empire: A Study in Nineteenth Century British Liberal Thought.* Chicago: University of Chicago Press, 1999.

Miller, Owen. "The Idea of Stagnation in Korean Historiography," *Korean Histories* 2, no. 1 (2010).

Min, Hyŏn-ku. "Koryŏ Politics under Mongol Control: Dynastic Continuity During the Period of Royal Absence." *International Journal of Korean History* 1 (2000).

Moore, Barrington. *Social Origins of Dictatorship and Democracy: Lord and Peasant in the Making of the Modern World.* Boston: Beacon Press, 1966.

Morgan, Lewis Henry. *Ancient Society.* New York: Henry Holt, 1878.

Mutsu, Munemitsu. *Kenkenroku: The Memoirs of Count Mutsu Munemitsu,* trans. Gorden M. Berger. Tokyo: University of Tokyo Press, 1982.

Myers, Ramon H., and Mark R. Peattie, eds. *The Japanese Colonial Empire, 1895– 1945.* Princeton: Princeton University Press, 1984.

Nahm, Chun-woo. "Discoveries of Hitherto Forgotten Sciences in Sŏkkuram Temple," *Chindan hakbo* 32 (1969).

Ngai, Mae M. "Transnationalism and the Transformation of the 'Other': Response to the Presidential Address." *American Quarterly* 57, no. 1 (2005).

Norman, Jerry. *Chinese.* Cambridge: Cambridge University Press, 1988.

Notehelfer, F. G. "On Idealism and Realism in the Thought of Okakura Tenshin." *Journal of Japanese Studies* 16, no. 2 (1990).

Numata, Jirō. "Shigeno Yasutsugu and the Modern Tokyo Tradition of Historical Writing." *Historians of Japan and China,* ed. W. G. Beasley and E. G. Pulleyblank. London: Oxford University Press, 1961.

Okakura, Kakuzō. *Ideals of the East with Special Reference to the Art of Japan.* London: John Murray, 1903.

———. *The Awakening of the East* [1938]. Tokyo: Seibun-kaku, 1940.

Oliver, Robert T. *Syngman Rhee: The Man behind the Myth.* New York: Dodd, Mead, 1954.

Osterhammel, Jürgen. *Colonialism,* trans. Shelley Frisch. Princeton: Markus Wiener, 2005.

Pai, Hyung Il. *Constructing "Korean" Origins: A Critical Review of Archaeology, Historiography, and Racial Myth in Korean State-Formation Theories.* Cambridge: Harvard University Asia Center, 2000.

———. "The Creation of National Treasures and Monuments: The 1916 Japanese Laws on the Preservation of Korean Remains and Relics and Their Colonial Legacies." *Korean Studies* 25, no. 1 (2001).

Pak, Che-ga. "Chonju ron," *Sources of Korean Tradition,* trans. Martina Deuchler, ed. Yŏngho Ch'oe et al. New York: Columbia University Press, 2000.

Palais, James B. *Confucian Statecraft and Korean Institutions: Yu Hyŏngwŏn and the Late Chosŏn Dynasty.* Seattle: University of Washington Press, 1996.

———. *Politics and Policy in Traditional Korea*. Cambridge: Harvard University Press, 1975.

———. "Stability in Chosŏn Dynasty Korea," *Occasional Papers on Korea* 3 (June 1975).

Palmer, Spencer J., ed. *Korean-American Relations: Documents Pertaining to the Far Eastern Diplomacy of the United States*, vol. 2. Berkeley: University of California Press, 1963.

Pang, Kie-chung [Pang Ki-jun]. "Yi Hun-gu's Agricultural Reform Theory and Nationalist Economic Thought." *Seoul Journal of Korean Studies* 19, no. 1 (2006).

Pang, Kie-chung, and Michael D. Shin, eds. *Landlords, Peasants, and Intellectuals in Modern Korea*. Cornell East Asia Series No. 128, Ithaca: Cornell University Press, 2005.

Park, Tae-Gyun. "Different Roads, Common Destination: Economic Discourses in South Korea During the 1950s." *Modern Asian Studies* 39, no. 3 (2005).

Pastreich, Emanuel. "The Reception of Chinese Vernacular Narrative in Korea and Japan." Ph.D. dissertation, Harvard University, 1997.

Perez, Louis G. "Mutsu Munemitsu and the Revision of the 'Unequal' Treaties," Ph.D. dissertation, University of Michigan, 1986.

Poole, Janet. "Colonial Interiors: Modernist Fiction of Korea," Ph.D. dissertation, Columbia University, 2004.

Pyun, Chong Wha. "The Visit of the Korean Mission to Boston in 1883 and the Beginning of Scientific and Technological Interactions between Korea and the United States." *Han'guk kwahak sahakhoeji* 4, no. 1 (1982).

Rhee, Syngman. *The Spirit of Independence: A Primer of Korean Modernization and Reform*, translated, annotated, and with an introduction by Han-kyo Kim. Honolulu: University of Hawaii Press, 2001.

Ricoeur, Paul. *Lectures on Ideology and Utopia*, ed. George H. Taylor. New York: Columbia University Press, 1986.

———. *The Rule of Metaphor: Multi-disciplinary Studies of the Creation of Meaning of Language*. Toronto: University of Toronto Press, 1977.

Robinson, Michael E. "Colonial Publication Policy and the Korean Nationalist Movement." *The Japanese Colonial Empire, 1895–1945*, ed. Ramon H. Myers and Mark R. Peattie. Princeton: Princeton University Press, 1984.

———. *Cultural Nationalism in Colonial Korea, 1920–1925*. Seattle: University of Washington Press, 1988.

———. "National Identity and the Thought of Sin Ch'aeho." *Journal of Korean Studies* 5 (1984).

Rosenberg, Justin. *The Empire of Civil Society: A Critique of the Realist Theory of International Relations*. London: Verso, 1994.

Rostow, W. W. *A Proposal: Key to an Effective Foreign Policy*. New York: Harper and Brothers, 1957.

———. *The Stages of Economic Growth: A Non-Communist Manifesto*. Cambridge: Cambridge University Press, 1960.

Rydell, Robert. *All the World's a Fair*. Chicago: University of Chicago Press, 1984.

Scalapino, Robert A., and Chong-Sik Lee. *Communism in Korea*. 2 vols. Berkeley: University of California Press, 1972–73.

Schmid, Andre. *Korea between Empires, 1895–1919*. New York: Columbia University Press, 2002.

———. "Rediscovering Manchuria: Sin Ch'aeho and the Politics of Territorial History in Korea." *Journal of Asian Studies* 56, no. 1 (1997).

———. "Tributary Relations and the Qing-Chosŏn Frontier on Mount Paektu." *The Chinese State at the Borders*, ed. Diana Lary. Vancouver: UBC Press, 2008.

Schmitt, Carl. *The Nomos of the Earth in the International Law of the Jus Publicum Europaeum*. New York: Telos Press, 2003.

Seager, Richard Hughes. *The World's Parliament of Religions: The East/West Encounter, Chicago, 1893*. Bloomington: Indiana University Press, 1995.

Shim, Jae-Hoon. "A New Understanding of Kija Chosŏn as a Historical Anachronism." *Harvard Journal of Asiatic Studies* 62, no. 2 (2002).

Shin, Gi-Wook, and Michael E. Robinson, eds. *Colonial Modernity in Korea*. Cambridge: Harvard University Asia Center, 1999.

Shin, Ju Baek [Sin Chu-baek]. "Perception of August 15 Remembered in and Forgotten from Korean Textbooks." *Review of Korean Studies* 8, no. 1 (2005).

Shin, Michael D. Introduction to *Landlords, Peasants and Intellectuals*, ed. Pang Kie-chung and Michael D. Shin. Ithaca: Cornell University Press, 2005.

Shin, Yong-ha. "The Revolutionary Movement of the Tonghak Peasant Army of 1894: Seen vis-à-vis the French Revolution," *Korea Journal* 29, no. 10 (1989).

Sill, John M. B. Letter to the secretary of state, January 4, 1895, in *Korean-American Relations: Documents Pertaining to the Far Eastern Diplomacy of the United States*, Vol. 2, ed. Spencer J. Palmer. Berkeley: University of California Press, 1963.

Smith, Sidonie, and Julia Watson. *Reading Autobiography: A Guide for Interpreting Life Narratives*. 2nd ed. Minneapolis: University of Minnesota Press, 2010.

Snodgrass, Judith. *Presenting Japanese Buddhism to the West: Orientalism, Occidentalism, and the Columbian Exposition*. Chapel Hill: University of North Carolina Press, 2003.

Sohn, Pokee. *Social History of the Early Chosŏn Dynasty: The Functional Aspects of Governmental Structure*. Seoul: Jisik-sanup Publications, 2000.

Son, Min Suh. "Enlightenment and Electrification: The Introduction of Electric Light, Telegraph and Streetcars in Late Nineteenth Century Korea." *Reform and Modernity in the Taehan Empire*, ed. Kim Dong-no, John B. Duncan, and Kim Do-hyung. Seoul: Jimoondang, 2006.

Stalin, Joseph. *Marxism and Linguistics*. New York: International Publishers, 1951.

Suh, Hee-Kyung. "Atrocities Before and During the Korean War," *Critical Asian Studies* 42, no. 4 (2010).

Suh, Jae-Jung. "Truth and Reconciliation in South Korea," *Critical Asian Studies* 42, no. 4 (2010).

Suh, Serk-Bae. "The Wanpaoshan Incident and the Anti-Chinese Riots in Colonial Korea," unpublished paper.

Tanaka, Stefan. "Imaging History: Inscribing Belief in the Nation." *Journal of Asian Studies* 53, no. 1 (1994).

———. *Japan's Orient: Rendering Pasts into History.* Berkeley: University of California Press, 1993.

———. *New Times in Modern Japan.* Princeton: Princeton University Press, 2006.

Tocqueville, Alexis de. *The Old Regime and the French Revolution*, trans. John Bonner. New York: Harper and Brothers, 1856.

Trachtenberg, Alan. *The Incorporation of America: Culture and Society in the Gilded Age.* New York: Hill and Wang, 1982.

Trautmann, Thomas. *Lewis Henry Morgan and the Invention of Kinship.* Berkeley: University of California Press, 1987.

Uchida, Jun. *Brokers of Empire: Japanese Settler Colonialism in Korea, 1876–1945.* Cambridge: Harvard University Asia Center, 2011.

United States, Office of the Provost Marshal General. *History of Military Government Training*, vol. 1. 1945. Microfilm.

Van der Grijp, Paul. "Pioneer of Untaught Anthropology: Recontextualizing Lewis H. Morgan and His Kinship Perspective." *Dialectical Anthropology* 22 (1997).

Van Lieu, Joshua John. "Divergent Visions of Serving the Great: The Emergence of Chosŏn-Qing Tributary Relations." Ph.D. dissertation, University of Washington, 2010.

Vermeersch, Sem. *The Power of the Buddhas: The Politics of Buddhism During the Koryŏ Dynasty.* Cambridge: Harvard University Asia Center, 2008.

Wales, Nym, and Kim San. *Song of Ariran: A Korean Communist in the Chinese Revolution* [1941]. San Francisco: Ramparts Press, 1972.

Weber, Eugen. *Peasants into Frenchmen: The Modernization of Rural France, 1870–1914.* Stanford: Stanford University Press, 1976.

Weinstein, Lucie R. "The Yumedono Kannon: Problems in Seventh-Century Sculpture." *Archives of Asian Art* 42 (1989).

Wells, Kenneth M. *New God, New Nation: Protestants and Self-Reconstruction Nationalism in Korea, 1896–1937.* Honolulu: University of Hawaii Press, 1990.

Whatmore, Sarah. "Dissecting the Autonomous Self: Hybrid Cartographies for a Relational Ethics." *Geographic Thought: A Praxis Perspective*, ed. George Henderson and Marvin Waterstone. New York: Routledge, 2008.

White, Hayden. *The Content of the Form: Narrative Discourse and Historical Representation.* Baltimore: Johns Hopkins University Press, 1987.

White, Trumbull. *The World's Columbian Exposition, Chicago, 1893.* Philadelphia: P. W. Ziegler, 1893.

Williams, Raymond. *Keywords: A Vocabulary of Culture and Society.* London: Fontana, 1983.

Yi, T'ae-jun. *Eastern Sentiments*, trans. Janet Poole. New York: Columbia University Press, 2009.

Young, Robert. *White Mythologies: Writing History and the West*. New York: Routledge, 1990.

Yun, Peter. "Rethinking the Tribute System: Korean States and Northeast Asian Interstate Relations, 600–1600." Ph.D. dissertation, UCLA, 1998.

INDEX